children under
CONSTRUCTION

PETER LANG
New York • Washington, D.C./Baltimore • Bern
Frankfurt • Berlin • Brussels • Vienna • Oxford

children under CONSTRUCTION

Critical Essays on Play as Curriculum

EDITED BY DREW CHAPPELL
WITH A FOREWORD BY JACK ZIPES

PETER LANG
New York • Washington, D.C./Baltimore • Bern
Frankfurt • Berlin • Brussels • Vienna • Oxford

Library of Congress Cataloging-in-Publication Data

Children under construction: critical essays on play as curriculum /
edited by Drew Chappell.
p. cm.
Includes bibliographical references and index.
1. Play. 2. Child psychology. I. Chappell, Drew.
BF717.C45   155.4'18—dc22   2009036590
ISBN 978-1-4331-0623-1

Bibliographic information published by **Die Deutsche Nationalbibliothek**.
Die Deutsche Nationalbibliothek lists this publication in the "Deutsche
Nationalbibliografie"; detailed bibliographic data is available
on the Internet at http://dnb.d-nb.de/.

Cover art: "Possibilities in Play" by Sharon Verner Chappell

The paper in this book meets the guidelines for permanence and durability
of the Committee on Production Guidelines for Book Longevity
of the Council of Library Resources.

© 2010 Drew Chappell
Peter Lang Publishing, Inc., New York
29 Broadway, 18th floor, New York, NY 10006
www.peterlang.com

All rights reserved.
Reprint or reproduction, even partially, in all forms such as microfilm,
xerography, microfiche, microcard, and offset strictly prohibited.

Printed in the United States of America

In memory of my grandparents, Armond and Laura Ault, who taught me the importance of lifelong play.

—DC

Contents

ACKNOWLEDGMENTS IX
FOREWORD: TOWARD CREATING A CHILDREN'S PUBLIC SPHERE XI
   Jack Zipes

INTRODUCTION
Colonizing the Imaginary: Socializing (Specific) Identities, Bodies,
   Ethics, and Moralities through Pleasurable Embodiment 1
   Drew Chappell

SECTION 1: PLAY AND IDENTITY

CHAPTER ONE
Online Girl Games, Identity, and the Creation of a Multimodal
   Consumer/Creator 21
   Amy Petersen Jensen and McKay R. Jensen

CHAPTER TWO
Exploring and Re-creating Indigenous Identity
   through Theatre-based Workshops 41
   *Warren Linds, Felice Yuen, Linda Goulet, Jo-Ann Episkenew,
   and Karen Schmidt*

CHAPTER THREE
Playing with Meaning in a Norwegian Language Immersion Village 63
   Valerie Borey and Tove I. Dahl

CHAPTER FOUR
Ñeovanga Poranguei: The Lucky Ones Who Play
   (*Mbyá guaraní* Children's Learning through Social Play) 87
   Noelia Enriz

SECTION 2: PLAY AND THE CHILD BODY

CHAPTER FIVE
What Are Little (Gender "Normal," Heterosexual) Kids Made Of?
   Performing and Subverting the Status Quo in the Dramatic
   Play Area 107
   Rebecca Howard

CHAPTER SIX
Children's Museums and Children's Bodies 127
Anna Beresin

CHAPTER SEVEN
We're All In This Together: Framing the Self-Representation
of Adolescence in Disney's *High School Musical* 149
Sean J. Bliznik

CHAPTER EIGHT
13 Going on 30: Adult Discourses of Femininity in Young Women's
Sports Training 167
Amy K. Way

SECTION 3: PLAY, ETHICS, AND MORALITY

CHAPTER NINE
Constructing Good and Evil at the "Happiest Place on Earth" 189
Matt Omasta

CHAPTER TEN
Whose Rights Are They Anyway? Examining Human Rights
Education with Young People Incorporating Theatre
Games and Dramatic Activities 215
Christina Marín

CHAPTER ELEVEN
Cyberculture, Multiculture and the Emergent Morality of Critical
Cosmopolitanism: Kids (Trans)Forming Difference Online 233
Maria Kromidas

CHAPTER TWELVE
Adversity in a Snowball Fight:
Jewish Childhood in the Muslim Village of Sillwan 259
Shimi Friedman

CHAPTER THIRTEEN
Success through Excess:
Narratives and Performances in Board and Card Games 277
Drew Chappell

CONTRIBUTOR BIOGRAPHIES 299
INDEX 305

Acknowledgments

First, I would like to thank my contributors. Their willingness to share their work and their dedication to the process of revision is commendable, and I hope for great things in their futures.

Johnny Saldaña, my professor at Arizona State University, provided much-needed guidance on the process of publishing with an academic press, and I thank him for this (and all of his) mentoring.

Daniel Cook, professor in the childhood studies department at Rutgers University-Camden, provided guidance on the initial call for proposals. I thank him for his suggestions.

I thank Jack Zipes for his generosity in writing the foreword.

Chris Myers and Sophie Appel at Peter Lang provided much needed support and guidance during the publication process, and I thank them, too.

Finally, I thank my wife Sharon, my daughter Gillian, and my sister Brooke for making this project a family effort!—DC

Foreword

Toward Creating a Children's Public Sphere

Never before has the scholarly and critical discussion about the value of children's play been so important as it is now. Not only has the play of children been overly regulated, commercialized, and colonized by adults, but children increasingly spend more time inside closed spaces and more time watching television or a computer screen than ever before. Schools emphasize rote learning and functional thinking more than ever before. Sports and the arts have become professionalized, that is, regarded as a means to make money, and children are often prompted by their parents to sell their talents as trained players to the highest bidder on the market. The transformation of play as a means for enabling creative self-development into a means for providing entertainment in the culture industry and for training children in conventional rule and role playing has entered a critical phase. In response, educators, social reformers, and critics have recently formed a National Institute for Play, which has been organizing conferences and symposia to discuss strategies for taking children's play more seriously and for restoring play to the children themselves. Fortunately, the Institute is not alone in its concern to re-create alternative forms of play that will foster the autonomy of children. During the past 20 years, researchers at universities have been producing excellent studies about play and the need for a redefinition of play to counter the negative trends in our culture. Consequently, Drew Chappell's superb collection of essays, *Children Under Construction*, is a timely book that summarizes some of the new thinking and approaches and also addresses the obstacles we face if we want to save play from the "spoil sports" of instrumental learning.

The significance of Chappell's edited volume lies, I believe, in the depth and breadth of the essays and in the propositions to "re-form" play so that it serves the needs of children. In the first part of the book, questions of identity formation are raised, and the essays offer some fascinating examples of how different forms of play can offer children concrete opportunities to re-create their indigenous identities or produce gender identities commensurate with their own needs. In the second part of the book, the authors examine how children must resist adult constructions and representations of their bodies. The emphasis here is on guiding children to learn through self-representation what roles they want to embody. In the final part, the essays are concerned with the ethics and morality of play. They involve a discussion of the rights of children and whether it is possible under the present dubious ethical conditions of regulated play in theater, the Internet, a snowball fight, and board and card games for children to mould their own belief systems and determine how they want to relate to one another.

It is easy today to become cynical when one regards how children are being branded and manipulated through advertising and indoctrinated through many of our cultural and educational institutions to sell their rights and identities. Such "colonizing of children," as Chappell points out in his introduction, is both sophisticated and brazen. Yet neither he nor the authors in this volume are pessimistic, and they provide numerous examples of how we can all work through alternative and resistant modes of play to restore more dignity and respect to children. The projects discussed remind me of early endeavors by progressive educators in the late 1960s and early 1970s to develop anti-authoritarian education based on imaginative free play. They also remind me of the many endeavors by reformers to develop a children's public sphere based on inventive and resistant forms of play.

One step in the right direction—a step that has always been argued for and explored by progressive educators following in the footsteps of John Dewey, Maria Montessori, and Loris Malaguzzi (Reggio Emilia schools)—would be to ask children themselves, to learn from them, and to develop projects of learning based on the ethics of humane development that also provide practical skill sets. Joan Almon, coordinator of the U.S. Alliance for Childhood, has remarked: "A tremendous wisdom is at work when children play; a kind of genius guides them to play out the very scenes they most need for their growth and development. I saw it over and over, in small ways and in large. It is a tragedy that so many of today's children have forgotten how to play and cannot access this genius and wisdom within themselves. I know that many people rave about how brilliant today's children are—at a young age they can write and read and use a computer and other high-tech machines, but so often they cannot relate strongly with other human beings or enter the deeper spaces of play. To me, they seem impoverished in the areas that matter most."[1]

---

1 Joan Almon, "Entering the World of Play" in *A Place for Play*, ed. Elizabeth Goodenough (Carmel Valley, CA: National Institute for Play, 2008): p. 21.

Children tend to be constrained and feel enclosed in spaces of play that adults construct for them. As I have already mentioned above, these spaces have become more and more controlled and tightly administered by adults so that children cannot forge their own identities based on their needs and desires in reaction to vested interests of adults who maintain the civilizing process. There is little room for critical thinking and reflection.

American childhood is bizarre in that childhood is never fulfilled, and we Americans remain stuck in it or in adolescence for most of our lives. Playing as controlled dis-play in all cultural realms of childhood does not allow children to gain a sense of themselves, of developing identities that will give them a clear comprehensive sense of what their talents and qualities are. Dis-play does not allow for critical reflection and the integration of one's virtues. Dis-play leads to an exploitation of talents and qualities on a commercial market.

If there is going to be a strong resistance to the current trends of dis-play, regulation, and colonization, I believe it will have to come from what the German theorists Oskar Negt and Alexander Kluge argued for some thirty-odd years ago: the development of a children's public sphere that resists the arbitrary societal control of children which depends on market forces. They maintained that education in the western world tends to reduce human beings to their productive functions within the capitalist labor process that involves performance at every level, not only to sell one's labor but also one's mind and disposition. In contrast, Negt and Kluge proposed that "if they are to realize their specific form of sensuality, to 'fulfill themselves,' children require a public sphere that is more spatially conceived than do adults. They require more room in which to move, places that represent as flexibly as possible a field of action, where things are not fixed once and for all, defined, furnished with names, laden with prohibitions. They also need quite different time scales from adults in order to grow. As it expands, such a public sphere does come up against substantial material interests. For the activity of children represents, once it begins to develop, a threat to adults' interests in their own lives."[2]

It is the threat of children playing on their own, in their own sphere that we must overcome if we are to understand the value of play. It is their resistant and innovative play that offers us the hope of transforming society that needs a renewal of substantial ethics and morals that the authors in Chappell's vol-

---

2   Oskar Negt and Alexander Kluge, *Public Sphere and Experience: Toward an Analysis of the Bourgeois and Proletarian Public Sphere*, Trans. Peter Iananyi, Jamie Owe, and Assenka Oksiloff (Minneapolis: University of Minnesota Press, 1993): pp. 284–85.

ume call for. If we listen and watch children at play, listen and watch carefully, we might learn that it is time to stop manipulating their lives for the benefit of institutions and corporations and to help them explore their bodies and their environments on their own terms.

Jack Zipes
University of Minnesota

Introduction

Colonizing the Imaginary:
Socializing (Specific) Identities, Bodies, Ethics, and Moralities through Pleasurable Embodiment

Drew Chappell

Children's play has historically been treated as a frivolity, an entertainment less worthy of serious scholarship. As manifested in material culture—toys and games, for example—such activity was (and still is) often separate from the adult sphere: "kids' stuff" to be "grown out of." Yet, adults are most often the creators of these toys, games, and other play structures. They define the kinds of play permitted and expected of young people and develop the source narratives that children encounter. As such, play is an ideologically-laden experience. Yet young people respond to these messages based on their own subject positions, either adopting, adapting, or resisting the narratives and performances as they see fit.

This book explores how play, as manifested in material culture and cultural performances, socializes young people. The chapters include interdisciplinary readings about the ideas that adult makers of toys, games, play spaces, and other play-based activities transfer to children from a variety of methodological standpoints but with a focus on the performative and educative power of play. The authors specifically consider play as performance, asking questions about embodiment at physical, relational and ideological levels. Following performance theorists such as Richard Schechner (2002), Erving Goffman (1959), and Judith Butler (1993), the authors consider "performance" to be part of identity construction as well as a method of enculturation into various societies. Of primary interest are the ways in which children try on various identities through their play, and how these identities may (re)define their attitudes, values, and beliefs.

As curriculum and instruction have become open to the use of play—and children's material culture more generally—as a forum for learning, intersections have emerged between schooling and culture at large. Following theorists such as James Gee (2003), Henry Giroux (1992), and Barrie Thorne (1993), this book also intends to broaden the scope of "learning" to investigate how cultural artifacts are open and/or closed to multiple perspectives and narratives, as well as how their use is constituted both in and out of formal educative experiences. I have divided the book into three sections that explore various ways in which play and learning function together as socialization: play and identity; play and the child body; and play, ethics, and morality. Although these "learning spheres" are interrelated, in the various sections they serve as points of departure for more focused analyses.

In this introduction, I use the contested term "culture" to explore notions of play in various communities of practice with young people. I situate my understanding of this term in sociologist Ann Swidler's (1986) vision of culture as a "tool kit" containing "symbols, stories, rituals, and world-views, which people may use in varying configurations to solve varying kinds of problems." This tool kit is used to form "strategies of action, persistent ways of ordering action through time" (p. 273). For Swidler, these strategies of action contribute to a view of "culture" that places its causal significance on societal processes rather than the ends of action. I use the term "culture" both in its traditional understanding as a label for a group of people sharing one or more identity markers (which is the end result of shared practices over time), and in a more dynamic way to focus on processes and strategies that are often otherwise obscured by a static view of culture as (singular) group. This allows me to analyze various shared identities/practices as "cultures" or "cultural." I also apply this label across large, disparate identity groups, imagining "cultures" based in gender or childhood. I do this not to suggest a monolithic experience within these identities but rather to hold in tension, for example, the way gender and childhood are traditionally understood, thinking of them in Swidler's terms as shared processes and strategies.

Play as Performance

The studies in this book analyze play as manifested in performance. Some of this performance derives from material artifacts; these cultural forms influence children's socialization and prior knowledge and inform their approaches toward embodiment, physical, relational, and ideological (I will discuss these aspects later in this chapter). The authors link play to critical theories, following Richard Johnson (1998): "[We] have to fight against the disconnection that occurs...when enthusiasm for (say) popular cultural forms is divorced from the analysis of power and of social responsibilities" (p. 79). When reading cultural artifacts and the performances they call for as texts, the play of children may be seen as theorizing—constructing particular visions of the past using adult-imposed narratives—and the artifacts/texts may be analyzed in a matrix of power relations including race, class, gender, age and ability.

The artifacts also occupy a space on the "circuit of culture" described by Johnson, a circular path linking production and consumption, in which "each moment or aspect depends upon the others and is indispensable to the whole." These moments occur independently from each other, and those at one point in the circuit (consumers, for example) are not necessarily aware of the ideas and actions taking place elsewhere (production, distribution). As Johnson notes, this can lead to *alienation*. "The forms that have most significance for us at one point may be very different from those at another. Processes disappear in results" (p. 83). Also important in this model is the idea that consumption influences new production, completing the circuit. This closure challenges the notion that play is "just a story" (or movie, or toy, or game), since it influences the development of new products—the narratives they tell, objectives they define, and representations they offer.

Material artifacts are often first encountered through their physical components: a book's cover, a game's board and components, a DVD's packaging, or an advertisement showing some artifact in "appropriate" use. These components create space for play to occur and a story to unfold. The components define the rules of interaction and the narrative; the children, working through this created space, actualize it. This actualization creates a "society in action" and constitutes a performative event, engaging the performers' mental, physical, and emotional capacities. The context thus created by the artifact is important in this temporary community of play; the event is partially governed by the children's expectations, experience, and prior knowledge.

"Play worlds" can be classified on a continuum from concrete to abstract based on their level and type of implementation, applied across narrative and role play. By narrative, I mean not only the storyline evoked but also those elements that support that story: play space, art, components, and scenic elements. By "role play," I mean (within the narrative frame) the qualities and voices of the character(s) players are asked to assume. Drama activities, for example, typically assign students characters with discrete objectives and backgrounds and might further define the characters with costumes or props, treating role play concretely. These classifications may suggest how open the artifacts are to interpretation—what kind of gaps they leave in the narrative or in performance to be filled in by the player/student's own cultural constructions and notions regarding history and culture (see Iser, later in this section). In this volume, authors from a range of disciplines explore these ideas as they relate to narrative and performance.

Performance scholar Richard Schechner (2002) defines some cultural artifacts as without authorship, carrying a kind of fluidity as they change with the times: "Rituals, games, and the performances of everyday life are authored by the collective 'Anonymous' or the 'Tradition.' Individuals given credit for inventing rituals or games usually turn out to be synthesizers, recombiners, compilers, or editors of already practiced actions" (p. 28). Although these performances may not constitute scripted performance, they share many of the qualities of what is traditionally thought of as theatre. Children's culture is filled with opportunities to learn about their larger culture's norms through practiced actions such as these.

To research children's play and/as ideological formation, the authors utilize this theoretical perspective, in which performance extends beyond acting for and on the stage. Following a particular strand of thought central to the emerging (anti) discipline of performance studies, we look at the ways theatre "functions as an episteme, a way of knowing, not simply an object of analysis" (Taylor, 2003, p. xvi) including analyses of embodied action, cultural agency, and pursuing character objectives, as young people interact with cultural artifacts and create performative texts. In my own work, I consider performance in terms of two key concepts: *embodiment*, the adoption and enactment of a prescribed role, and *power*, the relational act of making decisions, creating meaning, and controlling one's own actions or those of others. These concepts intersect in children's playing out of cultural norms and prescribed narratives as transferred to them via the colonized imaginary.

Fundamental to my understanding of performance is the concept of *embodiment*, a complex relationship involving a dialectical understanding of self and other, identity and role. As performers work through these relationships, they play out scripts as well as improvising moments (based on alternative scripts, still culturally bound) in unformed or unstable narrative moments. These improvisations, sometimes described as restored behaviors or twice behaved behaviors (Schechner, 2002), draw from the kinesthetic imagination (Roach, 1996) a collected set of cultural understandings and practices linked to Swidler's "tool kit" of culture (1986). The performances may have material consequences when compelled through institutional practices. The authors in this volume locate their analyses of material culture artifacts—and young peoples' performances with and through those artifacts—in the related dialectics of self and other, identity and role, and script and improvisation. We pay close attention to the physical performances called for by these artifacts, remembering that bodily practices are the end manifestation of embodiment, and that ideas and memory are strongly connected to physicality: "One tries out the very shape of a perception in one's own body; the musculature of the body is physiologically connected to percepts; and even ideational activity, not only perception, involves such embodying..." (Taussig, 1993, p. 46).

Early conceptualizations of performance, which focused on the enacted relationship between self and other, centered on the mimetic (imitative) act, which, for example, Aristotle used to differentiate drama from narrative. In Aristotle's (1989) definition, imitation is fundamental not only to storytelling, but to learning (p. 7). Through *becoming* the other—in a limited capacity and for an isolated period of time—the performer learns what it is to *be* the other, and makes choices about his or her identity-in-role, revealing those choices in bodily action and adherence to discursive practices.

Because performance manifests as both a thing done and the doing of it, it can be analyzed as both. Theorists such as Erving Goffman (1959) have subjected everyday activity to theatrical analysis. Goffman suggests that all individuals play roles in their daily lives, putting up a "front" in order to relate with others, marking themselves according to their specialized knowledge and abilities. Goffman points out that these roles can be more or less immersive for the players, that they may or may not be "sincerely convinced that the impression of reality which [they stage] is the real reality" (p. 17).

Richard Schechner (2002) more fully expands these connections between everyday practice and mimesis:

> Performances mark identities, bend time, reshape and adorn the body, and tell stories. Performances—of art, rituals, or ordinary life—are made of 'twice-behaved behaviors,' 'restored behaviors,' performed actions that people train to do, that they practice and rehearse (p. 22).

In this understanding, performance requires rehearsal, and rehearsal concretizes and naturalizes the behavior in question.

Yet, no matter how immersed the actor is in a liminal space—walking between the self and the character:

> To put it in personal terms, restored behavior means 'me behaving as if I were someone else,' or 'as I am told to do,' or 'as I have learned.' Even if I feel myself wholly to

be myself, acting independently, only a little investigating reveals that the units of behavior that comprise 'me' were not invented by 'me' (Schechner, 2002, p. 28).

Here, Schechner points to Judith Butler's (1993) reconception of the subject. In her work, Butler suggests that rehearsal is part of a process of *materialization* (as opposed to *construction*, a term she suggests is not grounded in materiality), which inscribes notions of power upon the subject during the process of self-becoming. This materialization "stabilizes over time to produce the effect of boundary, fixity, and surface we call matter" (p. 9). In the course of the reiteration, boundaries are both produced and destabilized, with the destabilization leaving "gaps and fissures." These gaps, like those in unfinished or abstracted narratives described by Wolfgang Iser (1980), are spaces in which improvisation—based on different cultural scripts—can occur, and new or resistant understandings might emerge.

The practice of *play*—whether bound by a board, a sports field, a classroom, or existing entirely in the body—is one of the ways cultural scripts are written and worked through. The authors in this volume consider play as both aspects of performance and acts of transfer. Sociologist Roger Caillois (1961) claims: "[...] A game that is esteemed by a people may at the same time be utilized to define the society's moral or intellectual character, provide proof of its precise meaning, and contribute to its popular acceptance by accentuating the relevant qualities" (p. 83). Through play, "real" and "imagined" life become intertwined, although theorists differ about the porousness of the border between these domains. Caillois calls them incompatible (p. 64), demarcating the play sphere as free, separate, uncertain, unproductive, governed by rules, and make-believe (pp. 9-10). Yet, Johan Huizinga (1971) claims that play and real life are "a single field of action where something is at stake" (p. 40).

Huizinga seems to have a stronger case. Often, play and players refuse to stay within neat boundaries. For example, disagreements may occur over procedural interpretations or outcomes. In *The Oxford History of Board Games*, David Parlett (1999) calls these the "ends" (objectives and/or victory conditions) and "means" (rules) of the game: "'Every game has its rules,' says Huizinga in *Homo Ludens*. But we may go further, and say 'every game *is* its rules,' for they are what define it" (Parlett, p. 3). And by extension, life can be interpreted as a series of playful engagements, with players pursuing ends within a series of overlapping and culturally constructed means. Disputes over ends and means often do not stay "in-game"; conflicts arise between players that are worked out through adjudication; a player's social status may change as a result of a given game (think professional sports or chess), and a player may remove him or herself from essential daily activities in order to continue playing. Additionally, players bring their own identities to their play, which affects the experience itself and its aftermath. So the temporal and spatial experience of play has porous borders with "life outside"—in fact sometimes it is unclear whether it is the playful identity or the life identity that is being performed in a given moment as players "get into" their roles.

Players and roles exist within a relational dynamic, enabling both a semiotic and cultural analysis of the several selves constructed through play. In discussing multiplayer computer games, Katherine McBirney (2004) posits that she negotiates multiple identities including her own, her persona in the online gaming community, and her character's: "The RL [real life] self controls these alternative identities, but the alternative identities are not merely circumscribed within the borders of the RL self" (p. 416). McBirney's identities exist at different levels of performance; her game character is both within and beyond the player (in the cultural imaginary), and it may provide McBirney an opportunity to momentarily exist "as someone else." Yet, as Ken Perlin (2004) points out, all play is negotiated and filtered through a player's own subject position:

> [When] I walk away from my computer screen, I cannot sustain the fiction that an actual Lara Croft continues to exist offstage, because I have not actually experienced her agency. All I have really experienced is *my* agency (pp. 14-15).

However, in both cases, to negotiate the game effectively, players must *become* characters, substituting a constructed narrative for their own reality. They dedicate their own agency to promoting the objectives of their character, intertwining the real and the imaginary for an established period of time. This embodiment places them into the game's world exactly as if they were performing a staged piece for an audience, but here player and audience are one.

Even when not asked to take on the physical aspects of a character, a player/student still engages in embodiment. Observers, audience members, and attentive learners exist in a *liminal* state; "stripped of their former identities and assigned places in the social world; they enter a time-place where they are not-this-not-that, neither here nor there, in the midst of a journey from one social self to another" (Schechner, 2002, pp. 57-58). Victor Turner (2002) notes that those in this state are open to ideological (re)formation, coming out of the experience changed by what they have been through. When engaging with a narrative, this observer embodiment functions on a *relational* level, as participants identify with, and build empathy for, characters they follow through a story. Yet, there is more at work in the "reading" process: Wolfgang Iser (1980) suggests that any given text is filled with what he calls "blanks" or "gaps" to be filled in by the perceiver. Through the process of reading (or experiencing),

> If the blank is largely responsible for the activities described, then participation means that the reader is not simply called upon to 'internalize' the positions given in the text, but he is induced to make them act upon and so transform each other, as a result of which the aesthetic object begins to emerge (p. 119).

Embodiment, then, works also on an *ideological* level, as audience members sort through the values and beliefs expressed in a narrative and position their own ethos relative to the narrative's (multiple) ideological strands.

As a cultural strategy, play stands in for events, rules, and norms that exist in memory and can only be called forth through a re-enactment. Joseph Roach (1996) calls this process a substitution or "surrogation," and the objects and artifacts of play "effigies." Play constructs a series of temporary social and cultural norms, behaviors, and expectations, all of which contribute to a scenario that exists outside children's experience of the artifact. The effigies become catalysts and texts for performance, thematically situated within a historical context of power relations. These relations continue to fascinate me. My analysis of sites and artifacts, as well as those of the other authors in this volume, includes considerations of how the sites and artifacts invoke relations of power. As catalysts, these elements of material culture call forth performances that may redefine and "other" cultural groups and periods of history; without an audience/set of players, they are incomplete. As texts, they provide the frameworks and supply the narratives within which the embodiment takes place. As catalysts for performance, they constitute a space where embodiment occurs, through recalled/recast and invented identities and roles.

Play, Power, and Ideology

In performance, power can be enacted through physicalization, as players/students consciously embody a character (or themselves-as-character) with an associated set of controlling knowledge, beliefs, and values. Michel Foucault (1977) labels this process *disciplining* the subject's body: "Discipline increases the forces of the body (in economic terms of utility) and diminishes these same forces (in political terms of obedience)" (p. 138). In formal schooling, a child is encouraged to increase his or her knowledge through exerting control over his or her own body (McLaren, 1999; Margolis, 2004). The opposite is also true; students' control of body is read as an increase in social and kinesthetic knowledge. This discipline is manifested in multiple sets of rules to which students are expected to conform. The rules construct an ideal learner, and adults reward those students who meet this ideal through various means, for example, time spent outside, prizes within a token economy, etc. The students' bodily discipline allows adults to supply them with sanctioned knowledge. Those whose bodies are unprepared are punished by removal of privileges or direct imposition of bodily constraints (detention, time outs).

This control works dialectically between the body and the mind, which (in a "good" or "behaving" student) participates in the construction of the disciplined ideal. The mind then exerts further control over the body and the dialectic continues. Louis Althusser (2001) frames this mental discipline as *ideology*, "the imaginary relationship of individuals to their real conditions of existence," (p. 37) and locates it even in seemingly benign spaces: "a small mass in a small church, a funeral, a minor match at a sports club, a school day, a political party meeting, etc." (p. 39). He notes that in the pervasive presence of ideology there is no practice except by and in an ideology, and there is no ideology except by and for subjects *of* that ideology (p. 39). Linguists George Lakoff and Mark Johnson (1980) note that ideology can be carried through metaphors used in everyday language, many deriving from embodied experience. Humans, they argue, use metaphor as an epistemological strategy, and power centers around creating and/or perpetuating these linguistic framing devices. Those who create (or make strategic use of) the metaphors infuse their values and beliefs into the conversations that derive from them.

So we live in and through competing ideologies, carried by various semiotic forms, and these attempt to influence us through a process of interpellation, or *hailing*: "*all ideology hails or interpellates concrete individuals as concrete subjects*, by the functioning of the category of the subject" (Althusser, 2001, p. 41). In order to achieve some effect—compel an action or belief—the institution (school, theatre, publisher) doing the hailing calls out to its subjects as a group, inscribing identities onto them. We as subjects are interpellated simply because we *are*—like fish breathing water, we cannot exist as subjects or have identities without ideology—and once interpellated, we perform the actions expected by controlling institutions. But like fish, we as subjects have agency to decide where we will swim—in which water, with what specific chemical content, with which other fish, and how quickly. Our agency enables us to make choices between the ideologies we encounter, and respond to those we find most resonant or compelling. Yet as Althusser points out, we are bound to respond to some. This again relates to Swidler's (1986) idea of culture as a "tool kit"—with the tools being certain ideologies shared by members of a given group and impressed upon the group as a whole. In the case of children's material culture, artifacts as ideologically-infused tools affect young people's understandings as they make sense of the culture(s) they inhabit.

As children progress through schooling and socialization, they traditionally are interpellated to undergo a series of "becomings" in a linear, developmental model of maturation into adulthood (Lee, 2001). Yet, proponents of a postmodern view of childhood such as Nick Lee contend that within these models and expectations, children exert agency and reinterpret culture to facilitate unexpected meaning making. This agency is located in the gaps and slippages of ideology within child culture. In addition to seeking out narratives that intervene into common understandings, Lee suggests that children may also increase their agency by creating *assemblages*—groupings of relationships, resources, knowledge, and discursive practices—that function to extend their influence over their societal positioning. As adults impose their beliefs on children, then, space exists for the children to redefine those narratives as parts of their own knowledge assemblages, extending themselves by joining a larger societal discourse, part of which refuses or recasts dominant cultural messages. They learn to play *resistantly*.

The studies in this volume explore the practice of play as a primary site for children's construction and maintenance of cultural norms as directed through imposed narratives and articulated through performance. Young people's interaction with cultural artifacts constitutes what Diana Taylor (2003) terms vital *acts of transfer*: "transmitting social knowledge, memory, and a sense of identity through reiterated, or what Richard Schechner has called 'twice behaved' behavior" (pp. 2-3). As players embody roles, their bodies are disciplined, allowing specific kinds of knowledge to be transferred. Referenced by games, curricula, and other scripts, this knowledge can both reinscribe and intervene in familiar cultural tropes. The pleasurable activities that serve as transfer agents may be more insidious than direct instruction in terms of indoctrination, as noted by cultural theorist Henry Giroux (1992) in his analysis of the work of Colin Mercer: "...consent is articulated not only through the structuring of semantically organized meanings and messages, but also through the pleasures invoked in the mechanisms and structuring principles of popular forms." Giroux argues that practices like these allow players to take pleasure in narratives and performances even if they know, "rationally and politically, [that they] are 'wrong'" (p. 195).

Reinscription of and intervention into cultural narratives occur through the interplay of memory and imagination. Eliot Eisner (1998) suggests that our abilities to remember and to imagine depend upon our own experiences of the world. These abilities then feed our capacity to contribute to culture and participate in its development (pp. 24-5). Paul Connerton (1989) and Joseph Roach (1996) both point to the importance of performance in the transmission of communal memory. Through rituals, performances, and play, societies perpetuate themselves and choose cultural moments to be remembered and forgotten. Roach introduces the concept of the "kinesthetic imagination," "a way of thinking through movements, at once remembered and reinvented" (p. 27). Like Diana Taylor's *scenarios*, these imagined moments become sites for communities to work through their past; reinscribe present values, norms, and beliefs; and perhaps envision their future. Imagination becomes culturally transformative as a process that contains multiple narrative gaps and slippages. When these gaps are filled in by individuals' memories and experiences, re-imaginings of history become possible. As Roach notes, to remember, we must first forget. Judith Butler (2004) would argue that in order to prompt positive cultural transformation, imagination should "interrogate the emergence and vanishing of the human at the limits of what we can know, what we can hear, what we can see, what we can sense" (p. 151). For children to engage in resistant play, they must have access to counter narratives that allow them to acknowledge and question the disappearance of humanity that can occur within the scenarios they are playing out.

Colonizing the Imaginary

I suggest that the playful narratives and performances analyzed in this volume participate in "colonizing the imaginary," an ideological process in which adults transfer their own culturally bound values, beliefs, and ideas using narrative structures and performances intended for children's consumption. As an invisible process enacted by (among others) adult art makers and educators, this colonization of children's imaginations greatly influences their emerging understandings of history and culture. Its seductive, pleasurable power only increases its ability to draw young people into its interpellating structures. Since children have little access to the historical record or influence over their own cultural practices, their understandings of historical and contemporary cultural scenarios depend on material that is produced for their consumption by adults. Children's performances are also contextualized by adult interventions—toys, stories, costumes, and other artifacts. While play can reconfigure and collage this material into new narratives, the initial stories they hear and the performances these stories elicit establish a foundation for these departures. The narratives and performances build a communal understanding, which might be seen as a "colonized imaginary," an ideological space inhabited by children in given cultural groups affected by particular artifacts. Think of children who, like me, grew up admiring Indiana Jones (Spielberg, 1981), framing him as a scholar and adventurer, rather than a thief and cultural intruder, for example.

When describing this process, I use the words "colonizing" and "colonized" deliberately. As in its historical manifestation, the colonization of children's minds is an act of settlement, a seizure of territory. It is a practice of power toward the maintenance of authority by a dominant group, a silencing of non-dominant/non-authorized identities and voices. The playful experiences analyzed in this volume reflect some of the spaces in which colonization of the imaginary occurs. However, there are many more. Although formed and reiterated by adults, these spaces are dynamic and often influenced by young people's speaking back to the narratives and performances.

To the extent that children's play and performance engage cultural modes of restorying events, these activities are complex and multilayered. Exploring constructions of history or contemporary life through playing roles or choosing actions that refer back to oppressive ideologies is a serious mode of performance that should be interrogated by scholars engaged in a critical analysis of socialization. This volume aims to contribute to an understanding of the ways that play and performance contain and (re)define particular cultural moments and trajectories with, for, and by young people. The individual studies call into question established ways of "doing things," whether designing and playing with toys and games, or other entertainment spaces, creating curriculum, writing scripts, or guiding young people's performance.

Liberatory Play

To play in a resistant way, young people must hold in tension what they have already learned. This subversion of adult ideologies requires: a) access to counter narratives, and b) the critical capacity to make distinctions and evaluate these counter narratives against the ones children have been playing through in the first place (or, perhaps, they may enter the colonizing process with such counter narratives already in place as prior knowledge). This practice of resistant play includes voices from multiple cultural perspectives—the presence of polyvocality forces listeners to make judgments about whose narratives have historically been included and whose have not. Such play engages perspective taking and moral judgment; it is not enough to simply read various narratives around a topic or event, there must be a critical lens applied—an examination of the matrices of power that surround the way that event is (re)performed.

Resistant play might also involve manipulation of the framing of performance in order to develop and employ counter narratives. Some of these strategies reflect the work of Bertolt Brecht (1977) and Augusto Boal (1985) cited by others in this volume. For example, children or critical adult facilitators might change a given artifact's use of space and time in order to disrupt the cohesion and containment that it employs or suggests. They might also change the scale of the performance space—miniaturizing a theatre performance that seems epic in scope, for example—or institute pauses in a performance for critical reflection or "talking back." In terms of mediation, children might change media/filter type or throw out game/performance rules. Instead of conforming to expected behaviors, they might refuse to play/watch/perform, behave resistantly, or change/create new behaviors not called for by scripted or disciplining material. Such transgressive behavior would likely bring disciplinary consequences from teachers or other adult facilitators, but would call attention to perceived injustices/misconceptions. Disruptions to narrative strategies might include genre changes, emphasis on alternative points of view or perspectives, or structuring the narrative episodically or circularly to disrupt a linear structure—outcomes of stories seem much less "inevitable" when presented as something other than the culmination of a long string of cause/effect pairs.

Why is resistant play important to consider? I consider it to be a form of utopianizing, in which young people are not arrested by the colonizing of their thoughts; rather, they are able to disrupt hegemonic narratives in order to build different futures more aligned with their own values. In his studies of science fiction, literary theorist Fredric Jameson (2005) calls disruptive narratives a discursive strategy, a "radical break... which insists that its radical difference is possible and that a break is necessary" (pp. 231-32). I believe that questioning and reframing are indeed socially necessary, that certain historical and contemporary tropes have outlived their usefulness and are too strongly tied to the unjust use of power. I hope that, with a set of strategies and knowledge, children will overturn these tropes, incorporating more "play" as Derrida (2002) would conceive it (exploiting narrative gaps, assessing various perspectives) within their imagined play.

While such reading against problematic cultural scripts is a worthwhile endeavor, it is too often temporary and private. "Mainstream" child culture rarely engages with or troubles the powerful scenarios that develop around historical events and contemporary sociocultural questions. I hope to see more public efforts at building awareness around these issues and a careful consideration of what exactly is being "carefully taught" to children through these "seductively pleasant spheres of children's culture" (Underiner, 2006, p. 1)

Chapter Contributions

Within each of this volume's interrelated sections are multiple chapters exploring that section's focus from various disciplines and methodological frameworks.

In Section 1: Play and Identity, Amy Petersen Jensen and McKay Jensen address how online environments, including games, structure "girlhood" and how these environments market themselves to girls, particularly "tween" girls. Warren Linds, Felice Yuen, Linda Goulet, Jo-Ann Episkenew, and Karen Schmidt describe a project in which the authors worked with indigenous youth from rural Canadian communities in order to explore their identity as First Nations people, particularly as it relates to health and wellness. Valerie Borey and Tove Dahl explore children's construction of a Norwegian language learner identity through play in a residential Norwegian language immersion village. Noelia Enriz analyzes child-invented games that socialize young members of the indigenous Mbya culture in South America into their multiple identities as adult community members.

In Section 2: Play and the Child Body, Rebecca Howard discusses the ways that pretend play areas in early childhood classrooms construct gender and heteronormativity through activities such as dress up, household tasks and occupations. Anna Beresin explores how adults frame children's physical explorations in children's museums through design and bodily limitation. Sean Bliznik looks at young people's recreations of songs from Disney's *High School Musical* series and the ways that their use of body is critiqued through online discussions. Amy Way writes about the ways that athletic female bodies are constructed through a non-competitive sports program aimed at elementary school age girls.

In Section 3: Play, Ethics, and Morality, Matt Omasta analyzes changing notions of "good and evil" in various attractions at the Disneyland theme park. Christina Marín looks at the impact of drama work on young people's understandings of the rights of children around the world. Maria Kromidas analyzes the development of a cyber multiculturalism based on young people's cultural identifications through online social networking. Shimi Friedman explores how spontaneous play enacts and helps to maintain tensions between Jewish and Muslim families in a shared settlement in Israel. Lastly, I analyze the values imposed upon players of three board and card games, including consumerism, work, and colonization.

Although these chapters employ different methodological frameworks and represent studies across a range of disciplines, they all demonstrate the ways adults (and sometimes children) use play to achieve some social goal. Through pleasurable activity, young people learn about themselves in relation to others, in ways both explicit and implicit. The authors in this volume believe such play deserves focused and serious study. We hope that these essays encourage further scholarly engagement with children's structured and free play activities. We hope, too, that artists, parents, teachers, curriculum developers, and toy makers will begin to imagine play as an opportunity to question "the way things are done" and develop new narratives and performances that cast young people as active and critical meaning makers.

References

Althusser, L. (2001). Ideology and the Ideological State Apparatuses. In C. Counsell & L. Wolf (Eds.), *Performance Analysis: An Introductory Coursebook* (pp. 32-42). New York: Routledge.

Aristotle (1989). *On Poetry and Style* (G. M. A. Grube, Trans.). Indianapolis: Hackett Pub. Co.

Boal, A. (1985). *Theatre of the Oppressed* (C. A. McBride & M.-O. L. McBride, Trans.). New York: Theatre Communications Group.

Brecht, B. (1977). *Brecht on Theatre* (J. Willett, Trans.). New York: Hill and Wang.

Butler, J. (1993). *Bodies That Matter: On the Discursive Limits of "Sex."* New York: Routledge.

Butler, J. (2004). *Precarious Life: The Powers of Mourning and Violence*. London: Verso.
Caillois, R. (1961). *Man, Play, and Games*. New York: Free Press of Glencoe.
Connerton, P. (1989). *How Societies Remember*. Cambridge [England]; New York: Cambridge University Press.
Derrida, J. (2002). Where There Is No Center, All Is Playing. In R. Schechner (Ed.), *Performance Studies: An Introduction* (pp. 99). New York: Routledge.
Eisner, E. (1998). *The Kind of Schools We Need*. Portsmouth, NH: Heinemann.
Foucault, M. (1977). *Discipline and Punish: the Birth of the Prison* (1st American ed.). New York: Pantheon Books.
Gee, J. P. (2003). *What Video Games Have to Teach Us About Learning and Literacy* (1st ed.). New York: Palgrave Macmillan.
Giroux, H. A. (1992). *Border Crossings: Cultural Workers and the Politics of Education*. New York; London: Routledge.
Goffman, E. (1959). *The Presentation of Self in Everyday Life*. Garden City, NY: Doubleday.
Huizinga, J. (1971). *Homo Ludens*. Boston: Beacon Press.
Iser, W. (1980). Interaction Between Text and Reader. In S. Suleiman & I. Crosman I. (Eds.), *The Reader in the Text: Essays on Audience and Interpretation*. Princeton: Princeton University Press.
Jameson, F. (2005). *Archaeologies of the Future: The Desire Called Utopia and Other Science Fictions*. New York: Verso.
Johnson, R. (1998). What is Cultural Studies Anyway? In J. Storey (Ed.), *What is Cultural Studies? A Reader*. New York: Oxford University Press.
Lakoff, G., & Johnson, M. (1980). *Metaphors We Live by*. Chicago: University of Chicago Press.
Lee, N. (2001). *Childhood and Society: Growing Up in an Age of Uncertainty*. Philadelphia, PA: Open University Press.
Margolis, E. (2004). Looking at Discipline, Looking at Labour: Photographic Representations of Indian Boarding Schools. *Visual Studies, 19(1)*, pp. 72-96.
McBirney, K. (2004). Nested Selves, Networked Communities: A Case Study of 'Diablo II: Lord of Destruction' as an Agent of Cultural Change. *Journal of American Culture, 27(4)*, pp. 415-421.
McLaren, P. (1999). *Schooling as a Ritual Performance: Toward a Political Economy of Educational Symbols and Gestures* (3rd ed.). Lanham, MD: Rowman & Littlefield.

Parlett, D. S. (1999). *The Oxford History of Board Games*. Oxford; New York: Oxford University Press.

Perlin, K. (2004). Can There Be a Form Between a Game and a Story? In N. Wardip-Fruin & P. Harrigan P (Eds.), *First Person: New Media as Story, Performance, and Game*. Cambridge, MA: The MIT Press.

Roach, J. R. (1996). *Cities of the Dead: Circum-Atlantic Performance*. New York: Columbia University Press.

Schechner, R. (2002). *Performance Studies: An Introduction*. London; New York: Routledge.

Spielberg, S. (Director) (1981). *Indiana Jones and the Raiders of the Lost Ark*: Paramount.

Swidler, A. (1986). Culture in Action: Symbols and Strategies. *American Sociological Review, 51(2)*, pp. 273-286.

Taussig, M. T. (1993). *Mimesis and Alterity: A Particular History of the Senses*. New York: Routledge.

Taylor, D. (2003). *The Archive and the Repertoire: Performing Cultural Memory in the Americas*. Durham: Duke University Press.

Thorne, B. (1993). *Gender play: Girls and Boys in School*. New Brunswick, NJ: Rutgers University Press.

Turner, V. (2002). By Their Performances Shall Ye Know Them. In R. Schechner (Ed.), *Performance Studies: An Introduction* (p. 13). London: Routledge.

Underiner, T. (2006). Introduction. *Early Interventions: Performance, Indigeneity and Young People* Retrieved 7 May, 2006, from http://theatre.asu.edu/791

SECTION ONE

Play and Identity

Chapter One

Online Girl Games, Identity, and the Creation of a Multimodal Consumer/Creator

Amy Petersen Jensen and McKay R. Jensen

Introduction

In the Fall of 2008 our family (Mom, Dad, and 8-year-old twin daughters) waited anxiously for the October launch of the Walt Disney Company's *Pixie Hollow*, an online virtual world designed for girls ages 5–8. The girls were excited because *Pixie Hollow* was specifically designed for (and marketed to) girls in their age range. They had heard all kinds of enticing stories from friends, handled collectibles in retail stores, and seen television commercials as well as web-based advertisements that led them to believe that this online game was particularly suited to their interests and abilities. Because of these encounters the girls were eager to participate, and we (the parents) were interested in observing this new transmedia experience.

Transmedia events, as defined by Jenkins (2007), are best described as storytelling processes where integral elements of a fiction (i.e., *Pixie Hollow*) get dispersed systematically across multiple delivery channels for the purpose of creating a unified and coordinated entertainment experience for participants (Laurel, 2001). For Jenkins, the transmedia experience (or product) equally involves each medium as unique and integral parts of the storytelling process. *Pixie Hollow* and many other websites, television shows and video games qualify as transmedia products because of their powerful integration of nostalgic characters, new online environments, widely distributed retail products, theme park attractions and feature films.

As co-researchers and parents we were intrigued by the opportunities that several media products gave us to reflect on the ways that young girls play in transmedia spaces. We were also interested in how play with transmedia products such as *The Avatar* televsion show, Wii video games, and the *Pixie Hollow* website might help us to understand investigations of identity, in and out of virtual spaces. We recognized early on that the notion of identity spans a variety of fields (psychology, sociology, anthropology, politics, etc.). Identity has been employed regularly and exhaustively by media scholars (Hall, 1996; Livingstone et al., 2004; Seiter, 2004; Buckingham, 2007) in their efforts to describe youth media consumption. Simply by the volume of comment, it appears safe now to say that theories of identity are central to understanding the attraction, reception, and interpretation of much of our mediated communication.

For the purposes of this chapter we will focus on the ways that young girls *perform* identity, or a conception of their social selves, through their engagement with transmedia products. Specifically we note the ways that our daughters, as representatives of other girls their age, engage with contemporary entertainment platforms as multimodal consumer/creators. This concept of multimodality is borrowed from Kress (2000) who asserts that to function in contemporary social worlds young people must make use of multi-modal opportunities; in other words, they must have the ability to simultaneously encounter and express ideas through a wide range of meaning making and bearing systems. Kress stresses the necessity of creating and interpreting in media such as graphics, print text, images (still and moving), sound, etc. More importantly he notes that children learn to thrive in these new environments only as they understand and value unique modes of representation.

Our chapter then, is a contemplation of the skills young people employ to successfully negotiate transmedia environments. We explore the ways that girls make meaningful choices about the best way to express and present their conceptions of their social selves (or identity) in these environs. We hope to illuminate how these skills, capacities, and techniques surrounding identity experimentation and formation seem to play a vital role in the designed interactions of transmedia products and the self-determinant choices made by those who consume these products.

Performing *Pixie Hollow*—Beginning with Brand Identification

In an effort to capitalize on the strategic opportunities present in virtual worlds, the Walt Disney Company launched *Pixie Hollow*. As an extension of their *Disney Fairies* group of transmedia products, *Pixie Hollow* is an online social networking website where young girls create and personalize fairy avatars that become members of the *Pixie Hollow* community. Housed in a home tree at the center of Never Land, characters in this multi-platform world grow out of J. M Barrie's original description of fairies from his novel *The Little White Bird*. In the work Barrie personifies his conception of a fairy world by saying, "When the first baby laughed for the first time, his laugh broke into a million pieces, and they all went skipping about. That was the beginning of fairies" (p. 32).

Describing the new generation of fairies, the *Pixie Hollow* website states that "Every time a newborn baby laughs for the first time, that laugh travels out into the world, and those that make their way to Never Land turn into a fairy." The central character associated with the franchise is the same Tinkerbell from Disney's 1953 film adaption of J. M Barrie's *Peter Pan*. Tinkerbell acts as the talisman for the franchise, but new fairies, not associated with the original film, now join her in Never Land. Inside the online community, fairies interact with other avatars, play talent games, collect curious objects, create fairy fashions and accessories, and earn special badges that showcase and keep track of adventures and accomplishments of each individual fairy.

Like most affinity-based Web sites, participants are welcome to play in *Pixie Hollow*'s online environs at no cost to the consumer. However, full participation in the online community is conditional to an annual membership fee. Concurrent with the launch of the *Pixie Hollow* Web site, Disney Consumer Products (DCP) also introduced the Clickable Fairy Collection (jewelry and toys) that more fully connects the digital world and the girl's own physical space. According to Disney's press release, these toys (which are worn or held by girl gamers) "unlock special content in *Pixie Hollow*, allowing girls to make online fairy friendships and add special virtual clothing, accessories and décor to their online fairies' world by simply clicking their Disney Fairies jewelry with their real world friends offline" (2008).

Through *Pixie Hollow*'s online community, DCP is intentionally marketing products (dolls, books, DVDs, and other collectables) to its target demography (five- to eight-year-old girls. This creates a sense that the Walt Disney Company is using technology to create a new multimodal consumer, one whom they are able to reach through a variety of transmedia platforms. Steve Wadsworth, president of Disney's Interactive Media Group describes it as the company's "first real effort at [a] more holistic approach to a franchise that includes an immersive online experience tied to consumer products, [and] physical goods… a world where all these things come together." (Nakashima, 2008).

Much of the research surrounding the development of the child-consumer concerns self/brand identification (Kinder, 2000; Cook, 2004; Chaplin and John, 2005; Mayo, 2005). This connection of identity to a range of transmedia products seems to be the overt aim of the *Pixie Hollow* virtual world. In effect, the young consumers participating in the *Pixie Hollow* world experience is what

Wickstrom (2007) would call "brandscaping" or an attempt by product producers to get their customer to tangibly identify with the brand they are staging. Wickstrom speaks of physical, site-specific mimetic experiences in commercial venues such as the American Girl Store, but the idea can certainly be extended into virtual environments, especially those that are designed to give an immersive experience. Wickstrom conceives of brandscaping as a "somatic epistemology," one that allows for a palpable, even sensuous "embodied comprehension" (p. 17) between the body of the consumer and that which they consume.

This type of behavior is common to the online interactions with virtual worlds designed by corporate entities and integral to the concept behind *Pixie Hollow*. Producers of many of the online virtual worlds designed for girls clearly hope to direct young consumers toward self-identification with their corresponding brands. *Pixie Hollow*, Barbie Girls, Ty Girlz, ePets, NeoPets, American Girl and Bellasara are all examples of this style of immersive environment where brandscaping is the goal.

While Wickstrom's ideas of brandscaping are wonderfully descriptive of the intents and strategies of the producers of transmedia products, they give only a limited picture of how consumers actually receive, interpret, and respond to those strategies and intents. The actions of the consumer/gamer, in most situations, remain powerfully unpredictable as he or she contextualizes personal experiences. The constraints of Wickstrom's ideas are demonstrated by the fact that even if Mattel is successful in making every girl an "American Girl," what it means to be an "American Girl" is still uniquely interpreted by each girl that assumes the label. Child consumers have proven themselves to be creatively self-determinant as they relocate themselves between local physical settings (home, school, community spaces, etc.) and more global, technological settings (social networking sites, virtual worlds, etc.).

This capacity to choose is commercialized by transmedia product producers by using opportunities for choices as a key attraction to their virtual environments. For example, in *Pixie Hollow* the user chooses everything about their fairy: hair style and color, eye shape and color, costumes, talents, and abilities. The point of a "virtual world" is to provide choices—where to go, who to meet, what to do. This virtual framework for endless choices and infinite customization is the primary point of attraction of little girls to virtual worlds. It is an attraction that is proving to be a marketing bonanza for transmedia corporations that specialize in virtual worlds for children.

According to Williamson (2007), there are currently 15 million children who are members of a virtual world and there will be 20 million in 2011. These virtual worlds allow kids to decorate bedrooms, play with online pets, shop for and collect virtual merchandise, and generally explore and engage in identity-play alone or with other users of the sites. This space for multiple choices and unpredictable action is precisely where identity can be performed. The choices connected to identity-play (or transmedia experiences that lead consumers to make individual and unique choices of self expression) are provided by producing entities, but remain ungoverned. This is their primary attraction as a commercial product, and a location where identity experimentation and formation can occur, independent of the intent, design, or strategies of the producing entity.

This type of "tactical" reaction to "strategic" intent is eloquently expressed in the work of Michel de Certeau. While not a direct refutation of Wickstrom, de Certeau's ideas of "strategies" and "tactics" can be used to identify how identity-play is offered but not controlled by corporate interest. It is our assertion that understanding identity-play is the key to fully comprehending the relationship between transmedia products and the children who consume them, especially girls who are the target of much of the virtual world marketing strategies that employ identity-play scenarios.

A document entitled "Generation Now and the Virtual Worlds of Girls, 6-12," produced by public relations and marketing firm MWW Group (2008) explains how they view children (especially girls of the 6-12 age group) and their relationship to virtual worlds, and the strategic possibilities connected to them, saying:

> Children age 6-12 are an influential part of "Gen Now," a generation that is accustomed to and expects instant communication and feedback. They absorb information like sponges, but the exchange of information is not just one-way. Consistent with the Web 2.0 phenomenon in other demographics, even the youngest web users participate in creating rather than simply consuming content. The Internet is increasingly an outlet for Gen Nows' creativity, curiosity and interconnectedness.
>
> This age group has a powerful voice in purchasing power. Gen Nows quickly master details of product categories and are especially adept at pitching their parents on products and practices. They are a generation most comfortable with using computers and other electronics.
>
> Virtual worlds are increasingly popular with Gen Now girls.... Among the hallmarks of successful virtual worlds is authenticity. Kids have an acute sense for recognizing sincerity.

MWW Group is the marketing and public relations firm that represents McDonalds, Hershey's, Sara Lee, Johnson & Johnson, and many others. Clearly girls in the age group of 6-12 are in their sights because of their "powerful voice in purchasing power." Their use of the word "powerful" is consequential as it demonstrates a recognition of a type of self-determinism that is fostered by identity-play in virtual worlds. MWW recognizes that for virtual worlds to be successful as commercial ventures they must provide an experience where the user must feel authentically powerful. This feeling of power stems from the self-determinant choices users make as they engage in identity-play and become not only consumers of a product, but creators of offline narratives and meanings.

This process of fostering consumer/creators has proven to be wildly successful for the Disney Corporation. In a story announcing a 13 percent year to year increase in traffic for Disney Games in 2007 to 2008, *Virtual World News* stated the following:

> According to Comscore, general U.S. online gaming grew 27% over the past year to 86 million visitors in December 2008 with time spent playing online games growing by 42%.... The increase in traffic, according to a Disney representative was "largely driven by our virtual worlds, and specifically by the popularity of the new Disney Fairies Pixie Hollow virtual world." (2009)

This demonstrated capacity for virtual environments like *Pixie Hollow* to attract mass audiences through identity-play has given the producers of transmedia products a powerful tool to engage pre-teen girls. That particular demographic has been a long-sought-after target audience for gaming companies who were thought to be limited to only half of the population because of their inability to attract female gamers. The development of pre-teen girls as the ideal multi-modal consumer/creators has moved this once-ignored portion of the gaming audience to a new position as the harbinger of future development strategies and the bellwether of the industry.

Girl Games and Intentional Identity Formation

In 1992, Brenda Laurel (2001) and her colleagues at Interval Research asked a very interesting question: "Why didn't girls play videogames?" Of one of the initial conversations that she had with Interval Research cofounder David Liddle, she recalls:

> Both of us were curious as to why there didn't seem to be any computer games for little girls.... Neither of us knew of any reason why girls would be intrinsically less interested than boys in computers or computer games, and both of us were deeply puzzled as to why no one had been able to make something that worked for them. Liddle's summary of the missed business opportunity was: "There's a six billion dollar business, with an empty lot next door." Most important, we agreed if this were an easy

problem, someone would have already solved it. In sum, it had all the characteristics of a good research problem—puzzling, consequential, and complex. (p. 18)

That "good research problem" served as the impetus for two-and-a-half years of inquiry by the team at Interval Research. They began with an extensive review of the literature in related fields like cognitive psychology, spatial cognition, gender studies, play theory, sociology, and even primatology. They also interviewed experts in academia and those that produced relevant literature. Most importantly, they interviewed 1,100 children, boys and girls, ages seven to 12, and surveyed another 10,000 children.

The result of that research was that there were clear differences in what girls expected and liked about video and computer games as compared to what boys expected and like. As summarized by Henry Jenkins (2001) in *From Barbie to Mortal Kombat: Further Reflections*, Laurel identified five key distinctions between the classic Boy Game and what came to be her vision for the ideal Girl Game.

First—Characteristics of leading characters:
- FOR GIRLS—Leading characters are everyday people that girls can easily relate to and are as real to girls as their best friends
- FOR BOYS—Leading characters are fantasy-based action heroes with "'super power' abilities."

Second—Goal of the game:
- FOR GIRLS—The goal is to explore and have new experiences, with degrees of success and varying outcomes.
- FOR BOYS—The goal is to win, and the play is linear. Outcome is black and white; die and start over; one 'right' solution.

Third—Pace of play:
- FOR GIRLS—The pace of play fosters multi-sensory immersion, discovery, and strong story lines.
- FOR BOYS—An accelerated pace is emphasized, and speed and action are key.

Fourth—Setting or environment where play takes place:
- FOR GIRLS—The game environment features everyday, 'real life' settings as well as new places to explore.
- FOR BOYS—The game environment features non-realistic, larger-than-life settings.

Fifth—Definition of successful game play:
- FOR GIRLS—Success comes through development of friendships.
- FOR BOYS—Success comes through the elimination of competitors (2001).

At the time of Interval Research's studies in the early 1990s, all of these ideas were in embryo—they were not testing produced products. They postulated at the end of their research that if such products existed for girls, these five features would be the key to their acceptance by a mass audience. While Interval Research's study introduces a problematic gender binary which pigeonholes girl gaming into passive and less competitive settings and situates boy games in more active and competitive environments, nevertheless, the subsequent decade and half that followed has much of that work. Today commercial entities and numerous game-producing companies employ these principles in products specifically designed for girls.

Pixie Hollow, for example, demonstrates a very close correlation between Laurel's principles and the virtual world design employed by Disney:

1. The leading characters of *Pixie Hollow* are avatars that the user creates, and are designed to foster virtual friendships. These friendships are extended to other avatars as they "friend" one another. Through the act of creation, the characters become generally the precise friend that the user is looking for—being the proper age and exhibiting the exact personality traits that the user is seeking in a friend.

2. There is no "winning" in *Pixie Hollow*. All game play is based around limitless experiences and virtual acts of consumerism. Users try new products, go new places, and meet new people.

3. Nothing is rushed in *Pixie Hollow*. All play is designed to extend the experience. The goal is clearly to create an immersive experience—especially when one considers that you buy actual products that interact with the virtual environment.

4. Like most virtual worlds, the setting for *Pixie Hollow* is grounded more in real life than in fairy abstractions. The fairy wood is easily recognizable as a community that the user might actually live in—there are homes and street names and (seemingly, most importantly) there are stores and shops. Bedrooms are featured as an important place to bring purchased things.

5. Certainly *Pixie Hollow* exemplifies how a virtual world defines success through the development of friendships. "Friending" other users is set up as a key goal of play and rivals virtual consumerism as the primary activity. Conversations are had, and invitations are extended. The lasting friendships, however, are usually between the users and their created avatars.

Clearly all of Laurel's marketing principles can be easily identified in *Pixie Hollow*. Additional experience with these principles has brought up the question of what these ideas mean in terms of identity and identity formation. For our daughters, *Pixie Hollow* quickly wears out its welcome in ways that actually reinforce Laurel's ideas. For them, the consequences of choosing all the characteristics of their virtual friends are that they instantly like their fairies, but they are easily bored with them. They tire of them because they are actually bored with themselves. In this way, *Pixie Hollow* is only providing different ways for our daughters to play with different versions of themselves. They are actually denied new knowledge because the scenarios they can create are rooted in their own experience. Thus, *Pixie Hollow* grabs our girls' attention for an hour or two, but then they put it down. *Pixie Hollow* doesn't challenge them with new information and narratives. The world of *Pixie Hollow* is actually their own world, and they seem to recognize that and are readily willing to trade it for something more exiting. For our daughters, identity play is clearly something that they want to engage in, but they require that play to stretch their identities, not just reinforce their own self-conceptions.

Gaming as Identity Experimentation

In retrospect it can be observed that identity was at the heart of what Laurel and her colleagues were observing and hypothesizing about. Girls were looking for computer gaming experiences that provided characters they could relate to, new experiences, opportunities for discovery, real-life settings, and new relationships. All of these game elements can easily be viewed as experiments in identity formation and discovery. Play centered on experiments in identity formation (or experimentation) seems to grab the attention of the mass audience of pre-teen girls that transmedia corporations market to and covet.

A story by Jason Ashley Wright (2009) in *Tulsa World* contains the following:

> A recent study showed that game usage among girls jumped from 50 percent in 2006 to 57 percent in 2008, said Ann Hamilton, a senior brand manager with game publisher Ubisoft.... In total, the Wii console has sold 15.4 million in the United States since it was launched in November 2006.... "What's driving the Wii sales is the use of Wii by women, girls and families," Hamilton said. "It's really a female-driven platform." (p. D1)

Wright's article did not speculate as to *why* the Wii is conducive to girls, or what led Ann Hamilton of Ubisoft to say that it was a "female-driven platform." However, direct experience with the device quickly demonstrates how the Wii leverages identity-play as a feature that might attract little girls. Even before gaming begins, there is a set-up process of creating individual player files to store game information, progress, and some preferences for specific players. Each player file, or identity, comes complete with a signifying avatar, or Mii (pronounced "me"). The set-up of the unique player file consists mainly of creating this new identity, or Mii, by selecting gender, height, weight, hair color, hairstyle, eye color, and facial features. These new Miis then gather in an on-screen courtyard and constitute the Wii's community of players.

Our household was one of the millions where the Wii landed lasted year, and this feature of created identities, or Miis, instantly and forcefully grabbed the attention of our daughters. They were equally delighted by the "Daddy Mii" whose hair, face, and body type shared little with the original, as they were with the "Mommy Mii," which was spot on with its hair color, hairstyle, and glasses. The creation of our girls' unique avatars also became a long and careful process of choosing and observing and re-choosing until they were finally satisfied.

To our surprise, this set-up procedure was not viewed by our girls as merely initiatory or even as a process that should be completed. Their immediate question as soon as our four-person virtual family was in place was: "Can we make another Mii?" Soon multiple variations of the Miis populated our Wii. There were several versions of our girls, each representing different identities that the girls wanted to try on. There were Miis that were more grown up, and Miis that mirrored nostalgic versions of their younger selves.

One new Mii was particularly interesting. "Who is that?" we asked, referring to a young male Mii that was new to our Wii.

"That's Kevin," responded one of our daughters.

"Who's Kevin?"

"Kevin is Sissy's," said the other daughter, gesturing toward her sister, "because she is a tom-boy."

From this it was clear that our girls were experimenting with their own identities—trying on longer or shorter legs, different hair, and even different genders. This type of identity experimentation has other tools in the Wii than simple identity substitution; for example, they also used our Wii to construct virtual relationships. Our Wii became the home of entire new families of Miis—some reflective of our own and others not. All of the Miis created were much more than a collection of simply body types and hairdos—our girls projected complete and complex personalities and narratives on them.

In addition to Kevin, there are Rose, Caroline, Aunt Dizzle and many others. They happily take different Miis to the virtual slopes of *Wii Ski* (a game by Namco) where they can be outfitted in unique clothing and ski equipment, and our daughters can interact with others and tool around the virtual ski village clothed in new identities. The Miis also appear as virtual celebrity endorsers on the billboards and signage along the racecourses in *Mario Kart* (by Nintendo), and as teammates or spectators in *Wii Sports*. All of these appearances by the Miis give our girls a sense of shared experience with them and therefore build their relationship. They recall when they ran into Aunt Dizzle in *Mario Kart*, or when Kevin made a spectacular catch in the outfield during a baseball game in *Wii Sports*. In short, they play with a constructed community were they make judgments and evaluate relationships that in reality are extensions of their own imagination, experiences, and assumptions. In effect, they play with identity in the same way that they played with Play-doh as toddlers: it is rolled out, examined, and touched through direct experience, shaped, and re-shaped. It has been a fascinating thing to observe because the technology provides a forum where our children's social assumptions and priorities can be demonstrated and observed.

Evaluating these experiences in the light of Laurel's five principles of girl gaming provides an interesting context of where the computer gaming industry has gone in the years since the question of what girls would like in computer games was first thoughtfully and thoroughly investigated. Certainly, the Miis on the Wii platform are "everyday people that girls can easily relate to"—they are in fact virtual representations of the actual player. Players are carried into the game through the constructed identities of Miis. The ideas of exploration and virtual opportunity for new experiences "with degrees of success and varying outcomes" are clearly demonstrated in game play on the Wii, as most of what our daughters viewed as important to the game took place before actual "game-play" began or outside of the game entirely in the narratives that they constructed in their own imaginations. The pace of play on the Wii also conforms to Laurel's idea of having a place for "strong story-lines" if the preparatory experiences to game play on the Wii and the imaginative construction of narratives outside of the game are taken into account. The settings of the Wii games vary broadly with each game, but the association of game play with a Mii that has been carefully constructed, and becomes a familiar friend to the player through shared experiences, means that "real life" is then carried into even the most fanciful of environments. Finally, if "success comes through development of friendships," then the Wii is designed to immediately deliver that sense of success through the interaction and shared experiences of the players and their Miis.

In this context then, it can truly be said of the Wii gaming system that it is a "female-driven platform," as it caters to the expectations and tastes of female players for engagement in identity-play. Certainly the very term "Mii" speaks to identity-play as being central to how users engage with the technology, and the process of creating "new Miis" is indicative of direct experimentation in identity conceptualization, formation, and interpretation.

Identity and Online/Offline Play

This type of identity-play and experimentation can be found in many more places than just the Wii systems settings. Another product that became an important part of our daughters' technology-aided identity-play is *Avatar: The Last Airbender*. First developed as a television show for the Nickelodeon network, *Avatar: The Last Airbender* has become a complete transmedia product line of action figures, video-games, costumes, websites, graphic novels, etc. The series was honored with a 2008 Peabody Award for its "unusually complex characters and healthy respect for the consequences of warfare" (Peabody Awards). An article by Ryan Ball (2008) for *Animation* magazine speaks to the show's popularity and its online and transmedia penetration:

Avatar: Sozin's Comet averaged 5.6 million total viewers, giving Nickelodeon a 195 percent increase in viewership over the same period last year. Wednesday's premiere of *Boiling Rock* grabbed 4 million total viewers, and all of the week's new *Avatar* episodes reached about 19.0 million viewers combined.

The property has also been popular online. *Rise of the Phoenix King*, the new *Avatar* online game of the week on www.nick.com generated almost 815,000 game plays and, in just three days, became the No. 2 online game for the week. In addition, *Avatar* had the most-visited message board of the week on Nick.com.

Oddly, our eight-year-old daughters' first contact with *Avatar* came in contexts far removed from any media at all. Children from our quiet neighborhood began introducing *Avatar* story lines, characters, and situations into the imaginative, outdoor play they regularly engaged in. An entire inventory of new names and interesting terms began to filter into our home, pricking our adult curiosity. A request for a DVD rental soon identified the source of their new vocabulary, and then the entire series was quickly devoured by our family in nightly viewing sessions of purchased DVDs.

The narrative for *Avatar* centers on the main characters' quest to rescue their world from the quasi-fascist rule of the Fire Lord and the tyranny of the Fire Nation. The protagonists' stated goal throughout the series is to restore the balance between the four nations of their world: the Earth Kingdom, the Water Tribes, the Air Nomads, and the Fire Nation. As mentioned by the Peabody Awards, it is the complexity of the characters, and how our daughters self-identify with them, that captures our imagination. The three central characters—Aang, Sokka, and Katara, each have personality traits that are easily identifiable to our daughters as things that they have in common with the characters. For example, all of the characters are children who are just beginning to feel some responsibility for their surrounding community and friends. Certainly the mission of growing to adulthood is as intimidating and mysterious to our daughters as Aang's stated mission to "save the world" seems to be for him—it seems distant and far off, if not impossible. Katara is a girl, but she is far from being a solitary female role model in the show, which is populated with many different female characters that span a remarkable range of different personalities, ages, and styles of social interaction. Sokka, though male, is a character that our girls can strongly identify with because he is what he appears to be—he has no magical powers; he is often underestimated, and his largest concern is often his hunger.

As evidenced by our daughters' initial imaginative play involving these characters, their identifying traits were much like identity handles for the girls to latch on to and carry for a while. These experiences are equivalent to effectively trying on different identities. This active identity play is not limited to gender roles (they do not always have to be the girl) or even appropriate behavior (they are free to be the villain or try personality traits that irritate or complicate their interactions). They both felt free to spend significant amounts of time as many different characters, because so many of the characters are so easily relatable to their own experience, having multiple identity handles for our daughters to identify and grasp.

This type of identity play (or self-character identification) is carried over directly to the video games by THQ that are based on *Avatar*. These games are experienced by our daughters on the Wii, but they are also available for Xbox,

PlayStation, and the hand-held Gameboy and PSP platforms. In each, not only is play as each character possible, it is required at many different points of the game. Each character's unique abilities come into play, and therefore the player sees himself or herself moving through the game in different identities. The result is precisely what Brenda Laurel would have predicted: close self/character identification through strong story lines, immersive experiences, and developed relationships (again through shared experiences) are part of an attractive product (*Avatar: The Last Airbender* in this case) which leads to more sales and therefore more revenue for the producers of the product.

As demonstrated by the Wii gaming platform and the *Avatar* family of transmedia products (and predicted by Interval Research), identity-play is being used as a central enticement for girls to new technology products. In turn, this targeted design to the tastes and preference of young girls is being used to elevate these products' market penetration to stratospheric levels of success. That empty lot that David Liddle saw adjacent to the multi-billion dollar game industry that catered mostly to boys is quickly filling up.

Strategic Environments, Tactical Play

It should be noted that this identity-play is being built into many transmedia products only for its attractive qualities in gaining and expanding market share. In our admittedly anecdotal experience, there appears to be no motivation to shape or drive identity formation in any particular direction. Indeed, limiting choices in identity-play, or guiding or influencing player identity formation seems entirely detrimental to the commercial interest of the producing companies. An excellent model for what is taking place with identity-play for games or transmedia products designed for (or attractive to) girls can be found in Michel de Certeau's description of strategic and tactical entities.

In the *Practice of Everyday Life* de Certeau describes an entity as *strategic* when it is widely recognized as an authority (i.e., an institution, government agency, mass media producer, etc). Such an entity defines the rules and regulations of a given space or community. It promotes and perpetuates itself through the things that it makes and distributes. The strategic entity, which uses large amounts of time, space, and resources to produce its products, is seen as inflexible. This inflexibility is related to its own need for efficiency in the distribution of its message and related products.

In contrast, individual consumers are said to act *tactically* to create space for themselves in environments defined by the strategies of the governing entities. Tactical actors are powerful because of their (re)combinatory power in interpreting rules, processes, and systems in ways that work specifically for them.

By this model, the game producers (or transmedia corporations) represent strategic entities. They have a demonstrated inflexibility in the motive—profit being the proverbial bottom line. Their message is similarly inflexible, being some version of "we're attractive, spend money on us." They use enormous amounts of time, space, resources, research, marketing, creativity and energy in perfecting their own unique (but still inflexible) adaptation of that message.

Game players, or transmedia consumers, represent tactical actors. They retain the (re)combinatory power for self-determination in the virtual space. They decide what the experience means. They make unique and unpredictable choices in identity-play that are not limited to the scope of the game or transmedia product. For example, our daughters act tactically as they navigate through the coordinated transmedia products associated with *Avatar: The Last Airbender*. They make active choices as to which character to play as in the video games, cheer for as they watch the show, or identify with as they seek purchases of consumer products such as costumes, action figures, and other toys. In other words, the strategic designs of the producers of the *Avatar* television shows, video games, and consumer products, though admittedly successful in attracting an audience, have little influence over the tactical decisions of consumers as they (re)combine images, story lines, ideas, and personality traits in the process of identity-play.

This phenomenon was clearly evident in the experience of our twin daughters. The marketing and design strategies of Nickelodeon, THQ, Mattel and others are manifestly successful in attracting our daughters' attention. However, the tactical decision by one twin daughter to self-identify with Toph (a blind, tomboyish female character), and the other twin daughter to self-identify with Sokka (a wise-cracking, male character) was made independently of the corporate strategies. The girls' (re)combinatory powers are in full display as they mix Kyoshi Warriors, Firebenders, the jocular Uncle Iro, the ageing Roku, the diffident Mai, or the athletic Ty Lee (all characters in *Avatar*) in imaginative play entirely removed from any type of electronic device or strategically produced product. Remember it was outdoor play where our children first encountered *Avatar*—outdoor play that continues as robustly as ever, richly populated with ideas gathered from identity experimentation, assessment, and play inherent to the transmedia experience they have been exposed to.

Tactical Open Space

This type of tactical success by consumers, or readers, of transmedia products should not be seen as a strategic failure by the producing entities. On the contrary, the strategic goals of *Avatar* producers are clearly successful—they attract an audience and generate a profit. We would assert, however, that creating space for tactical interaction (and therefore identity-play) contributes greatly to the success of the product, especially with girls. This strategy of attraction through identity-play and the creation of tactical open-space comes at a time when studies on consumption indicate that parents (and children themselves) are viewing adolescence as a period of active consumption in which children have a dynamic influence in the parents' decisions about materials that are consumed within the family home.

Writing for the British National Consumer Council, Mayo (2005) describes children as "active consumers" with power in the marketplace. He depicts young people as shoppers, collectors and brand identifiers. His research is supported by other consumer socialization research (John, 1999; McNeal, 1993; Kinder, 2000; Cook, 2004) which indicates that 21st century children are avid consumers who have been socialized into the role from an early age, developing the skills, values, and knowledge that they use in influencing and making purchases now and in the future.

The presence of tactical open-space (where identity-play is possible and even encouraged) in transmedia products drives not only commercial success but an increase in positive interpretations of the experience by the consumer/reader. For example, Microsoft's Annual Parent Survey released in 2009 shows that as the market grows and gaming devices are more readily available, parents view video games more positively and feel more informed about, and familiar with, both the games and the operating systems with which their children play. The recent increase in positive appraisal of video and computer gaming may very well be due to the increase in tactical open-space in transmedia products as companies try to feminize their products and therefore achieve greater market penetration. While not trying to draw any conclusions, we do think that it is noteworthy that this feminization through attention to identity-play and the creation of tactical open-space (through the adoption of Laurel's principles of girl gaming) has been contemporaneous to new attitudes towards gaming in general and record sales numbers.

Despite widespread warnings and public hand wringing over the reported negative effects of video gaming, sales are brisk and ever increasing. Current statistics that show 45 percent of heavy video game play occurs among 6- to 17-year-olds (NPD group, 2006). National reports also claim that 92 percent of all children and adolescents growing up in the United States play video games (NIFM annual report card). In addition the Annenberg Center for Public Policy found that children in the age group of 8-13 spend more time playing video games that any other segment of children, playing an average of 32 minutes a day with online and more traditional video game devices (p. 42). These statistics point to the ever-increasing video game market, which reached $31.6 billion in U.S. sales in 2006 with the projections for the worldwide market to grow to over $48.9 billion before 2011 (Scanlon, 2007).

The rapid expansion of this industry and its greater connection to female consumers are indicative of the impact that identity-play in tactical open-space has as a marketing strategy. The development of the multimodal consumer/creator, and that consumer/creator's ability to perform his or her own unique identity, has revolutionized how transmedia companies approach their audiences in general and their female audience in particular. This regular performance of identity is a hopeful sign that despite the profit-driven strategies of this industry, the child-consumers who engage with these products are free to act tactically and are increasingly encouraged to be the creators of their own identities.

Conclusion

Online games and other transmedia experiences clearly present new challenges for young consumers and their parents. It is generally held that the promotion and perpetuation of the multimedia industry through the things that it makes and distributes define the rules and regulations of a child's world, seeking to prevent that child from forming an authentic self through the establishment rigid binaries for girls' and boys' behavior. Transmedia environs, like those described in the chapter, certainly use large amounts of time, space, and resources to produce the inflexible message that consumption of multiple and various products determines one's identity. In contrast, we believe young girls' online/offline identities are more than simply a visceral, embodied comprehension shaped solely by the strategic efforts of gaming companies. Instead, aspects of virtual and physical identity can be shaped and reshaped by young people to their advantage as they embrace their own capacity for multimodality and therefore act tactically, creating space for themselves in environments defined by the strategies of the governing entities.

By acting tactically girls can resist prevailing gender scripts that devalue authentic selfhood and oppose codified notions of femininity, power relations, and other regulations of gender and childhood discourses embedded in the transmedia experience. As girls employ tactical skills that allow them to encounter and engage powerfully with and through consumer products, they are more likely to effectively utilize tactical open spaces to (re)combine images, story lines, ideas, and personality traits to form their own unique identities. This performance of identity, while commercialized as an attractive agent of transmedia products, is nevertheless powerful in its abilities to foster self-determinism through unique and unpredictable tactical responses to strategic environments.

References

Ball, R. (2008, July 23). Nick's Avatar hits ratings high. *Animation Magazine*. Retrieved April 29, 2009, from http://www.animationmagazine.net/article/8636.

Barrie, J. M., and Hollindale, P. (ed.), (1991). *Peter Pan in Kensington Gardens and Peter and Wendy*. Oxford: Oxford University Press.

Buckingham, D. (2007). Youth, Identity, and Digital Media. In *The John D. and Catherine T. MacArthur Foundation Series on Digital Media and Learning*, pp. 1–22. Posted online December 3, 2007. Massachusetts Institute of Technology Press.

Cook, D.T. (2004). *The commodification of childhood: The childrens' clothing industry and the rise of the child consumer*. Durham, NC: Duke University Press.

De Certeau, M. (2002). *The practice of everyday life*. (S. Rendal, Trans.). Berkeley, CA: University of California Press.

Disney Internet Media Group. (2008, October 23). *Disney Online launches Pixie Hollow virtual world; Magical destination brings enchanting fairy adventures to life*. Retrieved from http://corporate.disney.go.com/wdig/news_release/2008/2008_10_23_pixiehollow.html.

Giddens, A. (1991). *Modernity and self-identity: Self and society in the late modern age*. Cambridge, UK: Polity Press.

Hall, S. (1996) Who needs 'identity'? In S. Hall & du Gay, P. (eds.), *Questions of cultural identity*. London: SAGE Publications.

Holston, N. (2009). *Complete list of 2008 Peabody Award winners*. Retrieved April 29, 2009, from The Peabody Awards Web site: http://www.peabody.uga.edu/news/press_release.php?id=156. April 1, 2009.
Jenkins, H. (2001). *From Barbie to Mortal Kombat: Further reflections*. Retrieved April 29, 2009, from University of Chicago Videogames & Cultural Policy Conference Web site: http://culturalpolicy.uchicago.edu/conf2001/papers/jenkins.htm.
Jenkins, H. (2007). Transmedia Storytelling 101. Message posted to http://www.henryjenkins.org/2007/03/transmedia_storytelling_101.html. March 22, 2009
John, D.R. (1999). Consumer Socialization of Children: A Retrospective Look at 25 Years of Research. *Journal of Consumer Research*, 26(3): 183-237.
Kinder, M. (ed.) (2000) *Kids' Media Culture (Console-ing Passions)*. Duke University Press.
Kress, G. (2000). Design and transformation: New theories of literacy. In B. Cope & M. Kalantzis M. (Eds.), *Multiliteracies: Literacy learning and design of social futures*. New York: Routledge.
Laurel, B. (2001). *Utopian entrepreneur*. Cambridge, MA: MIT Press.
Livingstone, S. (2004). *Children online–consumers or citizens?* Retrieved from Cultures of Consumption Working Paper Series website: http://www.consume.bbk.ac.uk/publications.html. March 2009
Mayo, E. (2005). Shopping Generation. In *Young Consumers: Insights and Ideas for Responsible Marketers*. 6 (4): pages 43-49.
McNeal, J.U. (1993) Born to Shop. (Children's Shopping Patterns). *American Demographics*, 15(6): 34-39.
MWW Group. (2008). *Generation now and the virtual worlds of girls, 6-12*. Retrieved from MWW Group Thought Leadership Web site: http://www.mwwpr.com/images/thought_leadership/Generation_Now.pdf. Feb 2009
Nakashima, R. (2008, October 24). *Tinker Bell appears in act of marketing magic*. Retrieved April 29, 2009 from the Associated Press Archive: http://nl.newsbank.com/nl-search/we/Archives?p_action=doc&p_docid=124565A5A1F6D300&p_docnum=1.
Nguyen-Chaplin, L., & John, D. R. (2005). The development of self-brand connections in children and adolescents. *Journal of Consumer Research*, 32, June issue, pp. 119-129.
Pixie Hollow surge drives Disney online growth (2009, February 16). Retrieved April 29, 2009, from Virtual Worlds News website: http://www.virtualworldsnews.com/2009/02/pixie-hollow-surge-drives-disney-online-growth.html.

Scanlon, Jessie. (2007). The Video Game Industry Outlook: 31.6 Billion and Growing. Retrieved April 20, 2009 from www.businessweek.com/ innovate/content/aug2007/id20070813_120384.htm

Seiter, E. (2004). The internet playground. In J. Goldstein, D. Buckingham D., & G. Brougere G. (Eds.), *Toys, games, and media* (pp. 93-108). Mahwah, NJ: Lawrence Erlbaum Associates.

Wright, J. A. (2009, January 13) Design, baby-sitting video games target a growing market. *Tulsa World*, p. D1.

Wickstrom, M. (2007) *Performing consumers: Global capital and its theatrical seductions*. London: Routledge.

Williamson, D. A. (2007, September). *Kids and teens: Virtual worlds open new universe.* Retrieved April 29, 2009, from eMarketer website: http://www.emarketer.com/Reports/All/Emarketer_2000437.aspx.

Chapter Two

Exploring and Re-creating Indigenous Identity through Theatre-based Workshops

Warren Linds, Felice Yuen, Linda Goulet, Jo-Ann Episkenew, and Karen Schmidt

Introduction

Play, existing in the potential space between the individual and the environment, can be understood as a place where cultural experience is located. As Winnicott (1971) writes, "cultural experience begins with creative living first manifested in play" (p. 135). Play can also be conceptualized as a transformative context enabling participants to create, and practice, identities (Isenberg & Jalongo, 2001). Play is also seen as an important element of interactive theatre processes which can foster transformation of individuals and communities. Interactive theatre explorations draw on the experiences of the participants to create images and scenes to explore, through theatrical means, issues that the participants identify as relevant to their lives. Monks, Barker, and Mhanacháin (2001) outline how theatre provides opportunities for participants to test different relationships with the people around them. Participants can step out of their own bodies and try on others, providing a means of exploring the possibilities of other social relations (Auslander, 1994). Theatrical work becomes both symbolic and reflexive (Schechner, 1985), as what is shown is emotional, embodied, and based in the experiences of the participants. This chapter explores theatre workshops as a context for Indigenous[1] youth to play and to give voice to their experiences with a goal of identifying and examining the socio-cultural issues that affect their health and that of their communities. It also explores the data collected to date and situates our research in the context of the history of Indigenous peoples' experiences with colonization.

We are an inter-disciplinary team that has been working over three years with Indigenous youth[2] from an area served by one First Nations Tribal Council, which provides many services, including health to people living on

---

1. We use Indigenous as a general term that includes First Nations, Métis and Inuit peoples.
2. We worked with students from grades 8 to 12 who were between the ages of 14 to 21 years.

11 reserves, as well as those who live off reserves in the area. The research team is a partnership of the health educator from the Tribal Council, two academics from First Nations University of Canada, and two from Concordia University. We are a mix of Non-Aboriginal, First Nations and Métis who have personal and professional connections to this community. The health educator is from the community; one of the academics is married into one of the reserves, while another has connections to the many teachers in the community she has taught over the years.

Our team believes that engaging youth in an examination of the factors that affect their decision-making is foundational to the development of optimum health. We initially hypothesized that play, in the environment created by theatre-based[3] workshops, would foster growth in the Indigenous youth participants by supporting them in a process whereby they could become aware of and reflect upon factors that affect their decisions, and thus their health. This experience was an embodied and proactive process.

Our work with the youth involved seven workshops of two or three days in length beginning in the summer of 2006. After the initial workshop on the first reserve, there was enough interest at another reserve to organize two workshops the following winter, and then a follow-up workshop in late spring. In the spring of 2008, we brought together youth from several schools in a combined workshop at a central location and followed that up with a similar workshop in the fall of 2008.[4] This enabled us to expand the number of schools involved in the program. During the first workshops, many participants spoke with cynicism as they recited health information by rote: "Stay away from drugs and alcohol; peer pressure is bad." In our conversations with them, however, we learned that they did not apply these messages to their lives. In other words, current preventative measures, in the form of health education messages, were not being enacted by youth as part of their daily lives.

Our hypothesis was that theatre-based workshops would help participants to analyze the health issues that affected their communities and enable them

---

3   Although the roots of our workshop design are in workshops based on Theatre of the Oppressed (Boal, 1979, 1992, 1995) and Power Plays (Diamond, 2007), we use this term to indicate that our workshops involve everyone in interacting together in theatre games and storytelling rather than in producing a play for public performance.

4   At the time of writing, we had completed, but not analyzed, three more workshops in May and June 2009, and received four years of funding to continue and expand this research.

to become, in effect, health researchers and health advocates. Theatre games would be "warm up" exercises to build group cohesiveness and trust. Our primary objective was to create a Forum Theatre (Boal, 1979) play focused on health issues and provide the community with a "forum" to examine and discuss these issues through interaction with the play on stage.

Our project used elements of collaborative research (Goulet, Krentz, & Christiansen, 2003) with the youth participants in the delivery of theatre-based workshops. Games, combined with interactive theatre processes, built trust, developed voice, and shared power. The structure of the theatre workshops allowed participants to take leadership by directing the content of the research as they determined the stories they would share and the interpretation of those stories (Linds & Goulet, 2010). In the first workshops, we asked the youth to prioritize the health issues they were facing. We also responded to participants' voices in the initial data collection and focused subsequent workshops more on the theatre games and less on a forum theatre performance. These games enabled players to explore the reality and potential of their community and provided opportunities for increased awareness and self-esteem, and transformation.

Situating Our Research

Our work with Indigenous youth is situated within the context of colonialism. The serious health issues facing Indigenous peoples today are a direct result of colonization—colonization that continues to this day in the distribution of resources in Canada and globally—and in the relationships between Indigenous peoples and their relationships with governments and the corporate sector (Report of the Royal Commission on Aboriginal Peoples, 1996; Stavenhagen, 2005). Maori scholar, Smith (1999) identifies colonization as the process that facilitated the economic, political, and cultural expansion of European power and control by subjugating Indigenous populations. Adams (1989) and Paul (1993) describe the devastation and document the complex system of European colonization in Canada that used, among other things, trade and military power, combined with Eurocentrism and racism, to secure the resources, and especially the land, of the Indigenous peoples of Canada. The resistance of Indigenous peoples to colonization took many forms including armed struggle, political movements for self-determination (Adams, 1989; Paul, 1993), court challenges (Smith, 1999), and narratives that asserted Indigenous identity and histories (Said, 1993). The marginalized positions of Indigenous people living in Canada today lie in a legacy of colonialism. Colonization is argued as being significantly responsible for the drastic situation facing Indigenous communities (Monture-Angus, 2000).

Duran and Duran (1995) write that since the beginning of colonization, Indigenous people experienced a *soul-wound* that has continued through generations of Indigenous people who face the continual pressure to acculturate into settler society, the same society that created the genocidal policies and oppressive bureaucratic actions that have caused such harm. This soul-wound, manifested through symptoms of anxiety, depression, and violence against oneself or other Indigenous people (Duran & Duran, 1995), has also contributed to creating an Indigenous identity related to shame and powerlessness (Yuen, 2008).

Canada's Indian Act has severely weakened the Indigenous populations (Canadian Panel on Violence against Women, 1993; Lawrence, 2004; York, 1990). The Indian Act is, in effect, a regime of regulation that shaped, and continues to shape, the Indigenous identity and has permeated the ways in which Indigenous people understand their own identities (Lawrence, 2004). When traditional gatherings and ceremonies were banned by Canada's Indian Act, Indigenous peoples were essentially denied the spirit of coherence that kept their community together. The arts are where people developed social skills and engaged in their community, "collaborated, co-operated, co-ordinated, laughed and healed" (Amadahy, 2003, p. 145). Traditional ceremonies, which generally contained music, dance, and other arts, can be understood as social and political arenas to develop and maintain relations and solidarity among Indigenous peoples. As Backhouse (1999) explains, "ceremonial practices were inextricably linked with the social, political, and economic life-blood of the community, and dances underscored the core of Indigenous resistance to cultural assimilation" (p. 65). Music, dance and other arts in pre-colonial times were not perceived as separate entities in the lives of Indigenous peoples. As Amadahy explains, these experiences were "integrated into [their] daily lives, from the Sunrise Ceremonies that started the day to the Thanksgiving prayers that occurred at sunset" (p. 144). In other words, the abolition of such practices effectively destroyed the way in which Indigenous cultures created, maintained, and celebrated who they were. While play was not a word used to describe these rituals, various art forms such as music, dance and now theatre can be understood as exploring, creating, and celebrating identity, and giving expression to who you are as a person.

Arts, Theatre, and Community Health

An Australian study (Mulligan et al., 2006) suggests that community-based arts and cultural projects can enhance the well-being of isolated and marginalized communities to generate and sustain a different form of meaning for challenged and disrupted communities. Theatre appears to have significant power when applied in the areas of educational and community development. Taylor (2002) writes of the potential of "an applied theatre form in which individuals connect with and support one another and where opportunities are provided for groups to voice who they are and what they aspire to become" (p. xviii). Thompson (2003) adds that such programs "can be a vital part of the way that people engage in their communities, reflect on issues and debate change. They can be central to different groups' experiences of making and remaking their lives" (p. 16).

Theatre also creates the opportunity for "safe space" through which different relations can be built. According to Lumsden (1997),

> Theatre is perhaps the clearest example of an important resource—a transitional zone that acts as a 'safe space' for traumatized individuals and communities...[to work] through terrifying emotions and [try] new approaches to social relations—both of which may be invaluable in breaking the cycle of domestic and communal violence. (p. 263)

According to O'Connor, Holland and O'Connor (2007), theatre processes give youth an opportunity to share their knowledge from which adults learn:

> In making such connections, students are demonstrating their commonsense knowledge of their emotional world, or their emotional wisdom...it works because the moment you *give them a message* they turn off. In sharing this wisdom, they are giving, as much as receiving, powerful messages. (p. 9)

Similar to the participants in this study by O'Connor et al., youth in our workshops drew our attention to significant health concerns that directly affected their sense of safety and feelings of self-esteem, including peer pressure, addictions, suicide, and gangs. The scenes they created, as outlined later on in this chapter, revealed *the importance of relationships* in their communities and a problematic norm in social systems. Drugs and alcohol have a profound effect on their lives and their relationships, and decisions that have an impact on their health are too often made under those influences.

The focus on health issues also highlighted negatively constructed perceptions of community norms that clearly demonstrated how deeply these youth and their communities have been impacted by the processes of colonization, oppression and racism.[5] Some of the participants had internalized racialized negative stereotypes of Indigenous peoples, believing that change is impossible because "everybody on the reserve drinks," despite clear evidence to the contrary. Although some participants readily created short scenes emerging from their reality, many were not that interested in an analysis of the issues they identified. At the same time, they found the games engaging and wanted to play more.

Theatre-Based Workshops and Power Plays: The Process

> The Forum process focus is both educational and performative, whereby each participant develops their right to expression...Everyone has the right to speak, everyone has the right to question, and everyone has the right to be listened to... the power of creative representation becomes a democratic right for all. (Houston, Magill, McCollum & Spratt, 2001, p. 287)

Our theatre workshops were based on Power Plays (Diamond, 2007), an adaptation of Forum Theatre techniques, originally developed by Brazilian theatre director Augusto Boal (1979) to use in health and literacy education campaigns. Power Plays consist of a workshop approach developed for use in a North American context. Forum Theatre has spread throughout the world since Boal's early work. This dramaturgy has been used to structure dialogues around such issues as economic and health policy, race relations, school reform, and diversity and has proved extremely useful in grassroots education and problem-solving. It involves and engages communities directly and places high value on ideas, opinions, and proposals brought forth by the community's analysis of real-life experiences (Boal, 1992). The workshop process is designed to provide a performance-based, theatrical structure for dialogue on significant social, cultural, and health issues, to create imaginative "blueprints" for possible healthy futures based on appropriate interventions and choices. The process develops leadership skills as participants begin to question habitual thinking, enabling them to become aware of their power to be producers of knowledge and action, not just consumers.

---

5   For a more in-depth discussion of the impact of colonization on Indigenous peoples, see Goulet, Episkenew, Linds, & Arnason. (2009).

The Workshops

> Play does not have its being in the player's consciousness or attitude but on the contrary play draws him into its dominion and fills him with its spirit. (Gadamer, 1999, p.109)

Each workshop involved intensive experiences that introduced the rudiments of Boal's Theatre of the Oppressed dramaturgy using a graduated sequence of basic acting games and structures, image-making exercises and scene improvisations.

We began each workshop with a circle led by an elder from the community. Then we introduced ourselves and the project. We asked the participants to share something about themselves. To establish a sense of equity and to ease the youth into the day's activities, we asked questions that we thought would be nonthreatening, for example, "What is your favourite music?" Student participation was limited to a few words for those who responded. Yet, although the young people were reluctant to participate in discussions, they were enthusiastic about participating in theatre games where they could move around the space.

Following the circle, we asked youth to participate in trust, group-building, and theatre games. "Blind" games help develop trust as participants closed their eyes and moved around the room. These games encouraged the participants to pay attention to senses we normally ignore. The games were structured to move from simple to more complex. Participating in games helped youth express their ideas and feelings, developed group cohesion, and encouraged trust. They also brought together those who do not normally associate with one another, either in school or in the community.

These games were not separate from the methodology of our research; they built a sense of common purpose while unlocking issues the group was investigating. On several occasions, for example, a name game helped as we all began playing with our names, adding an adjective with the same initial letter as our first names, and then including a motion to describe ourselves. For example, one of the authors identified himself as "Wonderful Warren" while dramatically opening his arms. Everyone then repeated the name with adjectives, the motion causing much laughter among the participants and a subsequent lowering of barriers.

We briefly introduced the youth to moulding the human body—thereby creating images of actions, conflicts, or symbolic meanings. Then we guided the participants in constructing images of health concerns as well as ethnographic images that depicted unique community power dynamics and perceptions of risk. These images were configured as still photos or video freeze-frames, and used as a platform for animated short stories about a particular situation. Ultimately, the group improvised scenes that clearly showed how health issues were articulated in their real life situations.

During the workshops, we asked students to identify the health issues that they and their communities faced. Participants identified many issues but prioritized peer pressure, drug and alcohol abuse, and the resulting behaviours as the most pressing. Students then created images and short scenes of their experiences. Many of the scenes portrayed drinking or drug abuse at parties and the resultant negative actions of the youth that included drunk driving, fighting, and stealing.

We share the following scene created in one of our earlier workshops to illustrate the effects of colonization and oppression on the perceived world of the Indigenous youth with whom we worked. The scene opens with friends talking excitedly as they make their way to a party. When the characters arrive at the party, alcohol and drugs are being used and they are encouraged to join in, which they do. As the party progresses, some of the youth realize that they are running out of beer. Even though most of them are drunk by now, the youth decide that someone needs to make a beer run into town. A "volunteer" is selected who has a car and even though he is quite drunk, three other youth accompany him. As he drives into town, the driver continues to smoke marijuana, loses control of the car and rolls into a ditch, hurting some of the passengers. In debriefing this scene with the youth, the character that played a passenger was asked why she decided to get into a car with a driver who was obviously drunk. Her telling response was, "I don't know. I'm just along for the ride" (Goulet, Episkenew, Linds & Arnason, p. 112).

Stories were central to the learning process, as they act as mediators between self and others. As participants created different sets of images, they developed the capacity to give expression to experience. Not only does this emphasize the traditional aphorism of "show us, don't tell us," it also leads those looking to be able to interpret the images according to their own experiences.

Michael Rohd (1998) conceives of such games as collective activities that create a sense of comfort and enable people to interact together in a safe and energized space. However, we saw much more happening. The youth were engaging in these playful activities as explorations of their lives. In one such activity, *West Side Story* (Boal, 1992, p. 98), based on the Bernstein Broadway play, they talked in particular about how it related to life on the reserve. In this activity, two teams face one another with one leader each. One leader makes a sound and movement and advances against the opposing team which retreats. Once the team has retreated six steps, the roles are reversed. This goes on until all participants have a chance to lead their team.

Some of the youth were at first reticent to lead their team, but as each tried, the gestures and movements became more animated. Afterwards, during the debriefing of the activity, several participants linked their experience to being part of a group that supported each other and how sometimes that could take a negative turn. However, the participants emphasized that no one had used violent gestures while leading their team (even though they were divided by space and movement into opposing "sides"). Indeed, one participant subverted the expectation of aggressive and/or violent gestures by choosing to use humour as he mocked flatulence to drive the opposing team across the room. The youth also observed how their experience of the game, *West Side Story*, was different from their lives in their communities, where violence can divide members of families and community. As Boal (1995) points out, "the image of reality is the reality of the image" of the activities in which we engage (p. 43). The characters must forget the real world which was the origin of the image and play with the image itself, in its artistic embodiment, thus practising in the second world (the aesthetic), in order to modify the first (the social).

The Effect of the Theatre Process

> Dramatic play is in the dialectic between the actual, everyday reality and imaginative one...(in play) the former context is explored through the latter. (Landy, 1986, p. 63)

There is a growing recognition of role of drama in healing, "that artistic expression, symbolic acts and ritual have important roles and functions both for individual adults, and for families and communities" (Lumsden, 1997, p. 268). Liebmann (1996) believes art's approaches to dealing with domestic and inter-communal violence offer a number of additional benefits, such as understanding different points of view through activity participation and resolving conflict through cooperative projects, which essentially contribute to the development of participant's communication and cooperation skills. Episkenew (2008, 2009) observes that the inherently communal nature of theatre makes it a particularly attractive genre for Indigenous communities to use when grappling with the social problems that are a result of historical trauma.

Seidlitz (1994) explains that theatre is a medium that fits comfortably within Indigenous traditions, cultures, and ways of expression. Both Favel Starr (1997) and Manossa (2001) argue that contemporary Indigenous theatre is not merely an adaptation or appropriation of European theatrical tradition but rather a form of expression that easily fits within Indigenous traditions because it is rooted in traditional Indigenous performance arts. Wesley-Esquimaux and Smolewski (2004) argue that the "goal of any healing process is a recovery of awareness, a reawakening to the senses, a re-owning of one's life experience and a recovery of people's enhanced abilities to trust this experience" (p. 78). Drama can provide young people, who may be reticent to articulate their individual stories, with a safe, collaborative means to express the stories of the collective. In this way, they are able to begin the healing process. Importantly, the youth participants highlighted the *importance of relationships* to help them create healthy communities.

Our participants initially expressed a sense of acceptance towards certain misrepresentations of their community that had essentially developed into a racialized identity. Comments to support their claim that change was impossible were associated with stereotypical, colonized Indigenous identities such as lacking initiative and being drunk. Specifically, several young people stated that "everybody on the reserve drinks" and "no one on the reserve ever does anything" despite the fact that the researchers knew many families on that reserve who did not drink and took leadership in activities, such as a youth drum group, where no drinking or drugs were allowed.

Over time, particularly in the last few workshops, participants were able explore creative ways of initiating change through drama. For example, in one of the latter workshops that occurred in the spring of 2008, we conducted a three-day workshop with 25 Indigenous youth from various high schools in the area. Participants were engaged in the workshop process and provided us with insight regarding alternative debriefing techniques. At the end, we broke into smaller groups so the youth could provide inputs into future plans. Participants identified two directions for the project. Many participants wanted to learn how to lead similar drama games to help younger children "overcome shyness and develop confidence," which they identified as significant health issues; while others wanted to create and perform community plays based on their life experiences.

Inspired by that workshop, one person from the research team and four female youth participants co-facilitated two very successful, half-day drama workshops for younger children. The girls demonstrated developing leadership abilities and expressed a keen interest in continuing to plan and deliver these workshops. Phinney and Kohatsu (1997) cite several research studies that show that adjustments among ethnocultural adolescents are associated with "positive attitudes and interactions with members of their own group, of other groups, and of the larger society" (p. 438). Although a small step, the leaders of these workshops identified how they could participate in positive interactions with others and, with adult support, took action to make this happen.

How Does Identity Emerge through Play?

> The being of all play is self-realization. (Gadamer, 1999, p. 113)

One way to examine the emergence of identity through play is through the ancient rhetoric of community identity—belonging in a larger sense, which may present play more as an obligatory rite, whereby participation is less voluntary and determined by social context and community values (Sutton-Smith 1997; Turner, 1982). In *Ambiguity of Play*, Sutton-Smith discusses how play, in the form of ritual, festival, and other forms of community celebration, works to "persuade ourselves to adopt a communal view of ourselves" (p. 92).

Rules in play do not determine whether someone has won or lost but instead regulate the activity from within. In each instance of our workshops, the youth commented on the relevance of the activity to working with children younger than them. Even in one instance where the rules of the game were changed by the youth who were involved in it, it was done in a playful, and not competitive, manner. Whenever we played a game, we first modeled the game by explaining the rules and then demonstrating how to lead the game. In one instance, we played *Maria Maria Maria* (McCarthy, 2002, p. 50), a "name game" in which one person stands in the center of the circle and says another participant's name three times, very quickly, while pointing to that person. If that person says her own name before the person leading says it three times, then the person in the middle of the circle would have to try with another person. If the person cannot say their own name in time, she goes to the middle of the circle. One of the youth was put into the circle, and he immediately shifted the rules of the game so that he wouldn't be looking directly at the person he was trying to trick. He was playing the game but under his own rules, rules that were rooted in his cultural norms regarding eye contact with others, and in the use of deception, an important skill in traditional Indigenous gambling games. In this way, he playfully and culturally became the change he wished to see by taking control of the rules of play.

Gadamer (1999) considers "game" as a more specific form of "play": Qualities from "play" are inherited by "game." Game rules must interact with social rules—what is believed about fairness, niceness, cheating, friendship, generates the meta-rules of how to govern themselves in play and outside of play. Callois (1958) argues: "Games generally attain their goal only when they stimulate an echo of complicity" (p. 39). Sutton-Smith (1997) contends that children and youth need to express their special identity as well as their resentment of lacking power. These needs may be the point of reference for dealing with youth. That is, through play they become the change they wish to see. The development of scenes becomes "a 'play world' for 'fixing, 'un-fixing,' and 're-fixing' reality without the fear of social constructs or reprisal" (Chinyowa, 2006, Emerging implications, para. 2). Play operates beneath consciousness as it creates its own internal reality. In this way, the (playful) interactive creation of scenes by the youth changes the dynamics of the relationships between the youth by putting the responsibility on everyone to become more active participants.

Play allows us to transform ourselves into other people in order to be something else, Stories, as an esthetic form of communication, provide the "opportunity to anticipate, rehearse and contemplate [one's] own future" (Myerhoff, 1978, p. 19). How we perceive ourselves contributes to how we see ourselves within a community/social network/worldview. We build our life stories/identity thematically with an individualized narrative fitting within a larger community context (Kaufman, 2000). Further learning occurs by recapturing and sharing narrative play experiences through self-reflection, storytelling, and reflective dialogue with others bringing out new understandings of the meanings within the stories told.

Theatre-based Workshops and Identity Construction

> To control what is outside, one has to do things, not simply to think or to wish, and doing things takes time. Playing is doing. (Winnicott, 1971, p. 55)

According to Yuen and Shaw (2003), individuals involved in play can be considered active agents who learn from and influence their social environments. While their discussion is based in the reproduction and resistance of gender identities, they argue that certain forms of play (i.e., *unstructured play*) provide opportunities for empowerment and transformation that can deepen the understanding of youths' experiences of the theatre workshops. Unstructured play refers to "play that is guided by the [individuals] themselves. That is, the rules of play and how [individuals] are expected to behave during the play activity are typically dependent on [the participants]" (p. 13). Adults are present in the workshops to guide the experiences of the participants, but the young people themselves direct the creative process of play. In other words, in terms of creating an unstructured play environment, as recommended by Yuen and Shaw, the adults take on a more facilitative, as opposed to a directive, role.

In short, unstructured play experiences have the capacity to provide a sense of freedom that can help participants take advantage of the situation and construct rules of play that do not conform to societal norms and expectations (Yuen & Shaw, 2003). In this way, unstructured play experiences have the potential to interrogate, resist, reinforce or alter overlapping identities of race, class, gender, and ability. For example, in the fifth workshop, a group of girls were eager to discuss how they might take what they had learned in the workshop back to the younger students in their school. There was one young man in the group, but, because he was shy, he deferred to the girls leadership in the discussion. Most of the older girls in the group were all friends. Because of their bond and dominance in numbers, the girls were also able to exert the influence on the young man who was alone in terms of his gender, because he was still developing his confidence in his ability to speak out. This interaction contrasts with the typical decision-making process in their peer group, where males often led.

During the exploration of new realities in the workshops, participants are able to explore new roles and identities. For example, while youth resist possible identities, such as leadership through violence, they are able to explore leadership roles without the use of physical intimidation. The curiosity, imagination, and risk-taking associated with the creative aspects of play (Isenburg & Jalongo, 2001) in an unstructured environment, such as the theatre workshop, stimulate divergent thinking in its actors. As argued by Yuen and Shaw (2003):

> During their creative thought processes, participants of unstructured play may have an increased sense of freedom to explore and express themselves in a newly imagined world, without the boundaries and constraints of the current culture. The absence of predetermined...norms in unstructured play may help promote flexibility, originality and elaboration of ideas. (p. 15)

Popularly, play tends to be contrasted with work, and thus is often seen as chaotic and frivolous. Davis, Sumara, and Luce-Kapler (2000) observe that play is "generally regarded as what we do when serious responsibilities are fulfilled" (p. 146). The criticism of play as not work, and therefore nonproductive and potentially disruptive, brings up fears that unregulated play would lead to loss of control. In *The Therapeutic Powers of Play*, Schaefer (1993) lists the benefits of play as development of rapport, understanding, increased self-esteem, problem-solving, emotional release, adjustment to trauma, and practice of new behaviors and insight. Garner (1994) quotes Jacques Derrida who claimed that play itself is the "disruption of presence" (p. 40), which is evident particularly in the transition between sensory awareness and the improvised performance that we use to make the transition from playing with each other to playing with each other through the language of image.

Complete the Image (Diamond, 2007), which was used in every workshop, introduced the idea of a space of possibilities where the stability of the story is constantly challenged. This storytelling activity was first done in pairs and then in the large group. When in the large group, anyone who had an idea can jump up, tap one of a pair shaking hands and replace them, adding a new element to the story. This process continued until six or seven people participated in making a story out of the image. When the group understood the method, we began again, but this time we asked the group to use a particular theme when completing the image. In our workshops, the themes included life in our community and life in school.

The process involved in *Complete the Image* was an open and "writerly" (Barthes 1975) text as our bodies speak in a new language involving relationship and action with an audience. This awakens the sense of mindfulness but there is still initial resistance and discomfort. Some of this is due to the disruption Derrida speaks of. The work implicitly involves participants discovering their character-as-becoming in collaboration with those watching. Being "writerly" means the authors (in this case, the youth actors) do not attempt to control the actions or feelings of the watcher but, instead, create a structure where individuals can bring themselves into the text. When there is such room, there will be discomfort, ambiguity, and uncertainty about what we will discover about ourselves through the character that is being explored.

Play as Decolonizing

> Although "spinning loose" as it were, the wheel of play reveals to us (as Mihaly Csikszentmihalyi has argued) the possibility of changing our goals and, therefore, the restructuring of what our culture states to be reality. (Turner, 1983, p. 234)

While Forum Theatre is not a traditional form of art in Indigenous cultures, it does offer a space in which participants can experience similar practices that were once attributed to sustaining healthy and strong communities. Forum Theatre provides a space for decolonization in three ways:

- Reintegrating art back into community life as a social forum for engagement and collaboration
- Creating a space for self-expression, and
- Fostering much-needed discussions about community health and other issues to create healthier and stronger communities that move beyond the colonized images of Indigenous peoples portrayed by the larger society.

According to Fernández (2003), Indigenous peoples "must come to create a spiral, one that turns back to the past while at the same time progressing forward in order to survive in a different world" (p. 254). In other words, processes of decolonization require the reclamation of the Indigenous knowledge, practices and values of the past that can be applied to current conditions and used to guide our actions in addressing issues and solving the problems of today.

An important aspect of the workshop process that contributed to the spiral described by Fernández is the involvement of Indigenous elders. Many community members describe elders as respected role models who listen and offer guidance based on love and support (Yuen, 2008). In most workshops, an elder was present throughout the entire workshop. They not only opened our workshop but also provided connections for the young people to the Indigenous traditions of respect and listening. At times, they would provide us with the direction and structure to connect the participants to Indigenous traditions. One example that illustrates the connection to traditional values was when many of the participants came to workshops with an iPod in their ear. The elder began her talk with the statement that part of the tradition is respect, and in order to demonstrate respect, you must listen, so "earpieces out." In this way, the elder was able to ground the norms of workshop in terms of cultural values. Thus, with the involvement of elders, theatre-based workshops offer an arts-based context that has the potential to create stronger, healthier communities that are able to incorporate Indigenous traditions.

As Indigenous communities continue to resist and heal from Canada's colonial practices and as traditional ceremonies regain momentum, a theatre-based workshop provides another context for Indigenous youth to explore their identities and offers them the opportunity to adopt and celebrate, or resist and change what is ultimately discovered through their own performances. Through the workshops, the participants drew attention to their significant concerns, including peer pressure, addiction, suicide, gangs, and lack of self-esteem.

Social issues facing the communities have a strong impact on youth and ultimately contribute to their sense of hopelessness. There is increasing awareness and recognition for the importance of finding creative and different ways of looking at supporting youth as they struggle to overcome the ravages of colonization. The renaissance in culture that is facilitating the movement of Indigenous youth beyond the colonized, racialized stereotypes, and the impoverishment that their people have and continue to experience. Consequently, support and encouragement in their struggle to make good decisions in their lives are necessary. But rather than teaching the participants or giving them strategies for creating healthy communities, we tried to understand and discover new ways of support *with* the youth. In other words, we had to learn from the youth what their view of a healthy community was and what that meant.

We work with the imagination, and we work with content. For example, we wanted to look at healthy decision-making, so we asked the participants to create images that reflected issues they might have in their lives. When we asked participants to do an assessment of what they were learning and what was having the most impact on them, what they were really interested in was the drama games. Then we asked them, "Why drama games? What is so important about that?" The participants responded by highlighting the creation of a space where they could be themselves, and that is precisely what the group activities and the games did: create a community where participants could feel safe to take risks and do different things. We learned from the youth that the drama games helped participants be themselves and overcome their shyness.

For the Indigenous youth participants, the core of healthy decision-making required the confidence to be able to make their own decisions. If they did not have that confidence and know how to express themselves, then it was really hard to say no to peer pressure to engage in risky behaviours. We were not coming into the workshops to reinforce the status quo by teaching youth to "Say no to peer pressure" and "Say no to drugs and alcohol." Rather, the focus of our work was having the participants learn about self-expression and confidence and how they have the potential to contribute to the well-being of their own lives. In this way, the theatre workshop process can be understood as a vehicle that fosters human agency, cultural creation, and meaning.

We also learned that this kind of engaging process required a lot of time. The development of safe spaces requires lengthy periods where trust and openness can naturally develop. If such a space is created for youth, they can come up with some of their own solutions to their issues. During this process, an important caveat to remember is that after experiencing this safe space, participants may find it hard going back into the larger society, where there is little to no sense of safety.

As previously mentioned, some of the young people have already gone out and done workshops for younger children with one of the authors. This speaks to the character of the Indigenous youth participants. After their training, the first thing they wanted to do is give back to the community, to go and share it with others. This level of involvement is certainly something to be said for the strength of the youth. They are eager and ready to share their learning with the younger children in hopes that these children will not have to experience the same hardships as they did.

When engaging in artistic forms with any population, facilitators must provide the conditions and the structure for exploration. Flexibility is key, as there is no control over what is going to happen. This flexibility is particularly important to consider as adults working with youth, since the typical adult-youth relationship indicates that it is the adult who generally tries to control the behaviours and actions of youth (Linds, Goulet, & Sammel, in press), thereby minimizing the potential for youth to express themselves and be heard and take leadership to solve the problems they experience in their lives.

As mentioned above, the first three workshops were focused on issues youth faced in their lives. When we analysed and did a write up of our initial experiences, we began to see that there was a risk that we were perpetuating colonization rather than alleviating it by reinforcing negative stereotypes of Indigenous youth. In other words, in asking youth to represent issues and problems, there is a danger that we only represent their lives as "problematic" (no matter what the cause is). We thought to ourselves, "How would our world look to an outsider if we focused only on our problems?" Therefore, as researchers, we switched our focus to having youth represent times when they were able to make a decision that they were proud of or felt good about. We learned from the youth that they wanted to move towards the development of self-confidence and self-esteem, which are critical elements in supporting the youth's volition and agency for change. As researchers we have come to see the need to continue to move from a problem-based approach to strengths-based research that focused on health and healthy behaviours rather than unhealthy ones (Wilson, 2008). We will continue to listen to the youth as they share through the theatre work and the interviews we do with them.

One of the most basic human rights is the right to express oneself. Consequently, finding creative and alternative ways for expression, such as play through theatre, are important to the process of sustaining a healthy community where youth have the freedom to create and re-create their identities as contributing members of their community.

References

Adams, H. (1989). *Prison of grass: Canada from a Native point of view* (Rev. ed.). Saskatoon, SK: Fifth House Publishers.

Amadahy, Z. (2003). The healing power of women's voices. In K. Anderson & Lawrence, B. (Eds.), *Strong women stories, Native vision and community survival* (3rd edition) (pp. 144-155). Toronto: Sumach Press.

Auslander, P. (1994). Boal, Blau, Brecht: The body. In M. Schutzman & Cohen-Cruz, J. (Eds.), *Playing Boal: Theatre, therapy, activism* (pp. 124-133). New York: Routledge.

Backhouse, C. (1999). *Colour-coded, A legal history of racism in Canada, 1990-1950*. Toronto: University of Toronto Press.

Barthes, R. (1975). *S/Z*. Trans. Richard Miller. London: Jonathan Cape.

Boal, A. (1979) *Theatre of the oppressed*, trans. C. and M.-O. Leal McBride. London: Pluto Press.

Boal, A. (1992). *Games for actors and non-actors*. Trans. A. Jackson. New York: Routledge.

Boal, A. (1995) *The rainbow of desire: The Boal method of theatre and therapy*. (A. Jackson, Trans.). New York: Routledge.

Callois, R. (1958). *Man, play and games*. Chicago: University of Illinois Press.

Canadian Panel on Violence Against Women. (1993). *Aboriginal women: From the final report of the Canadian panel on violence against women*. Ottawa: Panel.

Chinyowa, K. (2006) Why theatre? A theoretical view of its centrality in HIV/AIDS communication, *Trans: Internet Journal for Cultural Sciences*, 16, July. http://www.inst.at/trans/16Nr/03_1/chinyowa16.htm. Retrieved August 31, 2009.

Davis, B., Sumara, D.J., & Luce-Kapler, R. (2000). *Engaging minds: Learning and teaching in a complex world*. Mahwah, NJ: Erlbaum.

Diamond, D. (2007). *Theatre for living: The art and science of community-based dialogue*. Victoria, BC: Trafford Publishing.

Duran, E., & Duran, B. (1995). *Native American postcolonial psychology*. Albany: SUNY Press, 1995.

Episkenew J. (2008). Contemporary Indigenous literature in Canada: Healing from historical trauma. In G.N. Devy, Davis, G.V., & Chakravarty, K. K. (Eds.), *Indigeneity: Culture and interpretation* (pp. 75-86). Hyderabad: Orient Blackswan.

Episkenew, J. (2009). *Taking back our spirits: Indigenous literature, public policy, and healing*. Winnipeg, MN: University of Manitoba Press.

Favel Starr, F. (1997). The artificial tree: Native performance culture research 1991-1996. *Canadian Theatre Review*, 90 (Spring), 83-85.

Fernandez, C. (2003). Coming full circle: A young man's perspective on building gender equity in Aboriginal communities. In K. Anderson & Lawrence, B. (Eds.), *Strong women stories, Native vision and community survival* (3rd edition) (pp. 242-256). Toronto: Sumach Press.

Gadamer, H. (1999). *Truth and method*. New York: The Continuum Publishing Co.

Garner, S. B. (1994). *Bodied spaces. Phenomenology and performance in contemporary drama*. Ithaca, NY: Cornell University Press.

Gonzalez, J. (1993). Directing high school theatre: The impact of student-empowerment strategies and unconventional staging techniques on actors, director and audience. *Youth Theatre Journal*, 13, 4-22.

Goulet, L., Episkenew, J., Linds, W., and Arnason, K. (2009). Rehearsing with reality: Exploring health issues with Aboriginal youth through drama. In S. MacKay, D. Fuchs & I. Brown (Eds.), *A passion for action in child and family services: Voices from the prairies* (pp. 99-118). Regina, SK: Canada Plains Research Centre.

Goulet, L., Krentz, C., & Christiansen, H. (2003). Collaboration in education: The phenomenon and process of working together. *Alberta Journal of Educational Research (49)*4, 325-340.

Houston, S., Magill, T., McCollum, M., & Spratt, T. (2001). Developing creative solutions to the problems of children and their families: Communicative reason and the use of forum theatre. *Child and Family Social Work, 6,* 285-293.

Isenberg, J, & Jalongo, M. (2001). *Creative expression and play in early childhood* (3rd edition). Upper Saddle River, NJ: Merrill Prentice Hall.

Kaufman, S.R. (2000). *The ageless self.* In J.F. Gubrium & Holstein, J.A. (Eds.) *Aging and everyday life* (pp. 103-111). Oxford: Blackwell.

Landy, R. (1986). *Drama therapy: Concepts and practices.* Springfield, IL: C. C. Thomas.

Lawrence, B. (2004). *"Real" Indians and others.* Vancouver, BC: UBC Press.

Liebmann, M. (1996). *Arts approaches to conflict.* London: Jesse Kingsley Publishers.

Linds, W. & Goulet, L. (2010). Acting outside the box: Using Theatre of the Oppressed in an anti-racism schools program. In P. Duffy & Vettraino, E. (Eds.), *Youth and theatre of the oppressed.* New York: Palgrave/Macmillan.

Linds, W., Goulet, L., & Sammel, A. (Eds.). (In press). *Emancipatory practices: Adult/Youth engagement for social and ecological justice.* Rotterdam: Sense.

Lumsden, M. (1997). Breaking the cycle of violence. *Journal of Peace Research,* 34(4), 377-83.

Manossa, G. (2001). The beginning of Cree performance culture. In A. Ruffo (Ed.), *(Ad)dressing our words: Aboriginal perspectives on Aboriginal literatures* (pp. 169-180). Penticton, BC: Theytus.

McCarthy, J. (2002). *Artpad: A resource for theatre and development.* Manchester, UK: Centre for Applied Theatre Research.

Monks, K., Barker, P. & Mhanacháin, A.N. (2001). Drama as an opportunity for learning and development. *Journal of Management Development, 20*(5), 414-423.

Monture-Angus, P. (2000). Aboriginal women and correctional practice: Reflections on the Task Force on Federally Sentenced Women. In K. Hannah-Moffat, & M. Shaw, *An ideal prison? Critical essays on women's imprisonment in Canada* (pp. 52-60). Halifax, NS: Fernwood.

Mulligan, M., Humphrey, K., James, P., Scanlon, C., Smith, P., & Welch, N. (2006). *Creating communities: Celebrations, arts and wellbeing within and across local communities.* Melbourne: VicHealth.

Myerhoff, B. (1978). *Number our days.* New York: Dutton Press.

O'Connor, P, Holland, C., & O'Connor, B. (2007). The everyday becomes extraordinary: Conversations about family violence through applied theatre. *Applied Theatre Researcher,* 8. Retrieved December 12, 2008 from http://www.griffith.edu.au/__data/assets/pdf_file/0007/52891/03-o-connor-final.pdf.

Paul, D. N. (1993). *We were not the savages: A Micmac perspective on the collision of European and Aboriginal civilization.* Halifax, NS: Nimbus.

Phinney, J.S., & Kohatsu, E.L. (1997). Ethnic and racial identity development and mental health. In J. Schulenberg, Maggs, J. L., & Hurrelmann, K. (Eds.), *Health risks and developmental transitions during adolescence* (pp. 420–443). New York: Cambridge University Press.

Richards, J. (2008). Closing the Aboriginal Non-Aboriginal education gap. Saskatchewan Institute of Public Policy. Regina, SK, March 4.

Rohd, M. (1998). *Theatre for community, conflict and dialogue: The Hope is Vital training manual.* Portsmouth, NH: Heinemann.

The Report of the Royal Commission on Aboriginal Peoples (1996). Ottawa, ON: Canadian Communication Group.

Said, E. W. (1993). *Culture and imperialism.* New York: Alfred A. Knopf.

Schaefer, C. E. (1993). *The therapeutic powers of play.* Northvale, NJ: Aronson.

Schechner, R. (1985). *Between theatre and anthropology.* Philadelphia: University of Pennsylvania Press.

Seidlitz, L.S. (1994). *Native theatre for the seventh generation: On the path to cultural healing.* Unpublished Masters thesis, Dalhousie University, Halifax, NS.

Smith, L. T. (1999). *Decolonizing methodologies: Research and Indigenous peoples.* New York: Zed Books.

Stavenhagen, R. (2005). *Report of the Special Rapporteur on the situation of human rights and fundamental freedoms of indigenous people.* Retrieved November 2, 2009, from http://cfsc.quaker.ca/pages/documents/RapporteurreportonCanada.pdf

Sutton-Smith, B. (1997). *The ambiguity of play.* Cambridge, MA: Harvard University Press.

Taylor, P. (2002). The applied theatre: Building stronger communities. *Youth Theatre Journal, 16,* 88-95.

Thompson, J. (2003). *Applied theatre: Bewilderment and beyond.* Berne: Peter Lang.

Turner, V. (1982). *From ritual to theatre, the human seriousness of play.* New York: PAJ Publications.

Turner, V. (1983). Body, brain and culture. Zygon 18: 221-245.

Wesley-Esquimaux, C., & Smolewski, M. (2004). *Historic trauma and Aboriginal healing.* Ottawa: Aboriginal Healing Foundation.

Wilson, S. (2008). *Research is ceremony: Indigenous research methods.* Winnipeg, MN: Fernwood.

Winnicott, D.W. (1971). *Playing and reality.* New York: Routledge.

York, G. (1990). *The dispossessed: Life and death in Native Canada.* Toronto: Little, Brown and Company (Canada) Limited.

Yuen, F.C., & Shaw, S. (2003). Play: The reproduction and resistance of dominant gender ideologies. *World Leisure, 45*(2), 12-21.

Yuen, F. (2008). Walking the red road: Aboriginal federally sentenced women's experiences in healing, empowerment, and re-creation. Unpublished doctoral dissertation, University of Waterloo, Waterloo, ON.

Chapter Three

Playing with Meaning in a Norwegian Language Immersion Village

Valerie Borey and Tove I. Dahl

The Construction Site

Villagers arrive, rolling oversized suitcases along gravel paths towards the registration tent. In other places they might be called "students" or "campers," but here at Skogfjorden, they are called "villagers" because they are here to participate *as if* this were true. They bring passports that enable them to cross the border when they arrive. Once through border security, they check in and select Norwegian names. Although they are still in the United States, they will convert their American dollars to Norwegian *kroner* at the bank, relinquish their American magazines, and learn to speak Norwegian by stumbling through the quarry of linguistic milestones that make a language speaker a speaker of language. This, at its very core, is the principle of language immersion.

But while this place, Skogfjorden, frames Norway as its primary point of reference, it does not claim, nor aspire to be, a mirror image of the country. Instead, it mindfully gathers together the bits and pieces of cultural realia (the historical data, the musical traditions and culinary precedents, the geographic terrain, the modern-day celebrities and old masters), and playfully stretches them to the point of distortion (also termed "creative tilt" by H. Hamilton and A. Cohen, 2004). In this place, then, time, space and method fuse into one another to create a world that is uniquely situated somewhere between the authentic and the fantastic, specifically designed to suit learners and their learning needs while expanding their Norwegian horizon. It is within this world that villagers learn to construct their identities as language learners and users.

The present chapter adopts a situated learning perspective,[1] as presented by Lave and Wenger (1991), to examine the role of meaningful play in second language acquisition. Specifically, we address (1) how cultural symbols are employed in creating a community of practice at Skogfjorden, a Norwegian language immersion program; and (2) how students in transitional states become active participants in the playful negotiation of meaning within this community as they take on the identity of a Norwegian speaker.

Skogfjorden as a Liminal Space

Skogfjorden is one of the 15 language villages currently run by Concordia Language Villages.[2] Spanish, German, Arabic, French, Chinese, and Korean are among the other languages represented, offering residential language immersion training to children aged seven to 18.[3] Located in the woods of northern Minnesota, Skogfjorden offers one-, two-, and four-week immersion sessions that are staffed by both native and non-native Norwegian speakers who communicate in Norwegian all day, every day in order to provide villagers ample opportunity to practice their emerging language skills.

Although it was relatively unique in insisting upon a principle of language immersion, Concordia Language Villages entered into an already thriving culture of summer camps in the United States when the first village opened in

---

1   In addition to researching the Skogfjorden community, the authors of this chapter are active participants in the program. Tove I. Dahl has served as the dean of the Norwegian Language Village since 1983. Valerie Borey has worked as a teacher and administrator with the Norwegian High School Credit Program since 2000. Our work with the program informs the research presented in this chapter, much as our research informs our work in the program. While we make no extraordinary claims on the objectivity of our stance as researchers, we can point out the benefits of participant-observation from the inside, which include access to key people and places, a wide diversity of opportunities for observational research, and the absence of gate-keepers restricting 'backstage' processes.

2   The villages have achieved international acclaim and support from leaders across the world, including UN Secretary-General Kofi-Annan, United Nations Under-Secretary-General for Communications and Public Information Kiyotaka Akasaka, U.S. President Bill Clinton, U.S. Vice President Walter Mondale, King Harald V and his father King Olav V, and the Norwegian Ambassador to the United States Knut Vollebaek.

3   The villagers who attend Skogfjorden during the summer come from all over the United States, although primarily from Midwestern states such as Minnesota, Wisconsin, Iowa and the Dakotas. Tuition varies by session, and various scholarships are available based on financial need. Approximately 25 percent of those attending the villages receive some financial assistance.

1961. In *Back to Nature: The Arcadian Myth in Urban America* (1969), Peter Schmitt noted that while the ideal notion of camps centered around the state of "communion with nature," in fact what they represented was a break with the routine of family and urban life and "served institutional needs little related to nature study" (p. 99). With military-style barracks and organization, the primary emphasis of these camps was oriented towards ideas of character formation and the development of useful skills; transformative in the sense that campers would return as better participants in their home communities. Indeed, camps in general have been documented to provide just the kinds of opportunities that offer a kind of social moratorium for personal growth (American Camp Association, 2005; Bialeschki, Krehbiel, Henderson & Ewing, 2003; Perret-Clermont, 2004; Resnick & Perret-Clermont, 2004).

This transformative nature of youth summer camps provides opportunities for "rites of passage" in which, as Victor Turner explains in *The Forest of Symbols* (1967), the subject of transformation departs from one stage of social existence and journeys to another. The subject of transformation is said to be liminal, occupying a role neither here nor there, but in between and unclassified, or not yet fully formed. Three stages characterize this state of transformation: separation, margin, and aggregation.

Separation involves the complete alienation of an individual from the stability of his previous self and social context. Extracted from his element, this subject of transformation undergoes the ritual death of his previous identity. At Skogfjorden, children are removed from their ecological contexts; parents, friends, and pets are left behind, belongings are limited to a few spare items of clothing and convenience, the trappings of American culture (music, junk food, and the English language) take on a forbidden status. The children exchange their given names for ethnic Norwegian ones.

A period of margin ensues, where an individual's resolute connection to their home identity begins to dissolve and for the subsequent one to four weeks, the liminal personae (the villagers) are ritually and functionally separated from the rest of society. Villager contact with the "outside world" is limited; they do not receive visitors or leave the site, and correspondence with family is primarily limited to the sending and receiving of old-fashioned letters. Even a villager's access to media is limited to that which is Norway-relevant (i.e., Norwegian magazines, newspapers, and websites instead of American sources).

The reality in which villagers are now operating does not recognize John as "the B average student from Roseville who plays video games with his best friend after school." It is an identity that simply will not bear the same weight at Skogfjorden, where the material and social fixtures enabling that identity simply do not exist. For most villagers, this transition is unproblematic. When the structural basis for one's identity is removed, a space outside of home life is created that allows one to play creatively with "the anti-structure" that is not home: to think, as Victor Turner put it, "not in cultural codes, but about them" (1969). This is an uncomfortable position for some, but over time, as villagers get to know one another and to share a common code for participation, a sense of communitas (or social solidarity) is established. Aggregation occurs at the end of the session, when villagers return to their home life with a new consciousness of what it means to speak Norwegian and to be a Norwegian speaker.

While this liminality is not unique to Skogfjorden (or to summer camps in general), there is some value in examining its significance to the development of a second language community. In this context, liminality has the effect of producing an anxiety-free model for learning, stripping normative behavioral anchors that might otherwise impede participation, highlighting or invoking referents that might otherwise be suppressed in day to day life, and finally, as a consequence of the first three points, reframing lived experience such that villager attention and participation are reconfigured to produce a sense of coherence with the target language community.

At Skogfjorden, these features of liminality converge into a sense of coherence between identity, experience, and meaning. While the villagers' native attachments (whether to Eminem or social expectations of the high school dance squad) are muted and held at bay, the Norwegian language and culture are made accessible both through authentic examplars and through exaggeration in both form and quantity. Just as languages parse the world into qualitatively different segments of experience, villagers come to apprehend the linguistic frame not as an object of study, but as a qualitatively different texture of experience. Because Skogfjorden is premised on villagers feeling safe and enjoying a sense of belonging (with the purpose of creating a low-stress and supportive learning environment), villagers find they may experiment not only with the form of language, but with the meanings which drive it as well; they construct their play in ways that are not only relevant to the language (i.e., with an understanding of grammatical rules and categories), but also to their own purposes (i.e., with an eye towards defining, for example, who they are in relation to one of the cultural symbols present at Skogfjorden).

When considering language instruction, it is useful to refer back to the idea that all linguistic signs (whether iconic, indexical, or symbolic) lie along a spectrum with two poles. At one end is the physical representation expressed at the formal level through utterance, pronunciation, gesture, written form, etc.. At the other end lies meaning, the semantic or pragmatic aspects of a shared or partially shared construal of lived or living experience. Language is not composed exclusively of form or meaning, but instead of a dyadic relationship between the two (Foley, 1997).

Despite this dualistic nature of language, the research on second language education to date has demonstrated an elaborate focus on form, often at the expense of meaning (Huttunen, 1996). This focus is an artifact of conducting research in the form-focused classroom where the goal of linguistic competence (rather than communicative competence) has traditionally emphasized an over-reliance on activities which have as their explicit aim the cognitive mastery of learner over the production (form) of language; these activities include translation exercises, reading aloud, underlining of structures and phrases, recitation, repetition, conjugation, and closed-answer questioning, in which the teacher already knows the correct response.

Although there is not as much information available on the effect of meaning-focused classrooms on second language learning, relatively recent initiatives such as the American Council on the Teaching of Foreign Languages (ACTFL) *Standards for Foreign Language Learning in the 21st Century* (1999) have given value to the exploration of meaning-focused strategies in the classrooms and ignited speculation on what such a classroom ought even to look like. The introduction of the Performance Assessment Unit (PAU) in 2000, with its shift from skills assessment in reading, writing, speaking, and listening to assessment of the communicative modes (presentational, interpersonal, and interpretive) has further propelled the field toward understanding the power of language as a meaning-maker (Thompson, 2000).

The Role of Play on Site

Activities at the Language Villages are characterized by hands-on activities that vary widely in form and content (Dahl, Clementi, Heysel & Spenader, 2007; Hamilton, Crane & Bartoshesky, 2005). By engaging in role playing, drawing, dancing, singing, playing a sport, writing for a newspaper or keeping a journal in a linguistic and cultural environment where these kinds of activities are the norm, villagers develop courage to invest in their language learning so that they may use the language for multiple purposes—including, or perhaps *especially*, for fun (Hamilton, Crane & Bartoshesky, 2005).

Fun is the basis of play, and village life, by its very nature, is essentially about taking on a new cultural and linguistic role and playing it out for what it has to offer.[4] If we think of this as a means to cultural learning—the kind of learning that involves coming to see things from others' point of view—there is a certain degree of identity-related risk associated with it (Dahl, 2009; Tomasello, Kruger & Ratner, 1993). The nature of the task becomes relevant for how willingly villagers engage in the game, and by embedding this kind of learning in play, the sense of risk is reduced. In play and in games, particularly those that involve role-playing or simulations, the parameters of the setting enable learners to freely experiment with who they are or wish to be and with how they spend their time (Pan, Cheok, Yang, Zhu & Shi, 2006).

Beyond using language for communicative purposes, language can also be used for play—a discursive tactic that can serve as a catalyst to increased language proficiency (Broner & Tarone, 2001). Research with children learning a native language indicates that proficiency in language play develops alongside one's overall language proficiency (Geller, 1985). Whereas language play is initially focused on sound and intonation, as children attain mastery over the poetic elements of language, they transition towards playing with verse, rhymes, rhythm, and ritual repetition. They begin to experiment with rhetorical conventions, creating puns and riddles, using non sequiturs and nonsensical utterances in conversational contexts and using alliteration, onomatopoeia, and tongue twisters. In so doing, children are actively "describing a world that doesn't exist—telling it like it isn't—as a way of exhibiting mastery over what is" (Geller, 1985, p. 41).

---

4   The gaps between the novel and the familiar invite acts of imagination:
    The power of the play of imagination is its ability to break traditional frames and dichotomies and allow us to explore a space where fantasy and play are no longer subordinated to reality and work and where we are able to find richer ways of identifying with the other (Thomas & Brown, 2007, p. 169).
    This is important for seeing possibilities and developing skills in how to engage with new communities of practice and learning to see and be in the world in new ways.

Situated Learning

The main proposition of Lave and Wenger's 1991 treatise *Situated Learning: Legitimate Peripheral Participation* is that learners, or "newcomers," benefit from engaging directly in a "community of practice," where the activity of learning is directly embedded in practical contexts and in association with others (for example, peers, near-peers, and "old-timers") who share compatible ways of *doing* things (not just compatible codes of representation). Note that this is not the equivalent of "hands-on" learning, where learning is applied but still takes on didactic forms of instruction and the teacher-centered perspective. Situated learning is conceived of as the natural consequence of participating in a community of practice, where efforts and attentions are differentially tuned to particular ways of doing and seeing things. The center of gravity for this kind of learning lies neither with the newcomer nor with the old-timer but with the gravitational pull of a particular community.[5]

Lave and Wenger make an important distinction between the teaching and the learning curriculum. While a teaching curriculum may or may not be present in any given community, the learning curriculum occurs wherever a learner is to be found. Applied to the field of second language education, this distinction between a teaching and learning curriculum reveals an important difference in how language classrooms work. From the learner's perspective, that difference rests on whether the end outcome is learning to be a language student (and to properly participate in the language classroom by raising one's hand when prompted or turning one's homework in on time) or learning to be a participant in the target language community (and to properly form and interpret meanings, to engage in the symbolic world of that community). The role of the instructor in this second case is to facilitate, rather than control, engagement and participation in the target language community, to assist learners in tuning their sensitivities to the symbolic field of that community and to continually orient and reorient the development of that community towards its end goal.

Central to this process of learning to participate in a community, Lave and Wenger propose, are the four key variables of identity, access, transparency, and control. A villager who is new to Skogfjorden, for example, begins by learning key details about the *identity* of the community, or how it works

---

5   Although there are differences between the terms "community of practice" and "communitas," for the sake of this chapter, we recognize both of these terms as at least addressing a shared code of representation.

(for example, you show up on time; you speak Norwegian; you participate with enthusiasm; you try new foods). His ability to *access*, or join the Skogfjorden community depends on his level of preparedness (to do these things) and whether the staff or other villagers meet his efforts with assistance or resistance. Her success in rendering the resources of Skogfjorden *transparent* (for example, how to say 'hi' in Norwegian, how to check books out of the library, or how to make an announcement at mealtime) will depend on the availability and willingness of peers or near-peers to demonstrate appropriate actions and to offer encouragement for others to try the same. His level of *control*, on the other hand, will depend upon his ability to notice opportunities for learning and his level of preparedness to take advantage of them (see also Dahl, 1997; Dahl & Jensen, 2003).

Over the course of the session, most villagers go beyond the mechanics of participation to engage in their own business of meaning-making; they learn to manipulate the cultural and linguistic symbols specific to our community and in so doing, become self-regulating, contributing members of the culture. They enter into and become a part of the imaginative universe, employing play to render the exotic familiar, and the familiar exotic.[6]

When this process gets personal, integrated into a villager's sense of identity as a speaker of a target language, the experiences become transformative and lead to lasting change, also beyond the village border. Part of what makes language personal is how language facilitates the building of relationships and a sense of intimacy with others (Giampapa, 2004). In order to perceive ourselves as masters of the knowledge, skills and values necessary to participate as full and valued community members, all forms of language are essential.

---

6   One example that best illustrates this puzzle of participation, from the staff perspective at least, is KU. KU is an acronym for *kompetanseutvikling* (skill development). This is a daily gathering that focuses on information and skill development in areas like language pedagogy, games and counseling that staff might find useful for doing their jobs better. The acronym KU is amusing for the fact that in Norwegian the word means "cow." If a counselor forgets to attend the meeting or is delayed, someone may MOO over the loudspeaker. A first-time staff member who is unfamiliar with how things are done at Skogfjorden may experience this as an utterly incomprehensible instruction. Whether or not he or she interprets the instruction correctly will depend on a number of factors, including her understanding of how the village works, her openness towards accepting an animal call as a decipherable message, whether another staff member is available to explain the message, and whether she has noted (and learnt from) similar experiences in the past.

On Norwegian Identity

The characterization of the Norwegian identity is, by necessity, an ongoing process. This is true both at Skogfjorden and in Norway proper, as globalization, immigration, and shifting political and economic situations continue to redefine what it means to be Norwegian.[7]

While there may be substantial disagreement about what it means to be Norwegian, many Norwegians recognize *Janteloven*, a termed coined by Aksel Sandmose (1953), as a deeply embedded value in Norwegian society. Described variously as a principle of egalitarian individualism and as a proclamation that "Thou shalt not think highly of thyself," *Janteloven* is credited with creating a society in which there are progressive legal provisions for equality and social justice. We see some evidence that *Janteloven* is a theme that emerges with relative regularity in the language play at Skogfjorden, and provide examples of this in the following paragraphs.

Though the ethnicity of Skogfjorden participants has never been formally surveyed, it is safe to claim from experience and villager surnames that a large proportion of the villagers have some ethnic tie to Norway, many of whom have ancestors who emigrated to the U.S. from the mid-1800s through the mid-1900s, largely to the Midwest, where Skogfjorden is located.

When the program first opened in 1963, it was perhaps more important for Skogfjorden to connect Skogfjorden villagers to their ethnic roots in the U.S.—roots that expressed themselves in their homes through particular foods, stories, songs, handicrafts and customs that were practiced by their immigrant grandparents or great-grandparents—many of whom were still alive at that time (Myklebust, 2003). That perspective has changed over the years as time has increased the gap between the majority of the first-generation immigrants and their current progeny. The emphasis in today's Skogfjorden has therefore

---

7 As a poor nation that was considered a developing country beyond the mid-1900s, Norway has, through its oil wealth social policies, advanced to a status recognized several times over in recent history by the United Nations as the world's best place to live (ranking first place in the Human Development Index for six consecutive years (2001-2006) by the UNDP, and in second place for the last couple of years). Norway is consequently experiencing increasing diversity as Saami indigenous groups continue to attain greater representation in the public arena, and as immigrants from Pakistan, Poland, Russia, Somalia, and other countries seek inclusion in a new cultural model for Norway, that of "the melting pot." At Skogfjorden, villagers encounter multiple models of Norwegian culture and, in a single day, may learn a Pakistani song, erect a Saami *lavvo*, and participate in an evening program about Norse mythology.

moved towards helping villagers to connect directly and personally with Norway (its past, present and future), and in that way (re)vitalize Norway's value for villagers in their home communities. Still, the reality is (and always has been) that not all villagers come for heritage-central reasons. This newer focus therefore has the added virtue of being broader and more inclusive of curious others and in that way giving greater relevance to Skogfjorden's overarching purpose.

Skogfjorden Geography

Skogfjorden lies just outside the town of Bemidji, where lakes and forests dominate the landscape, and where skunk and deer are frequently sighted by peripatetic villagers. Log cabins of varying sizes are nestled into the landscape amongst the fir and birch trees, accessed primarily through a simple network of dirt and gravel footpaths. One end of camp is occupied by a small beach on the Turtle River Lake shorefront (called Mjøsa at the village, named after Norway's largest lake), the other end features a soccer field and a spiral walking labyrinth formed of rock just like at Holmengrå on the coast of Northern Norway. Utgard, which houses an indoor gymnasium, a kitchen, the bank, kiosk, and an art room, is the largest building on site, with a peaked roof (featuring antlers at the apex), that hearkens back to pagan times. Other buildings, referencing various periods and regions of Norwegian history, dot the landscape, including a miniature medieval stave church; an immigrant farm yard; and traditional store-houses (small wooden cabins raised above ground to keep out vermin). Occasionally, a Saami *lavvo* (similar in appearance to a Native American teepee) is erected on the grassy fields out by the border to the outside world.

The playful qualities of Skogfjorden begin to a certain extent with its geography, which seems to defy the structure of everyday life: it is, in this sense, a site of anti-structure, a thinking space beyond the ordinary world and one that germinates creative play. Place names are selected on the basis of their relation to their namesakes in Norway. Adopted from the names of major cities in Norway, mythological spaces, and time periods in Nordic history, place names bring a sense of authenticity to the site but also carry a dream-like distortion, changing the spatial and semantic relationships between the named landmarks. The organization of the real world is condensed into a space that exists outside of real world structure. Thus, while spaces refer villagers back to the Norwegian world, the spaces are specifically, uniquely related to village life at

Skogfjorden. A first-time villager who finds herself one day walking through dry wisps of Minnesota prairie grass may weeks (or even years) later recall that experience within the context of simulating reindeer herding in Northern Norway. Skogfjorden geography therefore carries density of meaning that encompasses far more than the acreage or age of the site would initially suggest.

For example, in Norse mythology, Valhall was the hall of the gods, with 540 doors behind each of which lived 800 warriors (Pitt, 1893). At the coming of Ragnarok, the end of the world, it was believed that Odin—the eldest god who had once plucked out his own eye in exchange for wisdom—would open these doors to send the warriors out into battle.

On site, the place we call Valhall is an unassuming, two-story administrative building. It is the "hall" of staff offices and lounge, and it is here where general office supplies, confidential documents, and confiscated items are kept and strictly regulated. It is also here where counselors can work and have some privacy. Staff members use Valhall as a place to renew themselves in adult company and indulge in forbidden items—like treats and music not otherwise present in the program. For these reasons, villagers are not allowed into Valhall, shrouding it in mystery that the villagers imagine as the source of much of the magic that the counselors carry with them when they come through its doors and step into village life.

Long ago, a mischievous rumor was started amongst villagers purporting that the building concealed an underground roller coaster and bowling alley, among other things. Both villagers and staff delight in making references to the hidden pleasures of Valhall and engage in a certain amount of ribbing about the matter, although the counselors do their best to prevent villagers from knowing about what "really goes on" in there. On occasion, someone will feel inspired to stage a grand prank on the subject. One year, for example, the business manager downloaded roller coaster sound effects off the internet and played them periodically when villagers passed by, causing much tittering both inside and outside the building.

The meanings associated with any given place co-exist with one another but undergo distortion, displacement, and differences in interpretation depending on an individual's intent and level of familiarity with the place. The practice of meaning making is embedded in the very space of Skogfjorden, and villagers apprehend at least some of these meanings in a gestalt sense before they have even properly begun the task of learning to speak Norwegian.

The organization of spaces and their relations serve to help establish a framework for interpreting meaning, both at the individual and shared level of representation. A villager with no prior experience in Norwegian will readily grasp a simple mapping of personal experience; phrases such as *"Jeg heter Johanna og jeg bor i Stavanger"* ("My name is Johanna, and I live in Stavanger") are among the first to be mastered by new villagers, and place names are practiced and soon easily plucked from initially indecipherable announcements over the loudspeaker. Increasing participation leads to a density of personal experiences, all of which can be mapped for ease of reference with other villagers who share an appreciation of the affordances of each location at Skogfjorden. Because the places themselves also index a site or period of Norwegian geography or history, villagers also encounter an increasing sense of dimensionality or temporality in their understanding of Skogfjorden space, which in turn redirects them toward a mature field of practice in Norway.[8] For instance, the 2,000 lb metal paperclip in the center of camp will direct villagers toward its invention in Norway and its significance as a symbol of resistance during WWII.[9]

Second, it is through increasing dexterity in the use and manipulation of this frame that villagers learn to make and share sophisticated sets of meanings. To evoke locations at Skogfjorden such as *Ráfi Ája, Fagertun, Valhall* and the *Binders* is to evoke a collective understanding of the contrasting functions and meanings tied to those places, far more so than most language classes do in making use of generic locations such as "the bank," "the post office," and "the cinema."

---

8. In his book, *How Societies Remember* (1989), Paul Connerton acknowledges the significance of place in the formation of social memory. Places bind an individual to groups by inscribing a shared history onto the local topography. Places serve as a sort of shorthand for tying together disparate sequences of time and participation; they are both a way of organizing memory and a means by which memory is shared with others, whether present or not (see also Miller, 2004).

9. German forces occupied Norway from 1940 to 1945. Norwegian nationalists who opposed this occupation began wearing flag pins as a symbol of resistance. This practice was soon banned by the Nazis, forcing Norwegians to find other ways to express solidarity in their resistance. The paperclip was soon taken up as such a symbol, worn on the lapel. Called, in Norwegian, a *binders*, the paperclip expressed the sentiment that *"Vi binder sammen"* ("We bind together"). Like the flag pins of the early occupation period, paperclips were eventually forbidden by occupying forces, on threat of serious punishment (Stokker, 1995).

Timeplan Schedule

07.00 Morgenklubbene—*Elective clubs: swimming, jogging, etc.*
07.30 Oppvekking med MYGG radio—*Wake up to Norwegian music on the village radio.*
08.00 Før frokost jobber (morgentrim, kjøkkenvakt, Utgard)—*Before breakfast chores.*
08.15 Flaggheising og så frokost—*Raising the flag, breakfast.*
09.00 Byopprydding—*Cleaning cabins.*
09.30 Allsang—*Singing.*
10.00 Krets (OR Humaniora)—*Hands on theme-based activity or simulation.*
12.00 Matpause—*Snack time.*
12.45 Strenggruppe— *Content-driven language class.*
13.45 Kosetime I—*Free-choice activities.*
14.15 Kjøkkenvakt—*Kitchen patrol (KP).*
14.30 Middag i Gimle—*Midday meal.*
15.30 Middagslur—*Siesta/study/private time.*
16.30 Kosetime II—*Free-choice activities.*
17.15 Fritid—*Free time (store, bank, kiosk, café, health center and library open).*
18.00 Strenggruppe—*Content-driven language class.*
18.45 Kjøkkenvakt—*KP.*
19.00 Kveldsmat—*Dinner*
19.45 Fritid—*Free time.*
20.15 Flaggfiring og så kveldsprogrammet—*Lowering of the flag, evening program.*
21.30 Tilbake til hyttene—*Return to cabins.*
22.30 Lysene slukkes—*Lights out.*

The Daily Schedule

Like many camps, the daily schedule at Skogfjorden is highly structured. Villagers run back and forth between distant buildings and site locations to reach class in time or to find a good place at the meal table. While sports are offered only as elective activities, villagers nonetheless find themselves throughout the day engaged in a variety of running games, site-wide scavenger hunts, dancing, and swimming. Time is often measured in minutes rather than hours, and by evening, experiences from the morning often have the feel of having taken place days ago.

Specific parts of the daily schedule, such as meal-times, singing, and the raising or lowering of the flag are particularly conducive to villager contributions to community-wide play, and there are pre-existing "formats" that are structured to accommodate their playful input, according them access to community resources. Villagers participate in both large, mixed-level language groups and also small, same-level groups; they learn to "crack the code" of participation by observing the behaviors of their peers and near-peers. Returning villagers evidence greater control over this "code of participation"; they are more skillful in identifying these moments and demonstrate greater mastery over the play environment (and its legitimation) than their newer counterparts.

Language Play

In adopting a deliberate stance of playfulness with the language, the staff members at Skogfjorden implicitly encourage villagers to experiment with linguistic meanings, to explore the morphological and syntactic properties of the language, to understand how displacements and substitutions pervert or reify an intended message, and to actively wiggle words and their meanings around as linguistic tinkerers in the making. Villagers work to recognize and understand the playful models with which they are provided.

Down by the beach at Skogfjorden, for example, there is a small cabinet called the *venn-skap* that serves as an easily accessible model for language play. The beach is officially open for business when the lifeguard is in attendance and the doors to this cabinet are flung open. Nametags are collected in pairs and hung together on hooks inside the cabinet. When the lifeguard blows his whistle, all villagers must immediately find their *venn* (friend) and raise their clasped hands above the water so that the lifeguard may see and verify the headcount with those in charge of the *skap* (cabinet). While "venn" means friend and "skap" means cabinet, when joined together into the Norwegian word *vennskap*, the combination actually means friendship.

While the language play discussed represents deliberate tinkering at the level of the language program, the next set of examples involve observed, spontaneous tinkerings among villagers or villagers and staff members. Though not always as sophisticated as the previous example, they mark a more informal application of this playfulness in the program and demonstrate attempts to control meaning through form. The first example comes from a beginning learner who has managed to mutate the Norwegian word *matpakker* (literally 'food packets') into something equally evocative of what is to be served.

> At noon, villagers pack up their bags, getting ready for *matpause*, the snack before lunch. A boy, eight to 10 years in age, running after his friend calls ahead, "Is it time for *matpockets* now?"

The *matpakker* that are served during snack-time are open-faced sandwiches that are wrapped in wax-paper pockets. The villager, quite correctly, identified their physical similarity (basically pocket sandwiches) with the microwaveable product brand Hot Pockets, presumably available at his home grocery store. At the same time, he demonstrated an understanding of the morphological characteristics of the word (that 'mat' or 'food' could be recombined with another word to produce a shift in meaning), and further that the phonological characteristics of *pakker* resemble those of the English word 'pockets.' To a certain extent, the villager is showing some resistance to the Norwegian *matpakker*, but really, we see him on middle ground, here, establishing his own marginal terminology for something that is neither American nor Norwegian but somewhere in between.

The next example is a playful interaction between a counselor and a villager who has misplaced or forgotten his nametag.

> Stein, a counselor, walks up to a boy (about 12 years old) and says emphatically, *"Jeg heter Jo"* ("My name is Jo"). He very deliberately holds up his right hand, from which two nametags are dangling. The boy named Jo smiles sheepishly and grabs the nametag with his name on it.

In Norwegian, the name "Jo" is pronounced similarly to "You." The double meaning here lies in the idea that being in possession of someone's nametag is the conceptual equivalent of taking on their identity. In saying, "*Jeg heter Jo*" (My name is Jo), Stein is laying emphasis on the alternate meaning, "*Jeg heter you*" (My name is you). In this case again, we see a blurring of boundaries between the Norwegian and the American. It is a joke that only works between languages and cultural understandings.

"*Jeg heter Jo*" is also a joke that only works at the language villages, where wearing a nametag is both mandatory and enforceable (i.e., one cannot buy things at the store, exchange money, or go swimming without one). The counselor is thus asserting, albeit in a joking manner, his authority to enforce this rule. *Janteloven*, in the sense of "Thou shalt not think highly of thyself," is being subtly invoked here, as the villager is reminded that he is subject to the same rules as everyone else.

In just these few interactions, we see a proclivity among both villagers and staff to tinker with the formal characteristics of language. Sometimes these tinkerings occur by accident, a result of mispronunciation, the imprecise application of grammatical rules, or code switching (as when the director once publicly thanked a staff member who had made several new arrangements for the village band, praising him by inadvertently expressing that he had "put new life in the old *korps*," the Norwegian word for "band"). At yet other times, these tinkerings occur by design and contrivance, an attempt to cleverly manipulate meaning to one's own ends. Either way, the model of playfulness that is "out there" in the program serves to prime a state of attentiveness as to how the language is being applied (as with the last example) and, more importantly, to subordinate the role of form to the purposes of meaning.

Let us now turn away from this context and examine a unique series of events that took place in the summer of 2001 which vividly demonstrates how villagers synthesize information and become themselves "meaning makers" with Norwegian in the Skogfjorden community. In this series of events, villagers appropriated the name of a staff member named Gorm, playing with it in various contexts and using it imaginatively to place themselves within the Skogfjorden community.

Gorm is a long-time counselor at Skogfjorden who plays guitar at *Allsang*, the village singing time. As a business manager at that time, with cabin duties in Kristiansand and *Allsang* responsibilities in the morning for the whole village, he often appeared to be on his own schedule. This individuated plan was somewhat emphasized by his mercurial, sometimes distant, nature. Throughout the events of that summer, Gorm was vaguely aware that his name had been appropriated by villagers and was alternately amused and embarrassed by the situation.

There are a number of features of what we term "The Gormism Movement" that are of interest. The first is its spontaneous development outside of the formal curriculum and within the milieu of villager life, emerging at times as a commentary on social hierarchies at Skogfjorden and the egalitarian individualism of *Janteloven*. A second feature is that of transfer to peers and near-peers—Gormism—arose within a small, well-defined group of villagers who lived in Kristiansand and soon spread to their younger counterparts in Oslo. Third, we see demonstrated in this example the means by which Gormist ac-

PLAYING WITH MEANING IN A NORWEGIAN VILLAGE 79

tivity sought realization and actualization in formal aspects of the program (i.e., *Allsang*, meal announcements, geography) and, in a related sense, fourth, how village staff responded to and built upon these developments as "teachable moments." A final and more general point is how the Gormist movement sparked village-wide arousal that led other villagers to explore similar, legitimized means of expression.

> Per and Torbjørn are standing to the side of the balcony before meal time. Both are about 15 or 16 years old and live in Kristiansand. They are croaking to one another, "Gorm. Gorm. Gorm." It seems that they are trying to achieve the effect of the frogs in the Budweiser Beer commercial.
>
> There is an air of generalized arousal in the dining hall, with a certain giddy excitement underlying conversations at the various tables. The Kristiansand boys stand up on their chairs all of a sudden and pause dramatically for silence, making sure to catch the attention of everyone in the room. "GORM" they all say in unison, pause, then return to their seats. This induces raised eyebrows at our table and comments like, "What was that all about?"

Mealtime displays such as this one are not uncommon, although they are usually instigated by seasoned counselors or a particularly courageous group of older high school credit villagers. Younger villagers often express a desire to perform their own mealtime display but frequently fail to "pull it off" due to inadequate peer support or poor timing.

> The following day, Sverre leads a song called *La meg høre Bugaloo*, a song where an opening line teaser is followed by a refrain about the teaser. Midway through the song, he cries out *"La meg høre lederne"* ("Let me hear the counselors").
>
> Laughing, we yell for the refrain *"Jeg sier, Nei Nei Nei Nei Nei Nei Nei Nei Nei Nei Nei Nei Nei"* ("I say, no no no no no no no no no no no no").
>
> A counselor seated in the crowd calls out, *"La meg høre Torbjørn"* ("Let me hear Torbjørn").
>
> Everyone joins in laughing, "Gorm gorm gorm go-gorm gorm gorm go-gorm gorm gorm go-gorm."

Here, villagers revel in the opportunity to poke fun at staff members, first referencing their (as villagers sometimes see it) overbearing authority as rulemakers and nay-sayers on site, and then (with the second refrain), their affectionate (sometimes ambivalent) attitudes towards staff members.

After a simulation on Norse Mythology that evening, a group of boys have gathered to socialize:

> Lars is lecturing: "Well, it all started when Gorm was like 15 minutes late to *Krets*, and when he came in we all shouted, Gorm!" (Cheers reference?) "and then it just sort of evolved into a religion."
>
> Lars continues philosophically, "Yeah. And then we were gonna make this altar. We had a big piece of wood we were gonna roll up and we have a prayer...I'm still working on it. *'Kjære Gorm, hellig er ditt navn'* you know, I've got it all written down at home." ('Dear Gorm, holy is your name')

The popularity of the Gormist Movement soon spreads to the younger boys who live in Oslo. They discuss Gormism over breakfast:

> Tore says to another boy, "No. Here's how you do it." He puts two fingers together and draws an invisible G in the space in front of him.
>
> The boy copies the movement: "Like this?"
>
> Tore turns to Magna, "Are you a Gormian?"
>
> Magna: "Well, I'm pro-Gorm, but I'm not a fanatic or anything."
>
> Tore: "Then you're a Reformist. You do it from the inside out." (makes an invisible G starting with the cleft) "We do it from the outside in." he demonstrates the original G form.
>
> Tore says to the other boy, "Every real Gormian has to make a pilgrimage to Gorm's altar."
>
> Boy: "Where's that?"
>
> Tore: "Behind Kristiansand. I'm going to make a pilgrimage this morning."

If we treat the Gormism example as a cultural text that illustrates the development of self-regulated language use in the program, we can begin to understand how multiple factors interact in increasingly complex ways to achieve this effect. Gormism arose from a sequence of observations the boys had made about their environment and from which they had drawn conclusions about the *identity* and workings of their immediate world. Gormism was created from, for instance, a series of understandings involving, among other things, an idea that one ought to show up for *krets* on time (especially if leading *krets* activities), that pronouncing the word gutturally can achieve the effect of croaking and that this croaking could be evocative of a second reality (that of the Budweiser commercial), that pronounced with flatness the word could be Americanized and further evocative (through secondness), in the substitution of its initial phoneme, of a "regular guy" character, Norm, in the American television show *Cheers*. Thus we see this creative activity as engaged in multiple complex actions from the observation of normative behaviors at camp (expectations of behavior) to the comparative aspects of cultural symbolism (Gorm vs. Norm) to the effects of phonemic substitution and pronunciation.

We further see the transfer and refinement of this act of experimentation and hypothesis testing as peers and near-peers came increasingly to engage in the Gormist phenomenon (*transparency*). As the younger boys in Oslo became involved, Gormism took on a more rigid formality, with internal divisions (real Gormians, or pilgrims, and reformists) and appropriated for itself a ritual organization (prayer, hand signs) and a sacred space. What began essentially as a joke between a few boys transformed into a meaningful locus of communication and shared meaning in the wider community.

What in part contributed to the success of Gormism was the fact that its proponents sought to secure *control* over its legitimacy within the group by appealing to its resources and strategies. The mealtime display, in which the Kristiansand boys stood on their chairs and trumpeted Gorm's name across the room, is one such means for legitimate display at Skogfjorden and one that counselors often use to generate excitement about an upcoming event. Being sung about, establishing a ritual component and a play on meanings, and staking out a sacred spot on site, as we have seen in previous sections, are also means by which meanings may find a home at Skogfjorden.

We see also how the Skogfjorden staff was able to respond to the advent of Gormian activity without significant departure from the formal curriculum (*access*). Rather than ignore or prohibit such developments, counselors built upon the playful contributions of Gormian proponents by acknowledging their voice in situations like that at the next morning's song session. Thus, an inside joke was able to become at once a subject of casual contemplation and of comparisons between language and culture as well as a phenomenon which could easily and naturally integrate skills such as the writing (of Gormian texts), and natural repetition of language (in Gormian ritual).

We suggest that playful behaviors within the village are central to the construction of villager identities as Norwegian learners. By actively pursuing meaning-making activities, villagers come to understand language as a process of creative manipulation rather than a proper recitation of forms and words. From their liminal status as villagers, where ambiguity and a sense of "otherness" preside, participants learn, through access to opportunity, observation of peers and near-peers, and increasing control over their environment, to inhabit their newly emergent language skill and take on the identity of a Norwegian insider. This happens in many ways, and by no means trivially, through play.

We also note that language play at Skogfjorden, a place beyond the regular structure of things, can involve ideas about resistance and the social order on site. Play can serve to mark boundaries between the familiar and the unknown, as in the case of *matpockets,* or to anchor oneself to one or the other side of the linguistic fence, by relying on either American or Norwegian meanings. Play can also address the hierarchical differences between staff and villagers; staff can remind villagers to wear their nametags, they can and do say 'no' to some villager requests, they can have schedules that differ from the one villagers are required to follow. In this context, language play becomes an important way for both staff and villagers to negotiate roles in positive ways.

Clearly, learning Norwegian at Skogfjorden involves far more than the simple manipulation of grammatical categories and lexical constructions. It in fact involves the manipulation of a complex series of culturally significant symbols, of which language is but one subset. Unlike many second language programs, at Skogfjorden it is meaning making rather than language making that is the primary objective. Here the production of language is understood not to be the equivalent of the production of meaning but rather part of the tool-kit involved in making that meaning happen—particularly through play.

Through the creation of a community of practice with creative adaptations of geographical mileposts such as the country's major cities, manipulations of cultural symbols like the stave church and paperclip, and opportunities for playful language use like the Gormism movement, Skogfjorden provides a place where newcomers interact with old timers and together construct identities as Norwegian-speaking insiders. In so doing, the ever-present opportunities for learning and reinforcing new ways of speaking and being enable them to fully participate in Skogfjorden life—their bridge to understanding the greater community of Norway and Norwegian and their link to new perspectives on the world.

References

American Camp Association (2005). Directions: youth development outcomes of the camp experience. Martinsville, Indiana: American Camp Association. Original edition, Description of the study.

American Council on the Teaching of Foreign Languages (1999). *Standards for foreign language learning in the 21st century.* Yonkers, NY.

Bialeschki, M. Deborah, Amy Krehbiel, Karla Henderson, and & Dawn Ewing. (2003). The voice of the campers: Research findings through qualitative data collection. Paper read at American Camping Association (ACA) National Conference, at Denver, Colorado.

Borey, V. (2004) Skogfjorden observations 2000-2004. Unpublished raw data.

Broner, M. A., & Tarone, E. E. (2001). Is it fun? Language play in a fifth-grade Spanish immersion classroom. *The Modern Language Journal*, 85(3), pp. 363-379.

Connerton, P. (1989). *How societies remember.* Cambridge: Cambridge University Press.

Dahl, T. I. (2009). The importance of place for learning about peace: Residential summer camps as transformative thinking spaces. *Journal of Peace Education*, 6(2):, pp. 225-245.

Dahl, T. I. (1997, November). Situated learning in immersion environments. Paper presented at the 31st annual meeting of the American Council on the Teaching of Foreign Languages, Nashville, Tennessee.

Dahl, T. I., Clementi, D., Heysel, G. R., & Spenader, A. (2007). Start with a good idea and give it a world: Preparing young people to be lifelong language learners and users. In M. Mantero (Ed.), *Perspectives on language studies: Identity, culture, and discourse in educational contexts:* (pp. 143-158). Greenwich, CT: Information Age Publishing.

Dahl, T.I., and Jensen, B. (2003). Sociocultural theory in practice: Scandinavian language immersion in the American woods. Paper presented at *Sjätte konferensen om Nordens språk some andraspråk*, Lund, Sweden. May 22-24, 2003.

Foley, W. (1997). *Anthropological Linguistics.* Malden, MA: Blackwell Publishers.

Gee, J. P., Allen, A-R., & Clinton, K. (2001). Language, class, and identity: teenagers fashioning themselves through language. *Linguistics and Education*, 12(2), pp. 175-194.

Geller, L. G. (1985). *Worldplay and language learning for children.* Urbana, Illinois: National Council of Teachers of English.

Giampapa, F. (2004). The politics of identity, representation, and the discourses of self-identification: negotiating the periphery and the center. In A. Pavlenko & A. Blackledge A. (Eds.), *Negotiation of identities in multilingual contexts* (pp. 192-218). Clevedon, UK: Multilingual Matters Ltd.

Hamilton, H. and Cohen, A. (2004). Creating a playworld: Motivating learners to take chances in a second language. In: Jan M. Frodeson and Christine A. Holten Christine A. (Eds.), The power of context in language teaching and learning. Festschrift in honor of Marianne Celce-Murcia, pp. 237-247. Boston: Heinle & Heinle.

Hamilton, H.E. Crane, C., & Bartoshesky, A. (2005). *Doing foreign language: Bringing Concordia Language Villages into language classrooms*. Upper Saddle River, NJ: Pearson Merrill Prentice Hall.

Huttunen, I. (1996). The role of environment in language learning. Background paper for the Educational Research Workshop in the Effectiveness of Modern Language Learning and Teaching. Graz, Austria, March 5-8. Retrieved from ERIC database (ED394330).

Lave, J., and Wenger, E. (1991). *Situated learning: Legitimate peripheral participation*. Cambridge, MA: Harvard University Press.

Miller, J. (2004). Identity and language use: the politics of speaking ESL in schools. In A. Pavlenko & A. Blackledge A. (Eds.), *Negotiation of identities in multilingual contexts* (pp. 290-315). Clevedon, UK: Multilingual Matters Ltd.

Myklebust, M. (2003). Skogfjorden: Ethnicity and a contemporary foreign language camp. Master's thesis. Norwegian University of Science and Technology, Trondheim, Norway

Pan, Z. Cheok, A. D., Yang, H., Zhu, J., & Shi, J. (2006). Virtual reality and mixed reality for virtual learning environments. *Computers & Graphics*, 30(1), pp. 20-28.

Perret-Clermont, Anne-Nelly. (2004). Thinking spaces of the young. In *Joining society: Social interaction and learning in adolescence and youth*, edited by A.-N. Perret-Clermont, C. Pontecorvo, L. B. Resnick, T. Zittoun & B. Burge. Cambridge, UK: Cambridge University Press.

Pitt, R. (1893). *The Tragedy of the Norse Gods*. London: T. Fisher Unwin.

Resnick, Lauren B., and Anne-Nelly Perret-Clermont. (2004). Prospects for youth in postindustrial societies. In *Joining society: Social interaction and learning in adolescence and youth*, edited by A.-N. Perret-Clermont, C. Pontecorvo, L. B. Resnick, T. Zittoun & B. Burge. Cambridge, UK: Cambridge University Press.

Sandmose, Aksel. (1953) [1933, 1937]. *En flyktning krysser sitt spor*. Second edition. Oslo: Aschehaug.

Schmitt, P. (1969). *Back to nature: The Arcadian myth in urban America*. New York: Oxford University Press.

Stokker, K. (1995). *Folklore fights the Nazis: Humor in occupied Norway 1940-1945*. Madison, WI: Wisconsin University Press.

Thomas, D., & Brown, J.S. (2007). The play of imagination: extending the literary mind. *Games and Culture*, 2(2), pp.149-172.

Thompson, L. (2000). Foreign language assessment: 30 years of evolution and change. *ERIC/CLL News Bulletin* 23 (2). Available online at the Center for Applied Linguistics (www.cal.org).

Tomasello, M., Kruger, A. C., & Ratner, H.H. (1993). Cultural learning. *Behavioral and Brain Sciences 16*(3), pp. 495-552.

Turner, V. (1967). *The forest of symbols: Aspects of Ndembu ritual.* Ithaca, NY: Cornell University Press.

Turner, V. (1969). *The ritual process: Structure and anti-structure.* Chicago: Aldine.

Tønnesson, Stein. (1991). "History and national identity in Scandinavia: The contemporary debate." Trial lecture for the Dr. Philos. degree, University of Oslo, 25 October, 1991

United Nations human development index (2001-2008) http://hdr.undp.org/en/statistics

Chapter Four

Ñeovanga poranguei: The Lucky Ones Who Play: *Mbyá guaraní* Children's Learning Through Social Play

Noelia Enriz

Introduction

The *mbyá guaraní* religious vocabulary was transcribed by Leon Cadogan in the Ayvu Rapyta (1997[1959]) vocabulary and then organized by Bartolome Meliau (1992) in the Mbyá-guaraní-Spanish dictionary. There it is possible to find multiple *mbyá* words for the single concept of "childhood." The term in the *mbyá* religious vocabulary is *ñeovanga poranguei*, "the lucky ones who play." From this definition, we may say, playing games represents a central aspect of childhood development for this indigenous group. There are two specific vocabularies used by the *mbyá guaraní* people, one of them for their everyday lives, and another specifically for their religious experiences.

The *mbyá* is an indigenous group of 25,000 members who live in different Argentinean, Paraguayan and Brazilian territories. Nowadays 5.000 (Instituto Nacional de Estadisticas y Censos, 2008) people are living in Misiones (Argentina) in different communities and they define themselves as *mbyá*, speaking their own language. This represents a 0.5 percent of Misiones entire population, and the *mbyá* are the largest native minority.

The aim of this chapter is to describe *mbyá* children developing certain activities in order to understand which learning aspects appear in their games, how they play them, and what links with the universe these games establish. Particularly, most of the *mbyá guaraní* children begin and finish games in the middle of many ordinary situations in daily life, even interacting among other activities. They don´t have to develop activities connected to survival, such as hunting, setting traps, collecting fruit in the jungle and also praying. The idea of praying is considered by them as part of their survival. This could be because games are included in every activity of the *kiringue*, children between 3 and 10 years old. Perhaps, as *mbyá* adults say *"children time is a game* entirely."

The *mbyá* is a small group coming from the tupi-guaraní larger group. Some other groups living in these territories are the avá-guaraní (Argentina,

Paraguay and Bolivia) and the chiripa o paï (Paraguay, Brazil and Argentina); each of these groups has developed its own, specific linguistic mode. Historically, a common aspect for all of the groups is that they do not live in only one place but move from place to place within the same country. However, the *mbyá* group has abandoned this activity for the last 20 years because they live now in limited and enclosed territories. Later, I will explain how this issue has affected children's games.

The *mbyá* group living in Argentina is in rural areas, in small groups with different-sized houses. Although the *mbyá* language is commonly spoken, bilinguism with Spanish, Portuguese or Guaraní-jopara is generally used by them. About 60 percent of the group is younger than 18, and less than half of these children have the opportunity to go to school. There is no learning program for adults. In this social context children's play activities are varied. The activities allow them to learn several aspects about the environment where they are developed. It will base our research on this information in order to learn about *mbyá* knowledge categories and the experiences connected to learning.

Moving from one place to another in this territory does not permit carrying a heavy burden. So in the past, all the objects used as games or toys, were not carried by the *mbyá* when moving from one place to another. Only the knowledge used to build those objects was taken. Knowledge of games and the ways of playing them are still considered a priority for this indigenous group.

Since 2003, I have been working with different *mbyá* groups in Misiones province. I always live with them for a period of time, (approximately two months) in their houses or schools. I started this research after obtaining a scholarship from the CONICET (Consejo Superior de Investigaciones en Ciencia y Tecnología). This chapter incorporates material from about three different research sites from *mbyá guaraní* people (see Figure 1).

I agree with Aracy Lopes Da Silva (2002) that all children's games are multi-perceptive experiences going beyond words. Asking children about games in this study was not a very useful technique. One day I asked a group of girls about a game they were playing: a boy who was the same age, I assumed, was chasing them. The girls were trying to escape from him, but when touched by him, they kept on playing in the same way; roles never changed. While the boy was chasing the girls yelled. I tried to ask them about the game, but they only repeated it for me, this time with a girl chasing the group.

ÑEOVANGA PORANGUEI: THE LUCKY ONES WHO PLAY   89

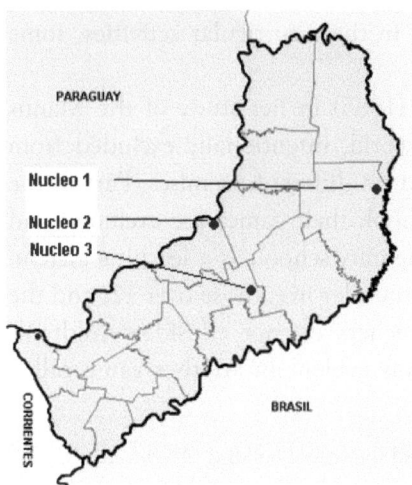

Figure 1. Map of the three research sites.

> When I asked them about the game they complained because the boy wasn't running fast and they called to him—*eju, ejuque* (Come, come in). Finally, one of the girls started the activity again running after the girls and the boy until another girl wanted to take control. At first, the first girl accepted the idea but then she refused it saying— *petei bicho* (you are an insect, or an animal) [n2 28/11/05].[1]

Some games include the possibility of modifying things; others do not. This game finished when the players saw some other children eating nearby, so they decided to stop the game to eat. The second time kids played a game gave me the opportunity to compare versions of it in a brief time. Roles and rules for this game were settled. One kid had to change the person playing the role of the leader, but this change generated conflict among the players even though they knew they could apply this rule. The conflict is a consequence of the lack of desire to play by the child.

This game was played in front of the school, where the headmistress' office was. Children were playing while other people were doing different activities such as filling in forms and reciting a poem in front of the national flag. This activity was a poem showing the beginning of school activities including hoisting the national flag and groups of pupils lining up. At that moment the confrontation between aspects of the *mbyá* identity and national identity was

---

1   In this format I include fragments from my field work diary, taking into account the indigenous group investigated and the date when this research was made in different periods between 2003 and 2009.

very clear. While the school was engaging in these curricular activities, some *mbyá* children were playing their games.

In some ways, as expressed by Mead (1985) in her study of the Manus population, *mbyá* kids live in their own world, intentionally excluded from that of the adults, and each world is based on different premises. Part of the *mbyá* kids' world won't be included at school; their games are excluded and ignored by the school agents. In fact, elementary school, as a learning system, keeps some people outside, such as children under five, those over 12, and the ones not attending classes every day. Teachers do not consider children's games. The disciplining force of school was evident in another game called *zapato ku' a*.

> Five children were running and jumping around the school building. They were also yelling *Zapato ku'a*. At that moment a teacher appeared and stopped the game. She took one of the kids inside because he had to attend classes. After that the rest of the kids kept on playing so I asked them about that issue." They answered—*Zapato ku'a* is broken shoe and she doesn´t like it—pointing at the teacher (n2: 28/11/05).

According to Mead (1985) children adjust the way to explain different situations to be accepted by adults, translating their own world using established activities. Observation as a research method has been used by the children themselves. In 2003, at the beginning of my research work, I was interested in children teaching me their own games. I used to stand near them trying to participate in order to acquire the necessary information. At that moment I was living with an indigenous group, (see Figure 1), in which kids played a very long game called *Kapichu'a*.

> When learning the techniques and rules of this game I could see the aim of it— watching to learn. Observation was their learning strategy. The children recommended that I watch them playing for a long time in order to understand the game itself (n3 27/04/03).

Observation, as a method, is not new in anthropology, but its use by children in order to learn to play is relevant. Observation was central in the consolidation of anthropology as a science in the last century. In research linked to games and play, observation is very important in order to make deep descriptions (Geertz, 1992) of a given phenomenon.

Games Connected to Survival

> Parents do not punish their children with no reason and they love them so much that they even adore them. –P. Ruyer. 1627 (Hernandez, 1913)

It is not just Jesuit priests, like Padre Ruyer, who think that *mbyá* parents' must use firmer methods to take care of their children. It is difficult to find indigenous parents keeping close watch on their children. Indeed, *mbyá* kids move freely along their territory and only in certain cases, due to age or gender, are they limited in their movements because they consider "it is not necessary for kids to be watched by a grown-up."

Children's routines in the *tekoa*[2] are not only based on a wide possibility of movements, they are even accompanied by other kids and have a great variety of tasks; they participate in looking for water, helping with meals, mate, etc. All these tasks are generally called for by adults, but in some cases, the actions are completely done by children.

> We are alone in Je's house. There were six of us; three little brothers, one of the older ones, she and me. I imagined kids would give me another place to sit because I was the only grown-up but we all sat around the fire place and Je, the older girl (*iñe' engue ramo va' e*) was moving the fire. (...) When the sun started disappearing, she began to cook. She needed some water so she asked for it from one of her brothers (...), she needed more pieces of wood and the same boy brought them. Je prepared the meal and gave it to us all. (n1: 17/11/06)

Is it strange to see *mbyá guaraní* children alone? As with Clarice Cohn's (2005) investigation of the Xikrin, it is very common for *mbyá* to learn things in groups. *Mbyá* people believe childhood learning should be developed in a collective way. Children used to being in groups with different ages have lots of experiences together. This group is called "game community" (Larriq, 1993) and is the base of our interest.

It is common to see a mother cooking and her little girl helping her and also girls around 10 years of age developing this activity without any adult participation. Until 11, the girls typically help their mothers or grandmothers in preparing meals and boys preparing mate. However, on certain occasions, when children are alone at home, the older girl can handle food. It is important to say that kids do not take these activities as games and that preparation of meals would never be an activity made by a visitor no-*mbyá*, as I was there. But, adults' *mbyá* consider these activities as games.

In the scene previously described, I read ethnic meanings of gender in use. While the girl was cooking, the other children were watching her, playing, or, in the case of the oldest boy, searching for water. When more water was neces-

---

2   *Tekoa*: literally "the place where we can be." The territory under their occupation and those who inhabit.

sary, I thought that I could possibly help get it from the river, but nobody asked me, and I stayed around the fire.

We could call this *ñeovanga-mbyá*, the word for games, if the meal wasn't the only opportunity for these kids to eat. If something went wrong in cooking, all the children would lose the opportunity to eat, so it wasn't a game for them. Maybe, that's why Je, the eldest girl at home, must prepare it. The *mbyá* girls must be socially instructed as future women who know how to cook meals. By contrast, boys should acquire experience moving around their territory. They should be able to get water even at night.

When the room with artificial light was set up for the first time (using an electric generator because there is no electrical system) I could share this experience with the children. All the children came into the room with their own animals. They made the animals come into the room, coercing a pig, until it started to chase kids around the room. After a while they let it go outside amid a lot of laughing and yelling. A dog came into the room on its own accord, and kids took it out. They used to be very unfriendly with dogs. A chicken could not sleep inside the room so children fed it. All of the children were surprised to see insects like mosquitoes and fleas attracted to the bulbs. I asked the children if they knew why this was happening, and they told me that the insects had just seen artificial light for the first time, like themselves. (n1: 15/11/ 06). *Mbyá* children have great knowledge of animals, and this knowledge was linked with games. Generally, when the children walk in the forest, searching for trees to climb, they must protect their domestic animals from wild ones. It is very common for kids to recognize the *chi'i* (wild cat), which comes to steal hens and which they chase away by screaming. Things like the interventions of the wild cat would happen in the middle of a game. When children face something new they often make their pets experience it first to see how they behave and then they draw conclusions, as when the electric light was turned on for the first time.

Mbyá girls play lots of games until they become *kuñava' era*, after their first menstrual period. Girls play games again when their first children are born. Boys stop playing games once they start learning survival skills in the forest such as looking for food, hunting, etc. *Mbyá* games and survival activities refer to very different experiences. Through play, kids may experience new things without risking calamity even if failure occurs. In survival training, kids must obtain skills or risk hunger or injury if something goes wrong.

Important abilities are acquired through group activities such as looking for water, making mate, providing food for the rest of the people, etc. All this allows children to gain knowledge of their environment (dealing with fire, the water fountain, etc.) others' needs and the structure of the community. This group planning is based on providing options.

Sharing is considered an important value, because *mbyá* live in communitarian groups where survival is based on giving answers for the whole group. We may say that children do not develop a poor imitation of adults' world, but create activities in a social context that will accompany them for the rest of their lives and that begin with the creation of games. Social relations are also evident when elder brothers and sisters take care of younger ones. Carolina Remorini (2004) comments: "Although we have seen five- and six-year-old kids watching out—*emae*—for younger ones, only those more than seven years old have the important responsibility of looking after little kids." (p.15)

From *mbyá* grown-ups' point of view, children's time is completely devoted to play, as the word for childhood makes it clear. In groups where kids do not attend school because they are too far away, adults explained that children play even during religious ceremonies. During these ceremonies kids are calm, sitting, listening with respect. But before the prayers begin, the children dance for a couple of hours, singing to the Gods and making smoke (with pipes) and sounds to get the attention of multiple Gods with different musical instruments.

According to the adults, play involves several everyday life activities (e.g., when kids collect fruit, in groups, near trees, they *mbokoa* (collect) by passing the fruit from hand to hand, some from tops of the trees and some others picking up fruit from the ground). These activities are never under adult supervision. The *game community* (Larriq, 1993) is involved in this, and children decide what to do in autonomous groups. For the children, climbing up trees and getting fruit is an ability acquired happily, laughing all the time. When children develop this ability they subsequently know which trees to climb— those near their *tekoa*, not trees in the middle of the forest. They learn which fruit to pick and how to eat it, combining the new task of climbing with their prior knowledge of fruit. I consider this activity a game because if something goes wrong, a child could ask another to bring fruit, because they search for it in ways that make light of the task:

> One girl was eating *pindo ra'a*—palm seed—with her little sister and she offered me some. She opened the fruit with a stone and explained: "you eat it all, also the insect," pointing at a worm inside the fruit (n2: 25/11/05).

The little girl laughed while she searched for seeds. Then she put into practice a technique to open them, showing her sister and me the appropriate way to extract the seed. Here, gender and age are connected to knowledge and games. Boys' outings in the forest are generally accompanied by men, because the forest is considered a place for men. Women only come out from their homes to accompany their husbands. But they generally stay in their groups. As Leon Cadogan (1997) said *"guaraní culture considers and defines women activities as being near fire"* (p.113). I may say, according to all the activities *mbyá* develop, their connection to the forest is extremely important. There are also adult group discussions about children and animals' relationships, sometimes including games between them. They may include a wide variety of points of view.

> A and L (a couple) moved to her mother's house, (the oldest woman in the group) because on that occasion, she was going to be alone for some time. They took everything with them: dogs, chickens, etc. But at night kids went to sleep to their own house. Children play with animals all the time. They play with piglets and they tumble them gently. Je bathed her puppy and then she brought it wrapped up. Ja was carrying some chicks in a hat trying to take care of them but they died later. When that happened, kids put them near fire and they told me "*this is much better.*" (n1 14/11/06).

Sometimes children's attitudes towards animals may be reprimanded by adults. Kids acquire knowledge of nature by themselves, but adult intervention and supervision are present in activities related to domestic animals. While boys are accompanied in their experiences in the forest, girls are together when they select seeds, and they pay close attention when they learn how to take care of farm animals.

> Vk, (another child of the same couple, around 8) is not treating an animal very well. In a family meeting they all agreed the child had attacked it. All of them expressed their disapproval: his mother, father and grandmother. The rest of the kids stared at him. The mother hit on the ground with a twig near the boy and she said he did not know how to take care of animals so he could not have one (n1: 14/ 11/06).

Games involving animals never can cause any damage as a result.

Religious Games

Knowledge of the forest is taught from men to boys; 7- or 8-year-olds start being included in outings to look for honey. At the age of around 12 a boy learns to check hunting traps. Girls, on the other hand, start experiencing housework tasks, such as cooking with their mothers, when they are 11 years old. Cohn (2000) opines: "children know everything and know nothing" (p. 211). Based on this concept I may include different areas of knowledge as being acquired gradually through play in a concrete way.

The *kiringue* group shows a great complexity of experiences. Their actions are based on age, gender and home location. But the *mbyá* idea of childhood expresses differences in categories according to the place where children are brought up. When a baby is born the oldest man on the *tekoa*–the place where the group lives–performs a ceremony called Ñemongarai (Ruiz, 1984). In this ceremony, the Gods teach them some knowledge about the baby's soul. Specifically, they learn characteristics of the place where the baby's soul come from.

There are differences connected to the developmental stages of *mbyá* children's lives. These concepts are linked to different meanings of childhood as a social concept. It is possible to know things about these different life moments by considering the relationship between children and play. *Mbyá* language delineates different childhood levels. Categories are the same for boys and girls: children move from *mita oikota va' e*, the baby who is coming, to *pyta'i*, a newborn baby, then to *kiringüe'i* or *kiri'i*, kids up to four years old. From this age on, children are gendered. These differences disappear, however, with old age, *tujai kueve* (old) or *guaimi'i kueve* (very old).

The different words mark periods of life at critical moments, in particular the period of time when *mbyá* stop being considered children and become adults. These moments are evidenced in natural changes: the first menstrual period for girls, and boys' voices changing to become rough and deep.

Virginia Caputo (1995), in her research, tries to work from the idea of "power" and expresses that "power has been an important issue to consider in children and adolescents' lives although this concept is pretty much connected to the last ones mentioned"(p. 35). This situation develops a wide variety of power strategies. Adolescents who try to be connected to adults and children show power through games. The value and attention given by *mbyá* people to religion and how it organizes their lives is well known. Children's participation in religious life includes learning concepts (the religious vocabulary) and the silent respect to the ceremony itself that adults demand. Children's participation in those religious moments is restricted to giving the adults mate or lighting the pipes for everyone. I consider all the play that the kids carry out before the religious ceremony—involved with dance—to be liminal (Tuner: 1980), because the children weren't included in the ceremony, but their activities served as a starting point to the ceremony. They are the ones who "call" the Gods or make sounds before praying. All this provides kids with "power," involved in games because they make a dance that helps in calling the Gods.

When girls are around 10 to 16 three words are used to categorize them. First, *iñe' engue ramo va'e*–the one who is going to listen to words; then, *kuña va'era*–the one who is ready to be a woman, and finally *kuña tai*–the one who is very young and has children. There are three words for boys–*kiringue as*, boy; *ñe' e nguchuramota va' e*, the one who is going to speak with a rough voice, and then *mitan ruchu*, young man. During these periods differences between genders are deeply stressed. Girls are divided into two groups *iñe' engue ramo va'e*, the ones allowed to play, and *kuña va'era*, those who cannot play and are to learn housework activities (they are not obliged to do so but are emphatically persuaded).

From the indigenous point of view, women are the ones more dedicated to childhood, and so they accept the idea of a woman ethnographer (me) being with their children more easily.

Games and Power

The classic anthropology bibliography contains many references to games (Tylor, 1879; Boas, 1899; Culin, 1899) but I found one mention by Marcel Mauss (2006) important. Mauss suggested considering games as a symbolic aspect of culture: "games are included into aesthetic aspects. Games are generally the starting point of (....) many high level activities, ritual or natural ones. Developed in the spare time of their activities" (Mauss, 2006, 122).

Gilles Brougère (1998) offers three aspects of games: first, the material aspect—all the interactive objects used for play. In this case every object used for play is included; they are not only toys, because there are common objects sometimes used in play, and some other play objects used for other purposes.

Second, the structural aspect—all the rules are applied to activities making some sense. It is not enough to develop a game or to call an activity a game if these concepts are not organized into a group of rules explaining to players what they are and are not allowed to do.

Third, the organization of the game itself—playing it, thus putting everything connected into an appropriate and specific context that offers different opportunities.

I considered this third playing stage as an analytical category, allowing me to emphasize the participants' experiences (connected to knowledge as a whole). I include transforming or creative activities developed for different reasons in their own cultural environment: job, art, social relationships, etc.[3] In addition, a playing experience often allows limits or boundaries to disappear because it is a way of approximating different situations.

Finally, I consider the native category as the starting point of this research. I work on *ñeovanga*–game—when some activity is defined that way, by *mbyá* children or adults (this idea will be developed later on).

I start by considering, as Nunes (1994) does, that playing games during childhood is an experience in which the main aim is to incorporate rules and values. Surprisingly, some domestic objects in the *tekoa* are used for different purposes, such as strollers (trolleys).

> One day I saw a child using a trolley: some kids were giving Fabiano (a boy around two) a ride around grandpa's house. Two or sometimes three children were pushing the trolley rudely and fast so Fabiano was running the risk of falling down all the time but they were laughing with no concern (n1: 13/11/06).

Another trolley was made with a big plastic container (similar to a can of gasoline), a piece of chain and some rope.

> This trolley was pulled aggressively by one child carrying another kid inside. The aim was, as in the previous case; make "the driver" (in general, younger than the rest) fall down (n1:10/07/05).

The most popular trolley is built with wood.

> This trolley was carrying everyday life objects inside: fallen fruit, young kids and even stones! Children call it *camion*, truck in Spanish. They pushed it to the middle of the forest, far away and they abandoned it there. Then, they came back running and laughing. The truck was far away, where it could not be seen. Real trucks are common objects for children because they can see them carrying wood from the forest for the wood industry every day (n1: 18/05/03).

---

3   This definition is given by Rubén Dri: "human being is essentially practice, a total practice and consciousness. It is a continuous, transforming practice of our natural reality. It creates products, such as pieces of art in which human beings are reflected and expanding themselves. Being through doing, creating. Nature is changing the world, the human world." (Dri, 1998, p. 195).

Leal Ferreira (2002) mentions certain indigenous children using medical waste products when they play. These *mbyá* children also view the activity of chopping trees as part of their lives (to them, another instance of waste—something is taken away and going nowhere). Ferreira says: "this is part of childhood universal autonomy" (p. 151). Allowing kids to play with these kinds of objects makes them understand some adult phenomena but in an abstract way; the *mbyá* childhood world does not go beyond play.

From the children's perspective, certain activities are not considered games by themselves (checking hunting traps as an activity for boys younger than 14, or cooking meals as an activity for girls before their first menstrual period). (Enriz & Garcia Palacios, 2008). These differences between one activity and the other are similar to the ones that Angela Nunes (1994) cites, when she establishes a difference between playing games and playing responsible games. Responsible games are played in the middle of housework and are productive activities: "real ones" (p. 163). It is important to add that this difference made by Nunes is only part of childhood activities described, and it is not considered by adults when describing their own activities.

Then, the playing games perspective is a premise expressing an order of thought. Organizing a game (setting rules and values) makes participants use and create social codes. They experience this social order through criticism or acceptance from other participants. Nowadays, playing games takes part in different contexts: schools (as a part of curriculum) and psychology (considering and using games for certain treatments). Playing games in these contexts includes manipulation as part of a historical and social process, and, as Ariés (1987) mentions, "games and school were part of the society but now they are inside a system with different levels" (p. 543). International organizations are dividing childhood into categories. UNICEF, for example, works on setting limits of different kinds for children, based on the research on the everyday lives of children. Every investigation made is applied directly to childhood and in many cases contributes to organizing and deciding kids' fates. And, for kids to play is a right.

Indigenous groups such as the *mbyá* can be considered differently, because native notions are historic productions. The occidental childhood notion comes from its historical development. Egon Schaden (1998) expressed that for *mbyá* people, there was no effort to develop childhood temperament; this was explained from *mbyá* acceptance of soul and rebirth, ideas establishing that people had characteristics of their personalities and these were innate.

ÑEOVANGA PORANGUEI: THE LUCKY ONES WHO PLAY

These concepts generate a transformation of *mbyá* kids' position within the group, because in the past, the process of learning was only represented by the oldest children who were carrying a vast knowledge with them. These changes take time to organize groups again; they bring a new stage of unbalanced knowledge. It is at this precise moment when *mbyá* old people appear. They go to schools to talk to teachers about what children need to learn and what must be taught.

> now he is not coming to talk to us about what we teach, but he used to come to school wondering if we had any questions. (Comment from a teacher talking about an old man in a private meeting: 10/ 06).

When I arrived for the first time at one *tekoa* (n 2), I asked about the *manga*, which is an *mbyá* traditional game well described by Leon Cadogan (1997). Briefly, the *manga* is a traditional game that *mbyá* (kids and adults) play when they are in a purifying situation. They play with a ball created by them, and the objective of the game is that the ball does not fall to the floor.

> By midday, a child brought me a *manga* ball used by children. He said, "Grown-ups use bigger balls to play, we are going to play later." I could also see catapults used by boys to hunt birds. "*Ka mirĩ* has one." the kid said. About *manga*, an old man told me "Adults play when they do not go out for several days; to do something. They stay in the *tekoa* when they cannot go out because they had a dream" (n1: 20/05/03).

Children play *manga* as an everyday activity; adults only play it when they cannot go to the forest, because a dream warns them not to abandon the group. Everyone has dreams, but only the oldest man will explain the meaning.

What *Ñeovanga* means.

Mbyá people use the concept of *ñeovanga* to send messages between kids and settle rules in a gentle way. Through the games, children learn how to search for meals. They learn the correct way to make contact with Gods. And they learn how to live in a community.

As mentioned by Christina Toren (1993), "learning categories used by children are as important as those ones used by adults." In my research I saw games defined by these young people. I compared their characteristics with some other activities, and from that I found the decisions used by children, such as: situations being developed in an unusual atmosphere, mixed with experimentation together with fixed rules. All these situations generate a particular mood related to time and place. From the children's point of view, during these practices their habitual places could be extraordinary and time flexible. Childhood development theories risk generalizing about children's specific, localized experiences. My research starts from children's activities, generating categories based on the local as a starting point.

We could say, from an adult perspective, that children's play time has no breaks. Indigenous adults talk about this issue in informal conversations and also when they are asked. Adults divide their time into three categories. None of them includes playing games. The first category of adult time is *jajagua* (what you must do). All of these activities are necessary in order to live, such as looking for water, finding and cooking food. The second category is religious activities, celebrated in ceremonies in the afternoon. The third is *trabajo*, (job in Spanish), the activities to acquire money and survive, such as *carpir* (to harvest manioc crops). This last one can be considered *trabajo* or *jajagua*, depending on the situation.

Children's time is not just spent playing games, when viewed from the children's perspective. There are certain activities—productive ones—called *jajagua* (such as checking hunting traps or grinding up wheat to make flour). As mentioned before, everyday games developed by *mbyá* kids are connected to hunting and gathering, handicraft, the school (when there is one), cooking and organization of religious ceremonies. From their point of view some of these activities cannot be developed separately. For example, hunting and gathering must be accompanied by religious ceremonies to be successful. So when children participate in one of these activities, they are obliged to take part in another. At the same time, those actions developed to survive are connected to family and welfare. So, linking activities provides children with an everyday understanding of causalities (cause-effect) among various aspects of social life. Adult tasks are usually accompanied by kids and defined as *ñeovanga* by children and adults.

I suggest that *mbyá* children experience many activities as *ñeovanga*. In this sense, as Mead expresses, every children's gathering is connected to games and their participation is completely voluntary (Mead: 1985). Another important activity, involved in *jajagua*, is washing clothes and bathing time. Kids participate in two different ways: bathing their little brothers and sisters and washing clothes from family members. This list of duties pretends to show some specific characteristics from *mbyá* childhood, with the aim of describing the environment where they experienced their knowledge.

Analyzing all this information we may then divide *mbyá* children's activities into three groups according to their importance. First of all, those activities developed to get food, as getting fruits from the trees; then, the activities showing power and strength, in order to find a way to be included in the community group, like the games with the truck, and finally, those religious activities in which the mutual dependence between children and adults is expressed, as the dances before prayers.

In religious experiences, the *mbyá* recognize a deep value in children's participation. Children prepare the place where religious words are said, and the girls and boys sing together to make gods listen to their prayers and songs. Religious knowledge has an important place in children's lives—when they sing an old song or dance a new rhythm they are acquiring new knowledge. Children know the purposes of these religious actions and they respect them. Through games they express their respect for religion, as we saw with the *mangá*. I agree with Cristina Toren (1993) that children are produced by culture and they, on their own, produce culture. Based on this, they express very different and sometimes incongruous ideas about their own culture.

Play, as shown in the example of the fruit or the animals, brings the opportunity to create games in group and to return to the experience. Information about certain issues (such as caring for animals or searching for fruit) only appeared in play. With religion, children learn in the ceremony, playing games—first jumping, dancing and singing—and then, taking a respectful role in the praying time. At this point it is very important to consider that in a messianic population, learning religious aspects by games is something very relevant.

This chapter argues that childhood, by itself, could be defined as "what is not adult," but for *mbyá* people, being a child is the opportunity to play. To play defines the condition of being a child, and is the most important everyday activity for *mbyá* kids.

References

Ariés, P. (1987). *El niño y la vida familiar en el Antiguo Régimen*. Madrid. Ed. Taurus.

Boas, F. Review of Mac Donald, A.: Experimental Study of Children. In *American Anthropologist*, New Series, Vol. 1, N° 4 (Oct., 1899), pp. 773-775.

Bortón, L.; Enriz, Nn; Hecht, A.C.; García Palacios, M. (2008). *Una aproximación a las representaciones escolares sobre el niño indígena como sujeto de aprendizaje*. 2008. Silvia Hirch comp. En prensa.

Brougère, G. (1998). *Jogo e educaçao*. Porto Alegre: Artes Médicas.

Cadogan, L. (1997) [1959] Ayvu-Rapyta. Textos míticos de los Mbya-guaraní del Guairá. Paraguay. Fundación León Cadogan. CEADUC.

Caputo, V. (1995). Anthropology's silent 'others': A consideration of some conceptual and methodological issues for the study of youth and children's culture. In *Youth cultures: A cross-cultural perspective*, edited by Vered Amit-Talai & Helena Wulff. London and New York: Routledge.

Cohn, C. (2000) Crescendo como um Xikrin: Uma análise da infância e do desenvolvimento infantil entre os Kayapó-Xikrin do Bacajá. *Rev. Antropol.* [online]. 2000, vol. 43, n. 2, (pp. 195-222). ISSN 0034-7701.

Cohn, C. (2002). A criança, o aprendizado e a socialização na antropologia. In: *Crianças indígenas*.

Cohn, C. (2005). *Antropologia da Criança*. Coleção Ciências Sociais, Passo-a-Passo, Jorge Zahar Editores, R.J.

Colangelo, M.A. (2006). La crianza en disputa. Un análisis del saber médico sobre el cuidado infantil. VIII Congreso Argentino de Antropología. Salta.

Culin, S. 1899. Hawaiian Games. *American Anthropologist*, New Series, Vol. 1, No. 2. (Apr., 1899), pp. 201-247.

De Carvalho, J.J. (1990). O jogo das bolinhas. Uma simbólica do masculino. *Anuario Antropológico* n° 87. Editore Universidade de Brasilia. Tempo Brasileiro.

Dri, R. (1998). *Los modos del saber y su periodización*. Buenos Aires. Ediciones Letra Nueva.

Enriz, N., & García Palacios, M. (2008). Deviniendo kuña va'era en *Mujeres indígenas*. Silvia Hirch comp. Editorial Biblos. Buenos Aires.

Enriz, N. (2006). Retorspectiva de los procesos de modernización de los Mbyá guaraní de Misiones. Núcleo Disciplinar: Ciências Políticas e Sociais: alterações sociais e institucionais produzidas pelas novas democracias no cone sul. XIV Jornadas de Jóvenes investigadores de la Asociación de Universidades del Grupo Montevideo. Campinas, Brasil 11-15 de Septiembre de 2006.

Ferreira, L., and Kawall, M. (2002). Divina abundancia: fome, miseria e a Terra-Sema-Mal das crianças Guarani. En: *Crianças indígenas*.

Geertz, C. (1992). *La interpretación de las culturas*. Gedisa. Barcelona. España.

Handelman, D. (1974). A Note on Play. *American Anthropologist*, New Series, Vol. 76, No. 1. (Mar., 1974), pp. 66-68.

Hernandez, P. 1913. *Organización Social De Las Doctrinas Guaraníticas De La Compañía De Jesús*. Barcelona, Ed. Gustavo Gil.

Huizinga, J. (1972). *Homo Ludens*. Alianza Editorial / Emecé Editores. Madrid.

Kelly, I.T. (1931). Reviewed work(s): *Ceremonial games of the south American Indians* by Rafael Karsten. *American Anthropologist*, New Series, Vol. 33, No. 2. (Apr.-Jun., 1931), p. 243.

Larriq, M. (1993). Ipytũma construcción de la persona entre los Mbya-guarani. Editorial universitaria. Universidad Nacional de Misiones.

Levi-Strauss, C. (1964). *El pensamiento salvaje*. Fondo de Cultura Económica. México.

Lopes Da Silva, A. (2002). Pequeños xamas: crianças indígenas, corporalidade e escolarização. In: *Crianças indígenas*.

Mauss, M. 2006. *Manual de Etnografía*. Buenos Aires. Editorial, Fondo de Cultura Económica.

Mead, M. (1985.) *Educación y cultura*. Paidos.

Nunes, A. (1994). A sociedades das crianças a'uwe-Xavante. Instituto de Innovação Educacional.

Quadrelli, A. (1998). Ejapo letra para'i. Educación, escuela y alfabetización en la población indígena de la provincia de Misiones. Tesis de maestría en antropología social. Facultad de Humanidades y Ciencias Sociales. Universidad Nacional de Misiones.

Remorini, C. (2004). Emae nde Kypy-i re! (cuida por tu hermanita!) Un análisis del papel de las interacciones infantiles en el proceso de endoculturación mbyá. VII Congreso Argentino de Antropología. Córdoba.

Ruiz, I. (1984). La ceremonia Ñemongaraí de los Mbïá de la provincia de Misiones. Temas de etnomusicología, 1, pp. 51-102. Buenos Aires: Instituto Nacional de Musicología.

Schaden, E. (1998). *Aspectos fundamentales de la cultura guaraní*. Universidad católica. Asunción.

Silva, H. (1999) Paradigmas y niveles del juego en RAMOS, José Luis (coord.), Juego, educación y cultura. ENAH: Conaculta, México, 1999, pp. 35-52.

Szulc, A. (2004). La antropología frente a los niños: de la omisión a las "culturas infantiles." VII Congreso Argentino de Antropología Social. Córdoba.

Toren, C. (1993). Making history. The significance of childhood cognition for a comparative anthropology of mind. *Man*. New Series, Vol. *28*, Issue 3. Sept. 1993.

Tuner, V. (1980). La selva de los símbolos. Siglo veintiuno, Madrid.

Tylor, E.B. (1879). On the game of patolli in Ancient Mexico, and its probable Asiatic origin. *The Journal of the Anthropological Institute of Great Britain and Ireland*, Vol. *8*, pp. 116-131.

SECTION TWO

Play and the Child Body

Chapter Five

What Are Little (Gender "Normal," Heterosexual) Kids Made Of?
Performing and Subverting the Status Quo in the Dramatic Play Area

Rebecca Howard

Story One: Casting Call

One of the greatest joys of being an early childhood educator is that you get to play at work. One of the advantages of being the owner of the facility is that you can choose to play whenever you get the urge (under the guise of checking in with the staff). Not long ago, I had the urge to spend some time with a group of eight 3- to 5-year-olds. It was near the end of the day, when the children have free play while waiting for their parents to pick them up. I had noticed earlier that three children, all girls, had been playing "house" off and on over the course of several days, sometimes with one or two of the boys, but mostly just with each other. I sat down at a table, child-sized in height but large enough to accommodate four small chairs, initially with the intention of simply observing. It wasn't long, however, before I was joined by the three girls, who seemed interested in continuing the game. As they were choosing "roles," I asked them if I could play and what I could be. One of them said I could be "the mom." Fully intending to model the disruption of the assumed roles of the standard "script," I said, "I have to be a mom all the time—can I be something else?" One girl suggested I could be the "little baby" (not to be confused with the "old baby," which was her part). The second thought I could be the "puppy," which I recognize as a coveted character in the domestic dramas of these children, so I was quite honored. However, since recent knee surgery made it difficult for me to crawl on all fours, I could not meet the physical demands of the role and had to decline. The third girl (the most cognitively and socially mature of the group), picked up on the more direct connotation of what is oppositional to "mom," and eagerly said, "you can be the dad!" I responded that I thought I could handle that, but was drowned out by the other two girls saying, "she's a girl—she can't be the dad." The third girl countered, "yes, she can," causing the others to reconsider and agree to cast me as the dad. I never got to fully realize the role, however, as parents arrived at that point, but the important part had been put in motion—the script had been introduced, critiqued, and rewritten with new rules.

Performing Play

One of the staples of Early Childhood Education and Care (ECEC) settings has long been the "dramatic play" area, especially in pre-K environments (where it was at one time better known as the "housekeeping" area). Traditionally, dramatic play areas are equipped with dolls, dress-up clothes and props, child-size "kitchen" furniture and toy "appliances," and other materials and equipment that constitute the immediately recognizable accessories necessary for young children to negotiate, recreate, and make sense of the domestic reality they experience in the home, the social reality they are part of in school and with friends, and the narrated reality they see on television. This narrated reality, of course (at least in the United States), is defined by the material standards and expectations of a Euro-American, middle- to upper-middle class, and assuredly heterosexual sensibility, and for many children, it is reflected in and reinforced by the domestic and social.

There is little dispute about the value of dramatic play in children's development. It enhances social skills, language acquisition, fine- and gross-motor development, logic/reasoning/problem-solving processes, creativity, and identity, to name just a few (Ary-De Rozza and Payne-Jones, 2004; Freeman and Brown, 2004; Piaget, 1962; Rosen, 1974; Sternberg, 2004; Sutton-Smith, 1967; Vygotsky, 1976). This chapter is particularly concerned with aspects of identity that are reflected, expressed, and occasionally challenged as children participate in "dramatic" play, especially those aspects that influence a child's understanding of their own and others' gendered bodies.

Perhaps more than any other location in an early childhood classroom, the *mise-en-scène* of the dramatic play area and its materials reflect the values and "norms" of the culture that is most dominant. Though class and race/ethnicity are inextricably interwoven with gender and sexuality, for the purposes of this chapter the focus will be on the latter, in consideration of the question of how gender identity and the foundations of sexuality tend to be very narrowly defined in traditional ECEC classrooms, and in what ways those definitions limit the full development of a sense of self, especially for children who do not experience their gender identity as falling within those narrow parameters. The visible (or, for children who are visually impaired, the "physically experienced") manifestation of this identity is the physical body, including the way in which it is clothed, decorated, regulated, and mobilized. It is through interaction with the physical environment, social contact, and cultural images that children are introduced to, and rehearse, their identity scripts and their embodiment (Alloway, 1995; Blaise, 2005; MacNaughton, 2000).

Approaching this topic as a site of "performance" offers an illuminating perception of gendered, heteronormative behaviors that children encounter in the course of their day outside of the home, especially those centered in the theatrically sounding "dramatic" play area. The tropes of dramatic play spaces are grounded in a cultural grand narrative that preferences and encourages predictable gender responses. By interpreting this narrative as a "script" that children "perform" through purposeful and/or subconsciously rehearsed choices, it is possible to understand the potential for positioning the dramatic play area as a site of resistance, offering children the space to develop notions of gender and sexuality that are more closely aligned with the way they actually experience their own sense of a gendered self, which may or may not coincide with the assumptions and expectations of the broader culture and of their more immediate social milieu. With such a performance-based approach, children (either in cooperation with or in spite of their parents, teachers, and caregivers) are better able to alter these cultural scripts, or to create brand new scripts that exist in alignment with, or counter to, the grand narratives of the dominant culture (Thorne, 2004).

Child Development, Dramatic Play, and Gender Scripts

The little girls in the opening scene of this chapter demonstrate these cultural scripts in production, in both their initial rehearsal of and their ultimate challenge to the grand narrative. Their "casting" process is based primarily on their understanding of the biological expression of what constitutes a "boy" or a "girl" and the ways in which feminine or masculine behaviors and actions are supposed to "match" the female or male physicality of the body. The two younger girls, who are in what Piaget would term a "pre-operational" stage of cognitive development, are rigidly bound to the simplicity of an either/or understanding of the world (Piaget, 1962; Thomas, 2000). Children in this stage are generally practicing the process of categorizing the world and see the categories as discrete and clearly defined even if those definitions do not always reflect the actuality of the child's world. For example, if you ask a group of four-year-olds how to tell if someone is a boy or a girl, there's a very good chance that one of the most common responses will be, "boys have short hair and girls have long hair." This response will occur even when there are boys with longer hair and/or girls with shorter hair in the group. The ability of pre-K children to create nuanced categories in which boys might have long hair and still be boys is limited, because their process of creating those categories is rooted in concrete binaries that are defined by the images and messages they absorb. On rare occasions, you might encounter a child who has been more attuned to the actual physical binary of "a boy has a penis and a girl has a vagina," but since those attributes are not readily visible, they don't carry the same cognitive weight for immediate categorization.

Many psychologists and early childhood educators believe that these concrete binaries are crucial to a child's development of a "healthy" gendered identity that is directly tied to a corresponding physical body and that the blurring of these categories will lead to gender confusion (known clinically as "Gender Identity Disorder" in extreme cases, a diagnosis that still exists in the DSM-IV, the diagnostic "bible" of clinical psychology and psychiatry). This belief is at the foundation of traditional ECEC curricular and classroom environment guidelines, which relies heavily on developmental psychology (Cannella, 1997; Dahlberg, Moss, & Pence, 1999). An example of this can be found in one of the most common tools for evaluating the quality of an ECEC program—the Early Childhood Environment Rating Scale-Revised (ECERS-R). This instrument consists of a number of categories that are rated on a numerical scale of 1-7, with seven reflecting the highest quality. One of the categories included in this instrument, not surprisingly, is "Dramatic Play." In states such as Ohio, it is a requirement for all licensed ECEC programs (whether they call themselves "day care" or "preschool") to include provisions for dramatic play, preferably in a specific, defined area, and the ECERS-R is recommended (though not required for licensure) as a valid tool for assessing the quality of these areas. The ECERS-R reflects this emphasis on dramatic play, explaining that, in order to achieve a perfect "7," a program must accept and reflect the belief that,

> [S]ince children are developing gender-role identity during the preschool years, they require concrete examples of dress-ups that are associated with being men or women. Thus, two or three gender-specific examples of dress-up items are required (such as ties, hard hats, or shoes to represent men's clothes; purses or flowery hats for women's). More generic clothing, such as sweatshirts or running shoes, can also be

provided, but these do not count as gender-specific dress-ups. (Harms, Clifford, & Cryer, 2005, p. 49)

This description not only exemplifies the overt influence of a specific branch of developmental psychology but also reveals what is, arguably, a generation gap in terms of fashion and occupations. Besides the fact that women in hard hats are increasingly common and visible, especially on road repair crews, one only has to spend a short time in a high school or college classroom to notice that "men's" shoes (presumably meaning box-toed and heavy-soled), and even ties, are not necessarily as gender-specific as they once were, and young women rarely wear the ubiquitous "flowery" hats that were already out of style for their parents' generation. The description of such props seems to be drawn straight from *Dick and Jane*, reflecting assumptions about gender stereotypes that are heavily influenced by a middle- to upper-middle class sensibility and which transmit to children storybook notions about gender that do not necessarily reflect the reality of their lived experiences—in essence, the script of the grand gender narrative.

The implications for the steadfast adherence to these outdated stereotypes on an embodied identity are profound, especially for children whose gender does not fit neatly or cleanly into one of the approved binary categories. Even though it is probably true that "most" boys exhibit certain behaviors and "most" girls exhibit the opposite (for example, aggressive, physical play for boys versus verbal, social play for girls), there will always be children who fall outside these expectations or who adhere in some ways but not in others (Blaise, 2005; MacNaughton, 2000; Thorne, 2004). For young children, transgressing these gender boundaries is seen as more acceptable for girls ("tomboy" is generally not a pejorative term for pre-adolescent girls) than for boys ("sissy" is never a compliment, no matter the age of the boy in question), but neither is encouraged past adolescence as a permanent facet of acceptable social behavior or an acceptable socialized body. The "tomboy-sissy" dynamic is one that is deeply rooted in notions of culture and social power, and is reflected in the artifacts of early childhood. "Sissies" (i.e., boys who emulate "girl" behavior) are perceived to be moving from a position of power to one of weakness, whereas "tomboys" (i.e., girls who "act like boys") are embracing a cultural construct that is imbued with greater power. Young children who are given the "flowery hats" and "ties [and] hard hats" of the ECERS-R as unchallenged examples of what it means to be a girl or to be a boy begin to comprehend the relative sense of strength and power (or weakness) that these items convey.

The ECERS-R description of the types of materials that should be available to young children reflects the ways in which a child's body is defined as acceptably male or female. In the description, the icons of femininity and masculinity (even if they are updated to reflect a more contemporary reality) provide the physical props for the gender script that is approved as "normal" and "healthy" by developmental psychologists and traditional early childhood educators. But it is not the only script out there (MacNaughton, 2000), and this sets up one of the most interesting paradoxes in ECEC.

On the one hand, early childhood educators and caregivers have, for the last 30 years or more, accepted the importance of diversity and inclusiveness in ECEC curriculum and materials. The wealth of picture books available to represent a broad range of ethnicities, religions, lifestyles, cultural practices, holidays, physical abilities, and non-sexist gender roles is testimony to the success of the commitment to multiculturalism evident in ECEC. This commitment is foundational in the position of the National Association for the Education of Young Children (NAEYC), perhaps the leading professional organization for early childhood educators and caregivers, in the latest revision of the *Developmentally Appropriate Practice in Early Childhood Programs* (often shorthanded as DAP), a document that many states, agencies, and boards of education have adopted as setting the standards for determining the quality of an early childhood program. As noted in response to a concern that DAP does not accommodate a variety of cultures, the authors note that, "Most important, the classroom must be a welcoming environment that demonstrates respect and support for all children's cultural and family backgrounds" (Copple and Bredekamp, 2009, p. 332). Presumably, this would include children from different gender and sexuality backgrounds as well, and sexism is often one of the most noted forms of discrimination that teachers and caregivers are frequently told to be aware of and actively counter.

On the other hand, dramatic play materials that are structured according to the ECERS-R guidelines would seem to encourage the perpetuation of gender role stereotypes and physical reflections of traditional "male-ness" and "female-ness." Even if the teacher encourages (or at least doesn't actively discourage), for example, boys carrying purses and girls wearing hard hats, children by the age of three have already begun to associate certain props with certain cultural expectations, especially if they spend any time watching television or if they live in a household where such associations are the norm for that family. Including these props in a traditional dramatic play area, accompanied by other familiar icons of adult role modeling, such as a toy sink, stove, and refrigerator (items which the ECERS-R also wants to see present in the classroom), makes it difficult for them to be viewed in any way other than with all of their gendered connotations.

Children certainly have agency to make choices about how to use these materials, but adults are capable of (and responsible for) shaping those choices and framing the context in which those choices become accepted as positive or negative ones. If these iconic props are to be included in a dramatic play area, one way to maximize the potential of these iconic props to appeal to children of all gendered possibilities and to thereby address the paradox of encouraging diversity with the limitations of traditional gender roles, is to "neutralize" the props by de-contextualizing them from their mainstream affiliations, allowing the children to create the meaning that they need for them to have. The following story illustrates this potential.

Story Two: Red Flag

Rather than a single "dramatic play" area, we accommodate the children's need for dramatic play by making props available in various areas of the room, at all times, and with different types of contextualizing experiences and information. Early in the 2008-09 school year, we brought in a box of fabric, clothing, and accessories and allowed the children to create whatever combinations they wanted. Since none of the clothes were "traditionally" male or female in an immediately recognizable sense, combining them with large pieces of nonspecific fabric made it necessary for children to bring meaning to their play defined only by their need, not by the limitations of the materials.

One of the pieces of clothing in this odd collection was a top that had been part of a Halloween costume that was originally intended to be a "Bratz" character (a hyper-feminized yet supposedly more "urban" response to Barbie® dolls). The shirt was a lavender, velour-type fabric with long sleeves made of a soft netting material that flared at the wrist. It was a very soft shirt, which gave the opportunity for a heightened tactile experience. The only child who showed any interest in this top was a three-year-old boy, who liked the color but mostly loved the texture. Over the course of the five days that this collection was made available to the children, he chose this shirt every time he had the opportunity. Since the collection did not include any Bratz dolls, and since it was not part of a traditional dramatic play area, the only context he and the other children had for the shirt was as a tactilely interesting fabric that was a nice color and felt good to wear while he was playing with his favored box of cars and trucks. No one derided him for wearing a "girl's" shirt, since no one else had the context for naming it as such. In fact, one of the older (after school) boys mentioned that he thought it looked kind of like the shirts knights wore in pictures (albeit not generally lavender or with quite the same flair to the sleeves).

In this instance, the potential for judgment of non-acceptability came not from the other children, even the older ones, but from adults who would see a boy wearing such a shirt as a red flag (or, in this case, a lavender flag), signaling the fear that wearing such a garment would, inevitably, mean this boy would turn out to be gay. Fortunately, neither his teachers nor his family were alarmed by it, and he eventually lost interest in the shirt. Whether or not he turns out to be gay won't be known for several more years, any more than we will know if his propensity for playing with cars will make him turn out to be a mechanic.

Froebel, Dewey, and Hill: Progressivism, Kindergarten, and Housekeeping

In order to understand the stability of the dramatic play area as a fundamental aspect of ECEC and its influence on the bodies and sensibilities of young children, it is helpful to understand the historical context that solidified it as a cultural and educational trope. The origins of dramatic play in education are not mystical or difficult to identify, but the process of codifying it as such an integral and recognizable part of ECEC is an interesting one to follow and helps to explain the implications for dramatic play on the development of a gendered and sexualized body.

Until the nineteenth century, children's play was generally seen as a frivolous waste of time or a necessary part of preparing for adulthood, even when their "games" were often what we would recognize today as "dramatic play." In other words, children typically acted out the experiences of the adult world that dictated their lives and destinies (Makman, 2004). Even with the Victorian invention of "childhood" as a distinct phase of life and the recognition that play served an inherent function that should be valued and nurtured, children's play still focused on emulating adults or recreating the real world around them in miniature (hence the Victorian fascination with realistic, detailed doll houses) (Formanek-Brunell, 1998; Burton, 1996). For very young children, even imaginative fantasy play has frequently been a reflection of what they know, or what they hear, or what they are trying to understand. For example, fighting off imaginary monsters, which may appear to adults as fantasy play, is probably less about fantasy and more about coming to terms with the manifestations of genuine fears and insecurities, which are very real to a three-year-old (Ary-De Rozza & Payne-Jones, 2004; Vygotsky, 1976).

The earliest structured educational program for very young children grew from the work of Friedrich Froebel (1782–1852), whose establishment of the kindergarten was heavily influenced by Pestalozzi (1746–1827) (Brosterman, 1997; Lascarides & Hinitz, 2000; Makman, 2004). During Froebel's time in Germany, education was a decidedly male-centered activity for both students and teachers. Froebel's emphasis on structured, active movement and engagement with the environment was accepted as appropriate for young boys, who were generally the only children allowed to attend school in the late eighteenth and early-nineteenth centuries. By the time the kindergarten movement had come to the United States in 1852, formal education for young girls had found growing acceptance, as had education for the poor, and it was increasingly the purview of women teachers (Solomon, 1985; Snyder, 1972).

With the establishment of free public kindergartens in the U.S. by 1873, the "kindergarteners" (as the teachers were known) had been forced to address the dilemma of gender in education: physical activity and enthusiastic exploration were acceptable for boys, but girls were still expected to be delicate and passive. One of the most notable and influential of American teachers to embrace the liberatory model of Froebel was Patty Smith Hill. In 1887, Hill was working with Anna E. Bryan, who had been trained in the Chicago Free Kindergarten program that was heavily influenced by the philosophy of John Dewey. It is this progression, from Froebel to Dewey to Hill, which led to the inclusion of dramatic play as a staple of kindergarten and, especially, pre-k programs.

An integral part of Dewey's theories of education rested on the recognition that education should be meaningful to all segments of society, not just those who were destined for college and/or lucrative careers in business. Under Dewey's model, children should be engaged in "manual education" (what we would (mis)label today as "vocational" training), in addition to traditional academic subjects, as a way of preparing all children to become equal participants in a democratic society (Dewey, 1916). For older children, alongside studies of math, science, and reading, this would include engaging in activities such as farming, machine operation and repair, building trades, food preparation, etc. For young children, these activities would be manifested through gardening, using tools, building with blocks, playing with kitchen utensils, etc.

Hill began developing, along with Bryan, a radically new approach to kindergarten, one that sought to blend Froebel's original ideas about the importance of organic unity and symbolic education with the Progressivist model of a less teacher-centered, more child-centered curriculum of free play with a wider range of materials. Hill later "claimed that reading a Dewey monograph and studying with Dewey influenced her view of creativity in children's artwork, the movement toward free play...and her approach to music. She gave up many of the traditional practices, on the principle that teaching involved creative thinking" (Lascarides & Hinitz, 2000, pp. 261-262).

The reason that this progression matters to the shape of dramatic play in contemporary ECEC settings is because Patty Smith Hill eventually took her approach, including her commitment to dramatic play, to Teachers College at Columbia, where she was in charge of developing the curriculum for training early childhood teachers (Snyder, 1972). Her model of teacher education and kindergarten instruction provided the basis for the familiar structure of kindergarten and pre-K classrooms in most areas of the United States today (Lascarides & Hinitz, 2000). The "manual education" aspects of Progressivism translated in the ECEC classroom to what we refer to now as "dramatic play," complete with blocks, utensils, tools, dolls, and the "gender-specific" clothing that the ECERS-R is so fond of.

In Hill's time, though, the emphasis on "gender specific" experiences was conspicuously less than it eventually became. The boys and girls in Hill's classrooms were encouraged to share all of the experiences available to them—girls built structures with blocks, and boys gave baths to the baby dolls. This began to change by the 1930s, when Progressivism became suspected as being in alignment with Socialism and Communism, and some of the more Progressive elements of education were discarded. Early childhood programs, including nursery schools and daycares as well as kindergartens, were able to retain those vestiges of Progressivism that emphasized play and exploration as long as they became more socially codified along lines of gender, class, and ethnicity (Holland, 2003). In other words, young children could continue to play and explore as long as the materials and expectations reflected the Euro-American, gender-specific, heterosexual, middle- and upper-class sensibilities that had come to dominate U.S. politics, culture, and curriculum.

Through this process of curricular and social evolution, children's bodies were increasingly regulated in accordance with new discoveries in science and psychology that reified traditional notions of gender and sexuality as a way of reassuring white, middle-class Americans that their values and desires were safely entrenched as the "norm" for the country. The dramatic play area became one of the most reassuring locations for the perpetuation of this mindset, and the materials and choices available to children became codified to ensure the status quo.

Story Three: Little Boxes

About 30 years ago, as a young teacher and administrator of the pre-primary program in a Progressivist-modeled private school, one of my tasks was to facilitate the process for obtaining a license under the newly established state requirements for day care and preschool programs. One of the rules that had been adopted was the articulation of the necessary types of spaces and materials that had to be part of the curriculum. One of these requirements was a "dramatic play" area, the new name for the "housekeeping" area traditional to ECEC programs.

The first licensing inspector I encountered was dismayed that we did not have a specifically designated dramatic play area and even more dismayed that we didn't have the recognizable tropes of such an area, especially a toy sink/stove/refrigerator, dolls, and "dress up" clothes. My challenge was to make the case that we highly valued dramatic play, and that we also highly valued creativity, and were very purposeful in our approach to facilitating both. I pointed out the blocks and puppets and fabric at various locations throughout the room, and told her the following story to make my point.

At one time, we had possessed a sink/stove/refrigerator unit that had been donated to us, and we put it in the room with the three- and four-year olds and carefully observed the children playing with it. Even though we placed no unreasonable limitations on how they could use it, with few exceptions the sink was always only a sink, the stove a stove, and the refrigerator a refrigerator, and the children used them to construct predictable domestic scenarios, using the blocks as food and the fabric as blankets. After we removed the unit, we replaced it with two sturdy, medium-size cardboard boxes that contained thick, heavy cardboard cylinders that had been used to hold the old-style roll paper used in copy machines of the time. The first day I put them out, the children found ways to use them that still met their needs for domestic re-creation but did not limit them to a single way of doing so. They stood the cylinders on end and placed a box on top of them, open side up, which became their "sink." When they turned the box over, it was a "stove," and placed on end, it was a "refrigerator." The cylinders were "milk cartons," "glasses," "salt shakers," "rolling pins," and many other things.

The most interesting part, however, was observing their play over the course of a few days to see them begin to use these materials in imaginative ways, moving beyond the predictable scripts of re-creative domestic play. The boxes became ships, and the cylinders telescopes as they imagined themselves pirates on the high seas. Another time, the cylinders were a stethoscope, x-ray machine, and medicine container as they played hospital. The next day, the boxes were racecars and the cylinders the tools to fix them. In each of these scenarios, the puppets, fabric, and some of the art materials were brought in to serve whatever function they deemed necessary.

Removed from the rigidly defined context of specificity, the children also found their way past predictable gender roles. Girls were pirates and doctors and mechanics, and boys were nurses and fathers who bathed and fed their puppet babies. It was this experience that convinced me of the value of non-traditional dramatic play.

The inspector was persuaded, and we got our license. Since then, with my own facility, every time I've had a new inspector, I've gone through the same routine of explanation, using the same example, along with new ones that I have acquired over the years, all supporting the idea that "dramatic play" has potential beyond the confines of traditional pedagogy. I also throw in a few references to Patty Smith Hill and John Dewey. I still don't have a defined dramatic play area, or gender-specific dress up clothes, or a permanent stove/sink/refrigerator, but I do have a license.

Challenge, Change, and the Performance of Gender

In order to fully appreciate the dramatic play area as a performative site of resistance, it is necessary to have a working definition for the intersection of play and performance. According to Henry Bial, who is referencing the work of Richard Schechner, one of the pioneers of performance studies:

> In performance studies, play is understood as the force of uncertainty which counterbalances the structure provided by ritual. Where ritual depends on repetition, play stresses innovation and creativity. Where ritual is predictable, play is contingent. But all performances, even rituals, contain some element of play, some space for variation.

And most forms of play involve pre-established patterns of behavior. Hence, as Schechner writes, "one definition of performance might be: ritualized behavior conditioned/permeated by play." (p. 115)

In this sense, play and performance are intricately related and interwoven. The definition of performance offered by Bial and Schechner could also be posited as a compelling definition of the activity in a traditional dramatic play space: "ritualized behavior conditioned/permeated by play." The ritualized behavior of dramatic play that is defined by traditional materials is evident in the re-creation by children of the domestic scenes they see and experience—in performance terms, dramatic play functions as a mimetic presentation of actions and behaviors that reify dominant social constructions of gender, sexuality, class, and race/ethnicity.

Performance theory provides us with the framework for extending the notion of a performance "text" as something not limited to an actual written script (Kirshenblatt-Gimblett, 2004; Worthen, 2004). Specific emphasis on the body in performance art also enables us to understand the immediacy of performance in the dramatic play area, where children, like performance artists, can base their characters "upon their own bodies, their own autobiographies, their own specific experiences in a culture or in the world, made performative by their consciousness of them and the process of displaying them for audiences" (Carlson, 2004, p. 71). Utilizing this focus on "consciousness" in the act of performing one's life experiences allows us to envision intervention in traditional dramatic play spaces by moving children away from the characters that society tries to script for them, and into the conscious enactment of their own gendered bodies. In addition, feminist performance theorists such as Peggy Phelan, Elin Diamond, Kate Davy, Jill Dolan, and Sue-Ellen Case, for example, provide a means for further focusing performance critiques on questions of gender and sexuality, especially in relation to dominant hierarchies and ideologies.

Theorists working in disciplines other than Performance Studies have also made foundational contributions to the field in general, and to this analysis in particular. The "ritualized behavior" and "pre-established patterns of behavior" that Schechner and Bial speak of are reflected in the work of Judith Butler. Her groundbreaking essay, "Performative Acts and Gender Constitution: An Essay in Phenomenology and Feminist Theory," was written nearly 20 years ago but is still a foundational work in the canon of performance theory, particularly as it relates to gender. Butler's revolutionary suggestion was that gender is a construct that is culturally scripted and "performed" through repetition, grounded in the cultural narrative that created and perpetuates it. She also suggests that understanding the performative nature of gender is the key to creating new possibilities for embodying gender. She writes,

> If the ground of gender identity is the stylized repetition of acts through time, and not a seemingly seamless identity, then the possibilities of gender transformation are to be found in the arbitrary relation between such acts, in the possibility of a different sort of repeating, in the breaking or subversive repetition of that style. (pp. 270-271)

As feminist theorists, poststructuralists, cultural theorists, sociologists, psychologists, semioticians, and others have posited strategies for subversion of these cultural gender narratives, the focus has primarily been on the awareness of adults as active agents who are reconstructing these performative gender acts with intent and forethought. But perhaps the most meaningful subversion may be when adults intervene in the topoi of that grand narrative in the daily experiences of children.

Adults are primarily responsible for the construction of and access to most of the spaces and contexts in which children play, especially in facilitating dramatic play. When adults intervene, with intent and forethought, in the arrangement and materials of children's play spaces, it can either be a function of control and regulation or an opportunity for exploration and liberation. When we provide children with rigidly defined materials in a context that supports the use of those materials in alignment with the status quo of the cultural script, we are deciding for them not only what they should play with, but how they should play with it, leading them through the "stylized repetition of acts" that define the "acceptable" embodiment of gender. Watching children in a traditional dramatic play area, these ritualized behaviors are readily apparent. Some of these ritualized behaviors include:

- Girls and boys "dressing up" in "gender appropriate" clothing, like the "flowery hats and purses" for girls or the "hardhats and ties" for boys described in the ECERS-R guidelines.

- Actions that reflect an unquestioned correlation between gender appearance and gendered behavior, such as girls taking their purses shopping or wearing flowery hats to parties, and boys wearing their hardhats or ties as they go off to work.

- The rigidity of family roles, such that boys are always "dad" or "brother" and girls are always "mom" or "sister."

- The enactment of family gender roles that recreate a heteronormative imperative—i.e., girl and boy as mom and dad, never mom and mom or dad and dad.

- The enactment of family gender roles that emphasize a "nuclear" family model which rejects extended families, step families, same-sex parent families, or single-parent families.

If we accept Bial's assertion that "play stresses innovation and creativity," then it is possible to argue that the traditional "dramatic play" area, with its dependence on pre-defined cultural topoi and material icons, may not really be "play" at all, since "innovation and creativity" are not the primary components of an activity that embodies "ritualized behavior" as it encourages children to recreate their domestic lives. Perhaps it would be more accurately descriptive to call a traditional dramatic play area a "dramatic performance" area.

In this sense, then, the redemption and reclamation of the dramatic play area as a space with the potential to maximize children's ability to challenge the status quo may lie in repositioning the emphasis on the "play" part, thereby restoring innovation and creativity to the process. In order to accomplish this, however, it is necessary to reconceptualize the way the dramatic play area is perceived, arranged, and equipped. As discussed earlier, one of the strategies for this reconceptualization is to not only broaden the creative content of the materials themselves, to make them less recognizable as discretely defined, gendered objects, but to also subvert the context in which those materials are made available. By removing the referential tropes of the context, the materials lose the immediacy of their "normal" definition, providing a conceptual space for children to create their own meaning.

But what of the ECERS-R assertion (based on the dogma of developmental psychology), that gender-appropriate dramatic play materials are required for children to "develop gender-role identity in the preschool years"? If we subvert these dominant paradigms, are we putting our children at risk for psychological or sexual confusion?

I am not aware of any definitive empirical studies that have proven the stability of gender role identity related to dramatic play materials. I am aware of theories growing from the observation of intersexed children over the last 50 years, such as the response to the work of Dr. John Money. Dr. Money counseled the parents of an infant boy, whose penis had been removed after a botched circumcision in infancy, to raise their son as a girl, with all of the attendant accessories of femininity. He believed that, with sufficient commitment on the part of the parents, they would be able to raise a daughter who was confidently socialized as a female. After questions were raised about the accuracy of his reporting and his methodology (which is still, however, validated today by many physicians) (Chase, 2003), it became apparent that the boy in question had never developed a firm identity as either male or female. More recent studies of intersexed and transgendered children seem to suggest that gender-role identity is not as neatly coincidental with biological sex as our cultural narrative supposes (Fausto-Sterling, 2000).

My professional experience and research lead me to believe that, given the freedom to explore, interpret, experiment, and rehearse their own gender performances and those of the culture around them, children will develop a confident conception of their own gender identity that embraces what "feels" right to them, meaning that it aligns with their physical embodiment of their gendered identity. As an educator, an academic, and a parent, this feels right to me as well.

Story Four: Make Room for Daddy

Just last week, I noticed one of the four-year old boys standing next to one of the shelf units that are used to store blocks, dinosaurs, and other larger items. This particular little boy generally exhibits gendered behaviors that would traditionally be considered as "normal" boy behaviors—he talks excitedly about the farm machinery and implements he watches his father use, he often wears a John Deere cap and t-shirts with various superheroes or sports themes on them, he is physically boisterous, he likes to play with blocks and cars and trains—he is, in most ways, what many people would refer to as a "typical" boy (meaning, of course, that he ably performs the reassuring scripted narrative of traditional gender).

On this particular day, he had collected an interesting array of items on the top of the shelf unit—a couple of small cars, a baby doll, a piece of fabric, and some dishes and utensils (and even a dinosaur). I observed him for a few minutes as he wrapped the doll in the fabric, used the utensils to "feed" the baby from the dishes, and then turned his attention to the cars, which he rolled in a circle around the doll. He then picked up the doll and removed the fabric, which he appeared to use as a washcloth or towel to clean the doll's face. At this point, he noticed me watching him. He clearly became more self-conscious, but did not stop his play; instead, he glanced at me every few seconds as he continued tending to the baby. I smiled at him, and made it obvious that I wasn't just watching him, but was looking around the room to see what the others were doing as well.

As I was preparing to return to my office, I stopped by the other side of the shelf unit, and asked him if he was having a good time. He simply said, "yes." I asked him what he was doing, and he said, "just takin' care of the baby and fixin' the car." I nodded, and asked him if he was the baby's friend, or dad, or teacher. He replied, "the dad." Before I left, I said to him, "I think you're going to be a really good dad some day, if that's what you want to be." He said, "yeah, I know," and continued on.

None of the other children in the room were reacting to his activity; there was no judgment, no teasing, and no snickering behind his back. In this room, this boy was free to figure out how being a boy can mean taking care of a baby as well as fixing a car. I am confident that, whether or not he chooses to be a dad someday, he will make that choice because it is a *choice*, and it's the best choice for him because he will have made it knowing that it's not the *only* choice available to him. He will have written his own life into the script the culture has given him, the same way the little girls at the beginning of this chapter will have explored different possibilities for their characters.

References

Alloway, N. (1995). *The construction of gender in early childhood.* Victoria, Australia: Dolphin Press.

American Psychiatric Association. (1994). *Diagnostic and statistical manual of mental disorders* (4th[th] ed.). Washington, DC: Author.

Ary-De Rozza, R. & Payne-Jones, J. (2004). A brief look at fantasy play. In R.L. Clements & Fiorentino L. (Eds.), *The child's right to play: A global approach.* Westport, CT: Praeger, (pp. 24-27).

Bial, H. (Ed.) (2004). *The performance studies reader.* New York: Routledge.

Blaise, M. (2005). *Playing it straight: Uncovering gender discourses in the early childhood classroom.* New York: Routledge.

Brosterman, N. (1997). *Inventing kindergarten.* New York: Harry N. Abrams.

Burton, A. (1996). *Children's pleasures.* London: V & A.

Butler, J. (1990). Performative acts and gender constitution: An essay in phenomenology and feminist theory. In S-E. Case (Ed.), *Performing feminisms: Feminist critical theory and theatre.* Baltimore: Johns Hopkins University Press, (pp. 270-282).

Cannella, G.S. (1997). *Deconstructing early childhood education: Social justice and revolution*. New York: Peter Lang.

Carlson, M. (2004). What is performance? In H. Bial (Ed.), *The performance studies reader*. New York: Routledge, (pp. 68-73).

Chase, C. (2003). What is the agenda of the intersex patient advocacy movement? *The Endocrinologist* 13:3. pp. 240-242.

Copple, C. & Bredekamp, S. (Eds.). (2009). *Developmentally appropriate practice in early childhood programs serving children from birth through age 8* (3rd ed.). Washington, DC: National Association for the Education of Young Children.

Dahlberg, G., Moss, P., & Pence, A. (1999). *Beyond quality in early childhood education: Postmodern perspectives*. London: RoutledgeFalmer.

Dewey, J. (1916). *Democracy and education: An introduction to the philosophy of education*. New York: Macmillan.

Fausto-Sterling, A. (2000). *Sexing the body: Gender politics and the construction of sexuality*. NY: Basic Books.

Formanek-Brunell, M. (1998). *Made to play house: Dolls and the commercialization of American girlhood, 1830-1930*. Baltimore: Johns Hopkins University Press.

Freeman, N.K. & Brown, M.H. (2004). The moral and ethical dimensions of controlling play. In R.L. Clements & L. Fiorentino L. (Eds.), *The child's right to play: A global approach*. Westport, CT: Praeger, (pp. 9-15).

Harms, T., Clifford, R.M., & Cryer, D. (2005). *Early childhood environment rating scale* (revised ed.). New York: Teachers College, Columbia University.

Holland, P. (2003). *We don't play with guns here: War, weapon and superhero play in the early years*. Maidenhead, England: Open University Press.

Kirshenblatt-Gimblett, B. (2004). Performance studies. In H. Bial (Ed.), *The performance studies reader*. New York: Routledge: (pp. 43-56).

Lascarides, V.C. & Hinitz, B.F. (2000). *History of early childhood education*. New York: Falmer Press.

MacNaughton, G. (2000). *Rethinking gender in early childhood education*. London: Paul Chapman.

Makman, L.H. (2004). The right to a work-free and playful childhood: A historical perspective. In R.L. Clements & L. Fiorentino L. (Eds.), *The child's right to play: A global approach*. Westport, CT: Praeger, (pp. 3-8).

Piaget, J. (1962). *Play, dreams and imitation in childhood*. New York: Norton.

Rosen, C.E. (1974). Effects of sociodramatic play on problem-solving behavior among culturally disadvantaged preschool children. *Child Development* 45(4) pp. 920-927.

Snyder, A. (1972). *Dauntless women in early childhood education.* Washington, DC: Association for Childhood Education International.

Solomon, B.M. (1985). *In the company of educated women.* New Haven, CT: Yale University Press.

Sternberg, P. (2004). Dramatic play for healing. In R.L. Clements & L. Fiorentino L. (Eds.), *The child's right to play: A global approach.* Westport, CT: Praeger, (pp. 359-369).

Sutton-Smith, B. (1967). The role of play in cognitive development. *Young Children* 22, pp. 361-370.

Thomas, R.M. (2000). *Comparing theories of child development* (5th ed.). Belmont, CA: Wadsworth.

Thorne, B. (2004). *Gender play: Girls and boys in school.* New Brunswick, NJ: Rutgers University.

Vygotsky, L.S. (1976). Play and its role in the development of the child. In J. Bruner, A. Jolly, and K. Silva (Eds.), *Play: Its role in development and evolution.* New York: Basic Books.

Worthen, W.B. (2004). Disciplines of the text: Sites of performance. In H. Bial (Ed.), *The performance studies reader.* New York: Routledge, (pp. 10-25).

Chapter Six

Children's Museums and Children's Bodies

Anna Beresin

> All museums tell narratives about culture...
> Amy Levin, 2007, *Defining Memory*

"Touch everything! This is your world and you don't have to ask mommy!" So croons the twenty-something staff member of the relocated and newly opened Please Touch Museum in Philadelphia. This line contains the central paradox of children's museums: they are places for children's independent play, yet unlike daycare or nursery schools, the children are there with their grown-ups. The children apparently know what to do with the museum as a play place, they run and climb and indeed touch everything, but the parents are mainly confused. The museum seems to understand this participatory paradox and appeals to the grown-ups through a display of toys and activities designed to elicit nostalgia. The parents respond by guiding their children through the exhibits with varying degrees of patience.

To offer a cultural critique for a place so enticing and positive for children seems harsh, like evaluating the benefits of ice cream. Yet, as there are art historians, and critics of education and its cultural assumptions, it is important to ask what frames the play at the museum? How do adults physically and verbally move children through the play space? What narratives about the body are privileged in the museum? How is the two-headed museum encouraging both development and a sense of cultural history?

There are 150 children's museums throughout North America, with a handful in Canada, and most major American cities boast one as a tourist attraction. In general, these are rich and inviting play worlds, from Alabama to Wyoming, from the Strong National Museum of Play in Rochester, New York, to the Children's Metamorphosis in Derry, New Hampshire. The focus of all of these places tends to be developmental enrichment, with the Please Touch Museum stating in its mission the connection between physical, sensory learning and growth. Yet, little attention has been paid to how children move through such places, the cultural framing of the children's bodies as objects in these unusual play sites, and the memories they elicit.

Several different literatures offer wisdom on our tour, all interdisciplinary: the study of toys, the study of education and cultural capital, the study of nostalgia and representation, and the study of the body, specifically the child's body, as cultural canvas and playful nexus. It is the goal of this chapter to introduce key frames of looking at children as they move through the children's museum and then describe my opportunity to follow children and their parents as they played and made sense of the newly redesigned Please Touch Museum in Philadelphia.

In *Designing Modern Childhoods*, historian John R. Gillis writes of "The Islanding of Children—Reshaping the Mythical Landscapes of Childhood" and suggests that children's experience is increasingly divided into geographies of disconnected time—the camp, the vacation, the activity, the grandparent's house (Gillis, 2008). Children's museums are themselves islands of romanticized family time, and like the middle class exotic vacation, come equipped with gift shops and photo ops. The challenge Gillis raises is how to connect childhood practices so they become social and ritualized rather than gifted and commercialized.

Beneath the paradox of the museum as romanticized alone time with your children lies the paradox of toys themselves. As toys are at the center of the experience at The Please Touch Museum, it is worth noting that toys are both culturally framed and psychologically charged, and as folklorist/psychologist Brian Sutton-Smith has noted, they are presented as a ritual of isolated bonding. The toy means both "be close to me" and "I leave you alone to play with it" (Sutton-Smith, 1986). So the toy museum is a place of dreamy isolation, with parents gifting the experience, but not the toy, to the child, and then leaving themselves outside the experience. This dance of togetherness and aloneness mixes with toy nostalgia, much to the satisfaction of toy manufacturers.

Corporate sponsors guide the exhibit designs, training preschool children for future purchases, and eliciting commands and nostalgic re-collection from the adults (see Calvert, 1992; Chin, 2001; Cross, 1997; Jacobson, 2008; Pugh, 2009; Schor, 2004; Steinberg and Kincheloe, 2004). The parent-child dyad of the museum necessarily expands to include the examination of both the design of displays and the market influences. The simple museum outing is anything but simple.

Much has been written of the body as artifact, with recent writing in feminist and queer studies about the child's body as a container of cultural signs (Butler, 1993; Fraser and Greco, 2005; Johnson, 2007; Orr, Mcallister, Lopez, Kahl and Earle, 2006; Springgay and Freedman, 2007). Folklorist Katherine Young reminds us how culture is "inscribed on the body," and although she meant concretely with decoration, it is interesting to see how gestures of projected work and sanctioned play also inscribe the young body (Young, 1993). Philosopher Connerton notes that "memory is sedimented or amassed in the body," echoing Freud. But dramaturge Diana Taylor takes it furthest. Memory itself is both "bodily" and "archival" (Connerton, 1989; Taylor, 2003). The museum stands therefore as a unique place to look at both sponsored artifacts on exhibit and the physical enactment of memory in its crystallized display.

Such intangibles then relate to a larger critique of education as cultural capital, and the study of opportunities for children as frames for the empowerment of specific ideologies (Bourdieu and Passerson, 1977; Foley, 1994; Giroux and McClaren, 1994; McClaren, 2007; Willis, 1977) Willis (1977, 1980) provides the clearest guide through his emphasis on power and the playful young body. The power narratives frame the child's play, and the child is both constricted by it and liberated to sneakily rebel against it.

Play serves as both "model" and "mirror," to use Handelmann's phrase, allowing the child to imitate and distort his reality in a manner aesthetically pleasing to him and his peers. Yet, play offers no robotic imitation, merely opportunity for interpretation and meta-commentary (Bateson, 1972; Handelmann, 1990; Sutton-Smith, 1997; Willis, 1990). Does the museum allow such playful distortions of the child's cultural framework? How do the children's bodies and words model, distort, and magnify the museum's cultural scripts?

The Study

Ten children, their good-natured parents and I set out to study their play at The Please Touch Museum, billed as the nation's first museum designed specifically for children under 7. We went during the first year of the new PTM's opening in its new location in the Spring 2009, by family group, one group per visit. The children ranged from two-year-old fraternal twins to a dreamy eight-year-old girl who enjoyed herself as much as her five-year-old sister. We have Chin, a pig-tailed six-year-old girl, who bopped her head side to side and skipped all the way to the museum entrance, Mary (eight), Amy (five-and-a-half), sisters, inseparable with their friend Peggy (six), and brother and sister team Joey (seven), and Ginny (five) who held hands and walked in circles until they figured out what to do first. Benny, (four) liked the museum so much he ran from his mother when he had to go. Eddie, (almost three) who is also known as Chase Utley and Bob the Builder and Robin (as his best friend is Bat Man), cried he liked it so much. Two-year-old twins Aviva and Noah ran away from their parents at escape velocity when they read their body language suggesting that it was almost time to leave. Noah declared, a true Piagetian, that at the Please Touch Museum, he "made ALL the stuff."

In addition to shadowing each family for its entire visit, I spoke with parents who had experienced the new museum and wrote down the muttered comments of exhausted-looking parents and grandparents as they trooped around the museum, led by their young ones. The families in the study were African American, Jewish, Asian American, European American, families with many generations on American soil and families that were the children of immigrants. All were highly educated and ranged from families who were well off to families that were struggling economically. All were known to me—either through my son's school or through my own neighborhood. Each was given a pseudonym to protect their privacy and all were eager to join me for a morning outing with their children. More than half entered the museum through my university-sponsored free membership.

I recorded their individual time on task, and overall am concerned about how to sustain sensory play and parental interest (see Borun, 1977, for more on time on task and museum evaluation). Sustained play is associated with a richer experience, a deeper emotional satisfaction, and a greater possibility of learning (Erikson, 1950; Sutton-Smith, 1997). In a sense, when play is sustained in an open environment, it indicates deep child satisfaction and suggests that it is the child who is in charge, and not the grown-ups. The contrast of sustained play and fleeting play indicates where there is engagement as opposed to power struggle.

Please Touch

The Please Touch Museum began in 1976 in a small corner of the Academy of Natural Sciences where children "played, weighed, and of course touched their way through exhibits that engaged their senses and ignited their imaginations, while parents fought the instinctive urge to warn, 'Don't touch that!'" (PTM Website). The link to Developmentally Appropriate Practice created by the National Association of Educators of Young Children makes the sensory agenda clear: "Children need years of play with real objects and events before they are able to understand the meaning of symbols.... Learning takes place as young children touch, manipulate and experiment with things and interact with people.... The child's participation in self-directed play with concrete, real-life experiences continues to be a key to motivated, meaningful learning in kindergarten and the primary grades" (1986).

John Dewey, the pragmatist philosopher, often cited as the founding father of experiential learning, wrote how the child makes approximations of the real and plays out his or her version of reality, but that adults need to be giving children access to real production, not approximations of the real thing. Real seeds, not imitation planting. Real sand. Real wood (Dewey, 1900). These are the roots of the "please touch" philosophy. But the museum seems to be sliding into a loop of cultural reference that is far removed from reality, linking play to the nostalgia of plastic toys.

The PTM runs two floors of the enormous Memorial Hall, former site of the U.S. Centennial Celebration, in the middle of Philadelphia's Fairmont Park. The original torch of the Statue of Liberty was housed there, before it was attached to the statue's arm. Now, in the PTM entrance, a torch made of old toys greets visitors, and every child who arrived asked if they could touch it. Bits of dolls and cars and tubes and tires were wrapped into the sculpture itself. Skis and smushed balls, with faded colors once bright were curiosity magnets. The children could climb a staircase around the sculpture's base, but it was, ironically, untouchable. Next to it are gigantic instruments, the "Big" piano, an oversized Taiko drum played without mallets, and a gigantic ukulele with a "Please Don't Climb on the Ukulele" sign. On the left is an exhibit of things that move (but don't) including fixed cars, diggers, a real Toyota Scion SUV, a Hess gas station, and a genuine half of a city bus, ready for pretend driving. Further left, there is a magnetic wall of art, and a monorail that doesn't move but provides a quiet space for reflection in this frenetic wing.

Toys are placed behind plexi-glass on the walls, in the monorail, and in tires as seats on the floor, much to the confusion of the children. The Barbie car, the Bat Mobile, all elicited comments: "Can I ride it? Can I have it?" The toys in the tire seats protected by plexi-glass were met with confusion. "Why are they there?" The eight-year-old quipped, "Today class, we will learn what toys are inside your tire seat."

Next to the pretend driving area, a room called "Flight Fantasy" has gross motor activities labeled "Flight Fitness": crawling and rowing and turning cranks. Beyond that is a Star Wars filled room with foam "Flying Machines" to build and watch as they float down when they tap the ceiling on a pulley. A foam mound in the middle provides a small hill to climb although it seems unlikely that was its intention. A quiet room for gooey art activities and dress up completes this half of the wing.

A pretend Shop Rite grocery store is available downstairs, complete with Shop Rite canned goods, a toy McDonalds, a shoe store, a medical center, and a construction site complete with foam bricks, conveyer belt, and punch clock. In the center hallway sits a Centennial exhibit that was mainly empty of people, leading to an Alice in Wonderland maze. Up the stairs on this side emerges the Alice in Wonderland tree top, which leads to an elaborate water play exhibit, a percussive rain forest with instruments, and the climax—a restored hundred-year-old rideable carousel, playing organ music with hotdogs for sale. It was as if we arrived at the beach, minus the sand, from a forest, minus the wood. All is plastic here.

Walker, in an architectural feasibility study of the former Please Touch Museum's home wrote "The goal of the (PTM) museum is therefore as fundamental as increasing the child's life experience...to help develop in young children an awareness of aesthetic, cultural, and scientific things" (1981). At the time that manuscript was published, the average visit to the PTM was an hour and a half. My sample of visitors spent around three hours there. Walker wrote: "Most children visiting PTM have almost no life experience outside the home or nursery school." It assumed the PTM was the children's "first museum," its first gallery, its first cultural event. This is no longer the case.

I asked my collected parents what the PTM could be compared to in their childhoods. Larry, Chin's father, used to visit his aunt and uncle in Chicago and loved the Museum of Science and Industry. "There was a coal mine and a mathematical soap bubble. The best part...was the focus on real world, real stuff, real coal mines and real cars and trucks. Museums are places to learn stuff." He notes that the Flight Fantasy area did not show much about real flight. "When they pedal, it made something turn. What does that have to do with flight?" He praised the water play area, though. "The great thing about the water area, no waiting around, something to do with water on every piece of it. Science museums are some of my favorite places in the world."

Daniel used to visit the PTM when he was a child and now is there with his two daughters. He remembers the plastic supermarket and liking it as a child. "It is a little like a theme park. The presence of the museum in a park near the zoo, feels like a theme park. It is an attraction, a tourist attraction." Willa, the mom of twins, remembers a Discovery Center in her Florida childhood. It was more "learning oriented" and notes the PTM is "a whole new category of experience."

Priscilla is enthralled by the PTM. "It is the neatest children's museum I have ever seen. It has a little town (downstairs). It is exactly what they want." Her husband muses that they used to have carnivals and go to the beach when he was a kid. We sat by the carousel while he photographed his daughter and wife. Is this like the shore? "This is not it. It is missing the smell of salt water and the feel of sand. A pale comparison." He snaps photos, encouraged by the wooden cutouts with open circles for the children to place their faces over the bodies of muscle men and ladies in poufy, old-fashioned dresses. Sally urges her son toward the carousel, a combination of guild work and amusement park nostalgia. "Ah the carousel. That's my childhood."

Two grandmothers walked by muttering, "a mad house," "There's too many things to do." A nine-year-old friend said the maze made him feel so wonderfully "dislocated," but several grown-ups called it "way overstimulating." I think of Piaget's notion of disequilibration, and Vygotsky's idea of the zone of proximal development (Piaget, 1952; Vygotsky, 1978). Play safely pushes the player to new levels of complexity and comfort. But there is more than a generation gap here, there is a different experience being presented for the young and for the grown. There are many conflicting scripts pulling the children and grown-ups in multiple directions.

With play comes the opportunity to integrate disjunctive worlds, both immediate and cultural into a dreamy mix that makes some sort of sense for the child. The grown-ups who do not play—either tune out and literally stare at the ceiling, direct their children quickly through the exhibits, or use photography as a type of activity for their own engagement.

A woman points to the timed moving rides in the flight of fantasy exhibit. "They have THAT in Chuckee Cheese." I wonder what the difference is between an amusement park and a play museum. Clearly, it has something to do with sustained play over time, the authenticity of the materials, and that the child herself controls the play. At an amusement park, the ride times the play. In a play museum, the adult is the vehicle that sustains or ends the play.

Please Wait in Line

"Sarah, what line do you want to wait in, hon? Come ON, let's wait in line." The mom steers the daughter in the foam flight room. In the next room, Chin points to the digger dozer scooping up plastic balls in a ball pit. It is protected on three sides by plastic, with only one entrance guarded by a young adult. "I want to go IN there." ("It is for diggers, you can't," says Dad.) She wants to try the digger dozer and there is a huge line. "How long is this going to take?" Aviva wants to drive the city bus. "We're waiting our turn." Noah is in the flight room: "I wanna do it." Another comes near: "No, wait your turn." Ginny wants to drive the bus. Mom instructs how and where to wait. Ginny walks in circles and walks away.

In the supermarket, parents are teaching children about territoriality and its opposite, politeness. "You're losing your shopping cart. You gotta put food in it. Put it over here." A seven-year-old places his plastic breads way high on a top shelf. "I'm putting it HERE so NOBODY gets it." A mother cautions, "Don't forget to say thank you to the cashier." "You have to wait your turn here."

Benny, the four-year-old, sees the ball digger. "I wanna do this." "You've got to get in line." He tries to squeeze in first. Four are ahead of him. "Wait, wait. This boy is next, next this one, then it is your turn." He figures out the motor is timed and most children exit the ride when the timer is up. He presses it for three turns in a row. When the staffer looks at him with a raised eyebrow he coyly remarks, "I started it for HIM" and he leaves to check out the exposed car engine. Another boy tries to share. Benny's mom cautions, "Let him finish it first. Let him finish it first." The boy's mom agrees. Instead, the boys overlap and both experiment, unplugging spark plugs and opening the oil tank. "You had your turn." "Everybody gets his turn." Eddie's mom sings, "You're good at taking turns. He's a good turn taker."

Several parents comment about the stress of turn-taking management. The parents of the two-year-olds become nostalgic for the quiet of their playroom at home. They seem most annoyed by the other children's parents. Another mom laments that in her neighborhood, she would know the children and their parents. Here, all are strangers.

Dreamy Play

This turn-taking experimentation is in direct contrast to the areas of suspended, dreamy play. Unlike the areas that required turn taking where the average turn was a minute or two, these areas let the children enter into the dream state we often associate with a rich play encounter (See Erikson, 1950; Geertz, 1973; Piaget, 1952; Sutton-Smith, 1997).

Two girls, previously strangers, play for twenty minutes imitating each other's water play. They laugh, splash their toys, and chase each other around the long, curved water trough. Their grown-ups look up at the ceiling while standing and wait for them to finish. Other adults snap photos, asking their children to look up, stop playing, and smile for the camera. Often, this is met with a confused stare. You brought me here to play, so why are you interrupting me?

Chin sings "boats, boats, boats" and plays with the model water lock for sixteen minutes, opening and closing the dock, changing the water level. "Are you the dock master?" Dad asks. She smiles knowingly. He turns and plays with the water screw and tests the buttons, while she plays with the water lock. He asks her questions about how she thinks it works and, when she tires, helps her press buttons she cannot reach.

Mary, Annie, and Peggy play with the Dollhouse Hotel in the Centennial Diorama Room, rearranging small dolls in semicircles, having meetings, laying them down, dressing and redressing them. They do this over and over for 45 minutes. One of the dolls is in a wheelchair; they all have different colored skin.

In the medical area the five-year-old hollers, "Get your babies! Get your babies here if you want to adopt one!" "Who wants to help me take care of this baby?" and this lasts for 10 minutes with much cradling and picking up and lying down of the doll. Noah is curious about the falling foam airplanes and watches them crank to the ceiling and cascade down, up and down repeatedly, as his father helps him. When he finds the baby area with fake water and plastic large trees he sits on a wooden swan in nonexistent water and declares, "I'm all wet." "Look, I'm all wet."

Aviva, his sister, coos next to him, "Mama, come to our party." "We're having a party." Ginny in the Supermarket is performing an elaborate ritual with an older boy pretending to exchange invisible money as he cashiers. For 20 minutes they hand each other plastic food and invisible dollars, the ritual of purchase carefully recreated.

In the Supermarket Bakery, she repeatedly puts "hot" bread in and out of the toy oven. "No more bread." "I helped the bakery!" 20 minutes baking.

Eddie loves the truck area and sings "Flat bed, flat bed," "I'm Bob the Builder." He stacks orange cones on the truck, off the truck. Mom helps him stack. He pretends to drive to the diner. As he drives home, he names the actual streets near his house. He drives to Atlanta to see grandma and repeats the cone stacking for 45 minutes. Benny tosses bricks in the Dump Truck area, calling, "I throw. I throw" for 10 minutes. His game is Hide and Seek with his mother, in the Alice in Wonderland area. "You have to count. That's how Hide and Seek goes." He stays where he can be seen when she covers her eyes. She gets lost. They repeat this endlessly. A new six-year-old girl joins in the game and they continue as a threesome for 40 minutes.

To the museum's credit, and to the credit of the parents in our group, every child I observed entered into a deep, sustained play session. Times not indicated in minutes below were spent flitting about the museum. The trio listed below for brevity includes Mary, Amy, and Peggy, who came together and were inseparable.

	Boats	Trucks	Market	Bricks	Flight
Chin	16 min		27 min		8 min
Trio					
Noah					20 min
Aviva					
Ginny			40 min		
Joey					
Eddie		45 min		10 min	10 min
	Maze	House	Baby	Hospital	Paint
Chin					
Trio		45 min		10 min	
Noah			20 min		30 min
Aviva			20 min		30 min
Ginny	10 min				
Joey	20 min				
Benny	40 min				

Several patterns emerged.

Time

First, attention span has little to do with age. Eddie could have spent the whole day on the flat bed, singing "flat bed, flat bed, flat bed" and stacking cones on his truck. Second, the main thing that sustained play was a play partner. Playing with a machine that needed turn taking was the quickest way to kill the playtime itself. The second-quickest play killer was photography (see West, 2000, on nostalgia and the development of the Kodak camera). The study suggests that the machines were interfering with the museum's primary objective to foster rich play experiences for children. The machines, flying machines, driving machines, even the carousel, were more associations for the parents rather than experiences for the children.

As the average visit to the museum was about three hours, the above chart suggests that for almost all of the children, two-thirds of the time was spent mulling about or flitting from one activity to another. Children seemed to settle in quicker when they had repeated visits to the museum and could anticipate where they wanted to spend their time. A challenge to the museum is the tension between overall exposure and the invitation to sustain engagement.

Play is fundamentally social, yet many parents stayed out of the play, or entered into dialogue to distract the player and go somewhere else. Dreamy play takes time, and players that sustained play had parents who respected their timing or asked play-sustaining questions. "Where are we driving to?" "How do you want to build that?" "Are you the dock master?" "What are you doing now?" Other parents helped by physically assisting the would-be boat captains, or chefs, by offering new materials. The key in sustaining play was the parents' willingness to serve as assistant rather than to lead.

The adults' attention spans appeared shorter than most children's. Unless the adults were directly involved in the child's fantasy, the adults stood by waiting or urged them on to the next experience. The fantasies that sustained the adults' interest were not necessarily related to a specific narrative. Alice in Wonderland was more often used as a backdrop for the discussion of illusions or to play tag around the large plastic tree. Adult interest was related to participation in a game or the patient observation of the child's own growth.

Space

Almost all of the dreamy play occurred in a private space or what appeared to be a more private space: the doll house was enclosed on three sides; the curved water table allowed for privacy and open access; the flat bed was enclosed and yet open. The bakery sustained the play in the small kitchen enclave, the area around the tree in Alice in Wonderland, the wooden fake forest for the babies. The flying machine room and art room were enclosed spaces, and each had small spaces within those enclosures.

The areas that had briefest encounters tended to have less accessible entrances with unprotected spaces. The areas around each vehicle, around each timed machine, each was a highway of activity. The body has to be invited in and, at the same time, offered protection.

Touch

Most tactile exploration is at the water area and art room. This is both by design and the nature of the medium. The water area is a cornucopia of touch, with a seemingly infinite number of access points for splashing, balancing, testing, dumping and turning. The art room was equally accessible. When Noah said, "I want to paint a picture," he put his nose right up to the easel, touched each color with a brush, and painted, enjoying the surprise of color that connected to his arm movements. When he was through, he shifted to the play-dough table.

His mom asked, "What are you going to make?" "I'm making a bear." "I made a pizza, let's share it." Mom then makes a Mickey Mouse and asks, "What will he eat?" Noah looks mischievous and offers to break him. "Break him? All yours." Dad makes a unicorn out of play dough and sticks it to his head. To their amusement, it actually sticks. He turns it into an elephant nose and they all take turns putting it on and making elephant noises. At the glue table, they squish the glue and rub it on the cut paper, arranging it to their satisfaction on the larger pieces. Dad grabs them and they hug.

The Carousel is all photo ops and snuggling. About a third of the parents ride next to or hold their children. The one-year-olds look the happiest, along with the parents. One dad clowns on a pretend bucking bronco, cowboy style. One little girl stares at her mirrored reflection. All wave to someone watching; most are photographed. This is the spot of parental laughter and engagement, more than any other in the whole museum. It is also the place of greatest touch and displayed bonding.

The littlest children touch each other and climb over each other's things, and the parents shoo them away. One toddler fondled the short, cropped head of the boy in front of her on the stationary monorail. Another one inspected each object with her hands in another child's market basket. In each case, the child was shooed away or picked up, apologies offered.

Touch may be primary for the youngest at the museum, but movement is central for all the children observed. Beyond the brief turn taking of the stationary scull and pedal boats and planes in the flight fantasy area, there were a few small slides with stairs hidden in the Alice in Wonderland section and baby area. The machine-led movement was often too large for some of the smaller children, who could not reach the pedals, and only one child could utilize the majority of the equipment at one time. The slides, although barely a challenge for those over three, were a magnet for the toddler set. Some children did these slides repetitively for long periods. Often there were handfuls of children negotiating their way up and through these slides, typically with an older child sitting precariously on its top, looking for some kind of challenge.

Movement

Peggy climbs on the carpeted demi-walls of the Alice in Wonderland maze, and mom announces, "Do not climb on the walls." Mary and Annie climb on everything in the Alice in Wonderland area, the Dodo, the roofs of the mini houses, the slides, and the caucus race racetrack. Mom: "I don't think you're supposed to climb on that." They all continue anyway. The caucus-race small toy racetrack, always an inviting mound for climbing, was removed by the third visit.

Half of the children literally danced their way from exhibit to exhibit. In the main entrance, Benny practices sliding on his knees. In the hallway, he pretends to ice skate on the smooth marble floor. These were benignly tolerated but clearly not in the design of the play space.

Sally, Benny's mom, is invited to join him in the brick area. "No, it's for kids." He sings, "we throw, throw, throw" and throws the bricks. He discovers the conveyer belt and experiments with it but returns to the bin area where there are piles of foam bricks. "I'm going in and here I go." There are 17 boys and 3 girls in the brick area. There is more foam brick throwing. One PTM staffer says loudly, "I want you NOT to throw bricks, okay?" The mom rolls her eyes and says to me, "Are you kidding?" It ends the play and he goes elsewhere.

Playing with a large dollhouse, Annie's head and half her torso is in the cubicle of the dollhouse's bedroom, literally entering the play scene. She crawls inside, like a giant directing the scene of figurines next to her sister. The tree house, the fun houses in Alice in Wonderland, the inside of the trucks and monorail, going inside these spaces allows for reflection. The children are trying to move their bodies through the exhibits, not just between them. The design tension seems to be to move, but not too much, as it might be dangerous. Yet in their desire to move, children were probably doing more dangerous things than if there had been actual climbing equipment.

With touch and motion comes territoriality. After hoarding practice in the Supermarket, Chin goes to have real lunch at the café and acts as if it is the plastic supermarket, hoarding dozens of drinks and sandwiches on her tray. Dad corrects her and they buy lunch. Then the hunt begins for a place to sit and eat. There are a half-dozen families sitting on the floor, jealously guarding spots. Nearby, a mom jokes about finding a free smock in the water play area. "Did you have to yank it off some other child?" "Hold on to your basket, or someone will take it from you."

Physical Labor

Most of the jobs at the PTM are blue-collar jobs, with the exception being the medical area. "It's funny what we're showing kids about work," muses Eddie's mom. She recanted his line heard at home while playing, "I'm busy, I have a lot of work to do. I'm getting ready for a meeting." We note it is interesting seeing so many white-collar families at the museum having their children do blue-collar work. She reminisces that her dad was a carpenter. Eddie, previously a truck driver, puts on an electrician's jacket. "You are an electrician. Go do some work." A mom passes by on the way to the mini hospital, "You know so and so is the head of the E.R..."

Eddie plays with the lawnmower push toy. She says he does that at home, too. He plays with the plastic flowerpots. "He planted our bulbs last year." Larry wonders about the origin of the PTM "a unique idea, bringing in real life into a museum for children." The garden area is a model of suburban landscaping, but it is dirt free, with plastic flowers and plastic tools in Astroturf.

As children's lives are more and more separated from the lives of their parents through the institutions of school and work, children long to connect and play with the imagined lives of their grown-ups. In the past children were part of the labor force, had a hand in farming or craft, and were in age-integrated settings (Zuckerman, 1985). The proliferation of toys to allow the fantasy of work goes hand in hand with this separation, further exaggerating the adult's lack of interest in this pretense (see Sutton-Smith, 1986, on the idea of toys, culture, and separation). Yet here there is a double separation;

these children have little contact with brick building, so bricks must be for throwing. Truck driving just is to guide the way to Grandma's house. The children swarmed the real Toyota SUV to pretend drive. This is something familiar. More than half of the children sat passively in the back seat, waiting for something to happen and enjoying the relative quiet of the sheltered car.

Nostalgia through Toys

In the Alice in Wonderland, there is a random Smurfs exhibit. "Smurfs. We have Smurfs!" Only one of the families have had their children read or hear *Alice in Wonderland*, but it was a source of recognition for most adults. There is a Humpty Dumpty on display. "Ooh, It is better than mine," says Mary, a fan of nursery rhymes. One dad photographs a giant Cupie Doll. Like the Star Wars figurines in the Fantasy of Flight wing, the parents reference the toys of their childhood, and the children occasionally connect their toys to the toys of their parents. "Woa, Etch-a-Sketch." Every dad I was with stopped to examine the elaborate drawings of animals displayed in an Etch-a-Sketch exhibit behind glass. "I have one of those, but it broke." None were available to touch.

Joey looks at the water toy display with its Barbie and Ken in Hawaiian beach wear, a range of toy boats behind glass. Joey glances at it and suggests, "let's go to the gift shop." Dad and Joey go off to the gift shop which looks like any other boutique toy store, Hello Kitty and Thomas the Tank Engine, Elmo and puzzles toward the back. The toys on display in a window of the monorail offer a surreal mix: a sewing machine, a dump truck, a Speak n Spell, a Garfield. "I wanna get i-in (next to the toys)" whines Eddie. "No these are closed cars." No explanation of why these toys are on display or what they are there for.

The stores are like "a tiny town," but the density feels more like a mall for small children. Two well-coiffed mothers with state-of-the-art strollers coo, "This place is unbelievable. You should see downstairs. When this place opened up I said THIS is the place for me."

On Display in the Shop Rite entrance

Cheerios Play Book Bingo Game, Candy Land Game, Frosted Flakes Play Set, Veggie Tales Mix Up Game, Snoopy Snow-Cone Machine, and a toy cashier. All product-placement in Shop Rite is of a Shop Rite brand. Nine kinds of Shop Rite crackers, eight kinds of Shop Rite Brownie or Cake Mix, Shop Rite Chicken Broth, Shop Rite Tomato Paste.... The large food signs offer "Bakery,

Dairy, Meat, Seasonal, and World Food." "World Food" consists of plastic bananas, kiwi, avocado, and pineapple, but the poster shows images of sushi, shrimp, and taco rice. One frantic mother-shopper calls, "Stay in the Shop Rite. Do not leave the Shop Rite. I'm going with your brother." Just what the corporation wants drilled into the heads of young children. It is a loop of product placement, name recognition and corporate name games.

Other museums, like the Children's Museum of Indianapolis offer images of folk toys around the word. The Strong Museum of Play offers "The Toy Hall of Fame." The PTM array of toys seems random, an untouchable array of mass-produced items from suburban childhoods. The Web site says 20% of its 12,000 toys are on display in Memorial Hall. Is the children's museum offering self-referential pop culture or presenting an idealized version of "culturally neutral" American play?

To quote Portia Hamilton Sperr, "the fundamental issues of child rearing are always ones of values and philosophy" (Zuckerman, 1985). It would then appear the PTM is now a model of suburban values of consumption for suburban children who already have access to many of its offerings. A challenge for the museum is how to reflect the worlds of the children who come and expand their minds toward a place of wonder.

The mother of a fourteen-month-old shares a table with me and my adopted family of the day. "We traveled over an hour here and he just wants to splash in the water." She looks annoyed. "And he's getting wet." Larry, the parent of the six-year-old I am with, counters gently, "He's engaged." The economics of visiting conflict with the ideal patience of letting the children lead where they are interested in engaging. Museum nostalgia is competing with childhood nostalgia and the untimed experience of sustained play.

"If we didn't push them exhibit to exhibit they'd just play. I don't have a problem with that, but I don't want them to feel they missed out. They've created their own world of play. I'm so glad. But if she doesn't get a chance to do the rainforest room, she'll be disappointed." There is a sense of financial urgency, that in order to make the trip worthwhile, one had to rush and experience it all. It is as if we are having them live our entire childhoods in one day. Play in fast forward, ages one to seven.

It seems this "whole new category of experience" is an expression of a new version of children's peer culture in the seven and under set. Children's peer culture, taught from child to child typically begins when children are on their own, ages eight and up, where games are central and parents fade to the background. (Beresin, 2010; Corsaro, 2005; Opie and Opie, 1997) It is culturally very American to foster independence at a young age, and at the children's museum it is this sense of independent childhood that is on display, a childhood with its own products, its own narratives, and its own rituals (see Schwartzman, 1978 for a contrasting view of childhood play cross-culturally). The children's museum emerges as a childhood communal experience of the individual family outing where children play by themselves. One way out of the paradox is for parents to carefully observe children while leaving them alone when they are deep in thought.

Observing Children

Priscilla gets a rather misty look in her eye, "I've been enjoying watching my five-year-old's negotiating skills. This is new. She said that we can work on the magnets together." The dad offers, "I usually don't get to see her playing in this kind of environment. The novelty. So many different things for her to interact with. One of the neat things about the PTM, some things intersect with kids' (own) experience, and some things don't."

For Willa, the mother of twins, the best part is "admiring my children. For me, it is the Please Admire My Children Museum." Daniel muses there is something exciting about a new environment "where other kids, new faces, are role models." As we exit, there is a Latino family, a traditional Jewish family, an African American family, an Asian family, and an Irish American family hopping on the cement bricks outside the museum, playing tag, avoiding cracks, giggling.

One has a sense of physical freedom and full breath going outside to play, and this physical play is the alternative common culture. The adults admire their own families and the health of the families around them. Two of the families, formerly strangers, play tag and laugh aloud, something that is rarely heard or seen inside the frenetic museum.

The PTM's cultural longing is twofold: the return to a suburban middle-class childhood of play, and the parental longing to preserve childhood, freeze it in a photograph, as a document of time well spent. Science museums take the journey farther back, with historical documentation about earlier journeys, or expanded journeys with more advanced materials available for examination. Art and culture museums tend to expand the journey with history or with a diversity of experience. As Kavanagh rightly observes, museums are "dream spaces," and the ideal is a sustained fantasy, in this case, one that works for both children and adults where objects, grown-ups, and other families are in an environment that playfully enriches. (Kavanagh, 2000).

The idea of a museum as dream space is doubly true for a museum devoted to play. "Get your babies here if you want to adopt one;" "I want to break him;" "Flatbed, flatbed, flatbed;" "Mama, come to our party..." The surrealism of the child's world and its exaggerated bodily narratives fall in a place that connects to bits of science, bits of art, bits of bodily grotesquery, hidden by unfamiliar storylines. One mother pointed to a spinning Alice in Wonderland on the wall, designed to simulate falling down a hole, and exclaimed, "Look, it's Willy Wonka!" as her six-year-old shook her head. One has this sense that parents are trying to connect their experiences to their children's, but are at a loss about how to do so. So they point to commercialized toys behind glass, a preserved former childhood, framed by the museum itself.

The children's museum stands at a crossroads, needing to decide if it will connect to the narratives of consumer pop culture, or if it will search for something more elemental—the growing body, the forces of nature, or conversely, the diversity of culture as it beckons us, young and old, to play.

At the time of this publication, the papers announced cultural organizations like this museum were soon to lose state aid. Does corporate funding mandate product placement? Does a child need to equate driving with Toyota, fuel with Hess, shopping with Shop Rite and meals with McDonalds? How will the museum open its cultural looping of symbols to children who do not have access to its wealth of toys and experiences? As art museums offer timed free admission, so too the Please Touch Museum can ideally open its doors to the less fortunate. The island needs to expand its opportunity and its cultural references, linking diverse childhoods to common themes.

The children themselves point to the next steps as they ride the objects, climb them, extending the physicality of please touch to please move, to manipulate their concrete symbols in their own way. Not just art or toys behind glass, not just toy sculptures to look at from afar. Touch your worldly objects, redefine them, re-move them. Otherwise, this museum is merely a rich man's toy store, a quick amusement park ride, a tourist island where only some of the grown-ups speak the body language.

References

Bateson, G. 1972. *Steps to an Ecology of Mind: Collected Essays in Anthropology, Psychiatry, Evolution, and Epistemology.* San Francisco, CA: Chandler Pub.

Beresin, A.R. 2010. *Recess Battles: Playing, Fighting, and Storytelling*. Jackson, MS: University of Mississippi Press.

Borun, M. 1977. *Measuring the Immeasurable: A Pilot Study of Museum Effectiveness*. Washington, DC: ASTC.

Bourdieu, P., and Passerson, J-C. 1977. *Reproduction in Education, Society and Culture*. London: Sage.

Butler, J. 1993. "Bodies That Matter." Reprinted in Fraser, Mariam, and Grego, Monica, 2005 (eds.) *The Body: A Reader*. London: Routledge.

Calvert, K. 1992. *Children in the House: The Material Culture of Early Childhood, 1600–1900*. Boston: Northeastern University Press.

Chambers, S.A. and Carver, T. 2008. *Judith Butler and Political Theory*. London: Routledge.

Children's Museum of Indianapolis, 1991. *Folk, Fantasy & Play: Selections from the Caplan Collection of The Children's Museum of Indianapolis*. Indianapolis, IN. The Museum.

Chin, E. 2001. *Purchasing Power: Black Kids and American Consumer Culture*. Minneapolis: University of Minnesota Press.

Chudakoff, H. 2007. *Children at Play: An American History*. New York: New York University Press.

Connerton, P. 1989. *How Societies Remember*. Cambridge: Cambridge University Press.

Corsaro, W. 2005. *The Sociology of Childhood*. Thousand Oaks, CA: Pine Forge Press.

Cross, G. 1997. *Kids' Stuff: Toys and the Changing World of American Childhood*. Cambridge, MA: Harvard University Press.

Dewey, J. 1900. *School and Society*. Chicago, IL: University of Chicago.

Erikson, E. 1950. *Childhood and Society*. New York: Norton.

Foley, D.E. 1994. *Learning Capitalist Culture: Deep in the Heart of Tejas*. Philadelphia, PA: University of Pennsylvania Press.

Fraser, M., and Greco, M. 2005. *The Body: A Reader*. London: Routledge.

Geertz, C. 1973. *The Interpretation of Cultures*. New York: Basic Books.

Gillis, J.R. 2008. "Epilogue: The Islanding of Children—Reshaping the Mythical Landscapes of Childhood" in Gutman, Marta and de Coninck-Smith, Ning (eds.) *Designing Modern Childhoods: History, Space, and the Material Culture of Children*. New Brunswick, NJ: Rutgers University Press.

Giroux, H., and McClaren, P. 1994. *Between Borders: Pedagogy and the Politics of Cultural Studies*. London: Routledge.

Handelmann, D. 1990. *Models and Mirrors: Towards an Anthropology of Public Events*. Cambridge: Cambridge University Press.

Jacobson, L. 2008. *Children and Consumer Culture in American Society*. Westport, CT: Praeger.

Johnson, M. 2007. *The Meaning of the Body: Aesthetics of Human Understanding*. Chicago, IL: University of Chicago Press.

Kavanagh, G. 2000. *Dream Spaces: Memory and the Museum*. New York: Leicester University Press.

Levin, A.K. 2007. *Defining Memory: Local Museums and the Construction of History in America's Changing Communities*. Lanham, MD: Altamira Press.

McClaren, P. 2007. *Life in Schools: An Introduction to Critical Pedagogy*. Los Angeles, CA: University of California Press.

National Association for the Education of Young Children. 2009. Position Statement—Developmentally Appropriate Practice. Washington, DC: National Association for the Education of Young Children (NAEYC).

Opie, I. and Opie, P. 1997. *Children's Games with Things*. Oxford: Oxford University Press.

Orr, D., Mcallister, L.L., Kahl, E., and Earle, K. 2006. *Belief, Bodies, and Being: Feminist Reflections on Embodiment*. Lanham: Rowman and Littlefield.

Piaget, J. 1952. *Play, Dreams, Imitation in Childhood*. New York: Norton.

Pugh, A.J. 2009. *Longing and Belonging: Parents, Children, and Consumer Culture*. Berkeley: University of California Press.

Schor, J.B. 2004. *Born to Buy: The Commercialized Child and the New Consumer Culture*. New York: Scribner.

Schwartzman, H. 1978. *Transformations: The Anthropology of Children's Play*. New York: Plenum.

Springgay, S., and Freedman, D. 2007. *Curriculum and the Cultural Body*. New York: Peter Lang.

Steinberg, S.R. and Kincheloe, J.L. 2004. *Kinderculture: The Corporate Construction of Childhood*. Boulder, CO: Westview Press.

Sutton-Smith, B. 1997. *Ambiguity of Play*. Cambridge, MA: Harvard University Press.

Sutton-Smith, B. 1986. *Toys as Culture*. New York: Gardner Press.

Taylor, D. 2003. *The Archive and the Repertoire: Performing Cultural Memory in the Americas*. Durham: Duke University Press.

Vygotsky, L.S. 1978. *Mind in Society*. Edited by Michael Cole. Cambridge, MA: Harvard University Press.

Walker, J. 1981. "The Please Touch Museum." Unpublished dissertation, University of Pennsylvania.
West, N.M. 2000. *Kodak and the Lens of Nostalgia*. Charlottesville, VA: University Press of Virginia.
Willis, P. 1977. *Learning to Labor: How Working Class Kids Get Working Class Jobs*. New York: Columbia University Press.
Willis, P. 1990. *Common Culture: Symbolic Work at Play in the Everyday Cultures of the Young*. With Simon Jones, Joyce Canaan, and Geoff Hurd. Boulder, CO: Westview Press.
Young, K. 1993. *Bodylore*. Knoxville: University of Tennessee Press.
Zuckerman, M. 1985. "Suburban Play." In Brian Sutton-Smith (Ed.) *Children's Play: Past, Present, & Future*. Philadelphia, PA: Please Touch Museum.

Chapter Seven

We're All in This Together:
Framing the Self-Representation of Adolescence in Disney's *High School Musical*

Sean J. Bliznik

Introduction

Considering theatre as a form of representation and a mode of creative play, this chapter explores the self-representation of adolescents on stage through the lens of the pop-culture phenomenon Disney's *High School Musical*. Disney's *High School Musical* is a direct-to-cable-TV movie (it aired on the Disney Channel only) marketed toward pre-teens and young adolescents. After the success of *High School Musical*'s release, Disney adapted the movie into a live stage version, which completed a national tour in August 2008. Other incarnations of this product include an ice show, an international concert tour, a second TV movie (*High School Musical 2: School's Out*), a feature film released in October 2008 (*High School Musical 3: Senior Year*), theme park "pep rallies" in Florida, California, and Paris, and more. How did *High School Musical* become a cultural phenomenon for young people, and how is this phenomenon being recreated by its target audience through different modes of creative play? Specifically, this chapter explores how adolescents have adapted the original movie and stage version to create their own interpretations of the show's musical numbers. In particular, I explore adolescents who recreate musical numbers and characters from the original and then publish these recreations on the self-broadcasting Web site, YouTube. I suggest that adolescents, through their embodiment and reinterpretation of the original product, reflect the show's anthem: "We're All in This Together." This embodiment occurs through the literal collection of bodies on the physical stage (or screen) and then virtually through their videos posted on YouTube.

Theoretical Approach

In light of the concept of creative play and constructed performance, I make use of several theorists who have explored the construction of meaning (and by extension the construction of self) in different modes of performance. First, evoking Erving Goffman (1974) in his work "Frame Analysis: An Essay on the Organization of Experience" explores and extends the concept of "role theory, a school of thought in social psychology which analyses human activity in terms of its enactment of socially determined roles," to the adolescent determining what role he or she should "play" and then how that role is enacted (Counsell and Wolf, 24-25). However, in dealing with such topics as self-presentation and social interaction, Goffman "focuses on the performative dimension of ordinary behavior, the way individuals adopt and enact given personae as a means of negotiating established interpersonal situations" (Counsell and Wolf, 25). In the case of Disney's *High School Musical*, the interpersonal situation is the high school environment. The adolescents recreate moments from the movie by negotiating the personae created in the film. They also create with the knowledge of how each persona functions in their own personal relationships with other contemporary peers by embodying the performance and posting it on YouTube. Goffman notes that in "play [...] those involved in it seem to have a clear appreciation that it is play that is going on" (25). This is certainly the case in the videos I surveyed on YouTube as the adolescent knows he/she is recreating a performance as do the other members of the YouTube community as seen through the viewer's comments regarding the video postings.

Finally, Goffman outlines the central concept in frame analysis: "I refer to the set of conventions by which a given activity, one already meaningful in terms of some primary framework, is transformed into something patterned on this activity but seen by the participants to be so quite something else" (27). I believe that this concept of the frame applies to the performances posted on YouTube. In this case, the primary framework is the environment of the high school depicted on the small screen. However, this frame is then transformed when the adolescent decides to recreate an image of self through these characters by posting an original video on YouTube. Once on YouTube, the adolescents recognize that they are not actually Troy and Gabriella but are "playing" Troy and Gabriella, thereby making these characters their own. In the process of creating these stories for the screen, the young people are aware that their bodies are now being watched by others. Ultimately, the young people are making these characters their own for the purpose of being gazed at (and rated) by others, thereby relating back to Goffman's assertion about how the participants alter and view the meaning of the activity as something different than the original source material.

In another theoretical extension, Clifford Geertz (1973), an anthropologist, examines the "meanings encoded in cultural practices" (Counsell 222). It is his "thick description" that entails "relating acts to their cultural context" in an attempt to determine the significance to a specific group of people (Counsell 222). What is the social and cultural significance of not only Disney's *High School Musical*, but of the recreations that appear on YouTube as defined by the re-creators themselves? Specifically, Geertz in "Deep Play: Notes on the Balinese Cockfight" employs Jeremy Bentham's concept of "deep play," but in a reversal. While Bentham believes that "any practical, utilitarian dimension to such entertainments makes them merely pointless," Geertz claims that the absence of utilitarian dimension in actuality demonstrates the events' symbolic importance (Counsell 222). It is Geertz's definition that I wish to employ in this chapter.

Through the seemingly impractical nature of recreating scenes from *High School Musical*, the adolescents create a symbolic importance and work to advance their interpretation of the original work in their own way for a different community of viewers. According to Geertz, the function of such events (referring to the Balinese cockfight) is "interpretive: it is a Balinese reading of a Balinese experience, a story they tell themselves about themselves" (Counsell 227). With *High School Musical*, the initial story is the movie, the story that the viewers and participants recreate to tell about themselves (by broadcasting for all to see) is the actual duplication of the initial source material. The adolescents are not only commenting on their beliefs and social structures, either by recreating the work literally or creating a parody, but they are leaving the created piece as a permanent remnant of a specific moment in their lives. This creation then becomes an archival trace of their performances for future audiences. The adolescents have positioned their physical bodies in a mediated environment for public consumption and critique by other young people, thus effecting an extension of young people's embodied identities. Goffman claims that it is through these experiences "that society is built and individuals are put together" (228). Indeed, a society is built both in the film version of *High School Musical* (literally in the movie in addition to the community of viewers) as well as within the smaller recreated videos on the on-line community of YouTube.

The Adolescent Body

Implementing the theories of Geertz and Goffman to help frame how to interpret these young people's recreations on YouTube, it is necessary to examine not only how the adolescents view these recreations but also how these recreations are inscribed on the body. *High School Musical* is a created world that is recreated using its own words while living in the real world of the adolescents doing the recreating. The idea that creating a nominal abstraction for another item in order to convey (and create) meaning does not remove the piece that wants definition from its surroundings. This concept reinforces Geertz's claim. In fact, many items are defined by their surroundings, and the meaning changes when the surroundings change. This is seen most clearly in the recreations that attempt to copy exactly the original and are praised by other YouTube users whereas those adolescents who recreate in the spirit of Disney's *High School Musical* are encouraged to work harder and rely on the original. Therefore, the viewer's experience is culturally constructed and formed by fusing multiple ways of seeing the performance as constructed on the body. *High School Musical* stands in as a reflection and a construction of contemporary society. Then, the adolescents recreate this construction through their viewpoint, either reaffirming the construction implicit and explicit in the movie or altering it ever so slightly (and sometimes in a major way) to reflect their individual perspective and constructing a new cultural context for this work. How is *High School Musical* presenting youth, and does this presentation reflect how youth are constructing and embodying various identities and representations as presented on YouTube? I examine the role of four musical numbers in the stage adaptation, and how adolescents recreate those musical numbers on YouTube while noting how these individual adolescents or groups of adolescents chose to interpret and embody a particular song. I compare the original incarnation of "Breaking Free," "We're All in This Together," "Start of Something New," and "Stick to the Status Quo" with that of its recreation on YouTube.

YouTube

A basic search on YouTube reveals that there are over 165,000 videos and threads related to Disney's *High School Musical*. Now, many of these videos are either scenes from the actual movie, interviews, TV spots with the actors, or videos of the theme park shows. All of these offerings are not considered in this chapter. However, by searching for the actual song title in conjunction with Disney's *High School Musical*, the search results reflect original videos created by adolescents. Another interesting facet of YouTube is that the interface is organic and alive. Most of the videos have comments from other YouTube members and sometimes even the original adolescent creator posts comments about the video and what inspired its recreation. Another consideration is who is posting the videos on YouTube? Is it the adolescent? Is it the parent? In the case of *High School Musical*, the original source seems to vary, but many of the videos I found that displayed pre-adolescent children were posted by adults and parents of the children in the video whereas the videos that featured preteens and adolescents were posted by the teen him/herself and was usually filmed in the teen's bedroom or other private home space. The videos discussed in this chapter were created and posted to YouTube between July 2006 and August 2007.

"Breaking Free" and the Controlled Body

Similar to the film version, the stage version of "Breaking Free" comes at the end of the production and is the moment where Gabriella has lost her courage and it is Troy who will encourage her. Gabriella claims that "I can't do it Troy. It was much easier when it was just you and me—" (Simpatico, 2006, 105). With Troy's encouragement both of them sing, reflecting that "There's not a star in heaven that we can't reach / If we're trying, so we're breaking free" (Simpatico, 2006, 105). As the song progresses the other characters join in realizing that they, too, can "break free." It is by experiencing this song that Coach Bolton (Troy's father) realizes how great his son is, and if his son wants to pursue a musical theatre career instead of a basketball career, that is okay, too. Coach Bolton claims: "You can be anything you want, don't let anyone ever stop you. Okay, son?" (108). After a shared hug on stage, the entire company (including Coach Bolton) sing the final verse of the song. The conflict of the play is resolved through understanding and an open mind. Diversity is celebrated and friendship and honesty prevail.

On "YouTube," "Breaking Free" was one of the most popular postings with 4930 related videos. Videos of "Breaking Free" ranged from same-gender lip-syncing to the song presented in several different languages including French, Spanish, German, Hebrew, and several Chinese dialects to animé versions of the song. The recreations of "Breaking Free" embrace the spirit of the song by envisioning the performances in ways not presented in the original material. The adolescents take ownership of the material. As a result, the material develops in ways that reflect the aesthetic of the adolescent, which separates the creation from the original. In addition, some of the videos are parodies (most of the same gender performances) while others are rehearsed and fully developed pieces. In many cases, the song was sung by younger children. In one case, Ally is falling asleep in her car seat as the song plays in the car. However, even though she is slowly falling asleep, she continues to mumble the words of the song as an adult captures all of it on video and encourages the child to continue singing. In two different videos, both the male and female singing parts were played by teenage boys. In both cases, the boy playing the female role embodied female characteristics either by wearing something on his head or by incorporating stereotypical female mannerisms as copied from the movie itself. The recreation of this song seems to allow for the least amount of staging and theatrics in the YouTube version. Most of the videos were simply sung or lip-synched without any additional props or costumes unlike "Stick to the Status Quo" in which, in all viewed cases, children staged the number and employed costumes as well as props like those used in the movie.

In one video, fifteen-year-old Chantelle plays the piano while singing live with the male voice dubbed into the recording. In the background, the viewer can see various types of recording and musical equipment. The room looks like a make-shift recording studio. She has several videos of her performing "Breaking Free." Other videos include performances at several school events and talent contests as well as different renditions of other *High School Musical* songs. After viewing the video, Chantelle asks the viewer: "What did you think? Rate it!" (YouTube). For Chantelle, performing the song is not enough; rather she wants her viewers to also rank her work as compared to other YouTube videos. This particular video has been viewed 314,444 times and has received 3,202 ratings (four out of five stars). In addition, Chantelle's piece has received 3633 comments and been listed as a favorite on 1652 other YouTube users' accounts. Clearly, Chantelle takes full advantage of the ability for viewers to comment on her work. One viewer, "JonasBrosRokUrSox33" claims "you are so good, wish you the best of luck with your music career, because you are going to be famous someday!!!" (YouTube). Many other comments echo this sentiment. They are encouraging and positive. Chantelle even has young admirers herself. "ashsadlerxxx" comments "accordin 2 every1 i look like her!! X but shes pretty" (YouTube). So, a subculture develops as Chantelle's viewers want not only to connect with the original *High School Mu-*

sical but also with Chantelle's recreation of the songs. Therefore, Chantelle now stands in as a representation of *High School Musical* itself. For Chantelle's viewers recognize her as a viable singer and performer on the same aspiring level of the actual performers from the movie and stage show. In addition, Chantelle's fans have created several Web sites showcasing her work and Chantelle appeared in local newspapers as she has over 1 million hits on YouTube.

In a final example, two teenage boys lip-sync the song. They are both shirtless, and there is a third teenager with his shirt open dancing in the background or "soaring" as the lyrics would indicate. The teens attempt to recreate the gestures and facial expressions of the original performers. However, their viewers know that the performance is just lip-syncing and is designed to be humorous. This video has been viewed 3317 times and has received eleven ratings—all of which acknowledge that the piece is funny and that the boys are hot. For example, "nikkikopp" states: "uh that's pretty hot i guess" and "liseisabelle" laughs: "hahaha the guys on the background! Anyway you guys are funny" (YouTube). In this example, both the creators of the piece and the viewing audience assess the material through the lens that it is not the original nor is it a legitimate entry as a performer (like Chantelle). The teenagers appear to be just playing—a reoccurring theme in the movie and stage version. Moreover, the comments are not complimentary as they were for Chantelle; rather these comments note the fun of the video, and it is not taken seriously unlike Chantelle's, for which viewers were providing career advice. In this example, each boy takes on one of the roles—one male and one female. There is no attempt to put one of the boys in drag or to indicate that one performer is female. The three teens create a light-hearted video demonstrating that this song is accessible to either gender and that it is not "off limits" because there is a female part. The role of gender in this song does not prevent either teen from identifying with the song or wanting to recreate the piece themselves. Rather, the teen boys do not see a "gender" in the piece and thereby subvert their preassigned gendered roles both in the recreation and in their actual lives. Ultimately, the teens are reinforcing Coach Bolton's claim (and Disney's too) that "You can be anything you want, don't let anyone ever stop you" (Simpatico, 2006, 108).

The Gendered and Sexualized Body

In the first example above, young Ally's body was being controlled by the adult (perhaps a parent) as the adult encouraged the young child to keep singing even when she is exhausted and falling asleep. In the second example, Chantelle is in control of her body and supplements the male part with a voice-over. In the final example, the three boys attempt to control the image of their own bodies by breaking from societal expectations of male and female. However, in this example, the two men are not taken seriously for their crossdressing interpretation. They find their performance humorous and the comments reinforce the stereotype. It is precisely because the two boys represent the heteronormative standard that their piece can be viewed through humor. However, if this piece was performed seriously by an adolescent gay couple, I cannot imagine that it would be assessed in the same manner. Chantelle, on the other hand, is not only being rated on her talent to execute the song well but also on her "pretty" and "talented" body. Therefore, the on-line community is stepping in to inscribe wants and desires underscored in the song on Chantelle's body itself. Chantelle's videos have become so popular because her interpretations seem to reify the message of the song and the movie as a whole when the desire to create the video in the first place could be for precisely the opposite reason.

Both male and female adolescents are recreating genders in their videos. These videos reinforce Judith Butler's idea that gender is a social construction that is performed. In Butler's *Undoing Gender* (2004), this mode of construction is called "doing." Butler notes that "[i]f gender is a kind of doing, an incessant activity performed, in part, without one's knowing and without one's willing, it is not for that reason automatic or mechanical" (1). I would contend that the "doing" and the "knowing" are connected and that the adolescents are, in fact, aware of what they are doing while knowingly constructing at the same time. However, the action of doing remains organic, fluid, and in many cases the opposite of the original construction in the film. This organic construction occurs when the role of performance and the performative nature of gender and sexuality enter the conversation. To do something is to perform it. Therefore, to be or do male or female, heterosexual or homosexual, is to perform those terms and to either reify their construction or deconstruct an accepted meaning. Moreover, it is through the continual performance of these roles that the meaning and normalized performance of those roles are questioned, explored, and expanded into a modern context and understanding not only of performance but of gender and sexuality specifically.

Butler continues by noting that "[t]o understand gender as a historical category, however, is to accept that gender, understood as one way of culturally configuring a body, is open to a continual remaking, and that 'anatomy' and 'sex' are not without cultural framing" (9-10). It is important to note the role of the body in constructing a performance. For me as a researcher, the role of gender performance and construction yields a series of questions that come out of the adolescent's performance. Their willingness to embrace a lifestyle and performance mode that reflects who they are and their personal artistic aesthetic while placing that aesthetic in a world that refuses to recognize it is exceptionally fulfilling. YouTube users note the elements of cross-dressing, and, for some undisclosed reason, the fact that the songs are recreated by two members of the same gender does not seem to affect their reaction to the recreation.

Butler claims that "[g]ender is the mechanism by which notions of masculine and feminine are produced and naturalized, but gender might very well be the apparatus by which such terms are deconstructed and denaturalized" (42). This "deconstruction" occurs through the construction of another gender and approach to understanding the construction of gender. Butler notes that "the alternative to the binary system of gender [male, female or heterosexual, homosexual] is a multiplication of genders" (43). The concept of a multiplication of genders is not only interesting in light of this essay but highlights the constructive and performative nature of gender itself. As Butler asserts: "I want to reiterate that displacing the binary model for thinking about relationality will also help us appreciate the triangulating echoes in heterosexual, homosexual, and bisexual desire, and complicate our understanding of the relations between sexuality and gender" (151). This triangulation is one of the successes of the adolescents created performance of self for they challenge how the viewer understands both the gender of the character being depicted as well as the gender of the performer on the video itself. This potentially conflicting image asks the viewer to come to a new understanding of not only the gender being performed in the movie and the recreated gender in the video, but also the gender being performed by the (silent) viewer.

The Proficient and Competent Body

High School Musical's anthem, "We're All in This Together" ends both the movie and the stage version of the show. The lyrics of the song suggest the ideas that "everyone is special in their own way" and that as individuals "dreams have no limitations" (Simpatico, 2006, 112). This song functions as an ensemble piece and involves the entire cast. Similarly, the recreation of this number on YouTube also relies on many people. Almost all of the recreations are lip-syncs because the focus is on the dancing and choreography and less on spotlighting individual voices. "We're All in This Together" stands out as the group video, whether that was in a dance class or out in the street with 1540 video threads. This song appears popular at local talent shows and in dance studios across the country. Also, due to the focus and attention to mimicking the choreography from the original movie, the comments posted by viewers usually noted whether or not the dancing was accurate or if more rehearsals would be helpful.

One example is two teenage girls dancing in their living room. They sing an occasional refrain of the song but nothing more. The girls are completely focused on the musical number's choreography. The video has been viewed 2218 times, received ten ratings (four out of five stars), and ten comments. The comments run the positive spectrum from "great vid" ("rubyhsm") and "that was awesome" ("samp92") to some viewers who are also *High School Musical* fanatics and note that they did not get all the moves correctly: "Hey umm yea the moves...my friend and i actually know all of them we might put a video on but hey u guys have good effort and are brave to put this on the internet" ("nibneb"). This viewer acknowledges that this number is difficult and should be done with great precision, but also includes herself in the recreation of the song by claiming that she, too, knows the moves and might put a video on YouTube.

Another video is composed by three teenage girls (Anna, Rosie, and Lauren) who create a performance space, assign each other specific roles in the song, and create a final video where the color of their costumes change as the video progresses. This video has been viewed 1247 times with three ratings (four out of five stars) and three comments. One comment reflects the theatrics of the performance: "How cool is that, changing coulours!" ("ureete26"). Another comment harkens back to the previous video's comments by connecting the viewer to the actual recreation of the material: "This has to be my 2nd fave 'High School Musical' song [...] I went back and watch this scene on the

DVD and you three actually do the dance really well" ("ChrisDilke"). This response underscores the importance of the original source material. "Chris-Dilke" checks the dancing in the recreation against that of the original so that s/he could accurately rate the new video and provide its creators with constructive feedback about their performance. So, s/he is both adolescent consumer as well as art critic and maintainer of the original source material. Most of the comments related to recreated videos of "We're All in This Together" provide the artist with critiques to ensure that the recreated material reflects the original as close as possible. These types of comments were not present in the cases of the other three songs.

Unlike the movie version, the stage version of *High School Musical* opens with a Wildcat cheer and then transitions into the ski lodge where Troy and Gabriella bump into each other at a karaoke contest and begin singing, "Start of Something New." The structural focus is the same. This song introduces the two leads in a romantic way immediately. They realize through the song that they were closed off, and now they have awakened something in each other that will come to fruition once they accidentally discover each other again at school. Troy sings: "Living in my own world / Didn't understand / That anything can happen / When you take a chance" (Simpatico, 2006, 6). Gabriella responds by proclaiming: "I never believed in / What I couldn't see / I never opened my heart / To all the possibilities" (Simpatico, 2006, 6). And then they both sing together about their realized friendship and perhaps something more: "This could be the start / Of something new / It feel so right / To be here with you / Oh, and now lookin' in your eyes / I feel in my heart / The start of something new" (Simpatico, 2006, 6). As clichéd as the lyrics might be, the song explores that moment when one gender awakens to their own individual sexuality and begins noticing how those feelings interact in the adolescent world—a theme to which all of the new video creations relate. Here again, the work of Butler is reinforced by the actions of the adolescents working to represent a version of him/herself as they understand that representation individually.

In one version of "Start of Something New," two gender-appropriate teenagers lip-sync. They both stand in front of a curtain covering a sliding glass door, creating a theatrical environment, and each holds a real microphone that is connected to an audio system. They perform the whole song with energy and intense facial expressions and commitment to the piece. This piece has been viewed 42,625 times and has received sixty-five ratings and is listed as a favorite on twenty-eight other YouTube users' accounts. The comments range from the simple and straightforward, "cute" ("Aprilscherzchen") to the more in-depth comment posted by "rhpsqueenforlife":

> This was beyond adorable. Im not too big a fan of HSM at all but I found this to be so worth watching. You two have cute chemistry and seemed to be having such fun. Plus, in my honest opinion, you did better than the original actors in the movie. Seemed to be more free and more confident in having a good time. I think you should definitely do more songs. Perhaps something from the 2nd one? Very good. (YouTube)

This comment not only makes a judgment on the recreation but compares the new piece to the original, concluding that the recreation is better. The viewer is so convinced of the performers' work that the viewer suggests that they create more videos. This comment moves the lens of representation from the creators lip-synching to suggesting a new work that would better reflect what the viewer wished *High School Musical* was really like. Although the viewer is not an avid fan of the movie, the viewer recognizes the work and passion behind this particular lip-sync.

Another version is created by two teenage girls who sing the song using the Karaoke track. This video has been viewed 7357 times and has received seventeen ratings (two out of five stars) with forty-two comments. The girls sit in chairs in the basement of a house reading the lyrics of the Karaoke prompter which is not visible in the video. Occasionally, each girl looks at the camera when she seems to be comfortable with the lyrics trying to connect with her viewing audience. There are several moments when the girls make a mistake and laugh at themselves but continue performing anyway. Since the girls are not standing up, they sway to the tempo of the song while sitting in their chairs. Unfortunately, both girls are off key and their viewers let them know it. Most of the comments are kind and suggest that more practice would make them better: "u wernt dat bad but remember practice makes perfect!!!" ("t123rulz"). Some comments are even apologetic: "ok, ummm. sorry!!!! kinda bad" ("biaspeich96"). Nonetheless, the girls felt comfortable creating this video that would be shared with an online community of their peers. Their created work is an example of unforced playful artistic expression, which makes them happy through its creation regardless of what others will say about it.

A final version of this song is another lip-sync by "idanmat." This video is of two teenagers playing out the roles of Troy and Gabriella. In the user's description, he lists the word "sing" in quotation marks to indicate that they are really not singing the song. This video has been viewed 25,877 times and received seventy-one ratings (three out of five stars) with eighty-nine comments including one video comment. Overall, the comments are not encouraging as "Peruanita28" notes: "ur not singing, at least learn how to fake it" (YouTube). Other comments echo the same sentiment: "bad lip synicking you guys suck I could hella tell" ("F4Luver") and "what talent does this show? you can read?" ("shankdrummer06"). These comments suggest that the viewing audience wants some level of performance and wants the new creation to take the original seriously. The viewers recognize that the performance is not professional, but wish to maintain a certain level of acceptable performance on YouTube. In addition, the video comment is actually posted as a response to the original video. The posting is by a young teenage girl who sings the song in response to previous video's lip-synching. Her video has been viewed 251 times, it received one star and seven comments. She sings *a capella* and with a close-up shot of only her face. The comments posted about her video are not complimentary or constructive. One comment attempts to be encouraging by telling her to "keep up d spirit ;)" ("clicheddisaster") while others tell her the opposite: "I have never laughed so hard" ("TakingBackSubway") or "you have GOT to be kidding me" ("slmh18") or the simple and straightforward "usuck" ("jackassnevermore").

This scenario is interesting because this particular member posted a video in response to another video, so her visceral reaction is not entirely from viewing the movie itself, but by being familiar with the product and having enough of a passion for *High School Musical* that she would subject herself to anonymous critics to express her version of "Start of Something New." Her posting asserts that lip-syncing is not a viable performance mode nor is it good enough to be labeled as *High School Musical*. So, she attempts to create a different and perhaps more accurate representation of the song by singing it live. Unfortunately, she is nervous and does not sing well as the comments posted on her video would indicate. Her willingness to provide an alternate option demonstrates that she is not sticking to the status quo—another pivotal theme of the play.

The Body as Parody

"Stick to the Status Quo" ends Act One of the stage version while appearing early on in the movie. This song identifies the cliqués and impenetrable groups of the average American high school. However, the song encourages each individual student to embrace his or her passion and "break free" from the constraints and regulations of the status quo. It is through this song that Troy decides to sing, Gabriella accepts her intellectual prowess, Martha raps, and Chad bakes. However, the play will have to run its course for each character to realize their individual journeys of self-actualization and acceptance. Ultimately, each character recognizes that: "inside I am stirring / Something strange is occurring / It's a secret I need to share" (Simpatico, 2006, 53). It is important to note that *High School Musical* encourages breaking from the stereotyped world all the while recreating and reinforcing stereotypes of another kind. A new status quo is instituted that does not alter the social structures that currently disempower youth. Rather the appearance of breaking down stereotypes through self-empowerment is conveyed, and the youth discipline themselves and their bodies by reinstituting cultural norms and expectations that have been informed by adults, but approved by young people.

Searching for "Stick to the Status Quo" yields the lowest number of submissions with only 387 videos. On YouTube, the adolescents take their work seriously. Most of the videos I viewed were not a parody of the original movie. Rather, the adolescents in the videos faithfully captured their own passion around the themes and music of *High School Musical*. One video recreated a full production number with eight adolescents while their parents sat in the background and watched. In another video by "hischoolmusicalover," she notes that "this is what happens when you put the 'High School Musical' shirt on! You can't help but dance!" (YouTube). One of the comments posted with this video claims "You made my life" (YouTube). Although the other adolescents in the room do not engage in her performance, their laughter and smiles reinforce the familiarity with the product and the normalcy that embodied play is an acceptable afternoon activity just like doing one's homework or baking cookies.

In one video, four teenage girls create a school environment where they can act out the entire song. The room is decorated with sports paraphernalia to match the opening of the song. Suddenly, the video cuts to an academic scene featuring four new teenage girls. The video cuts again to a group of five mixed-gender teenagers performing the third section of the song. The lip-synching is precise, the dance is well rehearsed, and the video appears to be professionally edited. The end of the song continues to transition between each of the three different groups performing different aspects of the song. In total, this video involved over twelve different teenage performers. This video has been viewed 21,528 times, received sixty-seven ratings (four out of five stars), and seventy-nine comments, in addition to being listed as a favorite on fifty-four accounts. The comments are pretty consistent: "that was good!" ("mamelottikala"), "better than awesome" ("coolgirl1209"), and "Oh My Word! That Was Amazing! And How You Made All The Different Bits Fuse Together It Was Wicked Good Go You Guys! You Should Make More! Wow!" ("xpaigexalicex"). This video incorporates the most performative aspects than any of the other videos surveyed. The creators use costumes, props, mimic the dance and gestures of the original to recreate their own high school cafeteria scene. This video is not just a random filming in one's bedroom, rather it required more intense thought, extensive planning, casting, rehearsal, and a large amount of "research" time with the original source material to appear to recreate the musical number so effortlessly and flawlessly. The commitment to play and the execution of this remake demonstrates the incredible impact that *High School Musical* has made on its youthful target audience.

In another video, two teenage girls recreate the entire song playing all of the characters. They sing aloud with the original cast recording and perform all of the choreography in the middle of a bedroom. This video has been viewed 16,608 times and received ninety-one ratings (four out of five stars) with forty-three comments, in addition to being listed as a favorite on thirty-one accounts. The viewer's comments are consistent: "haha you guys really know your highschool musical" ("dubsss22"), "FINALLY, someone who knows what they're doing" ("shedreamedforlife"), and "u can actuali both sing and dance nt many ppl cn do that" ("leahkerina"). These comments, again, reinforce that the viewing audience wants the videos to match the original or at least attempt to reach the same level of performance.

In terms of demographics, *High School Musical* attempts to represent all of the students in a culturally aware way even if the awareness is through stereotyping. The script breaks down the characters in terms of cliques such as "the jocks, the nerds, the thespians, the brainiacs, the skater dudes, and other students," while the representation on screen reflects a Latina and an African American girl in lead roles with another African American male in a supporting role (Disney Theatricals, 2007). Moreover, the script does not denote race or ethnicity in the casting. However, the representation of those ethnicities on screen has certainly influenced the actual casting of the production across the country and recently on tour. However, on YouTube, all racial and gender lines are blurred. The characters are universalized and unconsciously subscribe to a new form of cultural hegemony. Adolescents create new videos without adhering to the gender of the original singer (even if the video is a lip-sync where the change is obvious). They simply recreate a song that they connect with on an individual level and through this recreation create a cultural context (such as the claims of Geertz) for this recreation that is specific and is defined by the creator.

Conclusion

In all of the videos surveyed, there is a great attention to detail both on the part of the video participant(s) and the videographer. The recreation of songs from *High School Musical* appears to be a desirable activity by the creators. There is no indication that the adolescents take into consideration their "low budget" recreations (even though some videos had a high production value) as these recreations are in the mode of creative play and are not being produced for either TV or the commercial stage like the originals. The simple, straightforward, and familiar structure of the play makes it accessible to its target audience. Young adolescents can identify with the themes and the characters of the play. So, it is easy for them to recreate the world of the play for themselves in their own personal spaces through creative play. Evoking Geertz, *High School Musical* is the story of today's adolescents. Now, whether that story is an accurate representation of their individual overall lives is worth consideration. The overall message of the piece (stand up for what you believe and be who you want to be) makes the cross-gender recreations acceptable as young boys play girls and young girls play boys. After all, they are merely playing, not orchestrating a physical altercation.

Disney's *High School Musical* has served a need to present family-friendly entertainment that celebrates individuality and the self through either direct copycat videos as explored through lip-synching or through original pieces that include the performer's own voice. The belief that we, as adults, parents, scholars, etc., consider the *High School Musical* empire frivolous and reinforcing stereotypes and cultural hegemony is irrelevant to the target audience. The power of this new phenomenon is in its audience, and this audience (generally) is not composed of adults—it is an audience of pre-teens and adolescents who have connected with an entertainment offering that speaks to them on their level. For this reason, it is necessary for adults to be aware of the message being conveyed in the original product and engage an adolescent critically about the images represented in *High School Musical*. They are the Troys, Gabriellas, Kelsies, and Chads of the world. They want to be noticed. They want to be able to acknowledge themselves and their own passions in an oversexualized adolescent commercial world that celebrates getting to adulthood instead of experiencing one's adolescence.

Adolescents want to belong to a society that accepts them as they are and celebrates their passions and interests. *New York Times* theatre critic Charles Isherwood acknowledges that *High School Musical* proclaims that "it is O.K. to be yourself, even it means whipping up a mean crème brûlée after basketball practice. Especially, if it means whipping up a mean crème brûlée after basketball practice" (1). It is this acknowledgment that celebrates individual diversity in a sea of stereotypes that has made *High School Musical* successful (even though the movie itself reinforces stereotypes). Isherwood concludes that "whether this accords with current reality in American high schools I cannot say, and frankly doubt. But [...] devotion is not really about encountering the harsh truths of the world, but about seeking some solace for them and finding the inspiration to change them" (1). Ultimately, Disney's *High School Musical* is presenting the immediate needs of the adolescents who have chosen to make this production part of their popular culture. In all fairness, Disney did not set out to create a piece of theatre for social change or to reflect the potentially poor situations of youth in America. Rather, *High School Musical* represents an environment where the underdog, undervalued, and simply not noticed can achieve their dreams that popular culture prevents. The basketball player becomes a musical star; the nerd lands the lead; and the league of outcasts find their solace in areas of the school that were socially forbidden—Chad bakes, Martha raps, and Kelsie composes. However, *High School Musical* has become a phenomenon and with 165,000 *High School Musical* related videos on YouTube that represent both official materials as well as thousands of original adolescent copy cats from across the globe, it is nearly impossible to avoid the influence and the wide-reaching effects of Disney's pre-teen sensation, *High School Musical*.

References

Butler, J. (2004). *Undoing Gender*. New York: Routledge.
Calhoun, J., dir. Disney's "High School Musical on Tour." (2007). http://disney.go.com/theatre/highschoolmusical/#video (Accessed October 25, 2007).

Counsell, C. and Wolf, L., eds. (2007). *Performance Analysis: An Introductory Coursebook*. New York: Routledge.
Disney Theatrical Education Department. (2007). "Disney High School Musical on Tour." Study Guide. http://amedia.disney.go.com/theatre/highschoolmusical/pdf/HSM-StudyGuide.pdf (Accessed October 22, 2007).
Geertz, C. (1973). "Deep Play: Notes on the Balinese Cockfight." In Colin Counsel and Laurie Wolf (Eds.), *Performance Analysis: An Introductory Coursebook* (pp. 222-228). New York: Routledge.
Goffman, E. (1974). "Frame Analysis: An Essay on the Organization of Experience." In Colin Counsel and Laurie Wolf (Eds.), *Performance Analysis: An Introductory Coursebook* (pp. 24-30). New York: Routledge.
Isherwood, C. (2007). Review of "High School Musical on Tour." *The New York Times Online*. August 11, 2007. http://theater2.nytimes.com/2007/08/11/theater/reviews/11high.html (Accessed November 16, 2007).
Simpatico, D. (2006). Disney's *High School Musical*. Unpublished draft.
The Walt Disney Company. Disney Theatricals. "High School Musical on Tour!" http://disney.go.com/theatre/highschoolmusical (Accessed October 22, 2007).
YouTube. www.youtube.com. (Accessed October 10, 2007, November 15, 2007, December 5, 2007, November 22, 2008, August 30, 2009).

Chapter Eight

13 Going on 30:
Adult Discourses of Femininity in Young Women's Sports Training

Amy K. Way

Introduction

Though recognized in scholarly discourse as key to successful socialization, the importance of physical activity in a child's development is often underestimated with regard to the degree of its impact on the construction of a child's gender identity. Participation as part of a team (whether athletic, academic, or aesthetic) is often children's first experience of competition and cooperation and their first opportunity to embody their own strengths and weaknesses. Beyond the construction of individual identities, however, children's participation in physical activity has important implications for the construction of a gendered identity.

This chapter examines the involvement of young girls in a particular sports program model. Though potentially empowering, the analysis reveals that physical activity can also often be a site of discipline for young girls where competence is established in exchange for a girl's physical transformation. In many ways, sports socialize girls into adult narratives of femininity that can be confining and restrictive to the ways they physically inhabit their bodies. I employ a qualitative approach to examine the implications of sports and physical activity on girls' bodies through a character development program designed for elementary school girls. In the context of the program, women volunteer as coaches with the explicit goal of providing an alternate discourse for girls about what it means to transform themselves and physically enact femininity. Thus, the curriculum behind the program is framed as play and yet has important consequences for how it positions girls and creates spaces for agency. Rather than asking girls to change themselves physically, the curriculum encourages girls to transform the way they think and act in their bodies. Drawing on a curriculum focused on physical activity, girls are taught to use their bodies as a tool for their own success and development as strong women.

Run for Your Life (RFYL) is an organization that intervenes in the life of elementary school girls with the hopes of redefining what it means to be female. The program is based upon physical activity as a source of strength and empowerment for girls. Over the course of a school semester girls and their coaches meet twice a week to communicate about the challenges that face girls on their journey into adolescence. In addition to specified character development lessons, about half of each practice is set aside for girls to participate in physical activity. Running is a major focus of the program as it serves as a way for girls to embody strength. The final achievement for the girls in the program is to complete a three-mile run, which for the program is symbolic of the larger challenges girls will face in their lives. RFYL believes that if girls can succeed at training for and completing a three-mile run, they can use that experience and knowledge to overcome any challenge they might face in life.

Theoretical Framework

This chapter presents an overview of the social science literature addressing the construction of female bodies, specifically through sports. The notion of physicality is examined and discussed in terms of reconceptualizations that value feminine ways of engaging bodies and physical activity. I then conclude with a specific discussion of RFYL that offers the context for experimentation with these revised definitions of physicality and what they might look like in practice.

A Communication Perspective on the Discourse of Bodies

"Through communication, individuals over time, create, maintain, and transform the social realities they inhabit" (Eisenberg, 2007, p. 27). As social actors, we are constantly involved in a process of meaning making through discourse (du Gay, 1996). Discourse "refers to both the production of knowledge through language and representation and the way that knowledge is institutionalized, shaping social practices and setting new practices into play" (du Gay, 2007, p. 43). Thus, discourse has elements of communication and action that work in tandem to create and reflect the social order.

Like language, identity is a relational construct and comes to be meaningful only when considered in contrast to what it is not (du Gay, 1996). Femininity, for example, has significance in relation to it being not masculinity. Understanding gendered identity in this way further emphasizes the social construction of the meanings that we give to these constructions and not any essential meaning or value that may exist outside of discourse about them. "As feminist scholars have indicated, the idea that biology underscores the unambiguous authenticity of femininity and masculinity is itself a historical invention" (du Gay, 1996, p. 48). The meanings that we give to masculinity and femininity are just that—given, not essential or inherent. Individuals understand their subjectivities in the world by what they can physically enact (Nadesan & Trethewey, 2000). Thus, individual identities are enacted through the expression and use of our bodies. Bodies are not passive receptacles acted upon by discourses; instead individuals take a physical role in the construction of their identities (Butler, 1997); this physical representation of specific discourses is called embodiment.

Take for example a young child growing up in the world. Her/his first introduction is as a girl or boy, and important aspects of her identity are communicated in terms of gender for the rest of her life. Importantly, discourse refers not just to the verbal messages communicated across individuals and groups, but to the bodily displays and actions that manifest and reify these spoken messages. A communication perspective highlights the power of messages to impact our bodily comportment, the ways we think and eventually act in the world. When parents praise a boy for being strong or tell a girl to sit like a lady they are sending messages, which are in turn translated into physical representations of gender. The boy looks past his pain and continues to play while the girl physically positions herself in ways that generally take up less space and are often restrictive (think of a girl crossing her legs at the ankle).

Parents and immediate family members are not the only responsible parties in shaping a child's gendered expressions of identity. Schools, sports, and mediated representations of children that appear on television and written and visual literature have just as much of a reinforcing effect.

Construction of Female Bodies

One of the most salient aspects of a child's gendered identity is the physical expression of that gender. Much of the communication about one's gender takes place through physical comportment and interpretations of gendered bodily displays. By embodying the physical requirements for gender, boys and girls comply with gender norms and simultaneously construct and reconstruct them. Though boys and girls are born with differences in their physical bodies, it is the construction of masculine and feminine bodies that creates a noticeable difference in the way these bodies approach sports and physical activity, rather than the bodies themselves.

Socialization of girls' bodies as less physically inclined encourages girls to physically and mentally engage in physical activity differently than boys. Young (1990) describes the difference between the way men and women move their bodies in the context of sports, describing women's use of their bodies as "a failure to make full use of the body's spatial and lateral potentialities" (p. 32). As females are socialized to physically demand less space in the world, it impacts the way they interpret their ability to physically engage with the world. "[Women] feel as though we must have our attention directed upon our bodies to make sure they are doing what we wish them to do, rather than paying attention to what we want to do *through* our bodies" (Young, 1990, p. 34). Thus, in order for a girl to be as successful at sports as boys, she must rise above any gender socialization that directs her to be *reactive* in the world and take on a more *proactive* view of herself as a subject in the world.

Women and Sports

The literature examining the effects of girls' participation in sports paints a complicated picture. The outcomes of overcoming the challenges presented by a feminine body to participate in sports are mixed. Sports can prove beneficial to a girls' identity development while also proving confusing and constraining.

Much of girls' participation in sports takes place in the context of physical education or recess that occurs in schools; only about 30% of U.S. girls participate in organized sports teams outside of school (Pedersen & Seidman, 2004). Evans (2006) focuses on schools as the site of production for gendered identities and suggests that bodies be viewed as the "product of interactions" (p. 550), meaning that boys and girls learn to perform appropriate gender norms by watching and imitating their peers.

Beyond the guidance children receive through interaction with peers, findings indicate that teachers of physical education promote a "hidden curriculum" (Apple, 1971) which (perhaps inadvertently) values competition and cardiovascular endurance as a measure of physical "fitness" (Rønholt, 2002, p. 33). What counts as physical education is increasingly associated with power, speed, strength and aggression, favoring boys over girls. Female students are often discouraged by this bias and are called out as deviant or a problem; they may begin to dislike physical activity due to its association with competitive sports (Garrett, 2004).

Cockburn and Clarke (2002) note that in order for girls to truly succeed in physical education, they must perform in ways that run counter to other aspects of their identity work which they have learned they must perform to succeed in all other aspects of their lives as females; further, they must do it in public. Rather than being passive and non-threatening in the way their bodies are positioned, participation in sports requires active participation, freedom in range of motion and staking claim over physical space.

Evans (2006) found that in mixed-sex physical education classes, girls feel pressure to portray themselves to teachers and peers as both feminine (meaning passive and attractive) and competent. In single-sex classes, the pressure from the male gaze was not absent, however, as girls internalize the male gaze and measure themselves (and each other) through a masculine lens. Girls engage in strategies to compensate for their deviations from what is expected of girls by having "double identities" or "split lives" where they separate proficiency in physical activity from narratives of femininity. Instead of integrating physical activity into their feminine identities, girls feel they must choose between the two very different versions of their identities.

Crissey & Honea (2006) note that physical activity and participation in sports have been credited with positive outcomes in terms of self-esteem and academic success for girls but also with negative outcomes including an increased focus on physical appearance. Women's role in sports is understood to be passive and quite sexualized at times (Theberge, 1987). Research indicates that girls who participate in traditionally feminine sports, such as gymnastics or dance, are more likely to feel overweight and attempt multiple weight loss strategies as compared to non-athletes as they are "more likely to encourage behaviors and practices that reinforce dominant notions of appearance, thinness, and beauty than other sports" (Crissey & Honea, 2006, p. 253).

The social construction of feminine identities is not limited to the girls themselves but extends to others who exert significant influence on the construction of their identities. On the whole, male and female children who participate in team sports are judged by their teachers to be more socially competent, less shy, and as a group no more aggressive than their non-sporting peer. Interestingly, however, when the results are disaggregated to consider girls only, those who participated in team sports *were* judged by their teachers to be more aggressive than their peers not participating in sports while the opposite was true for boys (McHale, Vinden, Bush, Richer, Shaw & Smith, 2005). Interestingly, female athletes report more misconduct in school than male athletes; the reason may be due, in part, to cultural scripts that outline appropriate female behavior. Perhaps females who misbehave also find it easier to break the feminine mold and participate in more sports (Miller, Melnick, Barnes, Farrell, & Sabo, 2005).

This is not to say that girls' participation in school sports is entirely negative by any means. Shaffer & Witties (2006) suggest that the quality of one's initial experience with sports can determine later impact on self-esteem that continued participation in physical activity will have. Research shows that for lower-class adolescent girls from racially and ethnically diverse backgrounds, achievement in team sports was a predictor of higher self-esteem in later adolescence. This increase in self-esteem is thought to be a result of the individual accomplishment combined with support and encouragement from teammates (Pedersen & Seidman, 2004). While these findings are encouraging, other research indicates that previous findings linking participation in sports with positive academic outcomes may be overstated when gender and race are considered (Miller et al., 2005).

Noting the conflict for girls between socialized expectations for femininity and the traditionally masculine characteristics required to succeed in sports, Shaffer & Witties suggest that enjoyment of sports is determined by how girls manage competing expectations for their performance. Findings from a survey of 245 college-age women asked to reflect on their pre-college participation in sports, indicate that girls who had a positive initial experience with sports benefited from increased self-esteem and those who found less enjoyment from sports were at risk for declining self-esteem. The lesson to be learned is that participation in sports may not be beneficial (and may in fact be harmful) to girls who do not experience an increase in physical competence, body image, or masculine characteristics (Shaffer & Witties, 2006).

Even when not reaping the benefits of increased self-esteem, Rønholt (2002) found evidence for girls finding their own agency in the context of physical activity. Rather than participating in a traditional sporting activity which might make girls feel weak or lacking in some way, girls sometimes actively resist or change the entire structure of physical education activities to suit their competing identity needs. Others argue, however, that by resisting full participation in physical education, girls are submitting to societal expectations of how a girl should be, which reinforces expectations of weakness in females (Cockburn & Clarke, 2002). One unmistakable conclusion does emerge from these contradictory findings: when girls are active in reshaping the structure of sporting activities, a multiplicity of femininities emerge and provide female athletes a space for their own subjectivity (Young, 1997). Physical activity may indeed have empowering and emancipatory potential for girls, especially with collective involvement of females sharing similar interests and goals.

Physicality

The above discussion demonstrates females' participation in sports is fraught with implications for the construction of gendered bodies and identities. Physicality is a term that has been used to describe the embodied experience of participation in sports. Though lacking a clear conceptual definition, physicality has been understood, "at its most basic level, as how one experiences oneself physically" (McDermott, 1996, p. 16). The dominant narratives surrounding physicality however, construct a masculine understanding of the word.

> Due to existing cultural beliefs, ultimately, a self-fulfilling prophecy is apt to occur whereby physicality, because it has taken on a gender disposition, is associated only with men. Given this interpretation, sports-feminist analyses have identified physicality as a central aspect of the oppression of women within the context of sports and physical activity (McDermott, 1996, p. 14)

Beyond simply excluding females, the consequences for such a gendered interpretation of this concept result in a conceptualization of physicality that values "aggressive bodily usage, bodily contact, and confrontation" required for participation in a sports (p. 14).

Given the masculine connotation of physicality and the lack of a clear conceptual definition, McDermott capitalized on the opportunity to clearly define physicality in a way that celebrates feminine qualities of sports as much as masculine. Through her reconceptualization, McDermott (2000) defines physicality as "the complex interplay of body perception, agency and self-perception" (p. 331). In this definition, self-perception refers to an individual's understanding of her own ability to successfully participate in physical activity as well as the perception of her body as a reason for engagement in physical activity.

McDermott and others understand a redefinition of physicality as an opportunity to identify conditions in which new conceptualizations of sports can result in a redefinition of femininity as strong and empowered. Sports are an important place for efforts to transform notions of power from a masculine conceptualization, to one focused on capacity, which allows both sexes to "strive together" in competition and engage in activities which bring out the best in one another, rather than dehumanizing the opponent (Theberge, 1987). "By challenging each other to demonstrate certain skills, by calling out the best in each other, sports can be an ennobling process" (Birrell & Slatton, 1981, p. 4).

The following study proceeds from a communicative perspective on sports and children's play to explore how young girls embody adult narratives of femininity. Discourses surrounding girls' physical activity reflect the social norms and expectations for adult women.

Methods

Over the course of two seasons I volunteered as coach for a local RFYL team and collected data as a full participant. In addition to my participation as the coach of one team, I traveled to five other sites where the program was being implemented, to observe the interactions between the girls and their coaches. Through my participation and observations I was able to get a sense of the sanctioned organizational messages and how they ostensibly taught girls to be feminine while participating in sports. Finally, I conducted interviews with the coaches of several local teams to glean what they thought were the important messages communicated by RFYL and what their goals were for the girls.

In total, I spent over 60 hours collecting data and had contact with more than 20 adult participants in the organization. Between the RFYL curriculum, field notes from my observations, and interview transcripts, I accumulated approximately 520 single-spaced pages of data for analysis. My research was guided by a desire to understand the explicit messages communicated directly by the program and the implicit messages that resulted from the specific ways girls were positioned as a result of the intervention. My analysis reveals some of the key tensions that characterize feminine identity development for girls who participate in sports.

Findings and Interpretations

In an effort to parallel the process of socialization for girls in early childhood, RFYL aims to resocialize girls to experience their bodies in more physically empowering ways. RFYL demonstrates what physicality can come to mean if it is reconceptualized away from traditionally masculine connotations. Accordingly, in its explicit messages, the RFYL program emphasizes energy and movement and striving together for excellence instead of competition, speed, and winning.

While a majority of the coaches who volunteer for the program adhere to the mission of RFYL by helping girls explore their bodies in noncompetitive ways, there are those coaches who feel that girls are best served by developing their ability to compete. Interestingly these perspectives differently position girls/women to either emulate masculinity and "play the game" or to change the rules and value a more collaborative and cooperative style of interaction. Either approach illustrates the challenge of embodying resistance in ways that are not later reappropriated by traditional narratives of femininity.

Explicit Messages

Though it is not outwardly expressed in the curriculum, coaches learn through training sessions (and interaction with veteran coaches) that RFYL is completely noncompetitive in nature. Running and other exercises are never set up as a competition among the girls, only as a call for each girl's own best effort. Illustrating this noncompetitive orientation, one coach makes it a point to compliment the girls on one of their strengths as they complete each lap, telling them "I like the way you are pumping your arms" or that "it looks like you have really found your pace!" After the girls complete the workout, the head coach on my team would also try to praise the girls for what they excelled at as a team that day. The following excerpt from my field notes shows an example from late in the season when the girls had lost their sense of team unity, and their coach was trying to reestablish a connection among them:

> [The coach] asks the girls to get in a circle and hold hands—something we don't usually do. "This is your team," she says. "There's a reason we train together, because we need to support each other. We practice together because you all can help each other."

The RFYL program stresses teamwork and cooperation in an effort to achieve goals. Instead of competing with each another, the girls on a team encourage one another to perform their best. Running is simply a medium for girls to come to know their physical selves as strong, rather than experiencing their bodies as weak or awkward or something that stands in the way of their success. A girl's performance is never directly compared with anyone else's on the team, though there are physical indicators, such as lap counters, of what she has accomplished.

Physicality in Practice

RFYL focuses specifically on girls' bodies, which are often portrayed by family members, teachers, peers and the media as obstacles to overcome or sources of passivity and weakness, in contrast to boys' bodies which are seen as a resource for achieving success. Female bodies are generally characterized by deficit or liability (Young, 1990; Trethewey, 1999) as they are seen to be weak, leaky, and overly emotional, as opposed to male bodies, which are assumed to be adroit, strong, and skilled (Theberge, 1987).

In the space of the program under study, however, the communication surrounding girls' bodies demonstrates opportunities for empowerment. "The centrality of the body to athletic experience makes sports an important site for feminist efforts to transform power" (Theberge, 1987, p. 390). A stated goal of the RFYL is to change the way women and girls understand their bodies and they way these bodies interact in the world. Rather than serving as the focus of critique and criticism, girls are taught how to keep their bodies physically healthy and strong in order to overcome challenges and reach their full potential. Sports and physical activity are introduced to the girls as a way to come to know themselves physically, as an opportunity to embody what it means to be a strong female.

The talk among coaches and girls reflects the idea that training to run a long distance is meant to be a metaphor for overcoming any challenge they might face in their lives as demonstrated in the following field note:

> Kerry puts her arms around Raine, pulls her head in close and says, "Remember what we said in math class?" She whispers in her ear, "If you can run a 5K, you can do anything."

Using their bodies to work through a challenge allows the girls to feel what it is like to face a difficult situation and succeed in overcoming it.

In RFYL, the ideal female body is one that is physically, emotionally, socially, and spiritually sound. In addition to physical activity, the 10- to 12-week curriculum demonstrates healthy living in all areas of the girls' lives including strategies to keep their bodies, minds, emotions and relationships with others in healthy balance. The danger of such a broad focus is the potential for this degree of attentiveness to one's self to engender a need for strict control and discipline, which has always characterized the female body. Most of the messages aimed at girls about femininity ask girls and women to change their bodies to fit a certain ideal or norm, but program creators are careful to ensure this is not the case with RFYL.

However, transformation *is* central to the success of this program. But what is perhaps most unique about RFYL is that it does not ask girls to change their bodies at all—instead it asks them to change their *understanding* of their physical selves and their identities as girls thriving within those bodies. The curriculum directly addresses the mediated messages that target girls by teaching girls to be critical consumers of the messages they see. Rather than buying into the idea that girls must work on themselves to fit the ideal, girls are taught to question the goals of such messages and who benefits from them. Thus, rather than girls accepting the call to engage in physical activity as a way to achieve an ideal body, the program encourages girls find their own reasons for running.

Resistance and Reappropriation

As children enter school, they experience an intense interest in gender and gender roles (Stangor & Ruble, 1989); at the same time, increased exposure to mediated representations of men and women facilitate children's knowledge of these roles. One of the reasons that RFYL and programs like it target young girls is to take advantage of this critical time in the development of their gendered identities. Not only are elementary school age children hungry for information about gender-appropriate behaviors, but they are inundated with messages that teach and reinforce gendered ways of being. As children watch more television, their conceptions of gender roles become more traditional; women are portrayed as being most happy inside the home while men are seen as more ambitious (Freuh & McGhee, 1975; Morgan, 1987).

Perhaps the largest obstacle for resistance programs such as RFYL is the social environment in which they take place. For three hours a week, girls can find solace in the supportive messages communicated to them about their bodies, yet the rest of their time is spent in "the real world" where they are inundated with messages about femininity. And for the most part these media messages run counter to the supportive acceptance they receive through the context of RFYL. While the program itself steers clear of promoting the prototypical notion of beauty, the issue at stake is the degree to which organized resistance is reappropriated by dominant social narratives about femininity to construct mandates for a woman's body to be fit and adhere to a narrow construction of what is sexually attractive. Though running is presented to girls as a source of strength and empowerment, competing messages can confuse girls' interpretation of what is being communicated. Outside of this program, the dominant narratives that surround girls depicts physical activity as a way to lose weight and attain the ideal female shape, which is increasingly thin and sexualized.

For many of the girls who do not like to run, or find it particularly difficult, the combination of messages from RFYL and from their social environment (including friends and family members) can seem like another form of discipline. When running gets tough, some of the girls voice their dislike of running. In this situation, though they are pushing themselves to work through a challenge, their bodies feel pain and exhaustion and once again they experience their bodies as weak and unfit for the challenge, instead of as a tool for achievement. No matter how supportive and accepting the program intends to be, the messages communicated by RFYL and those communicated outside of the program blend together to construct a reality for girls where the reason for participating in physical activity is to conform to expectations about a woman's body.

In this case girls' play is co-opted by larger cultural narratives about what it means to be a girl, and girls must shift their focus from being children at play to adult women in training. As quickly as girls are given the space to try on new empowering feminine identities, these efforts are co-opted by larger cultural narratives in ways that discipline and constrain girls.

Competition and Sports

Competition is another narrative by which sports and physical activity are framed. Running is especially prone to characterization as competition. Children do not have a model of running that is not tied up in either exercise or competition. Trying to keep the competition out of running is a challenge. Typically, as a culture, we associate running with a race, especially as experienced by younger children, who may only run through school events or in competition with peers. Children are involved in track meets, or impromptu races against one another, but rarely do we ever encourage running for the sake of running, for its physical health benefits and the opportunity to use one's body in a positive way. RFYL provides girls with an opportunity to positively experience themselves physically, to know themselves by more than how they look, but by how they move and act on their own terms (not by what others tell them is appropriate).

It is because girls feel inept at using their bodies that RFYL takes a noncompetitive approach. Rather than emphasizing the weaknesses in a girl's body, the purpose of the program is to empower girls *through* the use of their bodies. Though most of the coaches are fully on board with a noncompetitive approach, there are a few that believe the girls should be taught how to successfully compete. One coach even explained that she joined the organization because she thought it offered healthy competition as a main focus for the girls.

These two very different approaches (helping girls explore their bodies in non-competitive ways versus teaching girls to be competitive) are being explored as possibilities for women to achieve equality with men. Interestingly, they position girls/women in different ways, by either learning how to emulate masculinity and join "the game" or change the rules and value each person's unique contribution.

The same message can be communicated to the girls if a larger focus is placed on goal setting. One coach explained that she and the women she coached with had turned their focus to goal setting, which allowed them to talk about (not) reaching goals and revising behavior to help attain a goal, saying in an interview:

> It kind of empowers the girls to um, be successful because every girl can basically work and achieve that goal and then they learn that gosh, if I can do a 5K, I can do math... you know, I can be a scientist. You know, it's... it's daily work, it's just putting one step in front of the other. (Head Coach, Goodwin Elementary)

In eschewing competition, RFYL attempts to embrace a very different narrative of running for girls. Perhaps by channeling revised notions of physicality, RFYL presents running as an opportunity for mutual achievement and success. On the first day of practice, girls are taught explicit messages of support for their fellow teammates and encouraged by coaches to communicate those messages throughout the season. As the season progressed, it was nearly impossible to pass a girl or be passed without hearing "keep it up," "nice job," "way to go," or other similar words of encouragement.

The RFYL training manual instructs coaches to teach the girls supportive behavior as it relates to expressing encouragement, gratitude, and positivity. In addition, many of the lessons required girls to work together to complete tasks. In one lesson, girls were split into teams and given a total number of laps to run as a team. It was up to the girls how many laps each team member ran and it did not matter how many each individual completed, so long as the team completed the entire amount. As girls completed the group activity, the coaches on the team asked the girls to go back out on the course to cheer on their teammates who were still running. Far from promoting competition, the structure of the program emphasizes success as a part of a team over individual achievement.

Though RFYL attempts to completely eliminate competition from its program, there is almost no way to do so. The coaches teach the girls to be supportive of one another and to measure their success in terms of their own progress, but the following excerpt from my field notes demonstrates that the girls still bring outside narratives of competition into the practices:

> At some point in the drills, I notice that Tonya is just running back and forth and not really completing the exercise. I yell ahead to her "hey those aren't lunges!" and I hear her say that she had to beat Krista. When the girls take off for the final sprint on their toes, Tonya and Krista and Amelia are all racing. I don't see who finished first, but I can hear them talking about who won.

Despite the program's emphasis on teamwork over individual achievement, competition did arise spontaneously among the girls. The girls who were the fastest or that ran the most laps were proud of themselves and often expressed their excitement by telling coaches or other girls how much they accomplished. It is understandable that these girls wanted to be validated for how well they had done, and at the same time, as a coach, I was afraid that it might make the slower girls feel inferior. It was a difficult balance to be supportive of the girl who has just run 15 laps in a way that did not belittle the girl next to her who was struggling to complete six laps.

While most of the coaches agree with a non-competitive approach, the following excerpt from an interview demonstrated that some still voiced a desire for girls to engage in competition in the same way that boys do.

> I believe that if we can teach girls how to be competitive in sports, they can be more successful in life. You know, and so that was my whole goal was that competition. But RFYL is not at all about competition. (Assistant Coach, Goodwin Elementary)

Rather than eliminating competition to create a level playing field for girls, this coach believed that the experience of competition was key for their future success. In this example, described in an interview with an assistant coach, competition provides a space for evaluation of one's own behaviors to understand past performances and improve future ones:

> You know, you set a goal today to run 10 laps; ok well you didn't make it. Well that's ok, but why didn't you make it? And who did make it and why did she make it? Not that she's better than you, but what did she do different[ly]? Did she eat a better lunch than you today? Did she drink water? Did she go to bed earlier? What did she do dif-

ferent[ly] that helped her achieve her goals and you didn't achieve yours? And is it important to you? (Assistant Coach, Goodwin Elementary)

What is also present in this view of competition, however, is the social comparison that comes with winning and losing. When competition is introduced into sports, individual performance only has meaning in comparison to others. Though the individual may feel good (or bad) about her own performance, this internal assessment is overshadowed by the performance of others.

Interestingly, the coach who did speak at length about the value of competition framed it as a way for girls to be on a level playing field with boys. "And my feeling about competition is that...and the reason that women lag behind men is just because men know how to compete and they know when the game is over, the game is over, right?"

The underlying assumption in this reasoning is that for men and women to be equal, women must conform to male standards. Masculinity is understood as the standard, to which the other gender should conform. When this argument is extended out into adult narratives of work and social interaction, it positions femininity as deficient when compared to masculinity. Thus, as Trethewey (1999) explains, women learn that in order to realize the same success as men, they must communicate a masculine demeanor, which includes eliminating any evidence of femininity in order to adhere to masculine bodily comportment.

Implications for Adult Identities

The debate over the value of competition for girls then becomes one of acting in compliance with the current structure or trying to break free from it. In the context of sports, it seems that girls must decide between "playing the game" by conforming to masculine standards of competition or totally disengage from competition and participate in ways that emphasize cooperation and teamwork. Each of these paths, however, reveals its own consequences for gendered identities.

By engaging in competition and learning to "play the game," women and men reinforce socialization into masculine ways of being as more valuable. The masculine again becomes the standard by which any person is measured, no matter her gender. Organizational discourses privilege masculinity in ways that "other" femininity and position it as less desirable. Women and men who do not conform to the masculine standard are seen as deficient.

This does not mean that the answer is as simple as rejecting competition altogether. When girls' sports shun competition and instead embrace models of teamwork and social support, they have the potential to essentialize feminine behavior and inadvertently reinforce the gender stereotypes that naturalize women as nurturers, which ultimately holds girls and women back. It is no secret that in organizations, women typically fulfill the support roles, while the leadership roles are occupied by men (Holmes, 2006). Women's encouragement and support of others often lands them less competitive jobs (Holmes, 2006), a second-rate income (Babcock & Laschever, 2007), and a greater number of responsibilities in the private sphere (Hochschild & Machung, 2003). Not only are support roles overwhelmingly occupied by women, but so is care work, which has been shown to lead to burnout in jobs (Tracy, 2008) and puts females at higher risk for anxiety and depression (Hinshaw & Kranz, 2009).

Conclusion

Women are constantly under scrutiny for how they embody the many social roles that constitute their identities; as mother, worker, or athlete, they must position themselves differently according to what is seen as appropriate for that role. The feminine subject is not the standard or the default (Acker, 1990), rather it is cast as "other" and requires discipline to minimize difference that is considered inherently problematic (Trethewey, 1999). When women deviate from what is expected of them, especially in their outward physical expressions, they are socially reprimanded (Cockburn & Clarke, 2002; Evans, 2006). Not only do women subject themselves to practices of cosmetics, dress, bodily comportment and even surgery in order to shape their femininity into acceptable expressions, they police one another into reproducing the disciplinary practices which subordinate them. Drawing on Tarvis (1992), Trethewey explains, "those disciplinary practices pit women against one another and drain time and energy" (1999, p. 425). The competition that many feel characterizes women's relationships with one another as antagonistic may be explained by their internalization of the disciplinary practices exerted on women and their regulation of other women in the same way.

Though the curriculum does not directly address the cattiness that often exemplifies the popular narrative for girls' relationships with one another, it does instruct the girls to outwardly encourage their teammates and includes lessons on cooperation and sportsmanship. In this way, girls are taught a different model for how to interact with other girls. An interview with one coach revealed her own positive affect toward the women she had come to know through the program:

> I love how this program reminds all of us women and also as coaches who we really are. It's just a real bonding experience, I think, for the women. And um, that's nice for women, I think, to have um, to be among women who are so supportive and nurturing of them. (Head Coach, Alcott Elementary)

In the RFYL environment, girls and women seem to internalize liking and support of their fellow coaches, embracing difference among them rather than policing one another to correctly appropriate a certain model of femininity. In this way, they provide a model for organizing according to feminist principles that resists the surveillance-based disciplinary practices so common in other contexts.

While this program represents progress, girls still find themselves in a double bind. Girls must choose whether to reinforce the value of masculine ways of being by engaging in competition and learning to succeed through this model, or risk constructions of femininity that are devalued and result in their own subordination by breaking free and enacting their own feminine standards.

References

Acker, J. (1990). Hierarchies, jobs, bodies: A theory of gendered organizations. *Gender and Society*, 4, 139–158.

Apple, M. W. (1971). The hidden curriculum and the nature of conflict. *Interchange* 2 (4), 27–40.

Babcock, L. & Laschever, S. (2007). *Women don't ask: The high cost of avoiding negotiation—and positive strategies for change*. New York: Bantam Dell.

Birrell, S. & Slatton, B. (1981). The embarrassment of competition: Why feminists avoid sports. Paper presented at the annual meetings of the North American Society for the Sociology of Sports.

Butler, J. (1997). *The psychic life of power*. Stanford, CA: Stanford University Press.

Cockburn, C., & Clarke, G. (2002). "Everybody's looking at you!": Girls negotiating the "femininity deficit" they incur in physical education. *Women's Studies International Forum*, 25(6), 651–666.

Crissey, S. R., & Honea, J. C. (2006). The relationship between athletic participation and perceptions of body size and weight control in adolescent girls: The role of sports type. *Sociology of Sports Journal, 23*(3), 248-272.

du Gay, p. (1996). *Consumption and identity at work*. London: Sage.

du Gay, P. (2007). *Persons and organizations 'after theory'*. London: Sage.

Eisenberg, E. (2007). *Strategic ambiguities: Essays on communication, organization, and identity*. Thousand Oaks, CA: Sage Publications.

Evans, B. (2006). 'I'd feel ashamed': Girls' bodies and sports participation. *Gender, Place and Culture: A Journal of Feminist Geography, 13*(5), 547-561.

Freuh, T. & McGhee, P. E. (1975). Traditional sex-role development and amount of time spent watching television. *Developmental Psychology, 11,* 109.

Garrett, R. (2004). Negotiating a physical identity: Girls, bodies and physical education. *Sports, Education & Society, 9*(2), 223-237.

Hinshaw, S. & Kranz, R. (2009). *The triple bind: Saving our teenage girls from today's pressures*. New York: Ballantine Books.

Hochschild, A. R. & Machung, A. (2003). *The second shift*. London: Penguin Books.

Holmes, J. (2006). *Gendered talk at work*. Malden, MA: Blackwell Publishing.

McDermott, L. (1996). Toward a feminist understanding of physicality within the context of women's physically active and sporting lives. *Sociology of Sports Journal, 13*, 12-30.

McDermott, L. (2000). A qualitative assessment of the significance of body perception to women's physical activity experience: Revisiting discussions of physicalities. *Sociology of Sports Journal, 17*, 331-363.

McHale, J. P., Vinden, P. G., Bush, L., Richer, D., Shaw, D., & Smith, B. (2005). Patterns of personal and social adjustment among sports-involved and noninvolved urban middle-school children. *Sociology of Sports Journal, 22* (2), 119-137.

Miller, L., & Penz, O. (1991). Talking bodies: Female body-builders colonize a male preserve. *Quest, 43*, 148-163.

Miller, K.; Melnick, M.; Barnes, G.; Farrell, M.; and Sabo, D. (2005). Untangling the links among athletic involvement, gender, race, and adolescent academic outcomes. *Sociology of Sports Journal, 22*(2), 178-194.

Morgan, M. (1987). Television, sex role attitudes and sex role behavior. *Journal of Early Adolescence, 7*, 269-282.

Nadesan, M. H., & Trethewey, A. (2000). Performing the enterprising subject: Gendered strategies of success (?) *Text and Performance Quarterly, 20,* 223–250.

Pedersen, S., & Seidman, E. (2004). Team sports achievement and self-esteem development among urban adolescent girls. *Psychology of Women Quarterly, 28*(4), 412–422.

Rønholt, H. (2002). 'It's only the sissies ...': Analysis of teaching and learning processes in physical education: A contribution to the hidden curriculum. *Sport, Education, & Society, 7*(1), 25–36.

Shaffer, D. R., & Witties, E. (2006). Women's precollege sports participation, enjoyment of sports, and self-esteem. *Sex Roles, 55*(3/4), 225–232.

Stangor, C. & Ruble, D. N. (1989). Differential influences of gender schemata and gender constancy on children's information processing and behavior. *Social Cognition, 7,* 353–372.

Tarvis, C. (1992). *The mismeasure of woman.* New York: Simon & Schuster.

Theberge, N. (1987). Sports and women's empowerment. *Women's Studies International Forum, 10*(4), 387–393.

Tracy, S. J. (2008). Emotion and communication in organizations. *International Communication Association Encyclopedia.* International Communication Association.

Trethewey, A. (1997). Resistance, identity, and empowerment: A postmodern feminist analysis of clients in a human service organization. *Communication Monographs, 64,* 281–301.

Trethewey, A. (1999). Disciplined bodies. *Organization Studies, 20,* 423–450.

Young, I. M. (1990). *Throwing like a girl and other essays in feminist philosophy and social theory.* Bloomington, IN: Indiana University Press.

Young, K. (1997). Short communication: Women, sports and physicality. *International Review for the Sociology of Sports, 32*(3), 297–305.

SECTION THREE

Play, Ethics, and Morality

Chapter Nine

Constructing Good and Evil at the "Happiest Place on Earth"

Matt Omasta

Introduction

The Walt Disney Company, as a producer of mass media for young people, acts as a cultural pedagogue; its products influence children's ideologies and attitudes throughout their lives. Scholars[1] and company executives[2] alike have opined that the narratives the company produces shape the minds of young people around the world. Walt Disney himself viewed children as Lockean *tabulae rasae*, and once explained: "I think of a child's mind as a blank book. During the first years of his life, much will be written on the pages. The quality of that writing will affect his life profoundly" (as cited in Giroux, 1999, p. 17). In this chapter, I explore how select attractions at the Disneyland Resort in Anaheim, California seem to "write" particular narratives for the children who visit the park.[3]

In his introduction to this volume, Chappell (2010) introduces the concept of "colonizing the imaginary," defined as: "an ideological process in which [adult art makers] write their own culturally bound values, beliefs, and ideas onto narrative structures and performances intended for children's consumption" (p. 11). I argue that Disney serves as one such "colonizer" and investigate how the company has "written" its ideologies into particular attractions. Specifically, I note how these attractions construct binaries of good

---

1   See, among many others: Brode (2005), Byrne & McQuillan (1999), DeCordova (1994), Fjellman (1992), Giroux (1999), Pinsky (2004), and Wasko (2005).
2   Former Disney CEO Michael Eisner once claimed that American media companies like Disney were responsible for the dismantlement of the Berlin Wall and the fall of Eastern Communism. (Giroux, 1999, p. 28).
3   While scholars have composed many volumes analyzing Disney's films, television programs, and other consumables, less has been said about the company's theme parks (a lengthy exception is Fjellman's 1992 work, which discussed every attraction in the Florida parks open at that time).

and evil and teach young people "correct" behaviors and identities by structuring their behavior as they engage playfully with Disney's creations. My analysis relies on critical interpretation of the empirical artifacts available to young visitors both before and during their trips, ranging from descriptions of attractions on the Disneyland website to narrations, images, and experiences within the park.

At the outset of this study, I experienced almost every attraction at Disneyland, then selected four particular attractions for closer analysis: "Pinocchio's Daring Journey," *Fantasmic!*, the "Buzz Lightyear Astro Blasters," and the "Innoventions Dream Home." The first criterion that informed my selection was children's access to the attractions; each of these experiences welcomes all park guests without discriminating by age or height. Further, the opening dates of these attractions range from the early 1980s to 2008, allowing me to explore how the company's ideological messages have changed over time. Finally, while no subset of attractions can be said to fully or authentically represent all of Disneyland's offerings, these four represent a diverse cross-section of experiences, including a traditional dark ride, a walk-through exhibit, an interactive game, and a stage show.

I have divided this chapter into three sections. I begin by discussing the theoretical frameworks that guide my analysis and then provide a narrative ride/walk-through of each experience, discussing the roles they construct for children and their ideological implications. I conclude by considering how young people might attempt to resist the narratives Disney offers.

Theoretical Frameworks

I draw primarily from four theoretical concepts to navigate the attractions detailed in this chapter and understand how they might impact young people. I argue that Disney exerts *hegemonic* power because many people treat the company's theme parks as *sacralized space*. I consider what *roles* the attractions call upon children to *embody*, and I explore how each creates *binary oppositions* of good and evil, frequently by employing *melodrama*. I also utilize Stephen Fjellman's theories *of de- and re-contextualization* to consider how attractions manipulate young people's extant understandings of phenomena.

Hegemony and Sacralized Space

The Disney canon conjures something akin to a "sacred" aura around the company. At times, its evocations of faith are overt, for example its "frequent, almost pervasive use of a theological vocabulary...words such as *faith, believe, miracle, blessing, sacrifice* and *divine*" (Pinsky, 2004, p. 1). Other times, the company links to the sacred realm more implicitly by evoking an assumed connection to childhood innocence. As DeCordova (1994) noted:

> Something like a sacred connection exists between Mickey Mouse and idealized childhood. However, as the occasional early references to Mickey's vulgarity attest, the connection was by no means natural or unproblematic. It was the result of a particular historical work. (p. 203)

This "particular historical work" includes Disney's deliberate efforts to revise its past and control its present and future through careful brand management adjusted to meet contemporary social standards. For example, few children today are aware that Mickey used to carry a shotgun or that Pluto has been drunk on moonshine.

If Disney constitutes a secular religion, Disneyland serves as a key house of worship. Writers have referred to the company's theme parks as "the Vatican with Mouse ears," "America's Sistine Chapel," a "playful pilgrimage center," and the staging grounds for a "morality play" (see Pinsky, 2004, pp. 229-230). Newcomb (2003) argued that visitors to Disney's parks treat them as "sacralized space":

> Ordered, organized space for the thoughtful, selective construction of social meaning and the mutual exercise of symbolic power, initiated in the creation of environment and experienced through ritualized activities and spatial movement, resulting in the recovery of the past and the possibility of a transformed future. (p. vi)

He noted that "things are sacralized in as much as they are intentionally set apart and invested with meaning by people" (Newcomb, 2003, p. 25). That is, people sacralize a space when they view it as sacred, engage in ritualized activity such as structured play, and use it to construct or interpret meaning. Millions of visitors do all these things during their pilgrimages to Disneyland, constantly marking the park as sacred by treating it as such.

Two important by-products of Disney's pseudo-sacred nature are that (1) it shrouds the company in a veil of innocence, assuring guests that they can trust any messages it presents, and (2) it actively discourages critical interrogation from investigators outside the company, including academics and the popular press. The company's ideologies thus escape criticism on two levels. First, visitors to the park are disarmed by the park's evocation of nostalgic virtuosity, reducing their resistance to the narratives presented there. Secondly, scholars and other writers who do attempt to challenge the company's teachings are often ignored at best or lambasted at worst.[4]

Visitors who treat Disneyland as a sacred space enter into a hegemonic relationship with the company; that is, they willingly consent to the dominance of Disney's ideologies and, through play in the park, participate in the reproduction of these values and beliefs. When Gramsci introduced the concept of hegemony, he observed that dominant regimes maintain their rule through both military force and ideological control. Those in power rely on a group of people who have earned the public's trust to serve as their "'deputies' exercising the subaltern functions of social hegemony."[5] These deputies work to ensure that the "great masses of the population" give their "'spontaneous' consent...to the general direction imposed on social life by the dominant fundamental group" (Gramsci, 2004, p. 673). Today, however, the Disney company serves simultaneously as a member of the "dominant group" (multinational corporate conglomerates) and as that group's "deputy," earning public goodwill and thus the ability to enforce ideological control without force.[6] Because "Disney products typically become a part of every child's life in one form or another, [Disney is] intimately and strongly associated with childhood and retain[s] a special place in people's memories of childhood" (Wasko, 2005, p. 222). These trust-building links to childhood allow the company to exert social control through "cultural hegemony," defined by Bruce McConachie as a process that "works primarily through legitimation, the half-conscious acceptance of the norms of behavior and the categories of knowledge generated by social institutions, public activities, and popular rituals viewed as 'normal' by the people whose actions they shape" (as cited in Chappell, 2008, p. 24).

---

4 For accounts of public resistance to critical scholarship of Disney, see Bell, Haas, & Sells (1995), Giroux (1995), or Wasko, Phillips & Meehan (2001), who noted that "taking a critical stance towards the company that has created the happiest place on earth may be considered overly pessimistic, not to say downright un-American" (p. 3).
5 Gramsci argued "the intellectuals" played this role during his time.
6 Though in some instances, the Disney company also controls "the apparatus of state coercive power which 'legally' enforces discipline" (Gramsci, 2004, p. 673). For example, the Florida State Legislature granted the company de facto authority (via the Reedy Creek Improvement District) to create a police force.

Roles and Embodiment

Just as actors on stage perform particular roles for their audience members, people perform a variety of roles for the others they encounter in their daily lives. Since its inception, the Disneyland Resort has branded itself the "Happiest Place on Earth." With this simple claim, the resort's "marketeers" have constructed an identity for guests who visit the Anaheim park: they are, in a word: happy. Visitors to the park become characters in a grand narrative as they interact with park employees (appropriately called "cast members") and attractions. Children adopt or "buy into" the role of "happy park guest" to various degrees: some conform and perform joyfulness throughout their stay; others resist and deliberately antagonize the dominant narrative, and many adapt the role as they see fit. All park guests will likely modify their "characters" several times throughout their visit.

While the "happy guest" is a macro-level role the Disney Company hopes children will adopt, the various attractions and themed spaces throughout the park each offer distinct identities for their young guests to perform. The "*Indiana Jones* Adventure" explicitly frames riders as adventurous explorers accompanying Indiana Jones's friends on an expedition through the Temple of Doom. "Star Tours," based on the *Star Wars* movies, tells guests that they are intergalactic tourists embarking on a pleasant journey to Endor to visit the Ewoks. At the "Mad Tea Party," inspired by *Alice in Wonderland*, children become guests at a un-birthday party with Alice, the Mad Hatter, and a drunken dormouse.

Schechner's concept of "restored behavior" offers one way to understand how humans enact roles in their everyday lives. He defined restored behaviors as "'me behaving as if I were someone else,' or 'as I am told to do,' or 'as I have learned.' Even if I feel myself wholly to be myself, acting independently, only a little investigation reveals that the units of behavior that comprise 'me' were not invented by 'me'" (Schechner, 2002 p. 28). Disney offers its guests many different "scripts" to "rehearse" throughout their vacations. Carlson (2004) noted that "from the point of view of the performer, restored behavior involves behaving as if one is someone else or even oneself in other states of feeling or being" (p. 47). Accordingly, in the sections below, I argue that Disneyland attractions call upon visitors to perform in both of these ways: as other entities and as themselves in some other state, as they play in the park.

Some attractions, including stage shows, may not seem to ask guests to take on roles, instead encouraging more passive engagement. However, since Plato developed his concept of mimesis, many theorists have believed that audience members embody roles simply by observing performances. Plato might argue that when we experience Disney content, "we enjoy it and give ourselves over to it. We suffer along with the hero and take his sufferings seriously" (Plato, 2004, p. 310). Similarly, Chappell (2010), following Schechner and Turner, notes in his introduction that

> even when not asked to take on the physical aspects of a character, a [person] still engages in embodiment. Observers, audience members, and attentive learners exist in a *liminal* state...those in this state are open to ideological (re)formation, coming out of the experience changed by what they have been through. (p. 7, emphasis in original)

That is, park guests embody roles and adopt their ideologies even when they appear to be passive spectators.

I examine Disneyland attractions that opened across several decades to consider how the company's presentation of social roles has changed over time. Lee (2001) argued that due to changing economic circumstances, adults and children have shifted from having a sense of stable roles to perform in everyday life to a more flexible plurality of roles. He noted that until the mid-twentieth century social roles were generally stable in terms of both employment (many people could expect to work one job for life) and romantic relationships (it was often assumed that marriage should last "forever"). Adults passed their social roles on to their children, perpetuating a family's role over multiple generations. However, Lee (2001) argued that in today's "flexible 'new economy'...one's geographical location, one's employment status, one's range of skills and, above all, one's self-identity now remain open to change" (p. 17). Thus, we might expect attractions developed at Disneyland during its early decades to offer singular and stable roles for visitors while more contemporary attractions offer a plurality of possible roles.

Binary Oppositions and Melodrama

Walt Disney once said: "The important thing is to teach a child that good can always triumph over evil, and that is what our pictures attempt to do" (as cited in Pinsky, 2004, p. 2). Disney offered a binary opposition of "good" versus "evil" that his company's attractions continue to manifest today. By presenting good and evil as dichotomous terms, Disney suggested they were mutually exclusive: all characters are good or bad; all choices are either right or wrong;

there are no in-betweens. As with most binaries, Disney consistently privileges the left-hand term ("good" or "right"). In the sections that follow, I explore how Disneyland's attractions perpetuate the idea that all people, things, and ideas can be firmly located in opposing camps of "good" or "evil." Just as scholars have exposed the problematic nature of false binaries such as "male/female" or "white/other," I consider how Disney employs this logical fallacy to promote particular ideologies for its guests who play in its theme parks.

Disneyland's attractions produce binaries so consistently in part because they rely on the melodramatic form.[7] Meyer (1999) defined melodrama as a heightened and highly stylized performance form,

> primarily concerned with situation and plot with little regard for convincing motivation, that calls upon mimed action extensively, employing a more or less fixed complement of stock characters, the most important of which are a suffering heroine or hero, a persecuting villain, and a benevolent comic.

Many Disney attractions employ melodrama, the simplified form of which polarizes issues so completely that it releases audiences from the "burdens" of thinking and critical discernment.

De-/Re-Contextualization

In his comprehensive review of Walt Disney World, Fjellman (1992) argued that one of Disney's most effective strategies for manipulation of meaning is its systematic de-contextualization of entities and phenomena. Disney removes them—connotations attached—from the places we expect to find them, and places them in new, often improbable contexts.[8] He noted:

> By pulling meanings out of their contexts and repackaging them in bounded informational packets, decontextualization makes it difficult for people to maintain a coherent understanding about how things work. Meanings become all jumbled together— separate in that all are abstracted from their different environments and equal in that their packaging destroys any sense of scale by which they could be measured against each other. Differences are glossed over, and 'differences that make a difference,' as Gregory Bateson puts it, are neutralized. (Fjellman, 1992, p. 31)

---

7   Or, perhaps Disney employs the melodramatic form *because* it produces binaries so efficaciously.
8   Perhaps Fjellman's best example is the "American Adventure" production's unproblematic depiction of a series of conversations between Benjamin Franklin and Mark Twain; the latter was born some forty-five years after Franklin's death.

For an example of de-/re-contextualization in action, consider "Soarin' Over California," an attraction that simulates the experience of hang-gliding over California. Riders soar seamlessly through more than ten disparate locations including the Napa Valley, the Golden Gate Bridge, and San Francisco. They fly over a golf course in La Quinta where they are almost hit by an errant ball, and finally travel just above Disneyland during the Christmas Parade, which heads down Main Street as evening's fireworks show erupts above. The ride begins in bright daylight, fades to dusk, and ends at night, giving the illusion of continuous travel and drawing attention away from the impossibility of gliding hundreds of miles in minutes. Although most guests who take a moment to think about the ride realize that it does not represent "reality," riders who are unfamiliar with Californian geography could leave with the impression that the various locations depicted are in close proximity. They might leave with the impression that the nightly parade features fireworks (it does not) or even recall having seen such a sight when they discuss their trip with friends back home. The attraction also splices clips of recreational activities such as kayaking or hot-air ballooning with images of Air Force Thunderbirds, wrapping together experiences of peaceful relaxation and military force. All are given approximately equal screen time, indicating we should pay no more attention to one than the other; perhaps all of these representations are more or less equally Californian and thus American. The attraction suggests that, at the very least, they all belong together.

In the following sections, I note how other Disneyland attractions consistently de-/re-contextualize both the company's own trademarks and other symbols in order to create particular visions of the world, its peoples, and constructs of good and evil. Fjellman (1992) offered a convincing rationale for why Disney utilizes such techniques:

> Control of contexts...is a very useful thing. It can make the arrangement and labeling of features inside these contexts seem reasonable and inevitable. One can pull features apart from their normal attachments and reconceptualize them in new patterns. With this ... it is possible to tell new stories and invent new legitimations. These new stories use familiar cultural elements that, if we are not sufficiently critical,[9] we understand as if they still carried their previous meanings. (p. 32)

In this way, de-/re-contextualization plays a critical role in legitimizing the false binaries (discussed above) that each attraction creates. By casting young theme park guests in specific roles, presenting them with melodramatic content

---

9   And, as I argue above, Disneyland's sacralized nature discourages such critical thinking.

aimed at creating or reinforcing particular dichotomous views of what is good and evil and carefully reconfiguring images and ideas from their real-life contexts, Disneyland attractions have the potential to subconsciously reframe children's ideologies.

The Attractions

"Pinocchio's Daring Journey" (Fantasyland, Opened 1983)

Based on Walt Disney's second feature-length animated film, "Pinocchio's Daring Journey" takes us[10] through recreated scenes from the movie. Disneyland's Web site[11] encourages riders to "dream along with Pinocchio as you ride along in his adventure-filled journey. With a little help from Jiminy Cricket, maybe you can save Pinocchio from the perils of Pleasure Island. And perhaps, if you wish upon a star, our little marionette will become a real boy after all." While this description positions us to journey along *with* Pinocchio, many portions of the attraction cast riders *as* Pinocchio; we literally see things through Pinocchio's eyes and make choices with/for him. In other words, we perform Schechner's "restored behaviors" by behaving as if we were someone else.

The attraction's first scene presents Pinocchio happily performing in Stromboli's circus, singing "Hey diddily dee, an actor's life for me!" We quickly see, however, that Stromboli is a cruel taskmaster who has imprisoned Pinocchio in a cage. Suddenly another massive cage descends over us, but forces we cannot see enable our escape.[12] We then come to a fork in the road, where signs point toward either Pinocchio's village or Pleasure Island. Here we are clearly meant to embody Pinocchio as Jiminy Cricket, our conscience,

---

10 I use the inclusive terms "we" and "us" throughout my narrative descriptions of the attractions in part to help readers envision themselves in the experiences but also because I believe the attractions are designed for a presumably homogenous group of guests. Because most attractions are not customized to particular riders, to be successful they must appeal to supposed human universals. While I recognize that each individual brings her unique subject position to an experience, those who designed the attractions may assume a more homogenous group of people from particular socioeconomic or racial backgrounds.

11 For all official attraction descriptions, see Disney Parks (2009b).

12 In the film, Pinocchio is released by the Blue Fairy only after a scene in which he learns that it is wrong to lie when she causes his nose to grow long. This is entirely omitted from the attraction.

warns us not visit the seedy island.[13] We promptly ignore the insect's advice and head on our way.

Figure 1. Jiminy Cricket warns Pinocchio/us not to head to Pleasure Island. We do not listen.[14]

We take a whirlwind tour of the island and head straight for Tobacco Row and the Rough House. Everything about the island is dark and ominous—it seems clear that we made a bad choice coming here. The evil Coachman quickly confirms this, revealing that he transformed all the other boys who came to Pleasure Island with us (there are no girls included) into donkeys and packed them into crates to be shipped to the salt mines. We see the Coachman ushering us into a crate ourselves to send us off to a life of hard labor, as depicted in Figure 2.

Once more we magically escape, only to find ourselves lost at sea. Jiminy Cricket warns us to beware Monstro the Whale, who suddenly leaps from the water intent on devouring us. Again, though, we turn a corner to safety. Gepetto finds us and whisks us home to celebrate. As the ride ends, we step out of role as Pinocchio and watch the Blue Fairy transform him into a real boy. After passing a large poster that reminds us "when [we] wish upon a star, all our [dreams] will come true," we return to the streets of Fantasyland.

---

13 See Figure 1.
14 All photographs by the author at Disneyland Resort in California in March 2009.

GOOD AND EVIL AT THE "HAPPIEST PLACE ON EARTH" 199

Figure 2. The Coachman prepares to send us to the salt mine.

"Pinocchio's Daring Journey" presents good and evil as a series of binaries. Nurturing authority figures such as Gepetto, Jiminy Cricket and the Blue Fairy are good, because (a) they care about us despite our bad decisions and (b) they give us things that we want, even if we don't deserve them. Evil is represented by the greedy liars Stromboli and the Coachman, who seek monetary profit at our expense. Stromboli imprisons us in order to sell theatre tickets; the Coachman sells us off as cheap labor. Even Monstro seeks to profit by turning us into food, the only commodity he values. The latter characters possess no redeeming traits, while the former do no harm. The ride reminds us that we ought to listen to our consciences, avoid pursuing a range of pleasures (from lives as actors to cigars and alcohol), and please those who care for us, while frowning upon those who exploit others for personal profit.

Disney's film version of *Pinocchio* deviates from its source material by undergoing what Schickel (1968) termed Disneyfication: "that shameful process by which everything the studio later touched, no matter how unique the vision of the original from which the studio worked, was reduced to the limited terms Disney and his people could understand" (p. 220).[15] Writers have debated how Disney's version defines "good" children. Pinsky (2004) argued that the story is one of redemption through one's works: "salvations through acts rather than grace" (p. 32), reasoning that in order to fully become a "real boy," Pinocchio must "prove himself to be brave, truthful, and unselfish" (Pinsky, 2004, p. 28). Though the Blue Fairy did indeed make these commands, Card

---

15 While Schickel referred in part to the simplicity of Disney's drawing styles, this simplification is also seen in the reduction of plots to simple binaries of good / evil along with the presentation of simplex characters.

(1995) argued that Pinocchio did not have to live up to them. Instead, the film teaches that "growing up is...becoming tamed [and] learning to please others, and...follow orders" (Card, 1995, p. 63). Disney's Pinocchio, to Card, "is an adorable child. Eventually he is led into smoking, drinking, and vandalism, which are presented as fun until it becomes ridiculous. Being bad has finally boiled down to making an ass of oneself" (p. 66).

The ride-through version of the movie has been even further simplified so as to be presented in just a few short minutes. On his "daring journey," Pinocchio rarely exerts agency; the only real choice he makes is to visit Pleasure Island and partake in its spoils. He does *not* save Gepetto from Monstro as in the movie; instead, unseen forces consistently save him. The attraction tells us we should listen to authority figures, but that even if we don't, we will somehow be saved. Pinsky (2004) argued that such faith "is an essential element" of what he calls the Disney Gospel: "faith in yourself and, even more, faith in something greater than yourself, some higher power" (p. xi). Not faith in any particular deity per se, but general "faith in faith"—faith that as long as we believe hard enough, our "dreams will come true."[16] Although it is Pinocchio who learns these lessons, because we experience this attraction *as* Pinocchio, it is we who are meant to "learn" as we ride this attraction.

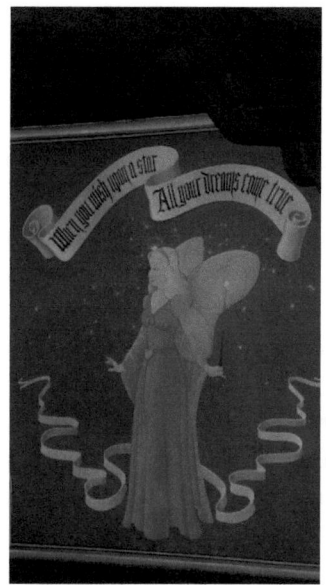

Figure 3. The Blue Fairy reminds us that when we wish upon a star, all of our dreams will come true.

Fantasmic! (Rivers of America, Premiered 1992)

Perhaps more than any other attraction, *Fantasmic!* creates explicit binaries of good and evil, noting in its official description that: "Mickey battles evil and conjures good in a musical pyrotechnic spectacular." The show premiered just a few years after what many scholars describe as a major ideological shift in the Walt Disney Company's ideologies in 1989. At that time the company, floundering after the loss of its founding brothers and the questionable management of Walt's son-in-law, Ron Miller,

---

16 See Figure 3.

came under the leadership of Michael Eisner. As Byrne and McQuillan (1999) argued, "there is something going on in...the entire period of Disney films dating from *The Little Mermaid* in 1989 which cannot be satisfactorily explained by the reapplication of old coats of critical paint (imperialism, sexism, etc.)" (p. 14). If we accept the notion that Disney underwent a significant ideological transformation under Eisner's leadership, then *Fantasmic!* is a particularly interesting subject of study because it draws heavily from movies produced prior to his tenure but was still shaped by his agendas.

Before the show begins, an announcement interpellates us into our role for the performance: we are about to "join Mickey" on a journey to discover if the powers of his "incredible imagination [are] strong enough, and bright enough, to withstand the evil forces that invade [his] dream."[17] Thus, we do not abandon our own subject-positions but rather become co-adventurers with Disney's hero (our "friend and host"), and experience trials and tribulations at his side. The performance begins when the signature mouse conducts a coordinated display of music, fountains, lights, and pyrotechnics that quickly morphs into a scene reminiscent of *The Sorcerer's Apprentice* from *Fantasia*, including errant fireworks exploding haphazardly as Mickey starts to lose control. This first "invasion" of Mickey's dream is resolved when the music calms and we are told: "see into your mind, and you will find in your imagination mysteries and magic, visions fantastic, leading to strange and wondrous dreams." (Not just in Mickey's imagination, but in ours as well.) Our dreams include beautiful flowers blooming and creatures from the *Jungle Book* roaming about, but our dream is invaded once more, this time by pachyderms: "They're here—they're there! Oh no! Look out! They're everywhere!"

The next happy scene features a dancing Pinocchio but is invaded when we see Jiminy Cricket trapped in an air bubble under the ocean, pursued by an apparently cricket-hungry Monstro. Audience members see and feel the beast's splash as he swims past and creates a tidal pool in which Mickey swirls perilously, crying for help.

The boom of a cannon then refocuses our attention on a massive pirate ship sailing into view. On board, a battle rages. Shots are fired and pirates plunge to their deaths while Peter Pan and Captain Hook duel high above the deck. Good conquers evil when Peter defeats Hook, leaving him swinging from a rope on the back of the ship, pursued by a hungry crocodile.

---

17 All *Fantasmic!* quotes from Healey (1998).

The show moves on to a romantic sequence featuring Snow White, Ariel, and Belle with their respective princes floating by to the sound of their well-known love themes. But these good, happy moments are soon disturbed by the Evil Queen from *Snow White* who, upon learning that her Magic Mirror sees three "lovelier maids" than she, casts a spell to transform herself into an old hag, then calls upon "all the forces of evil" to come to her aid. (Vain and jealous as the Queen might be in her beautiful state, *Fantasmic!* teaches that only physically ugly characters can be truly evil.) Determined to "turn that little mouse's dream into a nightmare Fantasmic," the queen morphs into different quintessential Disney villains including *The Little Mermaid*'s Ursula and Chernabog from *Fantasia*. A nervous Mickey is on hand to fight the intruding forces of evil but appears distressed when he meets his ultimate challenge: *Sleeping Beauty*'s Maleficent, who declares: "Now you will deal with me, and all the powers of *my* imagination!"

Spectacle abounds at the climax of the melodrama when Maleficent grows taller, eventually towering some fifty feet above the mouse. The evil fairy then transforms into a gigantic fire-breathing dragon and sets the entire lagoon aflame. Fortunately, Mickey remembers the powers of his own (inherently good) imagination, and tells the evil being: "You may think you're so powerful...Well, uh, this is my dream!" Brandishing a magical, firework-wielding sword, he defeats all of the villains (*vis-à-vis* the dragon), and a grand parade of happy characters emerges to celebrate in a picturesque scene complete with a giant steamship and rapid-fire pyrotechnics.

The performance exemplifies de-/re-contextualization and the perpetuations of binaries. To begin, all of the movies referenced are de-contextualized from their original contexts as separate motion pictures and re-contextualized as dreams taking place within our minds (although in one sense we see Mickey's dream, the show's lyrics repeatedly address audience members in the second person, referring to "your mind"). We are positioned as Mickey's friends embarking on an adventure. *Time* magazine once deemed Mickey "the symbol of common humanity in a struggle against the forces of evil" (as cited in Pinsky, 2004, p. 6)—and now, by using our imaginations, we can join him and fight all the forces of evil ourselves!

It thus becomes important to understand what evil is. Who are the villains we ought to be fighting? *Fantasmic!* links the good/evil binary to light/dark and beautiful/ugly binaries, privileging the former term in each. Consider the closing lyrics:

> When out of the night
> Dark voices ignite
> To blind you with frightening schemes,
> You use your might
> To brighten the light
> Creating a night of wondrous dreams.

Such allusions invoke Manichean dualism, conjoining darkness with evil. Earlier in the show, Snow White's stepmother (transformed into an ugly crone draped in all black) invoked "all the forces of evil" (including the all-black monster Chernabog and the decidedly dark-skinned, obese Ursula) to combat the "beautiful" and white-skinned (read: good) princesses Snow White, Belle, and Ariel. In this way, the production functions as an Althusserian Ideological State Apparatus—it "represent[s] the imaginary relationship of individuals to their real conditions of existence." That is, it creates "world outlooks" that "are largely imaginary, i.e. do not 'correspond to reality'" (Althusser, 2001, p. 37). There is no natural connection between attractive physical appearance and goodness; evil is not diametrically opposed to beauty, but *Fantasmic!* perpetuates these dualistic binaries nonetheless.

Finally, the decontextualization of many different villains from their original films and recontextualization as one metamorphic über-villain with a thousand faces promote the idea that all sources of evil are essentially the same, and can be easily distinguished from that which is good. Teaching children to think about good and evil in these terms may detract from their abilities or desires to see the world in more nuanced terms or to identify "evils" that don't clearly present themselves as such. Similarly to "Pinocchio's Daring Journey," *Fantasmic!* suggests that when we get ourselves into trouble, some higher power will always be present to protect us. It is not until the very end of the performance that Mickey exerts any personal agency in the fight against evil, and even then he relies on a magical sword to help him. He literally stands still while the sword's powers destroy the dragon for him.[18]

"Buzz Lightyear Astro Blasters" (Tomorrowland, Opened 2005)

While the "Pinnocchio" and *Fantasmic!* may teach passivity and faith in others, we are asked to perform more active roles when we play through the "Buzz

---

18 This is similar to the way Prince Philip defeats Maleficent-as-dragon in *Sleeping Beauty*. He is unable to defeat her on his own and relies on the magical spell the good fairies have cast on his sword.

Lightyear Astro Blasters" attraction. Our experience begins as we wait in the queue line, where a series of signs and audio announcements induct us into role as space rangers. We learn that Buzz Lightyear and all of Star Command need our help to defeat the Evil Emperor Zurg. "Attention all space rangers," we hear, "report to the briefing room. We need every space junkie we can get!" There is a war taking place, and we good guys (presumably we are all men—no women appear in the attraction), must battle the forces of evil—this time with Buzz instead of Mickey.

There is no doubt that Zurg is evil—it says so right on the box in which he is sold. But whereas some earlier attractions failed to offer rationales for their labels, "Astro Blasters" is quick to tell us *why* Zurg is evil: Buzz Lightyear himself informs us that Zurg is stealing our batteries, and "without power cells, we will be powerless and at the mercy of Zurg." Thus, we must climb into our "Star Cruiser," pick up our "hand-held laser cannon," and join the battle. The message is quite clear: if someone threatens our energy resources, we are undoubtedly justified in waging war against them. If we do not, we will surely be enslaved by those who steal the resources that we supposedly must have in order to survive.

Having been informed by the attraction's official description that "the fate of the universe is in [our] hands as [we] pilot [our] Star Cruiser through the treacherous terrain while zapping enemy targets and racking up points," we climb on board. Our objective is to hit a variety of targets with our laser cannons; the more we hit, the more points we receive. Those who earn the highest scores are publicly lauded on a screen at the end of the attraction and on the Internet.[19]

Interestingly, although the attraction's description noted that we would be shooting "enemy targets," many of the targets seem to have no particular connection to Zurg or his army of battery-stealing robots. On one planet, targets are everywhere, including members of the resident dinosaur population. In a time of war, the ride tells us, we must accept some indigenous casualties in the battle to prevent evil enemies from taking our resources. The attraction has so effectively re-contextualized the presumably innocent *Toy Story* characters within the scene of modern warfare that we are easily blinded to the implications of our actions; war becomes nothing more than a game. The perpetua-

---

19 See Disney Parks (2009a). Today (April 28th, 2009), for example, the highest scorer achieved 3,389,400 points at 3:26pm. This particular space ranger is anonymous since the website does not display the names of in-park players. Those seeking a bit more public glory can play the game online as well; their legacies are digitally preserved along with their usernames.

tion of the good/evil binary assures us that there can be nothing good about characters deemed "evil," thus we need not waste time thinking critically about how we interact with the world around us.

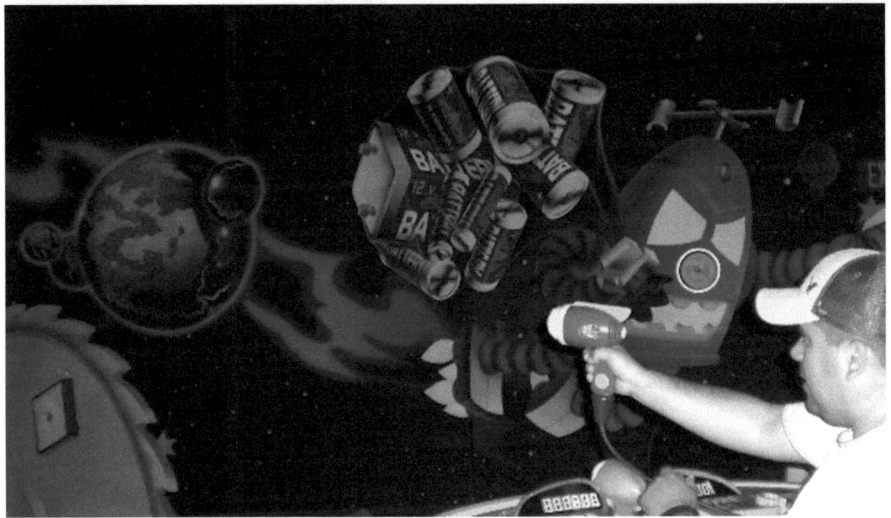

Figure 4. A "space ranger" fires his laser cannon while an evil robot tries to steal batteries.

Regardless of our score, we end the ride victorious. We have protected our energy resources from the enemy and liberated a race of three-eyed aliens from an oppressive dictator. Our victory is signified by Zurg's return to his box, and we observe our alien friends gratefully preparing for his return to the toy store.[20] Just in case we had begun to make connections between the attraction and real life, this scene reminds us that this has all been just a game. We should not take away any serious messages from the ride because Buzz Lightyear and Zurg are just harmless toys, available from retailers everywhere.

On that note, we step out of the attraction directly into a gift shop where we can buy all manner of Buzz Lightyear paraphernalia, as seen in Figure 6. Children wishing to further embody the space ranger role might convince their parents to buy them full body costumes or at least a special laser-equipped glove. Those who identify with the loveable but helpless aliens, or even with the evil Zurg himself, have plenty of options to choose from. While we might be encouraged to prioritize good over evil in some instances, when it comes to retail, Disneyland is willing to sell us whatever identity we desire.

---

20 See Figure 5.

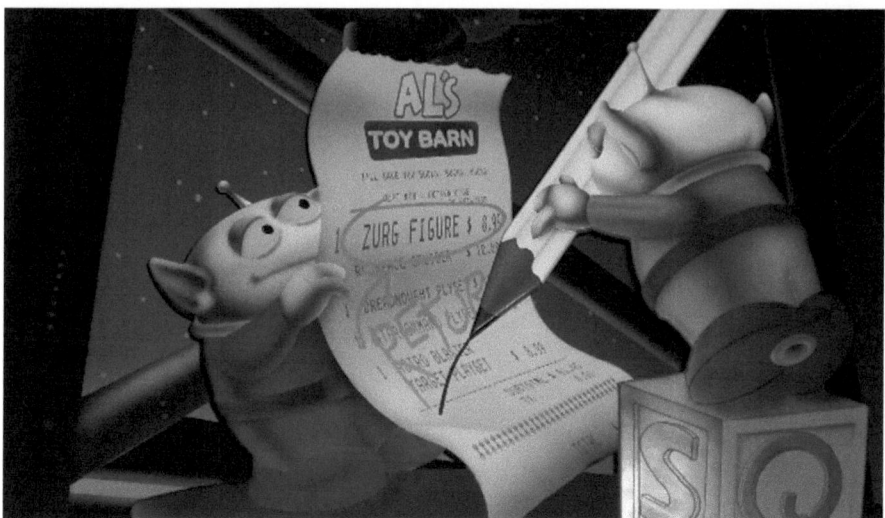

Figure 5. Aliens prepare for Zurg's return to the toy store.

I believe the inclusion of this gift shop is one of many indicators of the post-1989 ideological shift I discussed earlier. Though shopping venues have been available at Disneyland since its opening, more recent attractions seem especially designed to interpellate visitors into the meta-role of consumer. While riding "Astro Blasters," we are reminded that playing with toys is great fun, and that we can continue the fun by making a few quick purchases as we exit.

Figure 6. A variety of *Toy Story* merchandise is available for sale just beyond the attraction exit.

Further, although the Disney's re-contextualization of war within the frame of children's play might imply that there are "no serious messages" to be learned, children might very easily transfer the attraction's ideology and the lack of critical attention it promotes into their independent play with toys, whether they are purchased in the gift shop or elsewhere. Based on the model they played through in "Astro Blasters," they might assign some dolls to be valiant "heroes" and others "villains," and justify violent play between them based on the false good/evil binary presented by Disney's attraction. Such thinking could further structure their understanding of real-life war, both as children and in their later lives, especially if they do not experience alternative ways of seeing.

Innoventions Dream Home (Tomorrowland, Opened 2008)

As we wait to enter the Innoventions pavilion, our identity as consumers is taken to an entirely new level; playing this role is explicitly endorsed as "good." We are greeted by Tom Morrow, a robot spokesperson for the attraction, who explains that "innoventions" result from the fusion of innovation and inventions. He states that the pavilion is filled with "amazing new stuff that is going to make your life better." The innoventions we are about to encounter are *good*—they are going to make *our* lives better, regardless of our individual life situations and needs. If the innoventions themselves are "good," so must be their manufacturers: Microsoft, HP, LifeWare, and Taylor Morrison Homes.[21] These companies, we learn, produce "genius gadgets to take the hard work out of work." Whereas Pinocchio learned that excessive leisure was bad, today the Disney Company tells us just the opposite—work and toil are bad, relaxation is the key to happiness.

After we enter the pavilion, an energetic, youthful member of the Elias family[22] greets us outside the door to her home. She invites us inside to a party celebrating one of the Elias children, whose soccer team (the Astro Blasters, fittingly and synergistically enough) is headed to China for the world championships. His parents have, "naturally," thrown him an expensive party. We are invited inside, where our host notes that each room is equipped with a LifeWare panel—a digital system that controls everything in the room from the temperature to the lighting to the window shades. We can use the system to access the house-wide stereo system, or to peer through the lenses of the many security cameras mounted throughout the home. We are then set free to explore at our leisure and experiment with the various technologies. If we like, we can even head to the backyard, where guests are playing video games on large consoles installed for the party. "Playing outside" has been reduced to a virtual experience.

As we roam the house, the good/evil binary expands. We learn that not only is technology "good" because it makes our life easier, it also allows us almost complete dominion over our environment, which was meant to be con-

---

21 Disney has a long history of corporate partnerships with a diverse range of companies. See especially Fjellman (1992) and Wasko (2005) for details. Disneyland featured an earlier version of the Dream Home from 1957 to 1967, titled the "Monsanto House of the Future" and sponsored by the Monsanto Company, an agricultural biotechnology corporation.

22 Walt Disney's middle name was Elias, which was also his father's first name.

quered by humans. Anything virtual is ideal; the natural is undesirable. All of the artwork throughout the house is digital and can be changed at the touch of the button. Each photo frame can instantly display any image you like, so you need not see images that other family members enjoy but do not appeal to you. Cameras can be used not only for security purposes but for communication. In "Sister's" room we find her "magic mirror" that she uses to video chat with her friends, saving her the time and effort of meeting them in person.

Of course, the products throughout the house all bear the emblems of the various companies that have manufactured them. To sit in front of the fireplace is to admire HP logos on all of the artwork hanging above the mantel. It is impossible to look any direction in the den without seeing it several times. The photos in Figures 7 and 8 demonstrate the surfeit of emblems bearing HP's insignia.[23] Although the Elias family members are inundated by advertising at every turn, none of them seem to think this is unusual; they simply own many products, and of course each product has a logo. If visitors to the home adopt this view, then the Dream House has successfully hailed them into the role of techno-savvy consumer. That is, the attraction seems designed to make us accept as "obvious" the premise that our homes ought to be filled to the brim with technology. When an Elias family member tells us that the accumulation of expensive technological devices has made her life better, we are meant to have "the inevitable and natural reaction of crying out...'That's obvious! That's right! That's true!" (Althusser, 2003, p.41). Disney recontextualizes multinational corporations as benign friends we should welcome into our homes. It becomes only natural to live in a house with hundreds of HP products and to technologically mediate most aspects of our lives. Any negative conceptions we may have of the companies are sanitized by their presence at the "happiest place on earth." As former Disney executive Martin Sklar noted: "Industry has lost credibility with the public...but people still have faith in Mickey Mouse" (as cited in Fjellman, 1992, p. 350).

Skeptics might (rightly) note that most children do not have the fiscal resources to remodel their homes, but they miss two important points. First, young people often do have a significant impact on family spending—parents and others can be swayed by their children's views and may even turn to older adolescents to understand current trends in technology. Further, Disney posits that the Dream Home represents a house of the *future*. Although the products on display are often available today, the idea presented is that they will be

---

23 Each of the light gray circles in these photographs indicates an HP logo.

GOOD AND EVIL AT THE "HAPPIEST PLACE ON EARTH" 209

commonplace in the future. The message to today's children is that by the time they are homeowners, they will *need* these corporations to help them make their lives easier and keep up with the Joneses. While in the Dream Home, children may only be "playing" the roles of consumers in the sense of "pretending," but in the future they will be playing these roles by embodying them in everyday life, at least if the corporate sponsors have their way.

Figure 7. The HP logo appears 5 times above the Dream Home fireplace.

Figure 8. Seven instances of the HP logo appear in this photo. Microsoft and other corporate logos are also prevalent.

Conclusion: Spaces for Resistance?

In the preceding sections, I discussed the various roles and characters that Disneyland asks visitors to embody. In "Pinocchio's Daring Journey," we identify with a little wooden boy whose bad decisions get him into trouble but who is always rescued by unseen forces. *Fantasmic!* casts us as Mickey's friends whose imaginations are constantly invaded by dark, ugly, evil forces we must do battle with. "Buzz Lightyear Astro Blasters" situates us as space rangers fighting a war against those out to steal our resources, and the "Innoventions Dream Home" insists that we need expensive products to "make our lives better," ultimately interpellating us as consumers. While early attractions like "Pinocchio" shun greed and accumulation of wealth, later attractions embrace it.

Many Disneyland visitors likely embody these roles without conscious awareness that they are doing so, treating the park as a sacred space to escape from the harsh realities of the world and reconnect with "childhood innocence." Others may notice the roles Disney casts them in but accept them as part of a pleasurable vacation experience. But is it possible for children and other park guests to actively resist the narratives that surround them?

Chappell (2010) argues in his introduction that "for children to engage in resistant play, they must have access to counter narratives that allow them to acknowledge and question the disappearance of humanity that can occur within the scenarios they are playing out" (p. 11). That is, the only way young people can resist the roles they are offered is to know and deliberately adopt alternative roles. A particularly vigilant child watching the princes and princesses dancing the night away in *Fantasmic!*, for example, might realize that she is being presented with a vision of heteronormative sexuality and decide that in *her* dream, a blissful scene would involve Ariel dancing with Belle—the "invaders" of her dream might be Prince Eric and the Beast.

The Project on Disney[24] (1995) suggested that park guests can create counter narratives by partaking in what they termed "the Alternative Ride," defined as "a method of constructing visual drama that mocks a vision that is prescribed and stereotyped" (p. 166). They argued that if a visitor deliberately focuses on the aspects of their surroundings that the company does not intend for them to attend to, they may notice that "commonplace acts, not the Disney-approved attractions...provoke thoughts about history, science, technology, and sociology" (Project on Disney, 1995, p. 166). Thus, a child riding "Pinocchio" with her younger brother might focus not on the ride itself but on her brother's interactions with his surroundings. She might construct new narrative about a boy lost in a theme park attraction, for example, and thus creatively escape from her Disney-sanctioned role.

Nonetheless, I believe opportunities for resistance at Disneyland are rare because its attractions deliberately discourage the formation of counter narratives. Rides frequently employ the technique of forced perspective, making it nearly impossible to see anything other than the intended display. As Wasko et al. (2001) noted, "appropriate sound effects, music and even aromas are carefully manipulated throughout the park" (p. 166). Because many attractions are based on characters from Disney movies, young people may enter attractions with extant narratives about those characters that will only be further reinforced by the experience. Some children may have created alternative stories in their free play with Disney character dolls and such, but as Chappell

---

24 The Project on Disney team was comprised of scholars Jane Kuenz, Karen Klugman, Shelton Waldrep, and Susan Willis.

(2008) realized, even though "play can refigure and collage this material into new narratives, the initial stories they hear and the performances these stories elicit establish a foundation for these departures" (p. 19). If young people wish to partake in free play within the park itself, they will quickly learn that "play is all but eliminated by the absolute domination of program over spontaneity" (Project on Disney, 1995, p. 185). There is only so much room for deviation from Disney's intended narratives, and the sacralized nature of the park may preclude the desire to seek alternative stories; viewing a space as sacred implies acceptance of its creators' agendas and imposes a feeling that it is "wrong" to oppose them.

Visitors to the park are denied agency throughout their day. Riding "Pinocchio," their vehicle will always steer towards Pleasure Island and away from the safety of the village. They can choose what target to shoot on "Astro Blasters," or even refrain from shooting at all, but they will still see the same procession of scenes as everyone else. As Fjellman (1992) noted, the only real choices guests can make involve what food, drink, and souvenirs to purchase (p. 258), and even then the options are limited. Reducing the number of choices park visitors must make reduces their need to think, and all but eliminates the need to think critically, and resistant play requires critical thought.

I believe it is possible, with effort, to acknowledge and even resist the roles and narratives constructed at Disneyland, but it seems unlikely that this happens often. I confess that despite all of my critical training, I am still often drawn into Disney's stories—a part of my soul believes *Fantasmic!* when it tells me that "one day we'll find true love," and after a trip to the "Dream House," I agree that my life might be much "easier" if I owned the technology on display. I identify with the many scholars who note that, for all their criticism, they still enjoy viewing Disney's films and visiting the theme parks with their families. The question remains then: if those of us who deliberately set out to explicate Disney's narratives have difficulty resisting them, what is the likelihood that escape-seeking vacationers will be more successful?

References

Althusser, L. (2001). Ideology and the ideological state apparatuses. In C. Counsell & L. Wolfe (Eds.), *Performance analysis* (pp. 32-42). London: Routledge. (Original work published in 1970.)

Bell, E., Haas, L., & Sells, L. (Eds.). (1995). *From mouse to mermaid: The politics of film, gender and culture.* Bloomington: Indiana University Press.

Brode, D. (2005). *Multiculturalism and the mouse: Race and sex in Disney entertainment*. Austin: University of Texas Press.

Byrne, E. & McQuillan, M. (1999). *Deconstructing Disney*. London: Pluto Press.

Card, C. (1995). Pinocchio. In E. Bell, L. Haas, & L. Sells (Eds.), *From mouse to mermaid: The politics of film, gender and culture*. Bloomington: Indiana University Press.

Carlson, M. (2004). *Performance: A critical introduction* (2nd ed.). New York: Routledge.

Chappell, A.R. (2008). *Colonizing the imaginary: Children's embodiment of cultural narratives*. Unpublished doctoral dissertation, Arizona State University.

Chappell, D. (2010). Colonizing the imaginary: Socializing (specific) identities, bodies, ethics, and moralities through pleasurable embodiment. In D. Chappell (Ed.), *Children under construction: Critical essays on play as curriculum*. New York: Peter Lang.

DeCordova, R. (1994). The Mickey in Macy's window: Childhood, consumerism, and Disney animation. In E. Smooden (Ed.), *Disney discourse* (pp. 203-213). New York: Routledge.

Disney Parks. (2009a). *Buzz Lightyear Astro Blasters Online*. Retrieved April 28, 2009, from the Disneyland Resort Web site: http://www.disneyland.com/buzz

Disney Parks. (2009b). *Disneyland park attractions*. Retrieved April 27, 2009, from the Disneyland Resort Web site: http://disneyland.disney.go.com/disneyland/en_US/parks/listing?name=DisneylandParkAttractionsListingPage

Fjellman, S.M. (1992). *Vinyl leaves: Walt Disney World and America*. Boulder, CO: Westview.

Giroux, H. (1995). Memory and pedagogy in the "Wonderful World of Disney." In E. Bell, L. Haas, & L. Sells (Eds.), *From mouse to mermaid: The politics of film, gender and culture*. Bloomington, IN: Indiana University Press.

Giroux, H. (1999). *The mouse that roared: Disney and the end of innocence*. Lanham, MD: Rowman & Littlefield.

Gramsci, A. (2004). Hegemony. In J. Rivkin & M. Ryan (Eds.), *Literary theory: An anthology*. Malden, MA: Blackwell Publishing. Original work published 1930-32.

Healey, B. (1998). *Disneyland Fantasmic!: Good clashes with evil in a nighttime spectacular* [CD]. Disney Magic Productions.

Lee, N. (2001). *Childhood and society: Growing up in an age of uncertainty*. Maidenhead, UK: Open University Press.

Meyer, S.M. (1999). *Henry James and his appropriation and transformation of the melodrama*. Unpublished doctoral dissertation, The Ohio State University.

Newcomb, C. (2003) *Crossing the berm: The Disney theme park as sacralized space*. Unpublished doctoral dissertation, Florida State University.

Pinsky, M.I. (2004) *The gospel according to Disney*. Louisville, KY: Westminster John Knox Press.

Plato. (2004). *Republic*. (C.D.C. Reeve, Trans.). Indianapolis: Hackett Publishing.

Project on Disney. (1995). *Inside the mouse: Work and play at Disney World*. Durham: Duke University Press.

Schechner, R. (2002). *Performance studies: An introduction*. New York: Routledge.

Schickel, R. (1968). *The Disney version: The life, times, commerce, and art of Walt Disney*. New York: Simon & Schuster.

Wasko, J. (2005). *Understanding Disney: The manufacture of fantasy*. Malden, MA: Polity Press.

Wasko, J., Phillips, M. & Meehan, E.R., Eds. (2001). *Dazzled by Disney?* London: Leicester University Press.

Chapter Ten

Whose Rights Are They Anyway?
Examining Human Rights Education with Young People Incorporating Theatre Games and Dramatic Activities

Christina Marín

> My dear young people: I see the light in your eyes the energy in your bodies and the hope that is your spirit. I know it is you, not I, who will make the future. It is you, not I, who will fix our wrongs and carry forward all that is right in the world.
> —Nelson Mandela

The Right to Play

In wrapping up the introduction to his third edition of *The Development of Play*, David Cohen (2006) explains: "Today, few psychologists would argue against play or fantasy but the feeling still persists that such frivolous activities need to be justified by being in the service of reality. The right games should spur the best development" (p. 13). In this chapter, I offer a framework through which educational theatre can be harnessed for the purpose of Human Rights Education (HRE). I hope to shed light on how dramatic activities and theatre games have the potential to set the stage for profound dialogues among young people around controversial topics rooted in ethics and morality. I believe these games offer us a way to help students bear witness, albeit from a distance, to some of the most egregious acts perpetuated by humans against their own kind. Games may also help young people contextualize the numerous articles outlined in the original charters developed by the United Nations known as the Universal Declaration of Human Rights, ratified in 1948, and the Convention on the Rights of the Child, ratified in 1989. Through their engagement in theatre activities, we can offer young people a space in which to develop a critical consciousness.

This chapter is not meant to provide a catalog of game descriptions; there are many valuable resources that do an excellent job of outlining various requirements in terms of time, space, materials, number of participants, focus and energy levels as well as concrete goals and objectives for theatre and drama activities (Boal, 2002; McCarthy, 2004; Neelands & Goode, 2000; Poulter, 1991; Rohd, 1998; Warren, 1996). My intention here is to engage the reader in an innovative exploration of how these games and activities can foster intellectual curiosity, critical thinking, and sound educational experiences.

According to a document published in 2007 by the United Nations Children's Fund (UNICEF) entitled *A World Fit for Us–The Children's Statement from the UN Special Session on Children: Five Years on*, in 2002:

> At the Children's Forum, a "children only" event that lasted for three days before the [United Nations Special Session on Children] started, young people divided into groups to discuss the things that mattered to them most: child rights, exploitation, war, health care, HIV and AIDS, the environment, poverty, education and child participation. They then joined together to agree on a statement called "A World Fit for Us." (p. 3)

The UN document is filled with extraordinary stories of young people from around the world who struggle in their everyday lives against incredible odds. The young people gathered at the Children's Forum in 2002 imagined a world in which these problems would be eradicated.

Also in this document is a concise, one-page introduction to the charter known as The Convention on the Rights of the Child: "The Convention on the Rights of the Child (CRC) was adopted by world leaders on 20 November 1989. It spells out the fundamental human rights of all children. All but two of the world's countries have agreed to be bound by what it says" (p. 4). To date, Somalia and the United States are the only two countries within the United Nations who have not ratified this document.

The following is an abbreviated list of highlights from the original 54 Articles outlined in the CRC:

YOUR RIGHTS UNDER THE CRC

You [children around the world] have the right:

- To be free from discrimination
- To be subject to laws and treatment that put your best interests first
- To be protected and able to develop to your full potential
- To have your say in decisions that affect you
- To survive and thrive in conditions that enable you to grow into the healthiest and happiest person you can be

- To have your birth registered, with a legal name and nationality
- To protection from physical and mental injury or abuse, and from neglect, whether you live with your parents or with others
- To an education—and to primary schooling that is free of charge
- To freedom of expression, thought, conscience and religion
- To information that is important to your well-being
- To play (p. 4)

These final two words have had a tremendous impact on how I approach HRE. Young people have the right to play, even in a standardized test saturated society, even when they are engaged in educational enterprises.

I was not always aware that drama practitioners could use theatrical games and dramatic activities to inspire young people's learning. My own formal education was primarily implemented through the banking method. This is probably not surprising, considering I was born the same year Paulo Freire (1970) first published *Pedagogy of the Oppressed*. Needless to say, my elementary school teachers had not yet been exposed to what, even today in some educational circles, is considered radical pedagogy. I was not instructed to think critically but to memorize names and dates. I was not asked my opinion very often, but I did do well on multiple choice and true/false tests. I learned to fill in bubbles like an expert! But did formal schooling prepare me to think past the desk or beyond the classroom walls? It seemed, according to my teachers, that our textbooks contained everything I needed to learn. According to Singer, Golinkoff, & Hirsh-Pasek (2006), authors of *Play = Learning*, "Children need play alongside more traditional learning to build social and cognitive skills.... For Piaget and Vygotsky, play was an opportunity for children to learn more about their world, to stretch to accommodate new ideas, and to foster their imaginations" (p. 6). Fortunately, my parents understood the notion that education could be supplemented by experiences beyond the pencils and textbooks.

Memories of a Childhood Faraway

When I was young, my family traveled often from our home in New York City to my father's native country, Colombia, to visit his family. Sometimes we went for the Christmas holiday, and other times we went when school was out for the summer. These trips were about family; they were about revisiting the

Spanish language that was such an important part of our bi-cultural identity. My sisters and I were young, but we learned so much on these trips. We spent time in the countryside enjoying the fresh mountain air above the valley city of Medellín, and we walked through the busy streets that my father had known as a boy. Colombia was as much home to us as New York.

From all of these trips, there is a particular memory that has lived in my mind for many years. Whenever we walked through the downtown area of Medellín, El Centro, near the Metropolitan Cathedral, there were always numerous children running around in the streets. As a little girl in a frilly pink dress and patent leather shoes, I was jealous. I wondered why these little boys and girls could chase each other around in their bare feet, with their dirt-stained arms and legs. They had obviously been playing, and playing hard all day long. After all, I reasoned, only serious playing could get a child that dirty. Then there were the children with their little boxes of merchandise whose voices rang through the air shouting, "Marlboro, Marlboro!" or, "Chicle, Chicle, Chicle!" (gum, gum, gum). Others were selling newspapers to pedestrians on the street and to the people driving in cars. Where were their parents, I wondered? Why did mine keep a vigilant watch over me, never letting me get that dirty? I certainly was not allowed to run around screaming things at the top of my lungs. It didn't seem fair; why did they have the right to so much freedom? Why couldn't I be as free as they seemed to be?

In 1980, my family stopped traveling to Colombia for various reasons; but in my mind, the echo of those young voices haunted me, as I grew up in a world that could no longer hide the fact that those children on the streets of Colombia were not dirty because they had been playing all day, and they had not thrown off their shoes in a carefree, nonchalant gesture to celebrate their freedom. Many of them did not own shoes, and a warm bath was a luxury they did not often have access to.

When I was young, I saw the world through innocent eyes. My childhood was privileged: from the education I received to the travel my parents were able to afford. When we stopped traveling to Colombia, I admit, the haunting memories began to fade, and I focused on smoothed memories laced with smells and flavors, music and family. The Colombia I knew was green and lush; the Colombia I remembered was family and friends.

We returned to Colombia, after thirteen years, in 1993. The innocent eyes I had seen this city through as a little girl had grown up. I had gone to high school and then finished college. My upbringing was complemented with the kind of education afforded by a specialized high school in New York City and a private university in the Midwest. Returning to Colombia was the beginning of a whole new chapter in my education. My reading of this world at two such distinct time periods in my life is informed by Paulo Freire's negotiation with the terms *literacy* and *critical consciousness*. In one of his many dialogic chapters written with Donaldo Macedo, Freire observes:

> First, I think consciousness is generated through the social practice in which we participate. But it also has an individual dimension. That is, my comprehension of the world, my dreams of the world, my judgment of the world—all of these are part of my individual practice; all speak of my presence in the world. I need all of this to begin to understand myself. But it is not sufficient to explicate my action. In the final analysis, consciousness is socially bred. In this sense, I think my subjectivity is important. But I cannot separate my subjectivity from its social objectivity. (Freire & Macedo, 1987, p. 47)

I was coming into a critical consciousness of my place in this city my father had called home, a place for decades devastated by drug wars and violence, poverty and political problems, a place I realized I knew only from a distance.

As we walked again in El Centro, I heard the familiar intonation of young voices selling cigarettes, chewing gum, and newspapers in the streets. It seemed as if time had stood still here, but I knew, of course, that these were not the same children. The poverty in these streets seemed no better than it had been when I was ten years old. I began to wonder, who had the best interest of these children in mind? As I stood there in Medellín in 1993, the reality of the situation was that—according to the Web site of the charitable organization SOS Children's Villages, the world's largest orphan charity—local business owners in the capital city of Bogotá, Colombia, "hired 'death squads' to clean up the streets, and during the 1990s thousands of street children were just murdered" (*Street Children in Colombia*). As I read the world around me, I realized that there were children all over the globe who experienced this kind of poverty and violation of their human rights, living in developing countries and in some of the richest countries of the world, including the United States. I struggled to make connections between my work in theatre and the crippling circumstances that victimized children all over the world.

I began to understand that as a young girl I did not have the framework to comprehend the circumstances of the young children in the streets of Colombia or in other countries where children are the victims of child labor, conflict zones, and human trafficking. In today's global society, I believe children everywhere deserve better preparation to become active citizens in a world where social injustices still plague the lives of too many. But how could I have been educated in a manner that would not overemphasize these atrocities, yet still help me see the reality of the world beyond the borders of the United States? How could I have been introduced to the Universal Declaration of Human Rights (UDHR) and the Convention on the Rights of the Child (CRC) as a young person from a privileged background in a way that could help me understand that, even though I had never had the need to invoke these international charters, they outlined the universal, inalienable rights granted to every human being, no matter their age or where they lived? These questions triggered the central focus that fuels my work today; how can we engage young people through a pedagogy of hope rather than a pedagogy of despair? Freire (2007) reminds us, "Without a minimum of hope, we cannot so much as start the struggle. But without the struggle, hope, as an ontological need, dissipates, loses its bearings, and turns into hopelessness. And hopelessness can become tragic despair" (p. 3). He reiterates that hope must be paired with action: "hope, as an ontological need, demands anchoring in practice" (p. 2).

This self-reflexive, autoethnographic narrative has been a window into my own development as an educator poised to discover the power of theatre as a pedagogical tool for exploring human rights violations experienced by young people all over the world. I have come to recognize more deeply the inherent power of play to teach, with the understanding that, as the charter outlines, all young people have the right to play.

Theatre Beyond the Stage

In graduate school, I was introduced to the work of Augusto Boal and his Theatre of the Oppressed frameworks in a course called "Theatre for Social Change," taught by Professor Johnny Saldaña. When I picked up Boal's text *Games for Actors and Non-actors* (2002) for the first time, I felt like I had opened up a treasure trove of tools and methods to motivate dialogue around social justice issues, ethics, morality, and human rights. Boal is resolved that, "Theatre is a language through which human beings can engage in active dialogue on what is important to them. It allows individuals to create a safe space that they may inhabit in groups and use to explore the interactions which make up their lives. It is a lab for problem solving, for seeking options, and for practicing solutions" (quoted in Rohd, 1998, p. xix). As I studied, and later taught, the arsenal of Theatre of the Oppressed techniques, I dug deeper and deeper into this notion of how playing games could be one of the most liberating means of enacting critical pedagogy leading to social change. I realized that through games we could open up a space in which young people could grapple with complex issues in a potentially more relaxed environment. As Christine Poulter (1991) observes, "Many games assist group development by helping players to get to know each other and to feel relaxed in each other's company" (p. 4). She goes on to explain, "If the games are to be more than an end in themselves, if they are being used as part of a developmental process for the individual, the group and the project in hand, then it is important to foster trust, support and encouragement within the group as soon as possible" (p. 80).

Education researchers Nicolopoulou, McDowell, & Brockmeyer (2006) caution us, "The challenge is to integrate the play element *into* the curriculum in ways that are structured but foster the children's own participation and initiative, so that children infuse them with their own interests and concerns" (p. 125). While their chapter in *Play = Learning*, "Narrative Play and Emergent Literacy: Storytelling and Story-Acting Meet Journal Writing," focuses on the context of early childhood development in a Head Start classroom, I believe this challenge also applies to HRE with older children and adolescents.

When we employ games and dramatic activities for educational purposes we are not always focused on the presentational aspect of the theatre; in most cases we are more concerned with the processes involved. "Although many drama games originated as a means of training professional actors," Bernie Warren (1996) points out, "their usefulness has been extended beyond the theatre stage to a variety of therapeutic and educational arenas" (p. 3). In work where theatre intersects with Human Rights Education, I am often reminded of the sage observation Doug Paterson makes in his Foreword to Michael Rohd's (1998) book *Theatre for Community, Conflict & Dialogue*. He finds that "Theatre education, theatre experience, even theatre familiarity are not required. What is required is a desire to engage in dialogue about the oppressions in our lives and to use theatre as a tool to effect that engagement" (p. xi). We are not looking to develop talented actors; we are hoping to engage critical thinkers.

In *Adolescence: A Time That Matters*, educators at UNICEF remind us:

> When adolescents are supported and encouraged by caring adults, they thrive in unimaginable ways, becoming resourceful and contributing members of families and communities. Bursting with energy, curiosity and spirit that are not easily extinguished, young people have the potential to change negative social patterns of behavior and break cycles of violence and discrimination that pass from one generation to

the next. With their creativity, energy and enthusiasm, young people can change the world in astonishing ways, making it a better place not only for themselves but for everyone. (p. 1)

And aren't these the very characteristics that aid us in playing games: creativity, energy, and enthusiasm?

While I strongly support the employment of games in our work in HRE, I believe we must always keep in mind a very important distinction between competitive and noncompetitive activities. In his preface to the first edition of *Games for Actors and Non-actors*, Augusto Boal (2002) stresses that "None of the exercises or games should be done with violence, nor should any cause pain; all should be done with pleasure and understanding. Nothing should ever be done in a competitive manner—we try to be better than ourselves, not better than others" (16). This distinction helps us as we select developmentally appropriate activities to engage young people with.

In addition, as Boal suggests, "In Theatre of the Oppressed no one is compelled to do anything they don't wish to do" (p. 49). This tenet of the methodology echoes the teaching of one of my mentors, Professor Rives Collins, who first enlightened me to "the power of the egress" in his Creative Drama class almost 20 years ago. I have been employing this teaching tool ever since and have passed it along to countless students who have also recognized its effectiveness. The power of the egress gives students and participants the ability to step out of an exercise if they are uncomfortable in any way. They are encouraged to follow the work as active observers so that if and when they are ready to rejoin the group, they have the open invitation to do so. This teaching strategy is not meant to give students a free ticket to goof off during the lesson or activity; I believe that if the material presented is engaging, students will actively participate as long as they are in an environment that fosters trust and collaboration. According to Julie McCarthy (2004), "A good workshop enhances or maintains the physical and emotional safety of the participants and keeps them engaged through a planned and balanced structure" (p. 3). However, if for whatever reason, past experiences or emotional vulnerability, a student feels the need to step out briefly, they should be able to exercise that right. Warren (1996) counsels, "Be sensitive to the needs of individuals in the group. Do not force an individual to play—let them sit and watch. Then, before the next game, ask how they feel and suggest joining in" (p. 12). No form of education should be either coercive or oppressive.

While it is essential that participants not be required to share publicly why they have stepped out, the facilitator should foster a sense of confidence so that if the young person chooses, they may discuss their decision with the teacher. It has been my experience, with young people of all ages, that if the power of the egress policy is explained conscientiously then it is held in reserve for moments of necessity and not abused. I have found that young people are, more often than not, engaged by human rights issues and violations, but the reality is that some of the material can become overwhelming. That is why I find games to be especially powerful tools in this work. I agree with Robert Chambers who believes, "Theatre...accelerates, deepens and embeds learning and change; and it opens up areas and forms of experiences which are not accessible in other ways" (2004, p. v). It is crucial that we support young people through these learning experiences, focusing on child-centered pedagogies that invite young people to monitor their levels of comfort.

Education about, for and with Young People

According to UNICEF, "There are an estimated 1.2 billion young people aged 10-19 in the world—the largest generation of adolescents in history. More than four fifths of them live in developing countries, particularly in urban areas" (*Adolescence*, 2002, p. 2). If this is the bleak depiction of reality, how can we, as educators, help young people examine injustice and inequity without placing blame or pointing fingers? How can we teach about the experiences of young people in areas of armed conflict, such as Colombia, Uganda, and Sierra Leone? How can we facilitate learning about the human trafficking of children across international borders? All young people are guaranteed the right to an education. Furthermore, the Universal Declaration of Human Rights (2007), Article 26, Section 2 explicitly states: "Education shall be directed to the full development of the human personality and to the strengthening of respect for human rights and fundamental freedoms. It shall promote understanding, tolerance and friendship among all nations, racial or religious groups, and shall further the activities of the United Nations for the maintenance of peace" (UDHR, p. 10). There is hope outlined here in theory, and it falls to us, as educators engaged across disciplines, to implement the pedagogy that will anchor that hope.

Certainly there are government documents and academic resources, including current events articles from periodicals, which young people can read to learn about many of these issues; however, these often clinical, dismal portrayals of the world run the risk of having the majority of young people develop a hopeless, powerless perspective. These resources may also privilege the academically advanced students who perhaps have a more developed vocabulary, especially in the English language. As educators, we need to be prepared to address the diversity of learning styles in our classrooms and take into consideration the growing populations of immigrant children and adolescents for whom English is a new language. "Teaching in the spirit of human rights...encourages teachers to give learners the space and time to learn according to their needs. We may then become aware of our profiles as learners as part of our identities" (Gollob, Krapf, & Adzovic, 2006, p. 6). If the rights guaranteed in the UDHR and the CRC are considered universal, then is it not incumbent upon all of us, as socially conscious educators and researchers, to strive to develop educational tools that will reach diverse groups of young people? "When individuals participate in drama games, they are physically, mentally and emotionally active. This total involvement helps encourage imagination, spontaneity and even abstract thought" (Warren, 1996, p. 4). I would argue that scholastic resources such as the two documents above that deal with human rights issues can be brought to life through theatre games, enhancing the saliency of the issues and the connections young people make between themselves and children around the world.

As mentioned earlier, I believe the efficacy of theatre and drama games in HRE to be twofold. I strongly support the position that before we can introduce young people to the rampant violations of rights perpetuated against human beings all around the world, violations documented by organizations like Amnesty International and Human Rights Watch, it is crucial that we arm them with a solid framework through which to analyze these abuses. Introducing young people to the United Nations charters already mentioned, the UDHR and the CRC, is a first step in preparing them to examine both historical and current events more critically. Accepting that these documents are not flawless is also an important factor for young people to be able to confront before tackling context-specific human rights issues. And finally, taking into consideration the predominantly western lens that these documents were developed through, young people, especially in relatively privileged spheres, should learn to be critical about how the term "universal" is both employed and enforced.

Granted, these are not necessarily easy tasks to set for ourselves as educators. However, agreeing with Nelson Mandela's words that opened this chapter, I am convinced that it is only through the action of young people that we can hope for change. Perhaps, if we engage young people today about the UDHR and the CRC, tomorrow they will become voters who will finally convince U.S. government officials to ratify the Convention on the Rights of the Child.

Playing the Games: Student-centered, Participatory Education

One of the most significant resources I have encountered in my studies as a human rights educator comes from the United States Holocaust Memorial Museum Education Department. On their Web page, the USHMM offers resources for students, teachers, and university researchers/scholars to engage in a thorough, respectful, and age-appropriate investigation of one of the key human rights violations in history:

> The Holocaust provides one of the most effective subjects for an examination of basic moral issues. A structured inquiry into this history yields critical lessons for an investigation of human behavior. Study of the event also addresses one of the central mandates of education in the United States, which is to examine what it means to be a responsible citizen. Through a study of these topics, students come to realize that:
>
> - Democratic institutions and values are not automatically sustained, but need to be appreciated, nurtured, and protected;
> - Silence and indifference to the suffering of others, or to the infringement of civil rights in any society can—however unintentionally—perpetuate the problems; and
> - The Holocaust was not an accident in history—it occurred because individuals, organizations, and governments made choices that not only legalized discrimination but also allowed prejudice, hatred, and ultimately mass murder to occur. (n.d. Guidelines ¶ 1)

Within these resource pages, the USHMM outlines "Methodological Considerations" as well as "Five Guidelines for Teaching about a Genocide." I have returned to these resources time and time again as I prepare curriculum for my university courses or design workshops for young people around human rights issues. One key methodological consideration that I find particularly relevant to this discussion of theatre activities and drama games in/as HRE locates a specific type of theatrical engagement in educational contexts.

> In studying complex human behavior, many teachers rely upon simulation exercises meant to help students "experience" unfamiliar situations. Even when great care is taken to prepare a class for such an activity, simulating experiences from the Holocaust remains pedagogically unsound. The activity may engage students, but they of-

> ten forget the purpose of the lesson and, even worse, they are left with the impression that they now know what it was like to suffer or even to participate during the Holocaust. It is best to draw upon numerous primary sources, provide survivor testimony, and refrain from simulation games that lead to a trivialization of the subject matter. (Methodical Considerations)

While I agree wholeheartedly that students should not be asked in any way to simulate events or circumstances of suffering experienced by people during the Holocaust, I would like to point out the efficacy of other forms of dramatic role playing that include a level of abstraction from actual historical or current events to enhance educational experiences for young people.

Co-creating a fictitious environment through process drama is one example of how role-play activities can enhance HRE. According to Schneider, Crumpler, & Rogers (2006), "Process-drama techniques allow students to view the world from multiple perspectives, involving them in situations in which they must make informed decisions and live with the consequences of their actions" (p. xv). Elaborating on the potential of process drama to enhance students' learning, Cecily O'Neill (2006) writes, "Speculation, interpretation, evaluation, and reflection, all demanding cognitive activities, are promoted. Opportunities arise for both teacher and students to make the kinds of personal, social, and curricular connections that transcend the traditional boundaries of the curriculum" (p. ix). Students can be invited to go into role as academic conference attendees examining first-person narratives from the Holocaust; or they can take on the mantle of museum curators deciding which primary resources they should display for educational purposes. In their roles as experts, the students can share research they have conducted and engage in collaborative inquiry into ethical, political, and social contexts regarding one of the most difficult times in our history. These examples draw respectfully upon the work of Dorothy Heathcote, Gavin Bolton, Cecily O'Neill, Alan Lambert, Jonothan Neelands, and Tony Goode.

In reality, when I speak of the drama games and exercises I employ to teach about human rights issues, the spectrum of activities ranges from individual, introspective image theatre techniques, carried out in silence and subsequently discussed by participants in the whole group, to often rambunctious, interactive sessions of Alphabet Relay (described below). I believe in educational practices that imply collective ownership of the materials and experience; I believe in critical pedagogy and a problem-posing methodology. As Joe Kincheloe (2005) reminds us:

Critical pedagogy is enacted through the use of generative themes to read the word and the world and the process of problem posing. Critical pedagogy applies Paulo Freire's notion of generative themes used to help students read the word and the world. This reading of the word and the world [helps] students connect what they [decode] on the printed page to an understanding of the world around them. (p. 15)

I employ the following two examples of activities to illustrate how we can start from where the students are and build on the knowledge they already have.

The World Ball Exercise and Alphabet Relay

During the fieldwork for my dissertation research, I happened to come into possession of a small replica of the Earth, roughly three inches in diameter and made of the same soft, foam material that constitutes the average stress ball. This toy inspired one of the cornerstones of my educational theatre practices, an exercise I have been developing for the past five years. I call this activity the World Ball Exercise.

The World Ball is passed to participants seated in a circle and the facilitator asks: "If you had the whole world in your hands, what is one thing you would change?" It is important to emphasize that while there may be several, or many, things each of us would like to change about the world, for the purposes of this game, each participant should pick one they are committed to. Participants should also be reassured that there are no right answers in this activity. More recently, I have added another component to this exercise; I invite every participant to finish his or her turn by stating, "...and I am who I am." This construction results in contributions such as, "If I had the whole world in my hands, the one thing I would change would be violence against women...and I am who I am," and "If I had the whole world in my hands, the one thing I would change would be to provide HIV/AIDS education to everyone...and I am who I am." This activity can be followed up with a review of the articles in the UDHR and/or the CRC that apply to some of the topics shared in the circle. Connections like this are important to reinforce the UN charters and their role in Human Rights Education.

In response to this exercise, students have observed that they feel passionate about diverse issues, and they learn a great deal about their peers through hearing what they would change about the world. Participants engage one another's interests in new topics and issues. Finally, by adding the phrase "...and I am who I am," many participants in workshops and classes I have facilitated have shared that uttering this closing statement is like putting their verbal signature to what they have shared. It makes them feel more deeply committed to the issue; they experience a heightened sense of responsibility toward their topic of choice. They have also shared that this final phrase makes them realize that they are only one person and that they will only be able to have an impact on social change by partnering with other likeminded citizens. This stage of processing the activity is a time to critically reflect and examine, "What have we learned through this exercise?" If we do not leave time for deconstructing the experience, whether with the entire group, in pairs, in small groups, or even individually through a journal-writing exercise, then we are just scratching the surface. "In many cases the talking is as important, if not more important, than the activities" (Warren, 1996, p. 23). The game itself should never be the focus of the lesson plan; it is the dialogue that ensues as a result of the activity that fosters the development of critical consciousness.

The World Ball Exercise as an "ice-breaker" activity helps students to get some issues out on the table that they are concerned with as citizens. If it is used in a group that is just getting to know one another, another element can be added to transform this activity into a "Name Game." If students are asked to pass the world ball and share their names, as well as something they would change about the world, the facilitator can tie the exercise directly back to Article 7, Section 1 of the CRC: "The child shall be registered immediately after birth and shall have the right from birth to a name, the right to acquire a nationality, and as far as possible, the right to know and be cared for by his or her parents" (Gollob, Krapf, & Adzovic, 2006, p. 89). Young people should be given the opportunity to share with one another their interpretations of what each of the rights outlined in the charters means and how it applies to their own lives.

Alphabet Relay is another example of an exercise that has the potential to get students thinking about the different social issues and human rights topics they are already aware of. Depending on the number of participants, the facilitator prepares posters to hang in different spots on the walls, or spread out on the floor, that each have the letters of the alphabet listed along the left-hand side of the paper. In teams of 2-3, or 5-6, again depending on the size of the group, students line up and the first person in each line is given a marker. Signaled by the facilitator, the first student runs up to their team's poster and fills in a word, or short phrase, beginning with one of the letters, that has to do with a human rights issue they are aware of. The facilitator can choose to have students attempt to fill in the charts in strict alphabetical order or randomly, allowing more flexibility and freedom for the participants. When each team completes their list, they can sit down and discuss all of the entries, asking each other questions about phrases or words they are unfamiliar with. The term "relay" refers to the fact that each team sends one player up at time, passing the marker as a track team would a baton; however, this exercise should not be engaged in as a "race." If the atmosphere seems to get competitive, it is okay to remind the teams that they are not racing against one another, they are constructing a vocabulary list on which to build the human rights work you will be engaging in. Lists from workshops I have conducted have included words and phrases like, "abuse, borders, child pornography, disease, education, famine, government, human trafficking, intolerance...oppression, poverty, ineQuality, rape, solidarity... xenophobia...."

Games like Alphabet Relay offer students the opportunity to get creative. The example of the "Q" word illustrates a student team's negotiation with the fact that, even collectively, they were hard pressed to come up with a word that begins with the letter Q; as a result, they improvised. Bernie Warren points out that sometimes, "once participants understand the rules [of the game], they may try to bend them or even make up new ones" (1996, p. 4). I believe this sense of improvisation in response to the "rules" fosters an experience in which young people have the opportunity to encounter obstacles and collaboratively develop strategies to overcome those challenges. Another version of this game can be partnered with the reading of the UN charters, the UDHR and the CRC. As students become more familiar with the language in these documents they can fill in the alphabet lists with terms and phrases from the articles.

Reading the World, Making Connections

Another exercise I employ to introduce students to issues of power and oppression is the legendary game of Colombian Hypnosis. In *Games for Actors and Non-actors*, Boal describes this exercise in detail. To paraphrase him, participants work in pairs and one holds her hand up, palm forward, so that it is approximately 6 inches in front of her partner's face. The fingertips of her hand should line up with her partner's hairline and the wrist should line up with the partner's chin. The partner who is then hypnotized must follow the hand with their face, moving to maintain the constant distance of 6 inches between the face and hand, as well as the alignment and angle of the spatial relationship. The hypnotizer is allowed to move around the workshop space, avoiding collisions with other pairs but pushing her partner to limits based on levels and different speeds. It is Boal's recommendation that "the hand must never do movements too rapid to be followed, nor must it ever come to a complete halt. The hypnotiser must force her partner into all sorts of ridiculous, grotesque, uncomfortable positions" (2002, p. 51). During a session with young people examining the issues of genocide in Darfur, after participating in Colombian Hypnosis, one young person revealed that he had been made to feel like a dog, as if he was being led around on a leash. The students had been reading about the violent attacks that ripped through many of the villages and he made the connection that this exercise could be seen as a metaphor for the control the *janjaweed*, or armed gunmen on horses in Darfur, held over the villagers who were defenseless. He was not claiming in any way that he knew what that must feel like, or could empathize with their suffering, he was simply pointing out that the exercise had had an impact on the way he viewed the human conflict in that region. In their resource guide, Gollob, Krapf, & Adzovic (2006) remind us that "In phases of discussion and reflection, the students develop their general understanding and come to grasp the key concepts that the example has demonstrated.... By sharing their insights in class, the students will benefit from one another, as will the class community as a whole" (p. 6).

These Are Our Rights, Today and Tomorrow

In the work I do with young people, I make every attempt to employ games and activities that develop critical thinking skills, hone the power of observation, encourage creativity, enhance interpersonal communication skills, foster collaboration, strengthen group dynamics, inspire problem posing, and stimulate sensitivity and self-awareness. I believe that an environment in which games are actively engaged has the potential to foster trust and respect, important elements as we address difficult topics. I hope the collaborative activities promote the acceptance of different perspectives, and that through games that celebrate a pluralistic sense of agreement, we even come to accept the fact that we may not always agree on some of these controversial topics; and that is okay.

In the examples I have shared, my intention is to offer you, the reader, an introductory stepping-stone from which to plot your course. There are countless HRE resources and curriculum guides provided, often free of charge, by international organizations, such as Amnesty International (AI), Human

Rights Watch (HRW), and Human Rights Education Associates (HREA). Their Web sites offer numerous documents to download for educational purposes. In addition, as I mentioned earlier, there are excellent books and Web sites that provide step-by-step descriptions of theatre games and dramatic activities, which can be integrated into the HRE materials. Our challenge is to find the optimal combination of age-appropriate, arts-based activities that will enhance the experiences of young people learning about the Universal Declaration of Human Rights and the Convention on the Rights of the Child. I believe that as educators, researchers, artists, social and cultural workers, and parents, we owe it to our children to make these experiences accessible, educational, and entertaining.

Children all around the world are guaranteed the rights to education and to play. By combining these two rights today, we have the exciting opportunity to develop innovative teaching strategies to help young people realize a better tomorrow for all of us.

References

Boal, A. (2002). *Games for actors and non-actors*. (2nd ed.). New York: Routledge.
Chambers. R. (2004). Foreword. In J. McCarthy *Enacting participating development: Theatre-based techniques*. London and Sterling, VA: Earthscan.
Cohen, D. (2006). *The development of play*. (3rd ed.). London & New York: Routledge.
Freire, P. (2007). *Pedagogy of hope: Reliving pedagogy of the oppressed*. London & New York: Continuum.
Freire, P., & Macedo, D. (1987). *Literacy: Reading the word and the world*. Westport, CT and London: Bergin & Garvey.
Gollob, R., Krapf, P., & Adzovic, E. (2006). *Exploring children's rights: Lesson sequences for primary schools*. Strasbourg: Council of Europe.
Kincheloe, J. L. (2005). *Critical pedagogy primer*. New York: Peter Lang.
McCarthy, J. (2004). *Enacting participating development: Theatre-based techniques*. London & Sterling, VA: Earthscan.
Neelands, J., & Goode, T. (2000). *Structuring drama work: A handbook of available forms in theatre and drama*. (2nd ed.). Cambridge, UK: Cambridge University Press.
Nicolopoulou, A., McDowell, J., & Brockmeyer, C. (2006). Narrative play and emergent literacy: Storytelling and story-acting meet journal writing. In D.

G. Singer, R. M. Golinkoff, & K. Hirsh-Pasek (Eds.), *Play = learning: How play motivates and enhances children's cognitive and social-emotional growth*. New York: Oxford University Press.

O'Neill, C. (2006). Foreword. In J. J. Schneider, T. P. Crumpler, & T. Rogers (Eds.), *Process drama and multiple literacies: Addressing social, cultural, and ethical issues*. Portsmouth, NH: Heinemann.

Paterson, D. (1998). Foreword. In M. Rohd, *Theatre for community, conflict & dialogue: The hope is vital training manual*. Portsmouth, NH: Heinemann.

Poulter, C. (1991). *Playing the game*. Studio City, CA: Players Press, Inc.

Rohd, M. (1998). *Theatre for community, conflict & dialogue: The hope is vital training manual*. Portsmouth, NH: Heinemann.

Schneider, J. J., Crumpler, T. P., & Rogers, T. (Eds.). (2006). *Process drama and multiple literacies: Addressing social, cultural, and ethical issues*. Portsmouth, NH: Heinemann.

Singer, D. G., Golinkoff, R. M., & Hirsh-Pasek, K. (Eds.). (2006). *Play = learning: How play motivates and enhances children's cognitive and social-emotional growth*. New York: Oxford University Press.

SOS Children's Villages: The world's largest orphan charity. (n.d.). *Street children in Colombia*. Retrieved May 15, 2009, from http://www.streetchildren.org.uk/colombia

United Nations Children's Fund. (2002). *Adolescence: A time that matters*. New York: UNICEF.

United Nations Children's Fund. (2007). *A world fit for us—The children's statement from the UN Special Session on Children: Five years on*. New York: UNICEF.

United Nations. (2007). *Universal declaration of human rights: Dignity and justice for all of us* (60th Anniversary Special Edition). New York: United Nations Department of Public Information.

United States Holocaust Memorial Museum. (n.d.). *Guidelines for teaching about the Holocaust*. Retrieved June 1, 2009, from http://www.ushmm.org/education/foreducators/guideline/

Warren, B. (1996). *Drama games: Drama and group activities for leaders working with people of all ages and abilities*. (2nd ed.). North York, ON, Canada: Captus Press.

Chapter Eleven

Cyberculture, Multiculture and the Emergent Morality of Critical Cosmopolitanism:
Kids[1] (Trans)Forming Difference Online

Maria Kromidas

> In Cyberspace all positive properties are externalized in the sense that everything you are in a positive sense, all your features can be manipulated. When one plays in virtual space I can for example be a homosexual man who pretends to be heterosexual woman, or whatever: either I can build a new identity for myself or in a more paranoiac way, I am somehow already controlled, manipulated by the digital space.
> —Slavoj Žižek's About Me section of his MySpace profile.[2]

This chapter will explore how a diverse group of 9-, 10-, and 11-year-old kids in New York City played with ideologies of difference (in terms of race and culture) in the digital realm of MySpace. By play, I refer to actions and interactions that were purposive, laborious, and performative as well as enjoyable. It was in and through these playful practices that the young people navigated and (re)produced difference as well as subverted and transcended it. How did the particular digital environment of MySpace encourage or constrain specific configurations of difference, of Self and Other? And what do these specific configurations mean in terms of contemporary politics of difference? While the past few years have seen an explosion of studies on youth and digital technology very few of these studies also include a view of kids' social practices outside digital space. Based on 14 months of ethnographic work, this study contextualizes kids' digital practices within their everyday lives and experiences, allowing an analysis of the specific contours and constraints of the digital environment, an increasingly important realm in kids' lives.

---

1   My use of the term "kids" when referring to my interlocutors is one aspect of an overall politics of representation. The term is doubly advantageous in that it reflects how kids referred to themselves and each other and avoids the condescending if not derogatory connotations of the term "children."
2   Žižek's profile is public and accessible at: http://www.myspace.com/zizek.

Of specific interest in this chapter is how the digital environment affected the emergent morality of critical cosmopolitanism that was evident in the kids' informal talk, interactions, and social relations. This was a diffuse and playful set of practices, strategies, humor, and talk that defamiliarized and subverted the "facts" of race and culture and the very way that they are conceived, which also included introducing new valuations and meanings of specific categories of difference such as "Muslim," "Mexican," "immigrant" as well as "American" (Kromidas, 2009). This critical cosmopolitanism represents the kids' situated critiques of the established morality of multiculturalism, one of the dominant discourses of difference at the contemporary moment. When referring to the morality or moral lessons of multiculturalism, I use these terms in the broad sense defined by Nietzsche as normative or dominant ideas of what "Thou shalt" or Thou shalt not" do, believe, value, honor, and love, as well as his profound irreverence for all such established morals and received "wisdom" that denied life. He often referred to morals as "moral prejudices" (1967 [1887]). Multiculturalism's core moral lessons can indeed be considered prejudices: first, the normalized notion that different *types* or *kinds* of people simply exist, types that are absolute, essentialized, primordial, and fixed; and second that these differences are a matter of natural repulsion, the source of conflict, division, and inequality in society.

The kids' situated critiques challenged multiculturalism's core moral lessons. Their emergent moralit(ies) offered an alternative way of being *with*, *against* and *beyond* difference. In this way, it is of a profoundly different order than Nietzsche's object of criticism, for their moralities were not passive acceptances from the outside but worked out from the kids' own conceptions and experiences. The kids' experiences chafed against multiculturalism and provide a critical window on contemporary politics of race and multiculturalism: pointing out the limitations for expressing Self and Other at the dawn of the twenty-first century and revealing alternative visions and possibilities for a fuller and more robust humanity. As this alternative morality emerged from the mundane everyday face-to-face interactions, the task in this chapter is to explore how the specific technological interface of MySpace mediated the kids' cosmopolitanism. In the provocative terms posed by Žižek above were the kids able to rebuild their cosmopolitanism in cyberspace or were they controlled by the digital space? Before attempting to explore this question, I provide a preliminary sketch of the field site, the theoretical perspective on language and difference in everyday life and youth interactions in digital space.

Social Change and the Dialectic of Practice and Ideology

The analytic framework employed in this study is borrowed from a sociolinguistic approach that is ever mindful that all ideology, no matter how dominant or secure it appears, exists in continual tension with other competing unofficial and informal ideologies. It is an approach to social life that sees the relation between practice and ideology as fluid and dialectical and the source of all social change. At the heart of this theoretical apparatus is a view of language as "a set of symbolic resources that enter the constitution of social fabric and the individual representation of actual or possible worlds" (Duranti, 1997, 3). The concept of performance, based in part on J.L. Austin's speech act theory (1962), has been extremely productive in this regard, calling attention to how speakers also accomplish or "perform" some action when they speak. Performative statements vary enormously, but what is most unique about them is not any of their internal features but in terms of the total speech event, particularly in the heightened role of the audience. Heightened audience scrutiny means that performance has enormous potential for change and equal potential to function conservatively, a site for the reinscription of norms. In any case, performance is important in the production and reproduction of social life, no less so for kids and their playful use of language. While the nature of classrooms is certainly one of surveillance,[3] interaction in the networked public of MySpace makes the concept of performance that much more appropriate, especially in the context of kids' playful (trans)formations of difference and identity.

The analytic of performance has also been especially useful in analyzing the manner in which speakers construct gendered, racial, national and classed identities, deconstructing the essentialisms on which these categories are based (Bettie, 2003; Jackson, 2003; Ramos-Zayas, 2003, 2007). Judith Butler's (1993; 1997) re-articulation of Austin's work in her theory of the performative is certainly the most notable. For Butler, certain speech acts bring into being that which they name—thus gender (or any other identity) is the *effect* of performance rather than vice versa. However, this is not a view of a sovereign subject constituting reality through her speech, a view of individuals constructing this or that identity at will. Instead, Butler formulates the speaker's agency as "derivative," depending on the historicity of language for its performative power:

---

[3] I am decidedly not talking about adult surveillance of kids but kids' surveillance of each other. In fact, I thought of myself as but one of many participant observers of the kids.

> [T]he performative 'works' to the extent that it draws on and covers over the constitutive conventions by which it is mobilized. In this sense, no term or statement can function performatively without the accumulating and dissimulating historicity of force. (1997, 51)

Her key intervention is the emphasis on the derived power of performatives—they rely on prior conventions, structures, and meanings for their effect. These prior conventions, structures, and meanings interpellate or hail the subject (Althusser, 1971), with various sites of social life asking or rather demanding "Hey you, what is your gender?" Multicultural discourse functions in much the same way, in effect asking kids—"Hey you, what is your difference?"

These hailings are key sites whereby subjects are implicated in established ideologies, discourses, and moralities. While borrowing Althusser's anti-humanistic or deterministic language in order to keep power in focus, Butler theorizes alternative responses to the hailing. While incredibly constrained, subjects can respond in unexpected ways...or not answer at all. In effect, she implicitly (if opaquely) suggests a particular relation between practice and discourse, a relation that has been most productively mapped in an open-ended manner by the Bakhtin Circle. Vološinov's (1973) writings on the relationship between language and social interaction on the one hand, and ideology on the other provide a very useful framework with which to analyze how kids' practices articulate with larger discourses of difference and how this may or may not lead to social change.[4]

Briefly, Vološinov distinguished two broad levels of ideology (sets of practices, symbols, representations, meanings, and evaluations)—behavioral ideologies and established ideologies. Behavioral ideologies, representing the outward expression of everyday experience, are normally shaped and given meaning by more established ideologies. However, behavioral ideologies must give sustenance to established ideologies, "otherwise, without that contact, they would be dead, just as any literary work or cognitive idea is dead without living, evaluative perception of it" (ibid, 91). Because behavioral ideologies are grounded within human experience, they are more mobile, flexible and sensitive—and indeed it is from the creative flow of daily life that "partial or radical restructuring of ideological systems comes about" (ibid, 91-92).

---

[4] Ben Rampton's (1995) work with youth in a multiracial neighborhood in the South Midlands of England, discussed below, is the most exemplary use of Volosinov's insights in the analysis of ethnographic material.

This distinction between behavioral and established ideologies is parallel to Bakhtin's distinction between primary and secondary speech genres[5]; primary genres are those that emerge within everyday life and secondary genres being those complex and official, literary, or scientific genres. These distinctions shed light on how individuals can enact established ways of being in complex and unpredictable ways and how established ways of being can in turn absorb and digest the flow of everyday life. In other words, it is a way to see power operating in everyday life: the power of individual strategies and stratagems and the hegemonic power of institutions, directing us to the site of ideological conflict and struggle (cf. Philips, 2003).

Importantly, these social processes do not occur solely through the medium of language, but increasingly through the visual field. Indeed, there are scholars within the burgeoning field of visual culture that argue that the "world-as-a-text has been replaced by the world-as-a-picture" (Mirzoeff, 1999: 7). While there is no need to buy wholesale into this totalizing statement, it is clear that the domain of images cannot be ignored. While not expressed in precisely the same manner, the themes articulated in the field of visual culture productively converge with the framework from linguistics explicated above. Images, like language, are representations that are imbued with meaning, in fact, images can even tightly compress images and express them in more direct ways (Dubin, 1992). The point is that the visual field, just like the linguistic field, is a site of a struggle between hegemonic and counterhegemonic meanings. The framework employed here is productive precisely in identifying this point of struggle between the kids' playful verbal and visual performances and ideologies of difference. What is the conflict between established moralities and the kids' emergent ones? And what is the role played by the increasingly important realm of digital media?

The Larger Project: The Neighborhood, the School and the Production of Difference

The material presented in this chapter was culled from a larger fourteen-month ethnographic study that sought to produce an account of contemporary dynamics in racial formation (Omi and Winant, 1994) from the perspective of a diverse group of kids. As a major center of immigration with the most

---

5   Speech genres are types of utterance that are stable in terms of thematic content, style, and compositional structure. These can range from street greetings and lullabies to business documents and liturgical ceremonies.

diverse immigrant population in the country, New York City has a well-deserved reputation as a "global city." The geography of demographics tells a different story, for NYC neighborhoods and its school districts are among the most segregated in the country (Orfield and Lee, 2004). While no neighborhood or school proportionally represents the population demographics, there are a handful of neighborhoods in NYC are in fact *more* diverse. Augurville is one such neighborhood, a vibrant and unique working and middle class neighborhood in New York City's borough of Queens.[6] It is a neighborhood that represents what scholars are call the "new diversity"—unplanned, and more heterogeneous than anyone could have anticipated—"at no one's request and by no one's design" (Sanjek, 1998, 367; see also Maly, 2005). In Augurville, there are no numerical majorities. Residents hail from a stunning diversity of points of origin across the globe—Egypt, Croatia, Tibet, Nigeria, Mexico, Algeria, Bangladesh, the Philippines, Ecuador, Albania, to name a few—practice numerous religions and speak various languages, representing all socially defined "races" as well as many incipient racialized formations that defy conventional racial categorization. It is in contexts like these that we are more likely to see individuals "turning hegemonic beliefs upside down" (Bailey, 2000, 578), providing a laboratory in which to examine flux in contemporary dynamics of difference.

I collected the bulk of ethnographic data within one of Augurville's public elementary schools (P.S. AV), although the almost obligatory preoccupation with what kids "learn" or do not "learn" about traditional subject matters was notably absent. Rather, the concern was with what kids learn in the sense of apprehending and engaging with the world and their fellow human beings. One major aspect of this learning was the kids' production and transformation of difference as they construct selves and social relations. This is the unofficial curriculum of difference, often enacted within the space of the school through social relations forged in schools and largely ignored by the adults of the school. Of course, schools have their own curricula of difference. This curriculum is often enacted as part of the production of national subjects and the

---

6   The name of the neighborhood and all names of participants are fictitious in order to maintain confidentiality. Some nicknames or screen names are also altered as some invested in these identities. Some direct quotes from kids' MySpace pages are also altered so as not to be searchable. This is in compliance with the current ethical standards of Internet research with sensitive material or with minors, disregarding the fact that many of these statements are made in "public" (Bruckman, 2002; Ess and AoIR Association, 2002).

nation—that "impossible entity" (Balibar, 2002). Indeed, schools are one of the key institutions for this task (Althusser, 1971). Every nation has to build a "we," define its boundaries, its insiders and outsiders, and naturalize them—it has to continually and ceaselessly re-build itself as nation. The questions are: Who are "we" and who do we want to be as a "nation?" How is this "we" to be inculcated? And most pressingly, what will be done with those outside the "we?" These have always been questions that are anxiously asked of and in schools. If the answers to these questions are ever neutral, they have certainly not been so in the United States—any notion of "American" national identity is inextricable from a socio-political order that centers and privileges whiteness (De Genova, 2006, 2007). The seemingly benign official curriculum of difference in most U.S. schools, multiculturalism with its colorful foods, fairs and festivals, is no less neutral than any other national and racial formation of whiteness.[7]

Multiculturalism's seemingly neutral surface has been critiqued by numerous scholars under various rubrics, showing that it is an irreducibly moral and political discourse (Brown, 2006; Goode, 2001; hooks, 1994; Ladson-Billings, 2004; Lee and Lutz, 2005; McLaren, 1997). While the bulk of critiques are textual or discourse-based analyses, I focused on what the morality of multiculturalism meant in everyday life: what kind of subjects it produced and what this meant for social relations. What is the value of recognizing difference? What is the proper relation among constituent differences? The analysis of various multicultural events in the classroom revealed that behind all the celebratory discourse, core moral lessons of multiculturalism were directly and indirectly inculcated. Absolutely different types of humans exist and while it may be "natural," even preferable to "stick with your own kind," we must be tolerant or colorblind. That is, we must be taught by enlightened folk how to ignore our instincts and blind our very senses. Kids were fully proficient in

---

7   Of course, there are more radical or critical variants of multiculturalism that challenge the status quo, but here I refer to the mainstream or traditional version of multiculturalism (see McLaren, 1994 for the most cited typology). Multiculturalism does not just concern schools but is veritably the dominant ideology of difference for the past few decades, and was even called the perfect ideological counterpart to global capitalism (Žižek, 1997). While multiculturalism explicitly avoids talk of race (purporting that the racial era ended with the Civil Rights struggle), I argue that it is an explicitly racialized discourse that perpetuates racial inequality through its refusal to acknowledge the persistence of inequality and that ultimately reproduces race as ontological certainty (Kromidas, 2009).

this speech genre, fulfilling the tasks required of them, performing themselves as multicultural subjects and enacting the rituals of tolerance.

However, proficient does not mean fully or "properly" interpellated. Rather, it is the ability to use something in novel ways, for strategic goals and ends, even for subversion. Indeed, this transformative potential that inheres in the act of interpellation is quite similar to the qualities of kids' play—where order is challenged and taboos broken (Factor, 1988, 2004). And indeed, when the lens is moved to spaces where kids had more autonomy, where teachers' authority was not salient, the kids' playful proficiency becomes striking. For the restrictive confines of multiculturalism had to be stretched, collapsed, or undermined to be able to express the kids' everyday experiences, social interactions, and relations. These practices presented veritable challenges to entrenched forms of thinking about difference. Kids not only forged social relations across difference, but they bridged and crossed difference in creative ways that subverted the essentialism that inheres in multiculturalism and raciology. Rather than the alienating morality of these dominant ideologies of difference, an alternative morality emerged. This situated cosmopolitanism did not emerge from a conscious plan but from the long term, up-close and personal human encounters and social relations that were built in schools. If it was the human encounter that was productive of this cosmopolitanism, how did the digitally mediated nature of interaction of MySpace refigure this emergent morality? As Livingstone (2008, 400) noted, youth interactions within new media are constrained in two principal ways—"first, by the norms and practices of their peer group and, second, by the affordances of the technological interface." As such, I describe both these constraints and the possibilities they allowed in the two sections that follow.

Youth Interaction in Digital Space and the Architecture of MySpace

In the winter of 2007, MySpace caught on like wildfire among a significant number of the 4th and 5th graders in P.S. AV.[8] MySpace is a social network site (SNS) that was the most popular SNS for youth in the United States from

---

8 All data concerning kids' use of MySpace was collected within the school. Kids showed me their MySpace pages on their own or their friends' Sidekicks or PDAs or on my laptop. Most if not all were enthusiastic about showing off their efforts and creativity. Some kids took me on a guided tour of their own activities, verbalizing their interests as they clicked around. Data were also collected from informal talk about MySpace and from individual and group interviews.

about 2005 to 2007, even garnering the appellation of "the civil society of teenage culture" (boyd, 2007a, 3).[9] SNSs are an increasingly widespread communication tool with particular social resonance in the lives of youth. There is no doubt that part of MySpace's popularity was due to its emphasis on popular culture and music. MySpace was also much more responsive to user demands than other SNSs, quickly incorporating various multimedia features that are more attractive to youth (boyd and Ellison, 2008). More important is how MySpace provides a forum of interaction in light of the erosion of public space where youth could congregate (boyd, 2007b). For 9-, 10-, and 11-year-old kids whose spatial movements are significantly more circumscribed than teens, SNSs are the only way to extend the buzzing sociality of the school day. It is no wonder then that kids outright violated MySpace's restriction of use to those at least 14 years of age and gave false information that they were older.[10] Otherwise, confined to their homes, most kids would be engaged in solitary activities like watching television, playing video games, or on less-interactive sites on the Internet. Indeed, 9- to 17-year-olds spend as much time on SNSs as they do watching television, about nine hours per week (National School Board Association, 2007).

It must be made clear that, despite the label of *networking* tool, SNSs amongst youth are more of a *communication* tool, something that was completely true amongst my participants. Most youth are not using SNSs to meet new people.[11] They are simply using them as a place to interact or play, syn-

---

9   While there may be more registered users on MySpace now than there were previously (over 100 million registered users as of February 2010), its defining and cult status in the lives of youth is over.

10 Approximately two-thirds of my participants' parents were aware of their kids' MySpace use and most had no problem with it beyond the ordinary parental complaint concerning time expenditure. Many parents helped their kids set up their accounts and some even set up accounts themselves. Parents' more relaxed attitudes stand in sharp distinction to that of school officials. Teachers and administrators bought the line of MySpace as a shopping mall for sexual predators wholesale. They tried to censure kids with MySpace pages even though they were aware of many parents' approval. In the late spring of 2007 (admittedly a little behind), the school sent out a notice to parents warning them of the perceived dangers of exposure to "adult language and an adult community" and encouraging them to monitor their kids' Internet activity. Habiba was one user whose parents were unaware of her MySpace activities. When she saw the notice she folded it up, tucked it into a pocket of her bookbag and announced "My parents don't need to see this. They'll start to get ideas."

11 All of my participants were quite savvy and would reject "friend" requests from people they did not know. Girls were especially attuned to the possibilities of "molesters." Although I

chronously and asynchronously with their friends and other people they know. Interactions within SNSs thus have *continuity* with other processes of everyday life, making hard-line distinctions between the "real" world and a "virtual" one useless if not outright misleading (Livingstone, 2008, 395). This is not to deny the important shifts in both the face and substance of interaction within these media (Weber and Mitchell, 2008). The fact that many educators and other adults could perceive if not identify the shift in youth interaction, coupled with the stunning popularity and widespread adoption of SNSs among youth has predictably lead to moral panics, as occur with youth adoption of each new medium (Livingstone, 2002; Sefton-Green, 2006). In turn, many cultural studies scholars have responded in their own predictable ways, foretelling that the "virtual" world would usher in revolutionary transformations that overcome the "real" world (cf. Holloway and Valentine, 2003). Fortunately a more even-handed scholarship has emerged that rejects the technophobic/technophilic dichotomy,[12] as well as the virtual / real world binary, instead examining how processes within these new technologies "are still embedded in existing practices and power relations of everyday life" (Wilson and Peterson, 2002).

The celebratory / paranoiac dichotomy is perhaps most evident in discussions concerning race and the new information and communication technologies: the "democratizing" and "empowering" effects versus the "deepening digital divide" are familiar terms in public discourse. An important issue that has recently emerged involves the shifts in new media from text-based to visually driven (or graphic user interface): How might these serve to reinstate the raced human body (Everett, 2008a)? It is clear that we are a long way from the cartoon dog on the computer with the caption "Nobody knows you are a dog on the Internet" (ibid, 2008a, 5). Along with the increasing predominance of the image, the proliferation of questionnaires may also work to enforce or reinforce traditional identity categories (White, 2006). The point is to treat neither youth nor media as monolithic entities but instead to look carefully at how specific digital media present and represent race and how specific youth

---

do agree that the rhetoric of the child predator lurking on MySpace is definitely overblown (see boyd and Jenkins, 2006), I often gave kids advice on how to protect themselves. Notably, I urged an eleven-year-old girl to make private if not remove photographs of herself in a bathing suit in suggestive poses, photographs that her parents were fully aware of. She did not remove the photographs but made them visible only to her "Friends."

12 As Buckingham (2008, 11) perceptively points out, both poles of this dichotomy evince a profound technological determinism.

in particular sociohistorical contexts take up these representations (Everett, 2008b).

Thus MySpace, like any other social artifact, is embedded in existing structures, but also like any artifact has its own unique configuration which foregrounds particular constraints and agency. Although the kids' play was compelling in many ways, the exclusive focus here is the way that it provided a space for the (re)production and refiguring of difference. Did the specific technological interface constrain or coerce the kids into established moral code of multiculturalism, or did it allow their emergent cosmopolitanism to flourish?

There are three key features of MySpace's architecture that are pertinent to these questions: profiles, friends, and comments (see boyd, 2007; boyd and Ellison, 2008 for an overview). The most important feature is the profile. Upon signing up, one is asked to construct a digital profile of the self primarily by responding to questionnaire-like forms. The initial request is for "Basic Information" that is publicly visible: name or nickname; photograph; a "headline," or defining quote; gender; age; and location. The rest of the profile's visibility depends on the privacy-level setting: either publicly accessible or limited to one's "Friends." The profile continues with open-ended questions where one writes "About Me," "Who I'd Like to Meet" and various popular culture "Interests." Finally, in questionnaire-like fashion, one is asked to provide the demographic "details" such as the following: sexual orientation (bi, gay/lesbian, straight, not sure), hometown, body type, ethnicity (Asian, Black/African descent, East Indian, Latino/Hispanic, Middle Eastern, Native American, Pacific Islander, White/Caucasian, Other), Religion, Education, Occupation and Income. Notably, most kids did not bother with any of the open-ended questions, save for a few girls that wrote their "About Me" section, mostly to re-announce their best friends. In contrast, the kids responded to most of the information in the questionnaires, even the question of "Income" was answered, invariably with the "250,000 or higher" choice selected from the drop-down menu. Users are also provided space to upload audio and video material, more of which below.

The second integral architectural feature of MySpace is the Friend component. After completing one's profile, one is asked to invite friends. Once accepted, the friend's screen name and picture is visually displayed as one's

Friend.[13] The amount of friends is practically limitless but only a restricted number can be displayed on the profile, the "top friends." The choice of top Friends and especially the first spot can be considered performances in themselves—one is declaring and displaying one's social network while also enacting it. Rearranging the order of friends or deleting a friend are all acts with consequences and acts that declare something about the self. While most adults' lists are fairly stable, the kids' Friend display is constantly evolving and is thus subject to continuous surveillance.

The third related architectural feature is the Comments section, a public message board from one user to another that is visible by all. MySpace also has a feature similar to traditional e-mail where users can send private messages. In addition, the persistent nature of these messages in the Comment section makes them likely to reach a much larger audience. Consider the difference in the "public" quality of a comment made on a profile frozen in time and one made in the schoolyard. Kids are aware of their comments' persistence and use this feature strategically to make certain things public, to enact certain relationships, to perform certain acts. In the end it is the distinctive public aspect of MySpace and other SNSs' basic structure that distinguish them from other forms of communication—computer-mediated or otherwise. This basic structure also forms the architecture for the playing and (trans)forming of difference described below.

The Kids' MySpace Pages and the Production of Difference

Visiting any of the kids' MySpace pages is a sensory assault—brightly colored "wallpaper," blinking pictures, video clips of Family Guy, the hottest music video or the latest clip from YouTube, a playlist of songs, graffiti-like text falling like rain from the top of the screen, one does not know what to look at first. While most adults rely on the textual aspect of their profile, dutifully listing their favorite books and music, it is not surprising that the kids' energies are expended towards constructing the visual and audio components of

---

13 I capitalize MySpace Friend to distinguish from ordinary friends, as MySpace Friends may only be acquaintances. My participants were Friends with most kids in their class although they may not have interacted with these kids in terms normally defined as friendly. This should not be taken to be evidence of a "real" / "virtual" distinction but rather reinforces the sense of MySpace and other SNSs as a mediated public.

their profiles.[14] Not relying as much on MySpace's provisions for visual and audio, the kids have followed the path of teens in exploiting a programming loophole, which allows users to copy and paste HTML code to personalize their pages in nearly endless ways, adding or "embedding" graphics, video, and even games.[15] It is true that copying and pasting are technically simple, but as Perkel (2008) argues, this new form of literacy is also socially complex—media products are appropriated and disseminated and lines between producer and consumer are blurred (Ito [2008] thus prefers the term participation). It is this blurry line between production and consumption that bears heavily on the production of difference. In their heavy reliance on these commodified products, to what extent are the kids' new moralities of difference allowed to thrive, or to return to this chapter's epigraph, are they manipulated and controlled by these products?

Ashley, a 10-year-old girl whose parents were born in Bolivia and who visited there often, had her page decorated with Bolivian imagery: not only a twirling Bolivian flag but also a cartoon image of a girl in a mini-skirt and thigh-high boots surrounded by sparkling music notes and a twinkling border around "100% Boliviana"; another graphic that simply twinkled "Bolivian Mami"; and a graphic that said "REPPIN BOLIVIA FOR LIFE" in graffiti-styled lettering amidst a paint-splattered background. Amidst the twinkling and twirling and the equally distracting photographs of Victoria Secret models in their underwear, the syncopated rhythm of Daddy Yankee, a popular reg-

---

14 While there are certainly some convergences between adult and youth uses of MySpace and SNSs in general, there are widely recognized divergences. My description in this section is based on my own research as well as the overview provided by boyd (2007; 2008) and Livingstone (2008). One important divergence has to do with the purpose SNSs hold for adults versus youth. Youth use MySpace as a place to hang out or gather with their friends, while adults use SNSs to maintain, develop or solidify already existing, if weak, social relations. In the latter case, a profile lets you find out about a person one does not know whereas in the former, a profile is more spectacular and in the terms used here, performative—used to create certain personas with the available tools.

15 There are numerous sites (all commercial, selling advertising space) from which to copy code to embellish one's profile. Some contain the works of only one graphic artist and others collect and distribute works from many graphic artists, presumably many who are amateurs. Although it would have greatly enhanced this chapter to include some of these graphics, it is unfortunately difficult if not impossible to obtain permission. I direct the reader to some of these sites: crazyprofiles.com, doobix.com, hotfreelayouts.com, latinogfx.com, tagmy.com, coolchaser.com, layouts.fm.

gaetón singer at the time, blares through the speakers. It is hard to even notice the text in Ashley's "About Me" section, which simply says:

> IM ASHLEY U ALL NO ME I LUV MUSIC LIKE HIP HOP, REGETON I HAVE LOTS OF FRIENDS LIKE YANELY, SABRINA, LUISA, N LOTS MORE I LIKE THE SONGS FROM DADDY YANKE, DON OMAR, N MUCH MIORES SEE YAAAAAAA.[16]

Ashley was primarily performing a Bolivian-ness, but one that sharply differed from a more folkloric or "traditional" Bolivian-ness that official multiculturalism compelled. This Bolivian-ness was suffused with a heteronormative sexuality and femininity and at once evoked a broader Latinidad at the same time that it constructed this Latinidad with a tough urban sensibility. It was a Bolivian-ness that was in the end also quite American, itself refigured. This performance had some important similarities to the way that Ashley performed herself multiculturally when she was required by the apparatus of the school. For example, during Multicultural Day, an all-day classroom event where each kid was told to present their "culture," Ashley did bring in the requisite materials—maps, photos, currency, etc. But she also talked about her favorite boutiques, the campus where her sister was getting her medical degree and her favorite Chinese food restaurant. Although the teacher kept asking questions that tried to make Bolivia seem more *different*, more folkloric, "exotic" or even just "undeveloped," Ashley refused to present Bolivia in the frozen, essentialized or exoticized manner that her teacher expected.

Ashley was clearly (in)appropriating multiculturalism—putting the discourse to use in unintended ways. In both the classroom and in MySpace, she refused a particular construction of Bolivian-ness as Other. Furthermore, her MySpace profile rejected the morality of multiculturalism—Thou shall display your difference in regulated and circumscribed instances that will serve as spice or decoration to a hegemonic a-cultural "American" whiteness. Her profile was also a subversion of the core multicultural moral—Thou shall display and explain your difference so that we can tolerate you. The underlying motivation of Ashley's performance was completely at odds with this logic. She was not overly concerned with her peers' understanding or knowledge of the particulars of Bolivian-ness, but with conveying and *playing* with notions of affilia-

---

16 I avoid using sic for certain spellings that were not errors but purposively alternate spellings. As the kids became more acclimated in MySpace, they began to incorporate more creative or "cool" spellings.

tion, identification and belonging in a manner that multiculturalism did not allow.

The graphics used by Ashley are of a type popular amongst her peers. Michael, a 11-year-old boy with Albanian parents had his profile decorated with similar graphics—a waving (literally) Albanian flag as well as a graphic with an Albanian flag background overlaid with a handgun in the foreground with graffiti-like text that read "Albanian for life" and decorated with dollar symbols. Sabrina, a 10-year-old girl with Albanian parents also had her page decorated with the Albanian national symbol, a double-headed eagle, as well as an image of a cartoon girl with a glittering mini-dress and text that read "Proud to be an Albanian girl." Both Michael and Sabrina were refiguring dominant notions of what it meant to be Albanian in a way that was more in tune with their experiences, and in a manner that was for them ultimately playful and enjoyable.

Billy, a 10-year-old who was born in Greece and came to New York as an infant, had a profile that was playful in the manner defined above—purposive, performative, and enjoyable. His entire background or "wallpaper" was composed of the blue and white colors of the Greek flag, he had a section with a rotating photo album with pictures from Greece, the symbols from a Greek soccer team and an enormous amount of graphic material. One such graphic read "I'm no wanna be GOTTI. i set my own trends...a natural GREEK HOTTI,"[17] where the Gotti was written in diamonds as were parts of the words Greek Hotti, which also had the requisite blue and white of the Greek flag.

Billy's Greek graphics were interspersed with other types of graphics that are part of a "gangsta" or "ghetto" imaginary: an outline of a tilting figure with a cane and a wide-brimmed hat that read "Warning: Pimp Zone All violators will be bitch slapped," as well as real photographs and graphic images of so-called "tricked out" cars (cars with options or accessories). The use of this gangsta type of graphic on MySpace was widespread among the kids. I will de-

---

17 John Gotti was one of the more notorious mafiosos, head of one of the U.S. mafia's New York City based "Five Families," known alternately as the "Dapper Don" for his impeccable appearance and sartorial manner or the "Teflon Don" because he evaded conviction (cases were unable to stick so to speak) for such a long time. He looms large in hip-hop's iconography of gangsters. Outside of hip-hop, Gotti can arguably be seen as the precursor of the so-called "metrosexual" aesthetic of young males who consider themselves "tough:" weekly haircuts and intense daily hair styling, eyebrows shaped by waxing, manicures and the requisite "ice" (real or fake diamonds) on earrings and necklaces.

scribe a few graphics that made use of some of the predominant visual themes of this "gangsta" imagery: a drawing of a boom box in the background with a can of spray paint and a Nike sneaker in the foreground; a photograph of a toilet paper roll made out of twenty-dollar bills; a graphic of Mickey Mouse wearing sunglasses, baggy jeans, and throwing up a gang sign; one with a slightly malicious Bugs Bunny flashing a hand full of gold and diamond rings announcing "I'm Gangsta;" a diamond-encrusted tiara where the front read "Ghetto Queen" also in diamonds; a drawing of two skulls that read "Get Money, Spend Money, Stay Fly. Those 3 Codes I Live By."[18] There was a related type or subset of this "ghetto" graphic that celebrated authenticity, being "real" and castigated phonies and "haters," a general theme in face-to-face interaction as well. These were represented mostly by colorful graphic text ("What's worse than enemies? Fake Friends") or by a combination of graphic text and a simple picture (a bottle of green liquid that read "Stop Sippin Haterade"; a skeleton holding up its middle finger bones that read "for tha haters"; an outline of three female figures evoking the Charlie's Angels pose with the text "Me & My Girls are the Hottest Bitches You'll Eva See Don't Hate It's Just a Fact").

Many kids had profiles that solely relied on "gangsta" imagery, including Remzi, an 11-year-old boy whose parents were born in Turkey. He also had hip-hop songs and videos playing on his profile and a large picture of the rapper 50 cent. It is obvious that this "gangsta" style was articulated with and gained much of its meaning from Black or multiracial youth cultural forms especially hip hop subculture.[19] These stylistic features were related to other stylizations in dress, manners, and tastes that were associated with "coolness"

---

18 Some of these are obviously gendered. Although girls would display some of the more masculine graphics, it probably comes as no surprise that boys did not display the more feminine graphics.

19 Nomenclature here is important as different terms capture specific characteristics. "Hip hop subculture" indexes the point of confluence of the stylistic features, where they are represented and mass mediated and includes the commodities themselves. "Black youth culture" indexes the ownership and derivation of these forms in African American cultural production (with important contributions by Latino/as) at the same time that it signals their racialized status in the wider sphere. Both terms are necessary to signal the circuitous relation between on-the-ground forms and expression and their mass-mediation through media commodities. "Multiracial youth culture" specifically refers to how these kids, along with other youth, appropriate these forms to construct their own configurations which while somewhat disarticulated from Blackness are still an incipient racial formation.

and were the most valued ways of being and acting for most boys and some girls in the school, a value derived from the association with the vibrancy of Black youth culture. Some kids' stylizations were also attempts to symbolize and display affiliation with Black youth culture. In face-to-face interactions in school, one had to essentially gain permission to use these symbols—authenticity and legitimacy were heavily policed by those considered insiders as well as outsiders. Otherwise, one was considered a "wanna-be," a most demeaning slur. On MySpace, the restrictions were loosened quite a bit. At school, Remzi did not engage in conspicuous performances of gangsta-ness. He did try to subtly incorporate some stylistic elements—a NY Yankees baseball cap and T-shirts by name brands such as enycee or ecko, but it ended there. Clearly, Remzi's digital profile was a place to playfully experiment, a space that allowed him to signal affiliations that he was not confident or legitimate enough to signal in face-to-face interactions.

Much of the same can be said about other kids that employed multicultural-type imagery that was suffused with this "gangsta" ethos. We already saw how Billy's profile exemplified this and how Ashley's evoked it as well. While Billy donned the clothing and the posture, he was widely considered a "wanna-be" and thought to be "copying" kids that were regarded as authentic members of the multiracial youth culture. Steven, an 11-year-old Puerto Rican kid, and James, a 10-year-old boy, whose parents were born in the Philippines were two such boys. Accusations of copying aspects of Steven or James' profiles were frequent in the classroom. Notably, neither Steven nor James used many graphics that were text-heavy in the construction of their profiles. They relied instead on images of dollar signs, pictures of hundred-dollar bills, various iterations of the NY Yankees logo, photographs and drawings of sneakers, cars, and crowns. The boys were confident enough to let these images do their talking. Their online playful practices were extensions of their performances in school, assuring their place as the models of authenticity in this realm.

Ashley's MySpace performances were also experimental—some of her friends certainly performed themselves as "gangsta"[20] and with a certain type of femininity that was quite sexualized. Short skirts that sometimes got sent home from school, make-up, highlights in their hair, eyebrows waxed into an exaggerated shape—these were all elements of a Latina femininity amongst one

---

20 Notably, girls that cultivated this persona did it much more behaviorally than boys who relied much more on commodities to do their talking. The girls acted and spoke aggressively and were constantly on the offense as well as defense.

group of girls. These girls also used much of the same type of graphics—that boldly asserted they were 100% *Mexicana* or *Colombiana*—and sent each other chain-mail type comments that requested things like "If ur a real Mexican, pass this to 8 Mexicans u know!"[21] They often interspersed these with another genre of graphics—the young person in love theme—one also used by boys when they were "going out with" a girl. While there are many interesting threads to pick up on here, what is most interesting to me is the way that various ethno-national identities were hybridized with this gangsta ethos, thereby re-signifying both elements.

This hybridization had much continuity with the processes that occurred in school. I argue that for many kids who were migrants or had parents who were migrants, adopting these stylistic elements from Black culture was a way to become "American," a process that Ramos-Zayas also identified amongst Latino teens in New Jersey (2007). As with any other type of crossing (practice of appropriating aspects of an identity that one does not have conventional access to), this appropriation of elements associated with Black youth culture could be problematic or promising. The kids themselves were well aware of this, and the issues of authenticity and sincerity alluded to above were directed at precisely this issue. For Rampton (1995), crossings reveal the local and immediate structures of feeling as well as the wider political significance of racial stratification, identity, and social change and can challenge many of the essentialisms associated with ideologies of difference. Some of the kids' crossings certainly did symbolize heartfelt identifications with hip hop cultural forms as well as an identification and affiliation with Blackness. Steven and James both had Black friends, rejected whiteness and those who associated with its more hegemonic aspects and generally stood for a counterhegemonic racial politics. Indeed that is why they were considered authentic representatives of hip-hop culture. It was an unfortunate fact that a lot of kids that did appropriate these forms did not also reject the dominant morality. These kids' practices might be termed cultural plunders of sorts, and more distressing is how they reproduced some of the negative connotations of Blackness with aggression, masculinity and criminality. This selective appropriation allowed some kids to have their cake and eat it too: "a way of sharing vicariously in the plusses of that culture without having to experience the minuses associated with it" (Eble, 2004: 383). The asynchronous nature of interaction on MySpace, disregarding

---

21 Some of these chain-like comments were quite counter-hegemonic, not only claiming Mexican-ness but castigating whiteness.

the fact that any interaction or performance is potentially viewable by a larger public, allowed more kids to experiment with these risky cultural appropriations.

It is important to underline that although more kids dared to experiment with this type of performance, the experimental nature of performances was much more limited in MySpace than it was in ordinary face-to-face interaction. Informal interaction in the school was much more experimental *and* counterhegemonic. On MySpace, the hybridizations were mostly uni-directional—kids of various identities appropriated the "gangsta" imagery. In school, the hybrids were of various sorts and created in various ways. For instance, Jacinta, a 10-year-old Dominican girl who was best friends with two Albanian girls, Sabrina and Eliza, would sprinkle words of Albanian where she could, and all three of them would creatively and poetically bridge the difference between the Dominican Republic and Albania, recognizing each other's affiliations and constructing them as functionally equivalent. Lucas and Abdul, kids of Mexican and Lebanese parents respectively, also bridged and crossed between their identities creatively. Michael, whose Albanian-themed profile was discussed above, also engaged in these processes with Akil, his best friend of Pakistani descent. Jessie, a Puerto Rican girl that was best friends with a Mexican girl and a girl whose parents were from Montenegro also creatively crossed and bridged and performed herself to be Mexican and Montenegran. Notably, she was one of the few kids that participated in this cosmopolitan morality whose MySpace reflected this. In her "About Me" section of her profile, she wrote:

```
mY nAmE iS jEssIE . i aM iRrEsPoNsObLE . i
DoNt CaRe . i lIkE pEoPlE . i Am FiErCe StRoNg
AnD sMeXy. 22 i LiKe mE oR nOt {{cHoOsE oNe}} .
i LoVe bOySz . i hAtE bOyZs . i LoVe LiL bA-
bIeS *sO cUtE* . i LoVe sImPlE pEoPlEs . i Am
50% RiCaN 50% mExIcAnA aNd AlSo 50% FrOm MoN-
tEnEgRo BeCaUsE Of AdE My SiStEr/BeStFrIeNd .
My FaVoRiTe SoNg In HeR cUlTuRe Is "Guci Guci"
By Amet WiTch Is My SoNg >:) . ReTaRtED pEoPlE
lIkE mE rOk.
```

While she did not include this song, she did include images of all three flags: from Puerto Rico, Mexico, and Montenegro. Practices like Jessie's, Jacinta's,

---

22 "Smexy" seems to be a deliberate attempt to make sexy sillier and perhaps a more age-appropriate way to express her budding sexuality.

Eliza's, Abdul's, and Lucas' rejected the deepest cores of ideologies of difference—they rejected the notion that they had to *be* what they were assigned, this one identity and only that for all time. Along with rejecting essentialism, they also rejected the notion that "sticking with your own kind" was the right way to be—against not only the assumptions of ideologies of difference but often their own parents' wishes. Why were these more cosmopolitan formations infrequent on MySpace? Why were the hybrids created of only one type, one that was more hegemonic than most? Why did MySpace thwart the emergent cosmopolitanism that was evident in face-to-face playful practices?

It Ain't TheirSpace! Kids, Capital and the Submerging of Cosmopolitanism

One compelling answer to these questions has to do precisely with the very nature of MySpace—it is not just a communication or networking tool or a space for people to interact and exchange and enjoy various media. It is all those things but inserted into the overarching and overdetermining political and economic architecture of capitalism. It is a commodity. The media products that the kids exchange are not just images and graphics, they are also commodities. And within a capitalist structure, there are no free commodities. It is true that the kids are in a sense paying with their marketing information for a more effective and "all-knowing" capitalism (Beer, 2008), but I mean this in a different but no less important way. The kids are coerced to perform their selves with these already-given constructs, constructs that are often just as reifying and hegemonic as those from school multiculturalism. Indeed, this is corporate multiculturalism (McLaren, 1997), a type that converges in some ways with school multiculturalism but that also has significant differences. At core, they both reproduce essentialized difference as an ontological given. While school multiculturalism's celebration of difference is a screen for a deep suspicion and hierarchization of difference, corporate multiculturalism's fetishization of difference is truly benign. Constructing difference as marketable and marketed lifestyle choices, corporate multiculturalism privileges no color except green. The architecture of MySpace, arising as it does from the logic of the market, seriously delimits the complex and evolving morality that emerges within extended face-to-face interactions and everyday living in multi-racial multi-ethnic neighborhoods. It may be true that play contains liberatory potential, but it is also true that play can reinscribe lines of power and be a site for subjection and normalization.

To return to the opening epigraph of this chapter, it seems that the architecture of MySpace controls and manipulates or *coerces* the kids toward a more hegemonic morality. This is a morality where difference is essentialized, fetishized, pre-packaged, where the self is defined according to this essentialism. As Foucault (1989) remarkably noted, "Maybe the target nowadays is not to discover what we are, but to refuse what we are." Within schools, often unnoticed, kids in diverse neighborhoods are doing precisely that, rejecting their pre-given identities and cobbling together something new. If kids are taken seriously, as I do here, their playful yet serious interactions are not seen as absurd or surreal. Rather, they draw attention to how surreal and absurd the very ideologies are that violently split up humanity and prevent selves from realizing a full and liberated humanity. This is the moral crux of a critical cosmopolitanism, one that unfortunately remains hidden and submerged in cyberspace. The penultimate question then becomes: Will the kids' critical moral lessons be absorbed and neutralized by the de-humanizing established morality?

The task of critical scholarship does not end at critique but seeks to transform the stultifying and taken-for-granted realities that often seem insurmountable. Indeed, the alienating world of types and kinds of humans confronts us precisely as such. But kids in a multiracial neighborhood in New York City were able to subvert some of the most entrenched aspects of ideologies of difference. While their subversions and challenges were incomplete and fragmentary, the same could be said of scholarly accounts. To me, the kids' analyses of the social order are equally or perhaps more compelling than most articulations of cosmopolitanism that have been recently conceived in academia.[23]

I do not wish to romanticize the kids' perspectives but to reiterate that the foundation of any authentic emancipatory project, pedagogical or otherwise, must be collaborative. In that sense, educators, scholars, advocates, and activists of and for kids must take their cues from kids' everyday experiences. In terms of education, critical media literacy could help kids become producers rather than consumers of images in cyberspace. Furthermore, critical pedagogues' collaborative efforts could be geared toward productive dialogues that

---

23 It is true that some articulations of cosmopolitanism that call for a "detached" or "rootless" ethos have turned out to evince a classed and often raced parochialism (see: Hannerz, 1992). Much more useful are those that advocate indeterminate forms that are a result of interaction and co-existence (see: Bhabha, 1996; Gilroy, 2005; Hall, 2002).

engage with the normative ideologies that inhere in cyberspace as well as in other sites and artifacts that kids play in and with. More pressing, however, is the need for real spaces for kids, ones they could call their own, spaces where they can interact face-to-face, where they could encounter one another in real time, for it is in real time and space that all vitality and everything new in social life emerges.. In short, kids need places where they could play, where their imaginations can exceed the confines of the already-given.

Acknowledgments

I would like to thank June Factor for her helpful comments and criticism, for providing such inspiration in her own work and for allowing me to practice a little bit of cosmopolitanism with our cross-hemispheric exchange. I would also like to thank danah boyd for her advice and encouragement at the earliest stage in this endeavor, and Drew Chappell for helping develop this argument and making it more readable.

References

Althusser, L. 1971. Ideology and Ideological State Apparatuses: Notes Toward an Investigation. In *Lenin and Philosophy and Other Essays*, pp. 121-73. New York: Monthly Review.

Austin, J. L. 1962. *How to Do Things with Words*, Oxford University Press.

Bailey, B. 2000. Language and Negotiation of Ethnic/Racial Identity. *Language in Society* 29(4): 555-82.

Balibar, E. 2002. *Politics and the Other Scene*. London: Verso.

Beer, D. 2008. Social Network(ing) Sites...Revisiting the Story So Far. *Journal of Computer-Mediated Communication* 13: 516-29.

Bettie, J. 2003. *Women Without Class: Girls, Race and Identity*. Berkeley, CA: University of California Press.

Bhabha, H.K. 1996. Unsatisfied: Notes on Vernacular Cosmopolitanism. In *Text and Narration: Cross Disciplinary Essays on Cultural and National Identities*, ed. L. García-Moreno, P.C. Pfeiffer (pp. 39-52). Columbia, SC: Camden House.

boyd, d. 2007a. Why Youth (Heart) Social Network Sites: The Role of Networked Publics in Teenage Social Life. In *MacArthur Foundation Series on Digital Learning, Identity Volume*, ed. D Buckingham (pp. 119-42). Cambridge, MA: MIT Press.

boyd, d. 2007b. Social Network Sites: Public, Private, or What? *Knowledge Tree* 13.
boyd, d. 2008. *Taken Out of Context: American Teen Sociality in Networked Publics*. Ph.D. dissertation, University of California, Berkeley.
boyd, d, and Jenkins, H. 2006. MySpace and Deleting Online Predators Act (DOPA). MIT Tech Talk. http://www.danah.org/papers/MySpace DOPA.html. (Accessed May 4, 2009).
boyd, d., and Ellison, N. 2008. Social Network Sites: Definition, History, and Scholarship. *Journal of Computer-Mediated Communication* 13(1): 210-30.
Brown, W. 2006. *Regulating Aversion: Tolerance in the Age of Identity and Empire*. Princeton, NJ: Princeton University Press.
Bruckman, A. 2002. Studying the Amateur Artist: A Perspective on Disguising Data Collected in Human Subjects Research on the Internet. *Ethics and Information Technology* 4(3): 217-31.
Buckingham, D. 2008. Introducing Identity. In *Youth, Identity and Digital Media*. ed. D. Buckingham (pp. 1-24). Cambridge, MA: The MIT Press.
Butler, J. 1993. *Bodies that Matter: On the Discursive Limits of 'Sex'*. New York: Routledge.
Butler, J. 1997. *Excitable Speech: A Politics of the Performative*. New York: Routledge.
De Genova, N., ed. 2006. *Racial Transformations: Latinos and Asians Remaking the United States*. Durham, NC: Duke University Press.
De Genova, N. 2007. The Stakes of an Anthropology of the United States. *CR: The New Centennial Review* 7(2): 231-77.
Dubin, S.C. 1992. *Arresting Images: Impolitic Art and Uncivil Actions*. London and New York: Routledge.
Duranti, A. 1997. *Linguistic Anthropology*. Cambridge: Cambridge University Press.
Eble, C.C. 2004. Slang. In *Language in the USA: Themes for the Twenty-first Century*, ed. E Finegan, JR Rickford, pp. 375-86: Cambridge University Press
Ess, C. and the AoIR Ethics Working Committee. 2002. Ethical Decision-Making and Internet Research: Recommendations from the AoIR Ethics Working Committee.
Everett, A. 2008a. Introduction. In *Learning Race and Ethnicity: Youth and Digital Media*, ed. A. Everett, 1-14. Cambridge, MA: The MIT Press.
Everett, A., ed. 2008b. *Learning Race and Ethnicity: Youth and Digital Media*. Cambridge, MA: The MIT Press.

Factor, J. 1988. *Captain Cook Chased a Chook: Children's Folklore in Australia*. Ringwood: Penguin.

Factor, J. 2004. Tree Stumps, Manhole Covers and Rubbish Tins: The Invisible Play-Lines of a Primary School Playground. *Childhood*: 11(2): 142-54.

Foucault, M. 1989. The Subject and Power. In *Michel Foucault: Beyond Structuralism and Hermeneutics*, eds. H.L. Dreyfus, P. Rabinow. Chicago, IL: University of Chicago Press.

Gilroy, P. 2005. *Postcolonial Melancholia*. New York: Columbia University Press.

Goode, J. 2001. Teaching Against Cultural Essentialism. In *Cultural Diversity in the United States*, eds. I. Susser, T.C. Patterson (pp. 434-56). Malden, MA: Blackwell.

Hall, S. 2002. Political Belonging in a World of Multiple Identities. In *Conceiving Cosmopolitanism: Theory, Context, and Practice*, eds. S. Vertovec, R. Cohen (pp. 25-31). Oxford: Oxford University Press.

Hannerz, U. 1992. *Cultural Complexity: Studies in the Social Organization of Meaning*. New York: Columbia University Press.

Holloway, S.L., and Valentine, G. 2003. *Cyberkids: Children in the Information Age*. London: Routledge.

hooks, b. 1994. *Teaching to Transgress: Education as the Practice of Freedom*. New York: Routledge.

Ito, M. 2008. Mobilizing the Imagination in Everyday Play: The Case of Japanese Media Mixes. In *International Handbook of Children, Media and Culture*, eds. K. Drotner, S. Livingstone, D. Buckingham (pp. 397-412). London: Sage.

Jackson, J. 2003. *Harlemworld: Doing Race and Class in Contemporary Black America*. Chicago, IL: University of Chicago Press.

Kromidas, M. 2009. *Race, Multiculturalism and "Childhood": The Emergent Cosmopolitanisms of Kids in a New York City School*. Ph.D. dissertation, Teachers College, Columbia University.

Ladson-Billings, G. 2004. New Directions in Multicultural Education: Complexities, Boundaries, and Critical Race Theory. In *Handbook of Research in Multicultural Education*, eds. J.A. Banks, C.A. McGee Banks, 50-65. San Francisco, CA: Jossey-Bass.

Lee, J-A., and Lutz, J. 2005. Introduction. In *Situating Race and Racisms in Time, Space, and Theory: Critical Essays for Activists and Scholars*, ed. J-A. Lee: McGill-Queen's University Press.

Livingstone, S. 2002. *Young People and New Media*. London: Sage.

Livingstone, S. 2008. Taking Risky Opportunities in Youthful Content Creation: Teenagers' Use of Social Networking Sites for Intimacy, Privacy and Self-Esteem. *New Media & Society* 10 (3): 393-411.

Maly, M.T. 2005. *Beyond Segregation: Multiracial and Multiethnic Neighborhoods in the United States*. Philadelphia: Temple University Press.

McLaren, P. 1994. White Terror and Oppositional Agency: Towards a Critical Multiculturalism. In *Multiculturalism: A Critical Reader*, ed. D.T. Goldberg, 45-74. Cambridge, MA: Blackwell.

McLaren, P. 1997 *Revolutionary Multiculturalism: Pedagogies of Dissent for the New Millennium*. Boulder, CO: Westview Press.

Mirzoeff, N. 1999. *An Introduction to Visual Culture*. London and New York: Routledge.

National School Board Association. 2007. Creating and Connecting: Research and Guidelines on Online Social–and Educational–Networking. Alexandria, VA.

Nietzsche, F. 1967 [1887]. *On the Genealogy of Morals*, translated by Walter Kaufmann. New York: Vintage Books.

Omi, M., and Winant, H. 1994 *Racial Formation in the United States*. New York: Routledge.

Orfield, G., and Lee, C. 2004. *Brown at 50: King's Dream or Plessy's Nightmare?* Cambridge, MA: The Civil Rights Project, Harvard University.

Perkel, D. 2008. Copy and Paste Literacy? Literacy Practices in the Production of a MySpace Profile. In *Informal Learning and Digital Media: Constructions, Contexts, Consequences*, eds. D. Drotner, H.S. Jensen, & K. Schroeder, 203-224. Newcastle, UK: Cambridge University Press.

Philips, S.U. 2003. The Power of Gender Ideologies in Discourse. In *The Handbook of Language and Gender*, eds. J. Holmes, M. Meyerhoff, 252-76. Malden, MA: Blackwell.

Ramos-Zayas, A. 2003. *National Performances: The Politics of Class, Race, and Space in Puerto Rican Chicago*. Chicago: University of Chicago Press.

Ramos-Zayas, A. 2007. Becoming American, Becoming Black? Urban Competency, Racialized Spaces, and the Politics of Citizenship among Brazilian and Puerto Rican Youth in Newark. *Identities: Global Studies in Culture and Power* 14: 85-109.

Rampton, B. 1995. *Crossing: Language and Ethnicity Among Adolescents*. London: Longman.

Sanjek, R. 1998. *The Future of Us All: Race and Neighborhood Politics in New York City*. Ithaca: Cornell University Press.

Sefton-Green, J. 2006. Youth, Technology, and Media Cultures. *Review of Research in Education* 30(1): 279–306.

Vološinov, V.N. 1973. *Marxism and the Philosophy of Language*. Cambridge: Harvard University Press.

Weber, S., and Mitchell, C. 2008. Imaging, Keyboarding, and Posting Identities: Young People and New Media Technologies. In *Youth, Identity, and Digital Media*, ed. D. Buckingham (pp. 25–48). Cambridge, MA: The MIT Press.

White, M. 2006. *The Body and the Screen: Theories of Internet Spectatorship*. Cambridge, MA: MIT Press.

Wilson, S.M., and Peterson, L.C. 2002. The Anthropology of Online Communities. *Annual Review of Anthropology* 31, 449–67.

Žižek, S. 1997. Multiculturalism or the Cultural Logics of Multinational Capitalism. *New Left Review* September–October: 28–51.

Chapter Twelve

Adversity in a "Snowball Fight":
Jewish Childhood in the Muslim Village of Sillwan

Shimi Friedman

Introduction

This chapter deals with the design of a community identity composed of bi-directional socialization movements between adults and children, which operates in the children's encountering of the reality that has been constructed for them. Beyond their being passive absorbents of the social demands thrust upon their world, as constructed to them by their parents, I present the manner in which the children also actively contribute to the construction process of the community identity. With a natural continuity to this claim, I also investigate how through a shared Jewish and Muslim childhood in the mixed village of Sillwan, in Jerusalem, young people engage in building a different construct of identity from what the adults in their lives impress on them. In this research arena I spent four years of participant observation, taking part in the routine life of the Jewish families at the village. According to the anthropological method, I collected data from my stays; observations, conversations, and "open interviews" were my ethnographic base for understanding and analyzing the local culture.

Below is a short account of a conversation held with an 11-year-old Jewish girl and her mother, who have been living in the village for ten years:

> The girl: "We are facing the fence and talking with them, with our neighbors here, near the playground, near the fence, asking them 'How are you?' 'What's your name?' We don't really have a relation with the Arab kids, but merely talk; what's your name, and such questions. The Jewish kids know the Arab kids' names and vice versa."
>
> The mother: "Put the kids together, you think they care about Jews-Arabs? In the yard they constantly communicate—these from this side of the fence and these from the other, standing and asking each other, or merely watching and showing interest when one doesn't understand the language well enough."

Insights crucial for the discussion in this chapter emerge from this conversation. In an area where Jews and Muslims conduct a mixed life, the adult Jews feel a need to create a community whose ideological boundaries are clear for them but perhaps not clear enough for their children. First, the adults deal with the clarification of the borders for themselves—the founding generation of the Jewish community in the mixed ethnicity village of Sillwan—and, parallelly, attempt to organize and simplify dominant social and political ideas for their children. For the mother, the living area is undetermined and vague and needs to be clarified for the children. She refers to the existence of the boundary between the two groups and presents it as vague in the children's perception. For the young daughter, the children in the expanse are merely children. The girl's opinion is that the encounter is naive, challenging, and intriguing, and it has the potential to lead to simple friendship. But nevertheless, when the girl describes the "relation-non-relation" that the children live in on both sides of the fence, she speaks of the boundaries constructed by the adults and what she has learned about the local social network.

Riad, a Muslim inhabitant in the village, is a father of four kids. He too follows the Jewish mother's claim regarding the naivety of the children in the village. He words it even more clearly and sharply:

> The adults are in the way. It is clear. If the adults didn't come in between, and didn't interfere, the kids would manage very well among them.

With these words, Riad expresses his viewpoint regarding the mixed life in the village. Namely, we—the adults—prevent the creation of a calm and pleasant way of life. We have to learn from the way the children see the world and, perhaps, to behave like them. One way in which the strict identity boundaries may be redesigned is through children's games played in the village; this is the focus of my chapter.

Background

The first of the modern era Jews living in the village of Sillwan arrived in the eastern extension of the village, namely, the Western slopes of The Mount of Olives. Around 120 years ago, Jews arrived from Yemen and settled in these areas. With time, the Jewish settlement in Israel had assisted in expanding the neighborhood and the Jews arrived in the Western part of the village of Sillwan as well. The violent pogroms in Israel against the Jews in the years 1921 to 1929 around Jerusalem and Hebron undermined the idyll in the Yemenite Jews' neighborhood, and in 1938, the British police left the village notifying the Jews that they renounced their responsibility for the region's safety and recommended that the Jews leave the place with the hope of returning after the pogroms.

The Jews did not return to the area that had been occupied by the IDF (Israel Defense Forces) in the Six-Day War until 1991. During this year, the ELAD fellowship (Hebrew initials for To the City of David) bought two buildings in the village of Sillwan. The fellowship believes that this space is unique and invaluable for the Jewish people due to its history and religious ideas of a holy space and therefore a political issue between the Jewish-Muslim inhabitants. Therefore, the fellowship has been active developing tourism focused on the archeological sites which have been recognized by researchers belonging to the biblical period of the City of David (1006-586 BCE). The five Jewish families that entered the village that year (1991) shared two spacious complexes.

To this day, the fellowship has been taking measures to bring Jews to the village by buying houses from Muslim inhabitants of the village. The process of acquiring the houses is composed of a long and complex chain of bureaucratic, legal, and commercial actions that quite often get stuck during the negotiation with the owner of the property. The Muslim inhabitants are not allowed to sell the land they live on to the Jews, due to the *Waqf* rules (the lands belong to God, to give them religious value). Therefore, the Jewish fellowship uses a Muslim "Middle-Man" as a mediator who can bypass the *Waqf* rules and then pass the land on.

From 1991 until today, the fellowship has bought around ten additional buildings, where forty families now live among Muslim families. The Jews live in complexes consisting of two to four houses, and one complex that consists of one house only. Thus, some of the houses in the village are partially occupied by Jews and partially by Muslims.

The Jewish inhabitants avoid buying groceries in the village shops that are owned by Muslims, instead doing their shopping in the city center. The Israeli security institutions regard Sillwan as dangerous. As a result, there is a security net that consists of closed-circuit TV cameras, and armed security guards guard the Jews at their homes. There is also a nursery for children up to three years old. After this age, the children move to various educational frameworks in the Jewish Quarter, within the walls of the Old City of Jerusalem.

The majority of the sociology literature refers to the term "socialization" as the effort of society to convey rules, values, and norms to the individual who seeks to join it (see for example: Seginer, 1990; Shamgar-Handelman, 1991;

Marjoribanks, 1992). In this process, the community is interested in incorporating the individual into an existing cultural framework, so as to ensure that framework's survival. People seek to teach young individuals about the reality of their society, and to examine and encounter its complexities (Corsaro & Streeck, 1986; Miller, Potts, Fung, Hoogstra, Mintz, 1990).

An Israeli-Jewish childhood bears national meaning conveyed via family, school, and National youth clubs. Many of the national claims in this education are based on the Zionist collective ethos that encourages militaristic values as well, via the military service of the Israeli youth (Ben-Eliezer, 1995; Azaria, 1989). Henceforth, I will examine the adults' attempt to construct a world of ethnical-national boundaries by emphasizing the components of "the other" in the mixed village of Sillwan (Rabinowitz, 1996).

Most of the anthropological research that has been done up to date focuses on children's leisure games and studies the children's methods of internalizing the socialization through games (Schwartzman, 1976; Mead, 1928). The approaches that perceive the socialization process as one where the children discover a world of significations and turn a part of them into mutual significations show them how they mutually design a social order and a world of significations for themselves and for the adults around them. The social development of the children can be perceived as a continuous activity of social construction of a world of action and content. This world is anchored in the social circumstances the children encounter, and it assists them to cope with the knowledge, the demands and the constraints to which they are exposed via their contact with adults (Corsaro & Streeck, 1986). I studied how the adults use Sillwan as an expanse in the cultural construction process that they actuate on their children, so as to reinforce the ideological demand of the settlement project, for themselves. However, here I will also examine how the children's initiatives design the play environment as an area where there is constant negotiation, and not as an arena where the adults can ensure the conveyance of educational messages to their maximum extent. (Hadley, 2003; Bluebond-Langner & Korbin, 2007).

Orum and Cohen (1973) show how African American children in the United States who find themselves in day-to-day encounters with a charged political routine of racism show hypersensitivity in their understanding of the reality of mixed groups. The children seek to voice their opinions while having difficulties in containing their reality of being minority; in the case of Sillwan, this reality has been constructed for them by their parents. In my arena, in addition to all of the above, in the presentation of the children's encounters, they (the children) seek to add to and complete the picture of their handed-down identity.

Together with the children's language use and the adults' perception of the children, the children's games are a stage in which the socialization that the children and the entire Jewish community in Sillwan undergo is presented. Here I examine the children's games to study their mechanism of socialization. Via the games, the children seek to express something about the reality which will clarify the adults' claims regarding their efforts to construct the mixed life reality.

In the footsteps of Geertz (1973) and Goffman (1971), Handelman (1990) explains that via games, players express a certain reality. Games are an interpretive means for the social condition of the participants. In games, the central components in the circumstances of the players' lives are projected and emphasized.

The games in Sillwan express the clear reality of Jewish and Muslim social identity categories. Through their play, children exercise the boundaries of these categories which, at first sight, seem vague. The children receive the socialization from the adults and, parallelly, they organize the categories via the play, which simulates the reality for them. Via the games, the children examine the use of the categories in an imagined reality. The adults define the perceived hostile and dangerous expanse for their children so they will watch out for the menace, and the children process the danger and imagine solutions via the games.

When the children understand the construct that the adults seek to design for them, the picture clarifies and intensifies for the adults. The children assist the socialization of the community via the games that they created. The adults use the space to design for their children, in the cultural construction process that they operate on them in order to charge their community identity, but, at the same time, the children assist in the social construction process when they present the reality and confirm it, to the adults.

Levy (1998) adds another layer when adding his ideas to Goffman's game rules, claiming that playing enables the existence of permitted relationships and communication that would not have existed outside the framework of the games. Moreover, the games provide the opportunity for the groups to construct their uniqueness for themselves, or, as he put it, "their strangeness."

Via this communication, i.e., the games, the adults are able to design the identity of their community, through the negotiation that is maintained regarding the boundaries of the expanse.

Research Methods

This work was carried out according to the qualitative method, as part of an anthropological in-depth research study. The field work lasted four years between 2003 and 2007, during which I initiated conversations with Jewish families, stayed in the vicinity, and kept an observation diary around the routine social life of the Jewish inhabitants.[1]

Observation functions as a research method that brings forth the voice of the participants as they express it to the observer. Such observation is the method from which I expected it would be possible to obtain additional evidence regarding the culture that presented, namely, the culture as a staged document in its public display, as a shop-window for society. I watched for day-to-day practicalities that include metaphors, jokes, and people's actions, which are an expression of their perception (Geertz, 1973). Conversations or "in-depth interviews" are the second means that I used in the process of data collecting. I considered this method as a means via which I could complete the picture that I had witnessed during the observations, so as to reach the people's narratives and the way they learn about the manner in which they perceive and represent the reality (Zemon Davis, 1983).

Through participant observations of spontaneous games and the language uses of children, I will present my interpretation of the socialization process that the children undergo. Thus, this composition will examine the children's games for discussing the socialization mechanisms.

All names in this paper, adult's and children's, are pseudonyms according to their request. I watched and spoke with twenty Jewish kids, and with one Muslim girl, 10 years old. The Jewish kids' ages ranged between 6 and 11 years. These were the children who I could most often find outside the house playing around and could speak with and observe freely.

---

1 A methodological remark: As initially there had been only little reciprocity and relations between neighbors amongst the Jewish-Muslim families, I had difficulty maintaining a relationship with Muslim families in the village, as I was associated with the Jewish inhabitants. I did find one such family, with whose members I was pleased to do an in-depth interview in which they presented significant insights regarding the mixed existence in the village.

The Village Jews

When the Jews decided to come and live in Sillwan, they put their children under a "clasp." The children cannot go beyond a fenced area without being accompanied by a parent or a security guard. The children cannot roam in their village freely due to political reasons. The children know that they cannot leave one area and get to another, not because there is a physical gate which prevents them from leaving their Jewish yard, (often this barrier does not exist) but due to political restriction. They know that their yard is marked as "different." The political viewpoint is provided by their parents—"we are here, and they are there."

When I started theorizing before entering the field, I expected to find classical movement of uni-directional socialization processes, empowered and controlled by adults. This is one way to construct the identity of the community, as a community that is in the midst of its ideological formation. The adults have put themselves into a living situation perceived by them as dangerous. They are interested in monitoring their children via unilateral clarifications of identity, belief, and place, so that the children will not suffer doubts, fear and confusion.

However, as I progressed through my field work, this was not the way I found things. I did indeed see how the Jewish community in Sillwan attempts to establish itself via the routine life of its children. Via their educating power over their children, the socialization power, and the power of their circumstances—the lurking danger—the adults try to enlist the children to take part in the settlement efforts. But to the same extent, the adults depend upon the children's collusion in constructing and maintaining ideological mechanisms to defend their community from "otherness." Via the children's routine, the adults' aspirations are manifested and clarified. This is the "upward socialization."[2]

I will describe the children's everyday routine in Sillwan to show this socialization movement. When 7-year-old Tsilla's parents take her to see her friend Shir, they walk through the village alleys, hear the Arab language around them, watch the revolver of the security guard that walks by them and hear the sounds emerging from his walkie-talkie. Thus, the adults with the children physically study their relative location in the Muslim village.

---

2 "Upward socialization" is my way of expressing the *bottom-up* socialization movement, as a contrast to the classical socialization that communities use of *top down*; from the strong group down to the weak.

For instance, if Tsilla wants to visit her friend Shir who lives about fifty meters away from her house, she needs to wait patiently until one of her parents is available, or until an escort by a security guard can be found. The environment, whose components are the route she has to take to get to Shir, the security guard who marches next to her, together with the Muezzin sounds and the ringing of the church bells, all physically define the expanse for Tsilla as different and provide yet another insight for the understanding of her position in a dichotomic world, a place of good and evil, friend and foe.

Tovah, a Jewish mother of a few-months-old daughter, has recently arrived in Sillwan. She described to me how her Jewish neighbors are trying to protect their children from what they perceive as vague boundaries while she experiences doubts about the place where she is about to raise her children.

> The house of my neighbors, *Chohen* family, is a mini-cosmos. Their children have never known any strangers. I was the first stranger they met. Their parents take care that they do not leave the house. However, when they grew up to six to seven years old, they went out to the yard and discovered the gate through which they used to look, beyond the iron gate. They must assume that the world ends at the iron gate. To them, walking through the gate would be no less than discovering the world, the world beyond the iron gate.

Jewish-Muslim Shared Childhood

As I have previously stated, this chapter deals with the bi-directional socialization movement of the Sillwan community. On the one hand, the Jewish community members in Sillwan use physical force and socialization to signal and design the identity of their territory. On the other, within the routine that included encountering "the other" in the village, it is possible to examine the socialization movement on the children's part towards the adults, a movement whose aim is to express their different and complex opinions regarding the adults' ethnic claims. Here, I will present a few moments from my field work that illustrate the Arab and Jewish children's attempt to study the group of "others" facing them through self-directed play.

The Selfish Giant

Two Jewish and two Muslim families live in a spacious yard. In the heart of the yard, there are a small (around 20 square meters) lawn, a plastic swing tied to an olive tree, and two pomegranate trees. The yard is divided by a path where both of the families walk.

ADVERSITY IN A SNOWBALL FIGHT

It is afternoon, the yard is full of tumult; kids (less than ten) are running about, some are playing ball. My attention is caught by a group of kids playing together. Yahel, one of the mothers, is sitting at the entrance of her house, feeding a toddler on her lap, and, from time to time, looking at what is happening in the yard. Yehuda, a nine-year-old boy, is scolding everyone, shouting, and running in all directions, which seems like some kind of a catch-me game. He catches his 10-year-old sister Ayala. Ayala starts shouting, "rescue, rescue! Everyone out of the houses!" and Yehuda keeps chasing everyone.

Until now, it looks to me like just a chase game...but then, I start to realize that something is different....

Shifra and Dana, two 8-year-old girlfriends, are standing together in the yard, within one square meter of raised concrete. They call this "a house." "We are in our house, you cannot catch us here," they shout towards him. They are protected from Yehuda, who does not approach them. He approaches this piece of concrete and tries to make the two girls get out, but he himself does not get into the space where the players are protected; he cannot catch them. The rest of the children are running around the path and away from Yehuda when he approaches them. In the center of the lawn, Yehuda lies down and pretends to be wounded. He yells, "Ouch, ouch, my leg hurts." Then, when the rest of the children approach him he gets up and storms at them. They all run away from Yehuda, and some manage to get to the "house." Yehuda fails, all of the children manage to get to the concrete occupied by the two girls and everyone sings loudly, "We are at home, we are in the house." Yagil, a 10-year-old boy, joins the game and Yehuda yells at him, "you need to be the catcher, come on," and a row begins, which ends the game before it is over.

The children told me that this game is based on *The Selfish Giant* by Oscar Wilde, its plot consisting of children roaming around in the giant's garden. The giant wants to catch them, being dissatisfied with the presence of the children on his premises, and builds a wall around the garden to close himself inside. When the spring comes, all over the country there are little blossoms and birds. Only in the garden of the Selfish Giant, the land is still barren, and birds avoid it. One day the giant sees the kids playing on the trees, and the spring comes back to his garden. Then he understands his selfishness, and knocks down the wall to have the children in his garden forever.

With some small changes made to adjust the game to reality, the Jewish children managed to find a way to protect themselves against the giant—Yhuda—in the game.

The children know their identity position clearly, that is, who belongs to their social network and who does not; who is a friend and who is a potential foe. In their socialization process, via the games, they learn these categories also from the adults' rich experience. The children's socialization includes predetermined expectations that help them to act appropriately in situations they have not experienced yet.

The giant game expresses the binary nature of Sillwan social identity categories. These games construct the place of the Muslim "player" within those categories and describe what he can be to the kids. There is the protected "house" which the "giant" who does not want children in his garden may not enter. In the "house," a pastoral island in a stormy ocean, nothing happens. The children are untouchable. They are surrounded by invisible boundaries and, therefore, are protected. The existing "outside" rules do not apply here. The children are rehearsing real-life boundaries, which at first seem vague. An Arab neighbor walking on the path at their yards, an armed security guard standing on the roof of their houses—these create a danger that the children will face confusion, tension, anxiety and conflict. The adults define the hostile and dangerous expanse for the children so as to enable them to watch out for the threatening "giant," who does not really exist. The children process the danger and develop a solution via the game, building a virtual and categorical "fence." When the children understand the problem and implement their solution, the picture that the adults are presenting is clarified and enhanced for the adults as well. The children show the complicated reality back to the adults, not as a building of knowledge but as a confirmation of understanding of the community's norms. The children, through their play, contribute to the socialization process from "below."

Thus, when Tovah, the young Jewish mother, describes the world created for the children by their parents within the iron gates, she is expressing one of the adults' solutions for the preservation and protection of the individual joining the community: By illustrating a different world for them, a world without any "giants," a world of pure good, the parents teach the children the essence of a normal world, one which contains desirable components, without referring to "the giant," allowing the children to think that the world is a world free of worries, or as one neighbor put it, "a mini-cosmos," where the adults see to all the children's needs within the realm of the iron gates. The children can thrive as if they were in a world of their own. In fact, here, too, we can see the bi-directional socialization movement: from "the top" to "the bottom" and back again. Via the children's understanding of the "protected" world, imaginary as it may be, the adults construct for themselves a rationalization of the world they live in. As far as they are concerned, the iron gate is the same iron gate. They, too, live their lives as much as possible within the gate. There is no "giant" and if there is one, then the gate conceals him. The gate is an instrument that enhances the identity categories of us/them built by the adults. The parents depend on the children to ignore the "giant" so that they themselves will understand that he is simply away.

Conquering a Plastic Elephant

A game called The Elephant, played by Yishal and Liad, 7- to 8-year-old boys, also expresses the children's need to understand their identities and the way they attempt to control their social sphere via the adults' constructions.

Yishal and Liad are playing in the yard, assembling a giant (2 meter long) plastic elephant whose trunk is actually a slide. The elephant parts are scattered on the ground, and the children are trying to assemble them while singing "We are building in the Land of Israel" and "The Jewish People are alive." The conversation accompanying the construction of the elephant reinforces their spirit and awakens an aggressive attitude towards the passersby, such as a few 6- to 7-year-old Jewish girls who are stopping to watch. "Go away! Buzz off!" the boys shout towards the girls, till they retreat, looking anxiously at the boys. The boys ignore the girls and keep on with their business. Ultimately, the boys got tangled with some parts of the construction, with no success, so they struggled loudly with the plastic elephant, left the place frustrated, and went back home.

The game is a miniature model of the settlement project. The children play the role of the settler as they learned it from their parents who came here because of their linkage to Sillwan. The children sing about building and reviving The Land of Israel. This combination of physical and spiritual building fills the children with aggression and an air of militancy that helps them claim ownership over the toy. The building-the-elephant portion of the game is a metaphor for the building of a Jewish house in the Muslim village. The big gray elephant stands in for the massive block off by the Jewish settlers in Sillwan. A clumsy giant. The girls who pass by are comparable to trespassers of all sorts who penetrate the Jewish territory in the village. By using these symbols that express the adults' ideas, the children are able to understand and cope with their environment.

A Snowball Fight: When a Stone is Coated with Snow...

Another game demonstrates how relationships between groups that may not otherwise communicate may be established through play. Through this game, the players converse about the reality which they co-design. The game also provides the groups with the opportunity to construct their unique identities, vis-à-vis the other players.

Esther, a mother of six and one of the first Jewish settlers in Sillwan, tells me how, a few years ago, on the *Purim* holy day, it snowed in the city, and two of her sons who were 9 and 10 years old at the time went to play in the yard building a snowman. The children of Riad, a Muslim, also went to play outside and so, due to the circumstances, the children played together. They started a "snowball fight."

Esther explains that the fact that her sons were playing with the neighbor's kids did not bother her, but recalls:

> During the game, my boys noticed a few times that when they were hit by a snowball it hurt. They couldn't figure out why, till they realized there was a stone hidden in it. You see? They took a stone and coated it with snow! This is how they played! I'm not saying they hate Jews, and all. It doesn't interest me. But I'm talking about cruelty. I was happy, back then, that my kids learned it like this, delicately got to know the Arabs' mentality.

Esther is trying to understand the nature of the community she lives in. Via the boys' learning about who is "good" and who is "bad" in the tense environment, she identified essential characteristics and behavioral patterns of her neighbors. And now the picture regarding her own group is clarified. The strong, violent, and painful stone, coated with the white, pure and good snow, is presented as a cruel core hidden under a surface that projects innocence, naivety and purity. The reality hurts. Through the children's mutual game, they process the complex national and political issues in their space. By her sons' game in the snow, Esther receives another confirmation regarding the cruel reality she believes in. The game conceals the truth of the political situation by masquerading as a harmless, even beneficial, diversion, but it also exposes identity foundations, which, as the stone, are hidden under soft covers.

When I spoke to Riad about this incident he did not remember it and said that it must have occurred outside the residential area. Riad explained that due to such quarrels he is afraid when his children play with the Jewish children. In his explanation, Riad agrees that, through their play, the children are capable of constructing their reality in the manner of the adults' "disturbances."

Riad

> My children are not familiar with this the same way. I do not teach hatred. Our kids play with the Jews' kids, but due to the delicate relations between the Jews and the Arabs here, I am afraid something might happen and the child will be hurt, will get hit or something, and then people will say, "An Arab did that... because we are Jewish, etc." so I prefer that they not play together.

However, Riad's 10-year-old daughter echoes the voices of the children who seek to create more of these complex encounters.

> I truly want to play with the Jewish kids. I have no problem at all. On the contrary, we hardly ever play together. We play mainly ball, throw it back and forth, and that's it. It's fun, but not more than that. Also, because of the language barrier, we cannot talk that much but I would be happy to speak with them.

In this case, as in the 'facing the fence' description, the girl paints a picture of simplicity that is maintained throughout the games. According to her, the Jewish children are potential partners for playing and for friendship. The ball games do not satisfy her. She expresses her desire to achieve deeper relations, to know more, to touch "the people behind the fence" more.

The games, at first, are used by the children to clarify the sociological borders, which are constructed by adults. But then, we can see that the children are those who seek to present the reality as vague. The children disregard the national, political and social boundaries. To them, such identity-based constructs do not exist. The children who live "behind the fence" are merely children and do not hold any political position. Riad's words express the understanding that he, too, sees the potential lying within the children's games but it is his realistic perception of the charged living situation that makes him discourage the mutual games.

Implications

Because of the sensitivity and the complexity of the political and social issues in Sillwan and Israel as a whole, this chapter examines the region as one which is not only an instrument providing different meanings for people who seek to design the identity of their community (Bruner, 1994; Selwyn, 1996; Silberman, 1997) but also as an object that is reinforced via the people who live there, thus making it possible for them to stand on their own. That is, I have to examine the results of people's activity on the expanse itself, not only how they use it for their own sake.

This bi-directional movement of identity design by the community is part of a daily process of interpretation by the Jews who live in Judea and Samaria. The Jewish settlers are seeking to find influence and sustainability within a politically sensitive and a complex social life in these settlements. Under these circumstances, childhood becomes part of the identity design process of the settlers.

The children's games in the yards of Sillwan are an additional socialization instrument, via which the reality is processed for the adults and through which they clarify the boundaries of the community. Via the children's games, the adults better understand the boundaries of their community, and the marking and limit setting of their group along with the exclusion of the other group in the village are sharpened for them. In my field work I found that the picture of the children's world is part of the adults' discourse of the space they are living in. The children's routine is rich with symbols expressing the adults' ideas. The protection of the Jewish settlers' homes is a stage on which they present their understanding of Israeli identity. The adults are trying to teach this issue to the children but at the same time, to learn it for themselves.

We have seen from the "fence" anecdote and the "snowball fight" that the children seek to present a picture which differs from the one imposed by their parents. The children disregard the boundaries constructed for them and illustrate a simple world that avoids political complexity in this charged arena. In spaces like Sillwan, childhood functions beyond a classical adolescence process. It contains the possibility of associating the child with the struggle to design the values and norms of their society. The child is to undertake the goals of the community, present its creed, and become part of it, or—in my case—they are asked to perform for their parents, a different social construct Thus, we can find children who simulate and deal with their reality while playing, and adults who illustrate a reality that stops at the "iron gate."

Epilogue: "Hear Out My History"

While working on my research, the questions that came up in this chapter have only been a part of my learning process, complex and complicated as Sillwan is. In my field work, I became familiar with Riad, the Muslim neighbor of a few Jewish families who lives in one of the complexes in the village. When I turned up early in the morning, he used to serve me a cup of hot coffee, which he put on a stool near the security guard's post. When Riad left his house to attend to his business, he used to ask me whether I received the coffee and whether it was to my taste. On some occasions, he sent me a plate of freshly baked cookies with one of his children.

At first, the communication with him started and ended with mutual greetings and short conversations while standing. They were about daily affairs, mainly those of the Arab refugees in Israel. Later, I felt that I had many questions that needed to be answered and that I had to meet in a more formal way with Riad. I explained to him what my research was about and he was happy to host me and to converse about his feelings about the mixed life. I will present a short account of our conversation, where Riad describes his thoughts about life in the village of Sillwan in the past, present and the future:

> We have been living here before "the new war" [The Israeli Independence War, 1948]; hear out my history. My father used to say that we lived in the neighborhood of the Yemenites and if my brother made a mistake, the Jew would slap him on the face and if the Jew's son made a mistake, he would get slapped on the face by my father. We are brothers; we lived together, unlike now. Believe me, I'm dying for us to live together. Just as I live fine, let everyone live fine. It depends whether there will be a generation here that grows up going to school, studies how to behave with the Jew, leave the religion aside.

I am a human being, I was born out of my mother's womb, Jewish, Muslim, Christian, Buddha. I merely want to be able to live, that's all. What difference do all these questions make? Each one, on each side, needs to get the hatred out of their head. Do you understand? Not in our generation, perhaps in our children's generation.

> Riad's descriptions depict yet another aspect of the manner in which the Jews signify and design the boundaries between themselves and their Muslim neighbors, and his words also express frustration with the conduct demonstrated by his neighbors. Riad does not criticize the penetration of the Jews into the village. In his hope for a mutual future based on mutual life, he criticizes the way the Jews stretch the limits between themselves and himself, thus creating violence and tension in the area. The face slapping anecdote expresses the shared childhood that used to be evident in Sillwan;

when the kids here played together, their identities carried less meaning. Adults state that there is a shared childhood, and kids concentrate on playing. The kids state a desire to bring back Riad's childhood experience, to show the adults that life in Sillwan can be different.

I chose to conclude with this passage in order to express Riad's vision for the future, which is also my vision, linked by a long thin thread to my grandmother's life story. My grandmother lived her entire life and died in Jerusalem, and was probably familiar with Riad's face-slapping anecdote of the fathers, Muslim and Jewish alike, from both sides. Out of my desire for mutual respect, I wrote this essay, critically observing Jewish settlers' manners of designing their community, although, at the same time, I held (and still hold) feelings of ideological identification regarding the possibility of maintaining Jewish life in a Muslim village.

As a father, bringing up a young family with my wife, I thinking about our complicated and sensitive Israeli social life. Doing my research in the fascinating arena of Sillwan village, I was exposed to an essential issue—what is, or what should be, the Israeli identity?

I try hard to think about the different religious identities as a puzzle of social community. Like my grandmother who lived between Muslims and Christians while a child, I believe that mixed ethnic groups can live together. I can't form an opinion about my researched people, judging them as doing "good" or "bad." I can describe them, interpret them—and try to imagine my own life there.

I understand the perceived harm of Jewish children having a shared childhood with Muslim children. The Jewish try to construct a clear Israeli identity for their kids by drawing a sharp boundary between the groups, and in some ways, I find this important. On the other hand, it's a pity to avoid the kids on the other side of the gate. Clearly, there is a desire on both sides to get to know each other, even across language barriers, through play.

During this work I was happy to find a few cases of mutuality between Jews and Muslims in Sillwan, but as they were so scarce, both quantitatively and qualitatively, I chose to focus on the more prominent trends. I have tried to show here how the actions taken by the Jews and their construction of boundaries are their own creation, while giving the children voice when they spoke of another mode of mutual life.

References

Azaria, V. (1989). Civil education in the Israeli armed forces. In Krausz, E. (Ed.), *Education in a Comparative Context*. New Brunswick: Transaction Publishers.

Ben-Eliezer, U. (1995). A nation-in-arms: State, nation, and militarism in Israel's first years. *Comparative Studies in Society and History Years, 37*(2), 264-285.

Bluebond-Langner, M. & Korbin, J.E. (2007). Challenges and opportunities in the anthropology of childhoods. *American Anthropologist, 109*, 241-246.

Bruner, E.M. (1994). Abraham Lincoln as an authentic reproduction: A critique of post-modernism. *American Anthropologist, 96*, 397-415.

Corsaro, W.A. & Streeck, J. (1986). Studying children's worlds: Methodological issues. In Cook-Gumperz, J., Corsaro, W.A., & Streeck, J. (Eds.), *Children's Worlds and Children's Language* (pp. 14-35). Berlin: Walter de Gruyter.

Eisenstadt, S.N. (1967). *Israeli Society*. New York: Basic Book.

Geertz, C. (1973). *The Interpretation of Cultures*. New York: Basic Books.

Goffman, E. (1971). *The Presentation of Self in Everyday Life*. Harmondsworth, England: Penguin Books.

Hadley, K.G. (2003). Children's word play: Resisting and accommodating Confucian values in a Taiwanese kindergarten classroom. *Sociology of Education, 76*(3), 193-208.

Handelman, D. (1990). *Models and Mirrors*. Cambridge: Cambridge University Press.

Levy A. (1998). Controlling Space, Essentializing Identities: Jews in Contemporary Casablanca. *City and Society 9*(1), 175-199.

Levy, Jr. M.J. & Fallers, L.A. (1959). Some comparative considerations. *American Anthropologist, 61*(4), 647-651.

Marjoribanks, K. (1992). Ethnicity, family as opportunity structures and adolescents' aspirations. *Ethnic and Racial Studies, 15*(3), 381-394.

Mead, M. (1928). *Coming of Age in Samoa*. New York: Morrow.

Miller, P.J., Potts, R., Fung, H., Hoogstra, L., & Mintz, J. (1990). Narrative practices and the social construction of self in childhood. *American Ethnologist, 17*(2), 292-311.

Orum, M. & Cohen, R.S. (1973). The development of political orientations among black and white children. *American Sociology Review, 38*, 62-74.

Rabinowitz, D. (1996). *Overlooking Nazareth*. Cambridge: Cambridge University Press.

Seginer, R. (1990). Social Support: Application to early adolescent transition. Unpublished manuscript. Haifa, Israel: University of Haifa.

Selwyn, T. (1995). Landscape of liberation and imprisonment: Towards an anthropology of the Israeli landscape. In. Hirsch, E. & O'Hanlon, M. (Eds.), *The Anthropology of Landscape* (pp. 114-134). Oxford, England: Clarendon.

Shamgar-Handelman, L. (1991). Childhood as a social phenomenon: National Report of Israel. *Eurosocial Report*, 36.

Silberman, N.A. (1997). Structuring the past: Israelis, Palestinians, and the symbolic authority of archaeology monuments. In Silberman, N.A. & Small, D. (Eds.), *The Archaeology of Israel* (pp. 62-81). Sheffield, England: Sheffield Academic Press.

Schwartzman, H.B. (1976). The anthropological study of children's play. *Annual Review of Anthropology*, 5, 289-328.

Zemon Davis, N. (1983). *The Return of Martin Guerre*. Cambridge, MA: Harvard University Press.

Interviews

The fence (2004). An interview with a Jewish mother and her 11-year-old daughter.

The adults (2007). An interview with Riad. The Muslim inhabitant.

"The world beyond the iron gate" (2004). An interview with Tovah, a young Jewish mother about her children's neighbors.

The "Snowball fight" (2005). An interview with Esther, a Jewish mother.

"To play with the Jewish" (2007). An interview with Riad and his 10-year-old daughter.

The "Face slapping" (2007). An interview with Riad.

Chapter Thirteen

Success through Excess:
Narratives and Performances in Board and Card Games

Drew Chappell

My interest in board and card games is personal. I grew up learning them from my grandparents (I have fond memories of my grandfather's bridge lessons), played them with friends and family all through my childhood, and now continue to enjoy them with friends as well as other hobbyists in local groups. I believe that games—whether played on a board, a sports field, a computer, or entirely in the imagination—are an essential part of human existence, serving a need unfilled by other forms of interaction. They allow us to be playful, to learn about working as a team or as individuals toward a specific goal. They often compel fascinating performances, bringing out sides of ourselves that are not accessed in other ways. And they can cross boundaries, attracting players across divisions of class, race, gender, and age.

In this chapter, I analyze three games that occupy differing niches in terms of marketing and audience. *The Game of Life* (2007), a family game, has historical roots in the moral education games of the Puritan era (Parlett, 1999, pp. 98-100). *Life* sets players on a linear path through their adult development, with the objective of gathering wealth. *Magic: the Gathering* (Garfield, 2005a) is a collectable card game that enjoyed significant popularity in the 1990s and continues to be played widely. In *Magic*, players are rival wizards dueling through casting spells and summoning creatures to fight on their behalf. *Puerto Rico* (Seyfarth, 2002), is a newer "Euro game" that deals with the colonization of the island of Puerto Rico. Players are Spanish government officials who direct "colonists" (an amalgamation of Spanish colonists and native workers/slaves) to farm, produce goods, and work in government buildings."

In each of these games, there are dominant and subaltern character groups.[1] As part of the dominant group, through manipulating, sacrificing, or simply avoiding the subaltern characters, the players advance their own positions. This exercise of power is vital to the games' mechanisms; it is how the players reach their objectives. As these objectives have to do with the accumulation of power and the sacrifice or waste of resources, the games' moral value system centers around acquisition to excess, a fundamental principle in a capitalist/consumer society.

Play Theory and Games

The space games occupy in our lives is subject to debate. Anthropologist/sociologist Roger Caillois (1961) writes: "The structures of play and reality are often identical, but the respective activities that they subsume are not reducible to each other in time or place. They always take place in domains that are incompatible" (p. 64). Caillois' dividing line between "life" and "play" is perhaps too limiting, the boundaries more fluid than he admits, but his point is well taken regarding time set aside for leisure. Later, he addresses the impact play has on those who perform it: "[...] A game that is esteemed by a people may at the same time be utilized to define the society's moral or intellectual character, provide proof of its precise meaning, and contribute to its popular acceptance by accentuating the relevant qualities" (p. 83). He defines the concept of play using six labels: free, separate, uncertain, unproductive, governed by rules, and make believe (pp. 9-10). Caillois imagines a separate, unique space in which players agree to suspend the nature of "real life" in favor of a communally constructed, spatially and temporally bound society, formed for the sole purpose of competing toward an arbitrary objective.

This definition continues Caillois' philosophy of leisure as an activity separate from life, with no bearing on individuals "post game." Often, however, play refuses to stay within these neat borders. Disagreements may occur over procedural interpretations or outcomes, for example. Historian David Parlett (1999) calls these the "means" and "ends" of the game, with the ends being the objectives and the means the rules to be navigated toward those ob-

---

[1] The word *subaltern* was notably employed by Antonio Gramsci in his *Prison Notebooks* "as a code word for oppressed groups, such as industrial laborers and peasants..." (Apple & Buras, 2006, p. 4). Such groups are subject to physical and ideological control, and their identities are (re)formed through the dominant cultural lens.

jectives (p. 3). If disputes over ends and means refuse to stay bounded by the game, if fights break out between players in spite of the common plea "it's only a game!," it seems to me we cannot say that games are wholly bracketed off from real life. There are other such leaks; we might find ourselves thinking of new strategies for doing better at a certain game, or ruminating over an amusing scene from play that occurred days or months back. Or we might bring in-game narratives into our everyday language and thought—imagine a dance performance as "Twister-like," for example, or negotiations as "a game of chess."

Educational researcher James Gee (2003) links the process of game playing to learning. He points out that video game designers must develop games as problems or puzzles to be solved in order to keep consumers (children) interested in playing them. He suggests: "What we are really looking for here is this: the theory of human learning built into good video games" (p. 6). Gee outlines 36 principles of learning that occur through the playing of these "good games"—including active, critical engagement; levels and types of identities; rewards from achievement; and development of cultural models about the world (pp. 207-212). Gee cautions that for learning to occur, overt reflection by the player must occur or be called for by the game itself (p. 49), and identities and narratives must be carefully constructed (p. 66). He states that these games should "situate meaning in a multimodal space through embodied experiences to solve problems and reflect on the intricacies of the design of imagined worlds and the design of both real and imagined social relationships and identities of the modern world" (p. 48). Yet, few games offer players these metalevel opportunities. Instead the game often operates on an assumed, benign correlation between identities, values and behaviors in the real world and the game world.

Games are constructs, combinations of physical and abstract elements that relate to real-world counterparts in subtle and obvious ways. Even a game as simple as "tag," for example, has players (physical), a defined playing area (physical), and an agreed-upon set of rules (abstract). Board and card games include physical pieces—the board, cards, and other "bits"—and a printed set of rules for learning and reference. In what Parlett (1999) calls "theme games," the rules define a scenario that "simulate[s] or represent[s] some sort of real-life activity" (p. 348). These games "may involve elements of role-play and quasi-dramatic performances" (p. 7). Theme games' performative elements construct both in-game narratives and temporary social and cultural norms, behaviors, and expectations; all of which contribute to a scenario that exists outside the game. Since games exist in a cultural matrix, these scenarios may also play into colonizing children's imaginations. When players join in a game, they physicalize rules within a given theme (narrative) and create a temporary society in action.

One of the defining features of game play is the pursuit of an objective—the drive to "win" the game. Players seek to further their own positions relative to everyone else involved in the game. Sometimes this competition takes the form of a rank order of winners to losers, and sometimes winning means eliminating all other players and emerging as the sole victor. There are also cooperative games such as *Lord of the Rings* (Knizia, 2000), *Arkham Horror* (Wilson & Launius, 2005), and *Pandemic* (Leacock, 2008), in which the players' goal is to beat the game system, pooling their resources to stave off the end of the game until they have met a prescribed victory condition. This creates a different playing culture from a standard competitive game—a sense of communal threat, and a charge to work in harmony with the other players.

In pursuit of victory, games encourage players to accumulate—whether victory points, money or other tokens—in excess of necessity. If to win is to achieve dominance over other players, then the player must display quantifiable evidence of his/her power. This pursuit of excess echoes Joseph Roach's (1996) discussion of historical displays of power as the performance of waste:

> Human cultures somehow must cope with the profuse excesses produced by nature and reproduced by their own increasingly fecund manipulations of it. Their strategies for coping with this superabundance include such forms as potlatch, feasting, ritualized warfare, and sacrifice—performing the waste of excess objects, produce, and human life. (p. 123)

According to Roach, having too much was sometimes just enough to secure one's place in the social hierarchy. Games also ask players to waste resources—give up pieces, mortgage properties—in order to pursue abundance. There simply is no other way to win except to acquire more than anyone else at the table.

Pleasure in accumulation is accomplished through the games' defining of fetishes in the Marxist sense. As the games create token economies, "An abstract value system is grafted onto an imaginary investment in things, disavowing not only the origin of value but the process of symbolization that brought it into circulation" (Mulvey, 1996, p. 4). Players take pleasure in amassing these tokens that have no meaning except within the game. As they accumulate "power" or "wealth," the players gain standing, drawing ever closer to the victory condition to which they aspire. When related to real life referents, the fetishes engage what theorist Laura Mulvey (1996) terms "disavowal." As in Diana Taylor's scenarios, they stand in for rather than directly correlate to people, events, or objects:

> Disavowal maintains, after all, only a tenuous link between cause and effect while its investment in visual excess and displacement of signifiers produces a very strong texture that can come to conceal the need to conceal the relation between cause and effect. That is, the aesthetic of disavowal can easily provide a formal basis for a displacement which moves signification considerably further away from the problem of reference. (Mulvey, 1996, pp. 12-13)

Paper money is not really money. A token representing a worker is not really a worker. But what if, through playing the game, players are learning to treat these resources as expendable? How do these in-game performances affect young people's real life understandings of economics and culture?

Taking the token economy to another level, game publishers can manipulate supply and demand to their benefit based on internal definitions of game components. In the collectable card game model (employed by such games as *Magic: the Gathering*, explored later in this chapter), components are assigned rarities, and the rarer the item, the more power it holds in-game. Thus the rarest tokens become simulacra,[2] often commanding high prices determined by both by the manufacturer and fans of the game. This rarity system is analogous to character equipment in massively multiplayer online games, where players buy (or trade) weapons or magic items for use by their characters. Like the emperor's new clothes, the tokens' value only exists in the players' minds—and in the space of the constructed worlds.

Games as Moral Instruction

During the late 1700s and early 1800s in Europe and the United States, game publishers "shifted their attention to the expanding domestic market for moral and educational games that would instruct and inform the young" (Parlett, 1999, p. 98). Some of these games replaced dice with a "teetotum" (like a spinning top or dreidel) to do away with the appearance of gambling. Based on earlier South Asian game boards, many of the boards resembled race

---

[2] Simulacra have lost their original referents and refer back only to themselves. See Baudrillard (1994, p. 2).

courses in which the goal was to move along a circular or spiral path from start to finish (Lepore, 2007, p. 1). Along this path, players encountered certain spaces that set them back due to poor choices or bad luck, and others that would advance them due to moral choices or good luck, reflecting the moral instruction purpose. One of the first American-made games, *The Mansion of Happiness* (1832), included spaces such as "humility," "charity," and "generosity," as well as "cruelty," "whipping post," and "prison" (Adams & Edmonds, 1977, p. 368; Orbanes, 2004, p. 3). Moral instruction games were explicit in the messages that they conveyed; narratives were built around societal ills such as disease and drinking, and players' objectives were to navigate safely through a series of troubles and temptations.

In 1860, an early version of *The Game of Life* was published as a moral instruction game, called *The Checkered Game of Life*. Characters in the game started at infancy and moved through to happy old age, avoiding moral pitfalls and collecting points for virtuous behavior (Adams & Edmonds, 1977, pp. 373-374). Rather than didactically introducing issues of morality, the game required players to quantify their good behavior, trying to outdo their rivals in good deeds. In 1960, the game was republished, now with the objective of collecting money and reaching retirement, offering, as *New Yorker* author Jill Lepore (2007) opines, "a lesson in Cold War consumerist conformity" (p. 1). In a 1973 address to the Newcomen Society (a business support organization), James J. Shea, Jr. (1973), president of Milton Bradley, spoke about this change: "The original version had as its theme high ideas of morality and happy old age. The goal to be reached in the modern version is personal achievement and maybe, with some regrets, monetary success" (p. 16). Shea's glib "regrets" about accumulation of wealth are interesting in light of what the game has subsequently become, with modern moral instruction focusing around prosperity and achievement rather than avoidance of sin.

The Game of Life

In its present incarnation, *The Game of Life* (2007) is focused not on moral instruction per se but rather on the "path" of (middle class) adulthood, on careers and hobbies, and monetary risk and reward. The box cover illustration highlights the role of the spinner, which determines the players' fortunes throughout the game, and the importance of money. (Money flies through the air around the foregrounded characters.) *Life* is marketed at players 9 and above, and 2-6 players can participate.

Ostensibly, *Life* is a game structured around making life choices and dealing with their consequences. Players have the opportunity to choose a career, have a family, buy a home, and participate in numerous "life events." However, these choices are often limited and/or luck driven. The object of the game is to "Travel the path of LIFE making decisions, building a family, earning money (and paying some out too), buying homes and collecting LIFE tiles. Have the highest value at the end of the game and win" (*The Game of Life*, p. 1). Money is accumulated and lost as character tokens (driving cars) move along the game path, either through the purchase and sale of property or events that befall the players.

The *Life* board features three-dimensional components: buildings, mountains, and a bridge. These components give the board a geography, as opposed to having the players' pieces moving along a flat plane. Along the game track are various types of spaces, many featuring events that might occur in the average middle-class U.S. citizen's life (car accident, job loss). Others are highly unlikely to occur to an average citizen but are nevertheless represented on the board (win Nobel Prize, write best-selling book). At certain intervals, players collect salaries—whether or not they actually land on "pay day" spaces—ensuring that they will always have an income. Although jobs can be lost in *Life*, they are immediately replaced with different careers. The players' middle-class existences are never really under threat—if they need a bank loan, they can always take one out and will certainly be able to pay it off (with interest) when they reach retirement.

Several spaces along the game path are LIFE spaces; the rules state: "These spaces show pictures of LIFE tiles, and are all about family activities, community service, and good deeds!" (p. 3). The LIFE spaces are the heart of what moral instruction the game does offer. Each time players perform a good deed (by landing on one of these spaces), they are rewarded with a tile holding a monetary value, which adds to players' total values at game end. Some of the LIFE spaces could be considered ethically responsible: Volunteer at soup kitchen. Visit Old Soldiers' Home. Make new friends for life. Some deal with civic duty: Vote! Run for Congress. Players also accumulate children in the game, through either birth or adoption. When children arrive, their spaces grant LIFE tiles, as well as a $5000 gift from each player. Interestingly, as players continue to land on these "good deeds" spaces, and the stack of LIFE tiles is depleted, any player who lands on a LIFE space may steal tiles from a rival. So good deeds in themselves become a competitive factor in the game, as stealing is sanctioned and the tiles add dollar amounts to players' stockpiles—their only real contribution to the game's objective.

Life interpellates players by assigning them careers, which may change over the course of the game. A set number of career cards guarantees that each player has a career distinct from the others. Some careers require a college degree (with its accompanying investment of $100,000 at the beginning of the game); others do not, but their salaries have a lower ceiling. During the game, players perform "as if" they were members of their chosen career, embodying the adult roles of doctor, entertainer, police officer, and so on. In so doing, players foreground this aspect of their identity and de-emphasize others, serving as the sole representative of their profession throughout the in-game narrative.

As mentioned, players are physically represented on the game board by a small plastic car into which they place a pink or blue "people peg." Presumably these pink and blue pegs reference a female/male binary associated with player gender, though the rules do not directly address this issue. A girl player choosing a blue peg and playing a female lawyer, for example, is perfectly "allowable" under the rules. As their cars move along the game path, the people pegs "get married" and add a second peg to the vehicle. Marriage is a requirement; the game will not let players stay single. There is no rules-based obligation that a life partner be of the opposite gender (thus resulting in two pink pegs, for example, in the front seat of the car), but the phrasing of the "get married" space, its associated illustration of a heterosexual couple in wedding dress, and the "wedding gifts" marriage garners from other players all construct normative heterosexuality. Players' characters in *Life* also (usually) accumulate children, represented by more pink and blue pegs. As mentioned, there is a monetary bonus for adding each child (a gift plus a LIFE tile); conversely, children do not normally pull from players' monetary resources—there are only a few spaces that require players to "pay out" for their children (day care, summer camp). Thus, in *Life*, getting married and having kids is always advantageous, making it all the more insidious in its normalization of the traditional family structure.

The *Life* game board follows a linear track paralleling middle-class adult life events. The board begins with players' graduation from high school; their first decision is whether to attend college or begin working. Movement forward (always forward) along the track is accomplished through turning the large spinner in the center of the board, then moving the appropriate number of spaces along the track. The luck of the spinner might bring players a monetary windfall or cause them to lose their "hard-earned" cash. Although normally the entire spin is taken, certain spaces are marked with a "stop" icon, requiring players to stop there and follow the game's instructions, even if the number spun would have moved their pieces beyond the space. These "stop spaces" sometimes correlate with major life events—getting married, changing careers, and buying a home—and sometimes are jumping off points for life choices, including returning to school, having more children, and taking monetary risks to acquire more wealth.

The Game of Life ends not in death, but retirement. At the end of the game path, players choose to retire to either Countryside Acres or Millionaire Estates. Countryside Acres is the safe choice; rivals may not take LIFE tiles away from those who retire there. Millionaire Estates is riskier—LIFE tiles are vulnerable—but the richest player at that location receives four additional tiles at the end of the game. After all players have retired, they add their cash holdings and the dollar values from their LIFE tile achievements. "The player with the highest total value wins!" (*The Game of Life*, 2007, p. 6). Thus, the game's ultimate moral message conflates maturation with earning, consumption, and profit making, suggesting that nothing that we do during life has any value outside of the money it generates; furthermore, those with the most money are the true "winners." In addition, since the game is largely luck-driven, this wealth is gained primarily through chance.

Collectable Card Games (CCGs)

In 1993, a small company called Wizards of the Coast released a game combining the fantasy genre with the concept of sports trading cards. Bearing the cumbersome name *Magic: The Gathering* (Garfield, 2005a), the card game invited players to collect cards from randomly assorted packs, build customized decks, and compete with each other. Central to the game was the concept of rarity, a division of all the cards released into common, uncommon, and rare appearances in packs. Since the generally accepted notion was that the rarer the card, the more powerful and desirable, as players spent more money on cards, they had more at their disposal to build decks from, and their chances of doing well against other players increased. The ability to customize decks makes *Magic* an ever-changing game experience. By selecting different cards to compete with, players can try various strategies and modify them based on game outcomes.

The game's collectable quality and innovative deck-building system was an immediate success. Wizards of the Coast grew quickly and now owns two other major game companies: TSR, publisher of *Dungeons and Dragons* (Wizards RPG Team, 2008), and Avalon Hill, an established strategic board game publisher. In 1999, Wizards was acquired by Hasbro, one of the U.S.'s largest toy and game companies. After its introduction, *Magic* became a widespread cultural phenomenon: "Featured in film, television, and art, *Magic* has been a voice of postmodern culture for over a decade" ("About Wizards," 2009, p. 2). After *Magic*, many other collectable card games entered the market. *Yu-Gi-Oh* (Takahashi, 1996) and *Pokemon* (1999) are two of the best known.

Figure 1: Serra Angel image from *Magic: The Gathering*. Copyright Wizards of the Coast LLC. Image used with permission. Illus. Greg Staples

Magic: The Gathering

Magic is sold in starter decks (marketed as complete, playable decks) and booster packs (small sets of additional cards). To date, there have been ten "core sets" and over 50 other expansions, each with starters and boosters available. *Magic* is also available in an online incarnation, where players buy sets of cards that they "own" and duel online with these cyber decks. For my analysis, I used two of the 9th edition core sets: the Core Game Set (Garfield, 2005a) and the "Dead Again" Core Set (Garfield, 2005b). These sets play with two or more and are suggested for ages 13 and up. The Core Game packaging appeals to the competitive instinct: "Make new friends and then have fun taking them apart. Play for fame, from local events to global tournaments" (Garfield, 2005a, box back). The box features a picture of a sexualized female angel in ornate armor wielding a large sword over her head and holding a shield (Figure 1). Included in the Core Game set is a CD-Rom tutorial of the game as well as a hard copy walk-through in comic book form. The "Dead Again" Core Set deck—its cover depicting a ghostly black horse (Figure 2)— includes no rulebook, but instead a strategy guide focused around that particular deck's theme.

Figure 2: Nightmare image from *Magic: The Gathering*. Copyright Wizards of the Coast LLC. Image used with permission. Illus. Carl Critchlow

Magic incorporates multiple mythologies into its in-game narrative. In the two sets I researched, I identified the following cultural referents: Christian (angels, demons), Middle Eastern/Arabic (scimitar, assassin), fantasy/Norse (dragons, orcs, goblins), Greek (minotaur), and contemporary horror (zombie). These mythologies feed into a single fantasy realm where rival wizards engage in epic battles. *Magic*'s rulebook introduces the game's storyline as follows: "In the *Magic* game, you play the role of a duelist—a powerful wizard who fights other duelists for glory, knowledge, and conquest. Your deck represents all the weapons in your arsenal" (Garfield, 2005a). As a *Magic* player, you can damage your opponent by attacking with creatures you have summoned or by casting spells. You can also augment your creatures and spells, hinder your opponent's progress, or change other aspects of game play. Also in players' decks are land cards, which can be used to "pay" for spells and creatures with their "mana" (magical energy). In medieval fashion, all wealth and power in the game stems from this land ownership. So the game is a pastiche of historically recognizable details that are decontextualized and mixed with mythological content.

Spells, creatures, and lands are associated with one of five colors—white, blue, black, red, and green—with the exception of artifacts, magical constructions, which are "colorless." Players may play with cards from only one color, or more than one in combination, though it is more difficult to draw the cards you need with too many colors in your deck. Each of the colors is associated with a different land type and narrative flavor. White, the plains, is the color of law, order, and structure, or healing and protection. Its creatures are soldiers, clerics, and angels. Blue, the islands, deals in trickery, manipulation, and control. Sea and air creatures make up blue decks. Black, the swamps, focuses around death, disease, selfishness, treachery, power at any cost, sacrificing creatures and destroying other players' lands and creatures. Dark minions, undead creatures, and unspeakable horrors are native to the swamp. Red, the mountains, includes fire, frenzy, and storms of rock and lava, reckless spells and wild emotions. Its creatures include Norse-flavored dragons, orcs, giants, and goblins. Green, the forest, represents the power of nature: growth, life, and brute force. Green creatures are typically large animals or elemental forces (Garfield, 2005a, pp. 22-23). Of particular interest to me is the alignment of the colors white and black with a good and evil dichotomy. In a subtle way, Christian/feudalist ("law and order") philosophies are allied with whiteness and "good," while blackness is paired with death, destruction, decay, sacrifice, and "evil."

Each *Magic* card includes (among other things) a title, an illustration, and a description of what the card allows the wizard controlling it to do. Many cards also include "flavor text," quotations or original writings that create additional context around the card and game. Some flavor text is intertextual, referencing authors and sources players may be familiar with. As they interact with other cards and with the actions of the players, the cards create new narratives for every game. Some of these storytelling strategies have been described by Brett A. S. Martin (2004) in his ethnographic study of *Magic* players. Martin found that players "read" the cards and the game itself in various ways, including replacing images and spell descriptions with more personally satisfying interpretations.

As mentioned, *Magic* interpellates players as rival wizards engaging in individualized combat toward unspecified goals. In practice, this means players try to run each other out of either life points (recorded on a die, a sheet of paper, tokens, etc.) or cards in their draw pile, as creatures and spells are played. In other words, it is not enough to best a rival wizard; he or she must be killed or completely disempowered. Life points rise and fall during the game; a player may be at full health one turn and lose most of those points in the next. So injury and healing are often swift, and of course neither is "felt" by the player. Those who build decks including the color black are often required to subtract from their life totals in order to cast their powerful but "evil" spells—a nod to power gained through sacrifice, either of self or underling (creature).

To summon creatures and cast spells, players must first build up enough land holdings to pay for them. Land has no significant use except to produce mana, but players must include enough land in their decks to have a good chance of drawing the lands they need early on in the game. As land accumulates, it is normally stacked together to make record keeping easier, creating fiefdoms that the wizard controls. Land, like other cards, "resets" on the turn after it is used, available to be stripped of its resources again and again. The performance of economics, then, is one of sapping land's (renewable) energy in order to hire mercenaries or exercise power—in keeping with the feudal/medieval nature of the fantasy genre.

Conflict occurs using mercenary creatures that form a "battle line" in front of the wizards. Creatures attack as well as block, preventing opposing damage from sapping a wizard's life point total. Thus, the creatures in *Magic* perform the "work," and once paid for, creatures do not need to be compensated each turn. Like mercenaries or slaves, creatures serve their controllers to the extent of dying for them, and are unable to leave the wizards' service. The fetishism associated with ownership and manipulation thus becomes a large part of the game's performance.

The Rise of the Euro Game

In the mid-1990s, the German company Kosmos released a game called *The Settlers of Catan* (Teuber, 1995). This game had tremendous popular appeal and began what could be termed a "Euro revolution" in the board game hobby. The revolution brought European (mostly German) game makers into the U.S. market and introduced new game styles to U.S. gamers. As Todd Neller (2005) points out in his Web site examining current trends in gaming, this challenged the monopoly one American company, Hasbro, had over most of the board game publishers in the United States, including Milton Bradley, Parker Brothers, Wizards of the Coast, and Avalon Hill. Neller suggests that this monopoly led to what he calls "stagnation in gaming innovation." In Germany, where no monopoly exists, game designers have more freedom and the hobby is treated as a family activity (p. 2). The Euro game market continues to grow in the United States, with one company, Rio Grande Games, translating and distributing many games designed in Germany. The Euro game style differs from that of U.S. games, which are typically based on "area control" (domination of areas on the board) or "unit attrition" (slow destruction of enemy units), often manifested in militaristic representation. Euro games, on the whole, do not focus on military objectives. *The Settlers of Catan*, for example, is based in trading and commodity exchange (goods for money). As more of these games become available in the United States, "the trend of growing interest in imported games continues" (Neller, 2005, p. 3). Neller notes that U.S. hobbyists now commonly travel to game fairs in Europe, and share information on Euro games over the Internet.

Puerto Rico

The Euro game *Puerto Rico* (Seyfarth, 2002) is sold by Rio Grande Games in the United States, imported from the German game company Alea. Highly regarded in the gaming community, it was for several years the highest-rated game on the BoardGameGeek.com fan site.³ The game is for three to five players, ages twelve and up. *Puerto Rico*'s box art features a Spanish official supervising the shipping of goods. The text on the box reads, in part: "In 1493 Christopher Columbus discovered the eastern-most island of the Great Antilles. About 50 years later, Puerto Rico began to really blossom—through you!" (Seyfarth, 2002). This narrative alludes to the game's main mechanism—the choosing of roles associated with the colonization of the Americas in order to produce goods and ship them to Europe.

Puerto Rico takes place during the Spanish colonization of the island. Players participate in the colonial project in various roles, from a European identity and European concerns. Through the in-game narrative, the game renders invisible native identities, naturalizes colonization, and routes players through a single condition to victory—essentially: farm, populate, build, produce, trade, and ship.

Figure 3: The island of Puerto Rico, as depicted on the *Puerto Rico* player mats. Copyright Rio Grande Games and Alea Games, art by Franz Vohwinkel

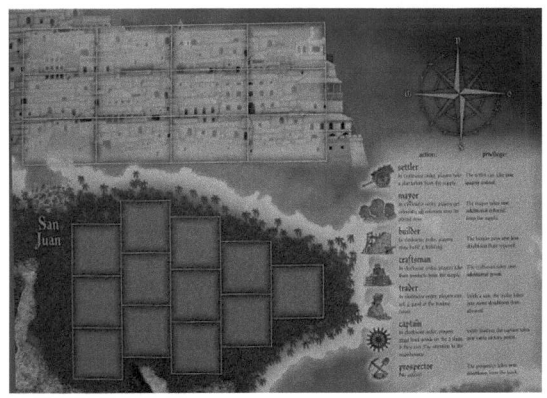

Game play takes place independently on player "mats" showing a field section and city section of Puerto Rico, specifically naming the city of San Juan (Figure 3). Colonization begins with the establishment of plantations—corn, sugar, indigo, tobacco, and coffee—which are represented by small plantation tiles and placed in the field section of the mat. Buildings, played in the city section, are divided into color-coded production buildings in which raw materials are processed into goods, and "violet" buildings that represent infrastructure such as universities and harbors. After establishing plantations and production buildings, players may produce goods, represented by color-coded octagonal wood pieces (blue for indigo, white for sugar, etc.). The

---

3 At this writing, it vies for the number one position with *Agricola* (Rosenberg, 2007), a game about medieval farming.

game also includes characters it calls "colonists," represented by small dark brown wooden discs. These colonists work both the fields and the buildings; production requires their presence. Other game components include a mat to hold the buildings and money in the bank; tokens to represent a colonist ship, a trading house, and cargo ships, as well as the player roles; cardboard doubloons; and victory chips (Figure 4).

Figure 4: Other *Puerto Rico* components, including role cards used by players to select their actions in a given round (on left of main board). Copyright Rio Grande Games and Alea Games, art by Franz Vohwinkel

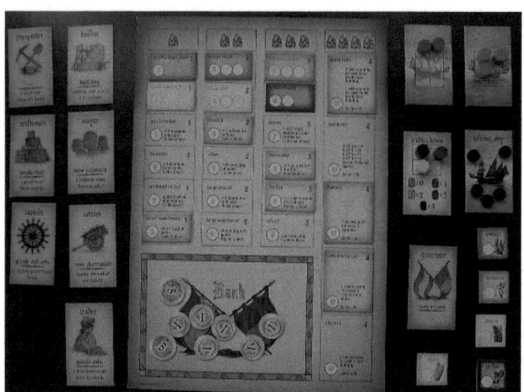

Despite locating the game in historical space, there are no components in *Puerto Rico* that reference native identity. Nor are there any references to native Puerto Ricans in the game rules. Interestingly however, players on BoardGameGeek.com discuss the "colonist" discs as having a dual reference of "colonist" (i.e., Spaniard) and "slave" (i.e., African or native). To me, the colonist pieces flatten and conflate the two identities, suggesting no distinction in the roles, treatment, and privileges of these two groups during the colonial period. There has also been discussion on BoardGameGeek around the color selection for the discs (dark brown), including a fan's sarcastic retort to critics of the game: "If you really have a problem with the little brown guys being slaves, you could always spray paint them white, with a rose-ish hue" ("Comments that Should Cost the Utterer GeekGold," 2007, p. 3). This posting points to Mulvey's (1996) disavowal, a conscious separation of referent and reference, a smoothing over of the historical experiences of diverse groups. As with *Life*'s people pegs, because the colonist pieces are abstract tokens and not complex portraits, players fetishize the human beings they reference into small, faceless, manipulable pieces. In the case of the colonists, even though the game does not establish native identities in its textual discourse, meta-game discussions demonstrate that fans perform intertextual readings based on personal understandings and scenarios around the colonial period.

In addition, the colonial project is represented through *Puerto Rico*'s components as an easy, engaging process. Establishing a plantation is a matter of placing a tile on a lush, green island space waiting to be filled. Erecting a building is a similar process. Produced goods are represented by colorful wood pieces that are traded for cardboard doubloons or victory chips, received from the faceless "bank." Winning the game hinges on shipping the most goods to Europe, acquiring victory chips that get tallied up at the end of the game. Missing from the narrative is any sense of the hardships or bloodshed associated with colonization and slavery. In *Puerto Rico*, colonization is about producing, selling, and trading, the slow buildup of an economic engine.

Puerto Rico's game play centers around the mechanics of role selection. On their turn, players select from a set number of roles and carry out one they've chosen, followed by all other players. Someone who selects the role of settler, for example, takes a plantation tile and places it on his or her mat in the field space. Then each opponent, in order, also selects and places a plantation. The ultimate goal of scoring victory points is a multi-step process, with each step requiring a different role choice. These roles must also be chosen and their functions carried out in a specific order, though this order may vary depending on individual players' circumstances. First, goods must be created from raw materials. This requires forming plantations (as a settler), earning money for building (as a prospector or trader), building a production building (as a builder), assigning colonists to work in the plantations and buildings (as a mayor) and producing goods (as a craftsman). Only then can players ship goods to the "old world" (as a captain) and earn victory points. To win the game, a player must have the most victory points when a game-end condition is reached—for example, the colonist supply is depleted, or one player's city section is filled with buildings.

One of the reasons given for the game's popularity on BoardGameGeek is that it incorporates very little luck. The only random element—besides seating order and the personalities and abilities of the players—is the availability of specific plantation tiles; the tiles are rotated at the end of each settler phase. This limited amount of luck allows players to become familiar with the workings of the game, develop strategies for play, and get better over time without— according to fans—the intrusion of random elements to "spoil" their plans. It also means that games of *Puerto Rico* will be somewhat static; that they will follow a familiar formula every time the game is played.

Performing the various roles in *Puerto Rico* reinscribes an economic system that dominated and necessitated the historical colonial project and its hierarchical division of labor—the desire for wealth leading to domination over native peoples. All player roles are middle- to upper-class Spanish administrative positions; the player who leads a given round is even called the "governor." Within these roles, players themselves do not perform manual labor; instead they order the colonist discs to produce goods and load them onto ships for the players' benefit. Players must manipulate the colonists and ship goods to Europe not only in order to win the game but to participate in it at all. There simply is no other way to play the game besides engaging in colonization as the colonizer.

Implications

Each of the three games, in its own way, rewards excessive accumulation. *Life*, for example, encourages the hoarding of much more wealth than is necessary in real life for retirement. In *Magic*, both lands and creatures are accumulated and used in order to overwhelm an opponent and run him/her out of life or power. The lives of the creatures are sacrificed (a term used in the game), or wasted, in order to secure victory. Recall Roach's (1996) link between the performance of waste—the destruction or overconsumption of excess—and the power necessary to produce or accumulate that excess. *Magic*'s language often speaks of overwhelming opponents with many small creatures or powerful large creatures, as well as their disposable nature; the *Dead Again* box reads: "Death is but a minor obstacle for this deck's denizens. Play your creatures, attack with them, and then get them back after they go to the graveyard. They won't mind! Your opponents' creatures, on the other hand, tend to stay dead" (Garfield, 2005b). In *Puerto Rico*, players accumulate plantations, buildings, colonists and barrels of goods to become undisputed economic masters of trade on "empty" land using pliable subjects. The game's cultural scenario creates an illusion of abundance, territory, and resources available for the taking without consequence. The game also constructs the waste of people and goods as relatively inconsequential. Out-of-work colonists simply bide their time in the city of San Juan until their player adds a building or plantation tile to which they are assigned. Goods that cannot be delivered "spoil on the docks" and are returned to the common supply. As in *Life* and *Magic*, real life consequences of waste and excess—unemployment, starvation, death, corruption—do not factor into the games' narratives. The games allow players to take pleasure in consumption and insulate them from the consequences of waste. Players may briefly lose a small token—a person, creature, or dollar amount—but their next turn will offer a myriad of opportunities to recoup that loss, and if they fall too far behind, there is always another game to play.

In addition to the pleasure derived from accumulation, players enjoy the game's rewards while performing no actual labor. By activating a spinner, they pass "Pay Day" spaces in *Life*. Their creatures do the fighting for them in *Magic*. And in *Puerto Rico*, their colonists produce goods and work buildings. The players perform intellectual work, tactically selecting actions to counter those performed by others. In this, they essentially take the role of bosses, issuing orders and reaping the benefits of others' (imaginary) labor. This again correlates with the fetish model—the ability to manipulate on a small, contained scale in order to vicariously experience what this performance is like in reality. And in this fetish model, the games reject (*Life*), sacrifice (*Magic*), and render invisible (*Puerto Rico*) subaltern identities. The players, representing the ruling class, engage in competition, trying to stay one step ahead of their rivals, in money or power. These performances become part of the colonized imaginary, training young people to live in a middle class, capitalist/consumerist colonialist model that values individual planning and aggressive pursuit of objectives and rewards quantifiable success.

I recognize that I have been strongly critical in this chapter, and I certainly don't want to suggest that either: (a) these games have no value or (b) enculturation is a monolithic, inescapable process. As James Gee (2003) suggests, games can be a wonderful starting point for rich conversations around (for example) the challenges faced by adults in U.S. society, the concept of feudalism, or the troubling history of colonization. In order to achieve these ends, restorying similar to the replacement strategy Brett Martin (2004) described for *Magic* might be necessary. When engaging in such play, those facilitating the play with children could ask: what does resistant play look like? What counter narratives can be layered on the game, both by adult facilitators and young players? And what happens if a group prefers the in-game narrative "as written," trumping more critical conversations? Through engaging these questions, a game can become an opportunity not just to share time together, engage in strategic play, and immerse oneself in a given narrative, but also to explore the various values extant in the in-game society and society at large.

References

About Wizards (2009). *Wizards of the Coast* Retrieved Sept 9, 2009, from http://www.wizards.com/Company/

Adams, D. W., & Edmonds, V. (1977). Making Your Move: The Educational Significance of the American Board Game, 1832 to 1904. *History of Education Quarterly, 17,* 357-383.

Apple, M. W., & Buras, K. L. (2006). *The Subaltern Speaks: Curriculum, Power, and Educational Struggles.* New York: Routledge.

Baudrillard, J. (1994). *Simulacra and Simulation.* Ann Arbor: University of Michigan Press.

BoardGameGeek Web site. http://www.boardgamegeek.com

Caillois, R. (1961). *Man, Play, and Games.* New York: Free Press of Glencoe.

Comments that Should Cost the Utterer GeekGold (2007). *BoardGameGeek* Retrieved 19 October, 2007, from http://www.boardgamegeek.com/geeklist/7853

Game of Life, The. (2007). Pawtucket, RI: Hasbro.

Garfield, R. (2005a). *Magic: the Gathering Core Set.* Renton, WA: Wizards of the Coast.

Garfield, R. (2005b). *Magic: the Gathering Dead Again.* Renton, WA: Wizards of the Coast.

Gee, J. P. (2003). *What Video Games Have to Teach Us About Learning and Literacy* (1st ed.). New York: Palgrave Macmillan.

Knizia, R.. (2000). *Lord of the Rings.* Roseville, Mn: Fantasy Flight Games.

Leacock, M. (2008). *Pandemic.* Mahopac, NY: Z-Man Games.

Lepore, J. (2007, 21 May). The Meaning of Life. *New Yorker,* 38.

Martin, B. A. S. (2004). Using the Imagination: Consumer Evoking and Theatizing of the Fantastic Imaginary. *Journal of Consumer Research, 31,* 136-149.

Mulvey, L. (1996). *Fetishism and Curiosity.* Bloomington, London: Indiana University Press, British Film Institute.

Neller, T. (2005). About Our Games/Welcome G'burg Game Enthusiasts. *Gamesurplus.com* Retrieved 7 May, 2005, from https://www.gamesurplus.com/site/about_neller.cfm

Orbanes, P. (2004). *The Game Makers: The Story of Parker Brothers from Tiddledy Winks to Trivial Pursuit.* Boston, Mass.: Harvard Business School Press.

Parlett, D. S. (1999). *The Oxford History of Board Games.* Oxford, New York: Oxford University Press.

Pokemon (1999). Renton, WA: Wizards of the Coast.

Roach, J. R. (1996). *Cities of the Dead: Circum-Atlantic Performance*. New York: Columbia University Press.

Rosenberg, U. (2007). *Agricola*. Mahopac, NY: Z-Man Games.

Seyfarth, A. (2002). *Puerto Rico*. Rio Rancho, NM: Rio Grande Games.

Shea, J. J. (1973). *The Milton Bradley Story*. New York: Newcomen Society in North America.

Takahashi, K. (1996). *Yu-Gi-Oh! Trading Card Game*. Carlsbad, CA: Upper Deck Entertainment.

Teuber, K. (1995). *The Settlers of Catan*. Skokie, IL: Mayfair Games.

Wilson, K., & Launius, R. (2005). *Arkham Horror*. Roseville, MN: Fantasy Flight Games.

Contributors

Anna Beresin is a multi-disciplinary scholar with two Ph.D.s, one in psychology and one in folklore. A regular Visiting Professor at The University of Pennsylvania, Anna serves as Associate Professor of Liberal Arts at the University of the Arts and teaches in the game design minor in multimedia. All of Anna's research focuses on play and creative processes, and she has published on a range of topics from toys to the history of movement games. Her book, *Recess Battles*, will soon be published by the University Press of Mississippi.

Sean J. Bliznik is a third year Ph.D. theatre for youth candidate and women and gender studies certificate graduate student at Arizona State University where he has taught courses in theatre for social change and improvisation with youth. His research interests include the construction of adolescent identity in commerical theatre spaces as well as through popular culture. Aside from research, Sean is an accomplished director and stage manager where his most recent work has been with Walt Disney Entertainment in central Florida. He holds an M.A. in theatre from the University of Central Florida.

Valerie Borey is a Norwegian teacher and curriculum writer at Concordia Language Villages, working with children from pre-school to high school. She holds a B.A. in Anthropology from the University of Minnesota and an M.A. in the social sciences from the University of Chicago, and is interested in ethnic performance/performance of ethnicity as well as the transformation of consciousness through the performing arts, including theatre, dance, improv, and the circus arts. Valerie is also a playwright in the Minneapolis area, writing works that center on the complexity of human behavior and motivation.

Drew Chappell teaches at California State University, Fullerton. He is a performance studies scholar with research interests in play, globalization, and ideological transfer, as well as visual and narrative research methods. He holds an M.F.A. from the University of Texas at Austin and a Ph.D. from Arizona State University. His published articles have analyzed topics including ethnodrama with middle school students, the *Harry Potter* series as postmodern cultural commentary, and historical conceptions of child audiences. Drew is also an award-winning playwright whose work focuses on the interrelationship of adulthood and childhood.

Tove I. Dahl is an associate professor at the University of Tromsø in Norway and serves as Dean of Skogfjorden, the Norwegian program of the Concordia Language Villages of Concordia College in Moorhead, Minnesota. Her research primarily focuses on how we learn the knowledge and skills relevant for responsible global citizenship, including the learning of language and of peace-relevant knowledge and skills. In 2009, the Norwegian government recognized her for promoting the Norwegian language and culture in the US by officially appointing her Knight of the First Class of the Royal Order of Merit, emphasizing the value of her academic grounding for the work she does at Skogfjorden. Tove earned her Ph.D. in educational psychology at the University of Texas at Austin.

Noelia Enriz has a degree in anthropology from the University of Buenos Aires and is a fellow of CONICET (Consejo Superior de Investigaciones en Ciencia y Tecnología-Ministerio de Ciencia y Teconología, Argentina). She is a member of a research team on "Indigenous and migrant children: identification processes and formative experiences" (Directed by Dr. Gabriela Novaro-UBA) and the project "On stage ratings: institutional rules and principles derived from ethno categories of humanity, otherness, sociality and history in indigenous societies of the Gran Chaco and adjacent areas." Her research, conducted since 2003, focuses on *mbyá guarani* children's everyday practices, deriving from her doctoral research referring to children's games. She has published several papers in journals and book chapters relating to this subject.

Jo-Ann Episkenew is an associate professor of English at the First Nations University of Canada in Regina, Saskatchewan, Canada. She is interested in the applications of Indigenous literature and drama as part of the healing of Indigenous communities from the intergenerational effects of historical trauma. Her book *Taking Back Our Spirits: Indigenous Literature, Public Policy, and Healing* was published by the University of Manitoba Press in 2009. Jo-Ann represents the Canadian Prairie Region on the national executive board of the Canadian Association of Commonwealth Literatures and Language Studies and is former President of the Association for Bibliotherapy and Applied Literatures.

Shimi Friedman is a Ph.D. student in the Anthropology & Sociology Department of Ben Gurion University of the Negev, Israel. He is interested in childhood and youth, education, cultural movements, Jewish-Muslim conflict, and the Israeli settlements. Shimi's chapter is based on his M.A. research that explored Jewish life in a Muslim village in Jerusalem, and concentrates on shared childhood between the groups. His current research is based on Israeli youth groups that have been moved from their parents' homes and are hanging around on the hills of the South-East Hebron settlements. Through that work he seeks to understand the youth generation as a social categorical movement.

Linda Goulet is an associate professor at the Department of Indigenous Education, First Nations University of Canada, Regina, Saskatchewan, Canada where she teaches classes in Indigenous pedagogy, anti-racism, and Indigenous health education. Her current research projects include the examination of the impact of "Elders in Residence" programs on school programming and the exploration of health issues with First Nations youth through drama. Her publications include journal articles on Indigenous education, chapters in books on anti-racism, health, and drama, and a co-edited book on collaborative research in education. She is currently co-editing a book on the role of adults who work with youth, to be published in 2010.

Rebecca Howard has been an early childhood educator for over 30 years, and is the founder and owner of the Oxford Early Childhood Center in Oxford, Ohio. She has a M.A. in theatre and is nearing completion of an interdisciplinary Ph.D. in educational leadership and women's studies. She is co-editor, with Dr. Shirley Huston-Findley, of *Footpaths and Bridges: Voices from the Native American Women Playwrights Archive*. She is also a part-time instructor at Miami University in Ohio, having taught courses in theatre, women's Studies, educational leadership, and interdisciplinary studies.

Amy Petersen Jensen is an associate professor in the Brigham Young University Theatre and Media Arts Department, where she coordinates the undergraduate Theatre Education Program and the Media Education Masters Degree. Amy directs Hands on a Camera, a service-learning project, in which university students work with in-service public school educators to teach young people media literacy and documentary production skills. She is the author of *Theatre in a Media Culture: Production, Performance and Perception Since 1970* (McFarland, 2007) and an editor of the forthcoming volume *(Re)imagining Literacies for Content Area Classrooms* (Teachers College Press). Her published articles discuss the use of multimodal and media literacies in educational settings. Amy is also the co-editor of the *Journal of Media Literacy Education*.

McKay R. Jensen is the coordinator of online learning initiatives for Alpine School District in Utah, where he also directs online curriculum creation and development for alternative education in secondary schools. McKay is also the principle consultant for Alpine Technology Consultants, which develops interactive technologies in support of human resource education.

Maria Kromidas recently received her Ph.D. with distinction from Columbia University's Teachers College. Her dissertation, titled "Race, Multiculturalism and 'Childhood:' The Emergent Cosmopolitanism of Kids in a New York City School" considers children's role in everyday processes of racial formation and transformation. She is an anthropologist interested in issues of social difference, post-humanism and cosmopolitanism, and how these sites can be rethought with and through the critical space provided by childhood. She is currently teaching at Hunter College, City University of New York.

Warren Linds is an associate professor in human relations and human systems intervention at Concordia University, Montreal, Quebec, Canada, where he teaches undergraduate and graduate courses on diversity, small group leadership and ethical practices in human systems intervention. He holds a Ph.D. in education from the University of British Columbia. His publications have looked at reflective practices in group and workshop facilitation, anti-racism education, performative inquiry, and the fostering of adult/youth partnerships for youth leadership development. For the past 20 years Warren has been a popular theatre facilitator and community educator using Theatre of the Oppressed in various community and educational settings.

Christina Marín is an assistant professor of educational theatre at New York University. Her research focuses on the use of theatre in human rights education through performance, dramatic literature, and dramatic activities in pedagogical settings. She is a Theatre of the Oppressed practitioner and scholar who has conducted workshops both in the United States and abroad. She holds a B.S. in theatre from Northwestern University and a Ph.D. from Arizona State University. Her dissertation, *Breaking Down Barriers, Building Dreams: Using Theatre for Social Change to Explore the Concept of Identity with Latina Adolescents*, was funded through an American Dissertation Fellowship sponsored by the American Association of University Women, and was honored with the Distinguished Dissertation Award from the Arts-based Educational Research Special Interest Group of the American Educational Research Association.

Matt Omasta teaches in the Department of Theatre, Dance, and Film at Providence College. He serves as co-chair of the American Alliance for Theatre & Education's College/University/Research Network, and has served on the Executive Committee of the American Society for Theatre Research. His research interests include corporate theatre for young audiences, educational drama across the curriculum, performance and cognition, and theatre for social change.

Karen Schmidt is the health educator for the File Hills Qu'Appelle Tribal Council in Fort Qu'Appelle, Saskatchewan, Canada. She has experience teaching in the public school system, as well as in a post-secondary teacher education program. As a health educator, Karen provides information to schools and communities for topics such as FASD, HIV/Aids, sexual health, smoking and healthy medication use. She is the driving force behind the Healthy Communities: Healthy Youth Project, where a committee of youth and adults gather regularly to address issues of self-esteem and healthy living for youth.

Amy K. Way (M.A., Arizona State University, 2008) is a doctoral student in the Hugh Downs School of Human Communication and fellow in the Project for Wellness and Work-life at Arizona State University. Her scholarship explores how gendered identities are organized in everyday life. Her master's thesis examined how extra-curricular intervention programs designed to enhance young girls' self-esteem often unwittingly reproduce the gendered problems they attempt to overcome. Since completing her thesis, Amy has served as a consultant to assist in the redesign of such program curricula.

Felice Yuen is an assistant professor at Concordia University, Montreal, Quebec, Canada, in the Department of Applied Human Sciences. Her research interests focus on leisure as a context for community development and social justice. Previous research examined the impact of Indigenous ceremonies on the healing and rehabilitation of Indigenous women incarcerated in a federal prison. Current research examines leisure and its impact on marginalized youth and civic engagement.

Jack Zipes is Professor Emeritus of German and comparative literature at the University of Minnesota. Some of his more recent publications include *Sticks and Stones: The Troublesome Success of Children's Literature from Slovenly Peter to Harry Potter* (2004), *Fairy Tales and the Art of Subversion* (rev. ed. 2006), *Why Fairy Tales Stick: The Evolution and Relevance of a Genre* (2006), and *Relentless Progress: The Reconfiguration of Children's Literature, Fairy Tales, and Storytelling*

(2008). He has also translated a collection of Kurt Schwitters' fairy tales, *Lucky Hans and Other Merz Fairy Tales* (2009).

Index

Academy of Natural Sciences, 130
Alice in Wonderland, 132, 136-137, 139, 141, 144, 193
Almon, Joan, xii
Alphabet Relay (game), 227-229
Althusser, Louis, 9-10, 203, 208, 236, 239
Amadahy, Zainab, 44
American Girl (brand), 24
Amnesty International, 224, 230
Apple, Michael W., 170, 278
Aristotle, 5
attention span, 136-137
Austin, J. L., 235
Avalon Hill (game publisher), 286, 290
Avatar: the Last Airbender, 21, 32-36
avatars, online and game, 22-23, 28, 30

Backhouse, Constance, 44
Balinese cockfighting, 151
Barrie, J. M., 22-23
Bial, Henry, 118-119, 121
binaries, gender, 28, 37, 110-111, 157, 284
binaries, good and evil, 189-190, 194-196, 199-200, 202-207
binaries, virtual / real world, 242
blue collar vs. white collar, 140
Boal, Augusto, 13, 42-43, 46-47, 49, 216, 220, 222, 229-231
board games, see games, board and card
BoardGameGeek.com (website), 291-292
boyd, danah, 241-243, 245, 254
brand identification, 22-23, 26
brandscaping, 24
Brecht, Bertolt, 13
Bryan, Anna E., 115-116
Butler, Judith, 1, 6, 11, 119, 129, 156-157, 159, 169, 235-236
Buzz Lightyear Astro Blasters (Disneyland attraction), 190, 203-205, 209

Caillois, Roger, 6, 278
Card, Claudia, 199-200
ceremonies, 44, 56, 93, 95-96, 100-101, 237
Chambers, Robert, 223
child-animal relationships, 92, 94, 101
Children's Metamorphosis (museum), 127
Chuck E. Cheese (family restaurant and entertainment center), 133
Cohen, David, 215
collectable card games, see games, collectable card
Colombia, 217-219, 223
Colombian Hypnosis (game), 229-230
colonialism, 43-44, 56, 291-295
Communism, 116, 189
competition, 28, 51, 167, 170, 174-175, 178-183, 222, 229, 280, 293, 295
Concordia Language Villages, 64
Connerton, Paul, 11, 74, 129
Convention on the Rights of the Child, 215-216, 220, 224-225, 227-229
corporate sponsorship, 138, 141-142, 209
cosmopolitanism, 233-234, 240, 243, 251-254
curriculum, "hidden," 170
curriculum, early childhood, 116-117
curriculum, formal language, 69, 78, 81
curriculum, Run for Your Life, 167, 174-177, 182

de Certeau, Michel, 25, 34
DeCordova, Richard, 189, 191
Derrida, Jacques, 14, 54
Developmentally Appropriate Practice, 112, 130
Dewey, John, xii, 114-116, 118, 131
Disney (media conglomerate), 21-23, 26, 28, 149, 155, 189-201, 206-208, 210-211

Disney Channel, 149
Disney, Project on. see Project on Disney
Disney, Walt, 189, 194, 207
Disneyland (theme park), 189-211
Disney's *High School Musical*, 149-165
dis-play, xiii
dollhouses, 114, 135, 137, 139
dramatic play areas, 107-109, 112-114, 117-121
dramatic play, 59, 107-110, 112-121
dreamy play, 134, 137
du Gay, Paul, 168-169
Duran, Eduardo and Duran, Bonnie, 44

Early Childhood Education and Care, 107-123, 221
Early Childhood Environment Rating Scale-Revised (ECERS-R), 110-113, 116, 120-121
Eisner, Eliot, 11
Eisner, Michael (former Disney CEO), 189, 201
Elephant, The (game), 269-270
Etch-a-Sketch (toy), 141
Euro game, 277, 290-295

Fantasmic! (Disneyland attraction), 190, 200-203, 209-211
First Nations, 14, 41-42
Fjellman, Stephen, 189-190, 195-196, 207-208, 211
Forum Theatre, 43, 46, 55
Foucault, Michel, 8, 253
Freire, Paulo, 217, 219-220, 227
friending (online interaction), 28, 241-245
Froebel, Friedrich, 115-116

game avatars, see avatars, online and game
games (board), 6, 278-295
games (collectable card), 277, 285-290, 294-295
games (computer / video), 7, 21-38, 279
games (drama), 41-58, 215-231

games (group created), 87-94, 96-101, 259-260, 262-274
games (religious) 95-96, 100-101
Game of Life, The (board game), 277, 282-285, 294
gangsta, 247-251
Gee, James, 1, 287, 295
Geertz, Clifford, 90, 135, 151-152, 164, 263-264
gender, xi, 2-3, 14, 27-28, 30, 33, 38, 52-53, 91, 94-96, 107-123, 153-183, 235-236, 243, 248, 277
Generation Now, 25
gift shops, 128, 141, 205-206
Gillis, John R., 128
Giroux, Henry, 1, 10-11, 129, 189, 192
Goffman, Erving, 1, 5, 150-152, 263
Gotti, John, 247
Gramsci, Antonio, 192, 278

Handelman, Don, 129, 263
Hasbro (game company), 286, 290
hegemony, 13, 164, 190, 192, 237-238, 246, 250-253
Hello Kitty, 141
High School Musical, see Disney's *High School Musical*
Hill, Patty Smith, 114-116, 118
HTML code, 245
Huizinga, Joseph, 6
Human Rights Education, 215-231
Human Rights Watch, 224

identity construction, 1
identity formation, 26, 29, 34
ideology, 1-4, 7-12, 119, 189-197, 200-203, 206, 233, 235-240, 250, 252-254, 260-265, 274, 278
Indian Act, Canada, 44
Indiana Jones (fictional character), 12, 193
Indiana Jones Adventure (Disneyland attraction), 193
Indigenous peoples of Canada, 14, 41-58

Innoventions Dream Home (Disneyland attraction), 190, 207-209
intersex, 121-122
Interval Research, 26-28, 34
Inuit, 41
Iser, Wolfgang, 4, 6, 8
Isherwood, Charles, 165

Jameson, Fredric, 13
Janteloven, 71, 78
Jenkins, Henry, 21, 27, 252
Johnson, Mark, 9, 129
Johnson, Richard, 2-3

kindergarten, 114-116, 131
Kluge, Alexander, xiii
Kosmos (game publisher), 290
Kress, Gunther, 22

Lakoff, George, 9
language immersion villages, 63-82
language play, 68, 71, 76, 82
Laurel, Brenda, 21, 26-29, 31, 34, 37
Lee, Jo-Anne, 239
Lee, Nick, 10, 194
leisure, 207, 262, 278
Levin, Amy, 127
Levy, André, 273
Liddle, David, 26, 34
liminal states and spaces, 5, 7, 64-66, 81, 96, 194
lip-synching, 154, 160-161, 164
Little White Bird, The (novel), 22
Lumsden, M., 45, 49

Magic: the Gathering (collectable card game), 277, 285-290, 294-295
Malaguzzi, Loris, xii
Mandela, Nelson, 215, 224
mangá, 99, 101
Martin, Brett, 295
Mattel, Inc., 24, 35
Mayfair Games (game publisher), 297
mbyá guaraní, 87-101

McBirney, Katherine, 7
McCarthy, Julie, 51, 216, 222
McDermott, 173
McDonald's (fast food restaurant), 26, 132, 144
Mead, Margaret, 90, 100, 262
Métis, 41-42
Mickey Mouse (fictional character), 138, 191, 200-204, 208-209, 248
Microsoft, 36, 207, 209
Milton Bradley (game publisher), 290, 292
mimesis, 15, 194
mimetic, 5, 24, 119
Money, John, 121-122
Montessori, Maria, xii
multiculturalism, 112, 233-236, 239-240, 243, 246-247, 249, 252
Museum of Science and Industry, Chicago, 132
museums, 127-144, 225, 236
MWW Group (public relations and marketing firm), 25-26
MySpace, 233-254

National Association of Educators of Young Children, 130
National Institute for Play, xi
Negt, Oskar, xiii
ñeovanga, 92, 97, 99-100
Newcomb, C., 191
Nickelodeon (television network), 32, 35
Nietzsche, Friedrich, 234
non-competition, 15, 179-180
nostalgia, 127-128, 131, 133, 137, 141-142

O'Neill, Cecily, 226
online avatars, see avatars, online and game

Parker Brothers (game publisher), 290
Parlett, David, 6, 277-279, 281
parody, 151, 154, 161-162
performance studies, 4, 118-119

performance theory, 1, 119
Perlin, Ken, 7
Peter Pan, 23
physicality, 5, 109, 144, 168, 173–174, 176, 179
Piaget, Jean, 108–109, 130, 133, 135, 227
Pinocchio (Disney character), 197–201, 203, 209
Pinocchio's Daring Journey (Disneyland attraction), 190, 197–200, 203, 209
Pinsky, Mark I., 189, 191, 194, 199–200, 202
Pixie Hollow (fictional environment / online game), 21–24, 26, 28–29
Plato, 194
Please Touch Museum, 127–144
Poulter, Christine, 216, 221
Power Plays, 42, 46
prayer, 44, 80–81, 87, 93, 96, 101
Progressivism, 114, 116–117
Project on Disney, 210–211
Puerto Rico (board game), 277, 290–295
Puerto Rico (place), 251, 277, 290–294
purchasing power, 25–26

race, 3, 46, 53, 108, 119, 163, 172, 233–234, 238–239, 242, 253, 277
racial formation, 237, 239, 248
Rampton, Ben, 236, 250
religious games, see games, religious
resistant play, 10–13, 210–211, 295
Rio Grande Games (game publisher), 290
Roach, Joseph, 4, 8, 11, 280, 294
Run For Your Life (sports program), 168–183

sacralized space, 190–191, 196, 201
safe spaces, 45, 57, 220
Schechner, Richard, 1, 4–7, 10, 41, 118–119, 193–194, 197
Schickel, Richard, 199
Selfish Giant, The, 266–269
Settlers of Catan (board game), 290
sexism, 112

Shea, James J. Jr., 292
Shop Rite, 132, 141–142, 144
Sillwan (Jerusalem village), 259–274
Skogfjorden (language village), 63–82
Smith, Linda Tuhiwai, 53
Smurfs, 141
snowball fight, 270–272
social change, 41–58, 213–254, 215–231, 235–236
social networking website, 15, 22–32, 240–254
SOS Children's Villages, 219
soul-wound, 44
Sperr, Portia Hamilton, 142
sports program, 167–183
Star Wars, 132, 141, 193
Strong National Museum of Play, 127
subaltern, 192, 278, 295
summer camps, 64–66, 128
Sutton-Smith, Brian, 51–52, 108, 128–130, 135, 140
Swidler, Ann, 2, 4, 10

tactical open space, 36–38
taking turns, 134
Taussig, Michael T., 5
Taylor, Diana, 4, 10–11, 129, 281
Taylor, Philip, 45
Theatre of the Oppressed, 42, 47, 220, 222
Thorne, Barrie, 1, 109, 111
THQ (videogame developer and publisher), 33, 35
Time Magazine, 202
Toren, Cristina, 99, 101
Toy Story (film), 204, 206
transgender, 122
transmedia experiences and products, 21–25, 29, 32, 34–38
Turner, Victor, 7, 51, 55, 65–66, 194

Underiner, Tamara, 14
United Nations Children's Fund (UNICEF), 98, 216, 221, 223

United States Alliance for Childhood, xii
United States Holocaust Memorial
  Museum, 225
Universal Declaration of Human Rights,
  215, 220, 223-225, 227, 229, 231

Victoria's Secret, 245
virtual worlds, 21-26, 28, 242
Volosinov, V. N., 236

Warren, Bernie, 216, 221-222, 224, 228-
  229
Wickstrom, Maurya, 24-25
Wii, 21, 29-34
Williamson, Debra Aho, 25
Winnicott, D. W., 41, 52
Wizards of the Coast (game company),
  285-287, 290
workshops, theatre-based, 41-58, 222
World Ball Exercise (game), 227-228

Young, Katherine, 129, 170
YouTube, 149-155, 157-158, 160-164,
  244

Zizek, Slavoj, 233, 234, 239